THE PHILOSOPHY OF FOOTBALL

Human beings are the only creatures known to engage in sport. We are sporting animals, and our favourite pastime of football is the biggest sport spectacle on earth. *The Philosophy of Football* presents the first sustained, in-depth philosophical investigation of the phenomenon of football.

In explaining the complex nature of football, the book draws on literature in sociology, history, psychology and beyond, offering real-life examples of footballing actions alongside illuminating thought experiments. The book is organized around four main themes considering the character, nature, analysis and aesthetics of football. It discusses football as an extra-ordinary, unnecessary, rule-based, competitive, skill-based physical activity, articulated as a social (as opposed to natural) kind that is fictional in character, and where fairness or fair play – contrary to much sport ethical discussion – is not centre stage. Football, it is argued, is a constructive-destructive contact sport and, in comparison to other sports, is lower scoring and more affected by chance. The latter presents to its spectators a more unpredictable game and a darker, more complex and denser drama to enjoy.

The Philosophy of Football deepens our understanding of the familiar features of the game, offering novel interpretations on what football is, how and why we play it, and what the game offers its followers that makes us so eagerly await match day. This is essential reading for anybody with an interest in the world's most popular game or in the philosophical or social study of sport.

Steffen Borge is Professor of Philosophy at UiT The Arctic University of Norway, Tromsø.

ETHICS AND SPORT
Series editors
Mike McNamee, University of Wales Swansea
Jim Parry, University of Leeds

The Ethics and Sport series aims to encourage critical reflection on the practice of sport, and to stimulate professional evaluation and development. Each volume explores new work relating to philosophical ethics and the social and cultural study of ethical issues. Each is different in scope, appeal, focus and treatment but a balance is sought between local and international focus, perennial and contemporary issues, level of audience, teaching and research application, and variety of practical concerns.

Sport, Ethics and Philosophy
Edited by Mike McNamee

Philosophy and Nature Sports
Kevin Krein

Emotion in Sports
Philosophical Perspectives
Yunus Tuncel

Sport, Ethics, and Neurophilosophy
Jeffrey Fry and Mike McNamee

Doping in Cycling
Interdisciplinary Perspectives
Edited by Bertrand Fincoeur, John Gleaves and Fabien Ohl

Sport and Spirituality
Edited by R. Scott Kretchmar and John B. White

The Philosophy of Football
Steffen Borge

For a complete series list please visit: https://www.routledge.com/Ethics-and-Sport/book-series/EANDS

THE PHILOSOPHY OF FOOTBALL

Steffen Borge

LONDON AND NEW YORK

First published 2019
by Routledge
2 Park Square, Milton Park, Abingdon, Oxon OX14 4RN

and by Routledge
52 Vanderbilt Avenue, New York, NY 10017

Routledge is an imprint of the Taylor & Francis Group, an informa business

© 2019 Steffen Borge

The right of Steffen Borge to be identified as author of this work has been asserted by him in accordance with sections 77 and 78 of the Copyright, Designs and Patents Act 1988.

All rights reserved. No part of this book may be reprinted or reproduced or utilised in any form or by any electronic, mechanical, or other means, now known or hereafter invented, including photocopying and recording, or in any information storage or retrieval system, without permission in writing from the publishers.

Trademark notice: Product or corporate names may be trademarks or registered trademarks, and are used only for identification and explanation without intent to infringe.

British Library Cataloguing-in-Publication Data
A catalogue record for this book is available from the British Library

Library of Congress Cataloging-in-Publication Data
A catalog record has been requested for this book

ISBN: 978-0-367-18091-1 (hbk)
ISBN: 978-0-367-18092-8 (pbk)
ISBN: 978-0-429-05947-6 (ebk)

Typeset in Bembo
by Taylor & Francis Books

CONTENTS

Preface   *vii*

Introduction: A funny old game   1

    Football and the human condition 1
    About the book 3

1   The character of football: This is Anfield   9

    Introduction 9
    Preliminaries 10
    Some kinds of make-believe 13
    Sport is extra-ordinary 15
    Aliefs, football behaviour and the purpose of football 19
    Football and proto-pretence 30
    Objections and replies 46
    Conclusion 58

2   The nature of football: A game of two halves   69

    Introduction 69
    The variety of formalism and social kinds 70
    The social kind of sport 83
    The social kind of football 94
    The football form and functions 100
    Objections and replies 107
    Conclusion 119

3   The analysis of football: Four four two   122

   Introduction 122
   An outline of Suits's analysis of sport 123
   Football and prelusory goals 124
   Football and limited means 129
   Football and constitutive rules 133
   Football and the lusory attitude needed for playing the sport 138
   Football and physical skills 157
   Football and wide following with a wide level of stability 160
   Refereeing and match minding and maintenance 160
   Objections and replies 165
   Conclusion 186

4   The aesthetics of football: Football, bloody hell   190

   Introduction 190
   Fairness of result vs. the drama of football 191
   Free beauty and football 193
   An agon aesthetics of football 199
   Real values and fictional values 215
   Aesthetic engagement resistance 220
   Silly questions and the football fiction 223
   Objections and replies 226
   Conclusion 248

Conclusion: They think it's all over   256

References   *260*
Index   *278*

PREFACE

This work has benefited from colleagues and friends who have read it and given feedback at some stage or other of the writing. I am very grateful to all who gave of their valuable time. In particular, I'd like to thank Jussi Haukioja and Paisley Livingston, who meticulously laboured through the whole manuscript; Graham McFee and Bill Morgan, who gave Chapters 3 and 4 a thorough going-over; and Lev Kreft, from whom Chapters 2 and 5 have benefited. Others who have come to my rescue by reading parts of this work are Mitch Berman, Gunnar Breivik, R.A. Briggs, Gordon Burghardt, Stephen Davies, Paul Davis, Marzenna Jakubczak, Filip Kobiela, Scott Kretchmar, Signe Højbjerre Larsen, Alyssa Ney, Jim Parry, Tony Pellegrini, Murray Smith, Deborah Vossen, Margrethe Bruun Vaage and Brian Weatherson. Thank you! Parts of this book have been presented at various conferences and talks at Cardiff Metropolitan University, Cardiff University, Norwegian University of Science and Technology, Pedagogical University of Cracow, University of Brighton, University of Gloucestershire, University of Kent, University of Milan/Vita-Salute San Raffaele University, University of Porto, University of Sunderland, University of Tromsø and University of Turku. I am grateful to the people who accepted me at their conference or invited me to talk at their university, and to everyone who showed up to my presentations and talks and tried to show me the errors of my ways. A special thanks goes to Mike McNamee for his encouragement and continuous support of my work. Without Mike, I doubt this book would have been written. Some of the material in this book has already been aired in written form. Most importantly, Chapter 5 builds on Borge 2015c, while parts of Borge 2010a, Borge 2015b and Borge and McNamee 2017 have also found their way into the book.

INTRODUCTION

A funny old game

Football and the human condition

This is a book about the human condition. In particular, it is about what appears to be a unique feature or quality of human existence found nowhere else in the animal kingdom – our ability and willingness to engage in sports as practitioners and spectators. It is a book about association football, which is known throughout most of the world simply as football. It is about how we can understand our fascination with the so-called beautiful game within a broader theoretical framework. We are, as far as we know, the only species that plays football.

The uniqueness of humans, which until fairly recently was more or less taken for granted, has turned out to be surprisingly hard to pin down. There have been many attempts to pick out a feature (quality) or features (qualities) of humans that set them aside from all other animals and make them special. Obviously, it may be the case that humans are not special or that our uniqueness does not lie in there being a feature or features that no other living creatures have, but rather that an amalgam or collections of features give the assumed unique end result of human beings. Sticking to the game of identifying that unique human feature or features, perhaps the most famous attempt is the definition of humans as *rational animals* – a demarcation associated with Aristotle. Unfortunately, trying to understand rationality is a notoriously slippery business; so one way of approaching the question without falling into the quagmire of attempting to define rationality has been to focus on capabilities that serve as good indicators of a rational mind. One prominent candidate here was the definition of humans as *tool-using animals*.

> [T]ool use has long been considered to be an indicator of rational thought. Because tool use involves finding or constructing an object that is utilized as an extension of the body to achieve a specific goal, some think that tool use

> requires identifying a problem, considering ways of solving the problem, and realizing that other objects can be used in the manipulation of the situation.
>
> *(Andrews 2011: 7)*

That definition was exposed as flawed by Jane Goodall's famous field study of chimpanzees in the Gombe Stream Reserve; and as researchers looked more carefully at nonhuman animal behaviour, other studies showed that a whole host of nonhuman animals use tools (van Lawick-Goodall 1968). Indeed, it has turned out to be rather difficult to find that allusive defining feature or features that make humans stand out in the animal kingdom. Derek Penn, Keith Holyoak and Daniel Povinelli tell us that, among the features previously thought to be uniquely human, but which have been contested, we find: "complex tool use, grammatically structured language, causal-logical reasoning, mental state attribution, metacognition, analogical inferences, mental time travel, culture and so on" (Penn et al. 2008: 109).[1] Researchers in comparative psychology have tended to agree with Charles Darwin that "the difference in mind between man and higher animals (...) is certainly one of degree and not of kind" (Darwin 1872: 101). Irene Pepperberg gives voice to this Darwinian line:

> For over 35 years (...) researchers have been demonstrating, through tests both in the field and in the laboratory, that the capacities of non-human animals to solve complex problems form a continuum with those of humans.
>
> *(Pepperberg 2006: 469)*

Even the ability to have moral responses and attitudes has been challenged as not uniquely human (Bekoff 2004, Bekoff and Pierce 2009). Unsurprisingly, not all agree with the idea that the difference between humans and nonhuman animals is merely one of degree, but it is worth noting the range of the features mentioned above – including both behaviour and cognitive abilities – that are no longer taken for granted as uniquely human.

Nevertheless, when we move to the realm of what I, in the next chapter, call the extra-ordinary, we find several candidate features that do not seem to have counterparts among nonhuman animals. Leaving aside the risky business of defining a human essence, in the domain of the extra-ordinary there are several features of human existence that do seem unique to us. Among those we find religion, which seems uniquely human. To my knowledge, no nonhuman animals produce literature, and humans are the only animals that engage in sport. Nonhuman animals play, but they do not play sports. That is, nonhuman animals do not arrange sport competitions. Humans are *sporting animals*. Again, this is not suggested as a definition of human essence – not all humans play or watch sport – but merely to point out that the sport phenomenon seems restricted to the human sphere. Not only are humans sporting animals, but throughout the twentieth century and thus far into the twenty-first, participating in sports, both as practitioners and spectators, has become a huge part of our lives. Sport is a global phenomenon that demands attention. Unless you understand it, you do not fully understand the human condition. This is why a philosophy of sport in general and a philosophy of football in particular are needed. The latter is the topic of this book. A philosophy of football, being a subset of philosophy of sport, will also be about sport, and many of the arguments and considerations presented here on how to understand football will apply to many other sports as well.

Then there are football philosophies and there is the philosophy of football. The former concern the more or less reflective outlook on the game that people have, or the style of play a football team chooses to follow, whereas the latter – to philosophize about the practice of playing and watching football – is what I will aim to discuss here. When, after his club had been given a 4–0 beating on their home turf Allianz Arena in Munich by Real Madrid in the 2014 Champions League, Bayern München's Spanish manager, Pep Guardiola, told the press that "[f]ollowing this defeat I am even more convinced of my philosophy", he was talking about style of play, not a philosophical position akin to, say, existentialism or realism (BBC 2014a). So football philosophies aside, what might a philosophy of football look like? The answer is simple: It will look like any other philosophy. The only difference between the philosophy of football and, say, the philosophy of biology or the philosophy of film, is that in the former case we apply tools from our philosophical toolbox to the phenomenon of football and not, as it happens, to biology or film (or any other area). That is all.

The question of what it means to be human through an inquiry into our sporting nature can be approached in at least two manners. One can address sport as a general phenomenon and then use the various sports as ways of illuminating one's theory, or one can study a single sport or type of sport in depth, while having a keen eye for similarities and dissimilarities between one's object of study and other sports. I have chosen the latter path and my sport of choice is football. Sport-specific considerations have the advantage of forcing one to take the details of the practice seriously. That also functions as a good method for bringing out both similarities and dissimilarities with other sports and neighbouring phenomena such as play and fine art.[2] Notwithstanding the niceties of sport-specific considerations, both approaches, I believe, have the same aim: *understanding the sporting animal*. The choice of football as the target sport is a simple one. Football, or "soccer" as it is called in some parts of the world, is both the biggest global game – measured by the number of people playing and watching the sport at various levels – and surely the largest sporting spectacle on earth. In order to understand the sporting animal as we find it today, it is a fitting choice.

About the book

So, this is a book about football. Football is all about the football. The ball is the main protagonist or antagonist of the game, all depending on how it falls for your team. The drama of the game ultimately revolves around the ball. Win, lose or draw, it all depends on the movements of the ball during the game. The actions of the players mostly relate to the ball. Players' actions and formations seemingly not about the ball still tend to depend on the ball – not as a question of where the ball is now, but where it might be shortly thereafter. Likewise, the rules of the game give the dos and don'ts regarding handling of and challenging for the ball, while at the same time defining much of the game by stipulating which movement and subsequent position of the ball count as, for example, a goal, a corner kick, etc. The rules of the game are flexible to a certain degree. There are various versions of the sport. A pick-up game in the park between friends is just as much a game of football as the World Cup final. I will describe what we might call the standard version of the game and how it is played at a senior level in official matches. That is, I will describe the game that is played during the sport spectacle of the Football World Cup. No matter how uninterested in or ignorant of football you are, when the World Cup circus comes rolling in it is difficult to avoid at least catching a glimpse of the game on a television, either at home or through the windows of bars, cafés, pubs, etc., around the world. Furthermore, I will describe the single match, even though most matches we encounter are played as part of a league or a cup tournament like, for example, the Football World Cup. Importantly, the topic of this book is mainly the game played and watched by grown-ups as adult entertainment. Sports in general and football in particular were originally adult activities and still are. A full treatment of questions concerning children and sports like football would require a very different book and will have to wait for another day.

The basic motivation for the discussions in Chapter 1 is the simple observation that winning football matches does not matter for most of the people playing or watching the game. Win or lose, life goes on for most in the same way it did before Saturday's match or the end of a league campaign. Still, footballers and their audiences care. What a queer fact that is. In order to unpack this odd aspect of our ball game, we need to note that football and other sports are extra-ordinary. They are an extra added onto the ordinary everyday world involving a decision to play a game that would otherwise not happen in the everyday trouble and strife of making a life for ourselves. Furthermore, and unlike neighbouring phenomena in the realm of the extra-ordinary such as fine art and religion, football and other sports do not address and are not seen as addressing everyday life concerns. Sport in general and football in particular are extra-ordinary and unnecessary. We *make* football matter by make-believing or pretending that it matters. Part of the psychological basis of this make-believe notion that winning football matches matters is the basic activation of a fight-or-flight state when faced with physical confrontation and struggle, which a contact sport like football is. This reaction stirs the emotions and readies us for a fight-or-flight response. What happens, however, is that we do not act on this mental state. In the normal case, footballers do not fight or take flight, but instead play the game of football. On the terraces, we do not clutch our fists in anticipation or look nervously around for the exit signs, but instead enjoy the sporting spectacle as it unfolds in front of us. We engage in the game, while also clearly being aware that our excitement does not track a real-life, ordinary world, fight-or-flight situation. This is the essential make-believe involved in playing and watching football. This is football's fictional character. This make-believe should not be equated with the sort of make-believe we find in pretence play or engagement in fiction, such as when reading literature or watching a fiction film. Rather, the make-believe in football, as we play it, involves the simpler, more basic proto-pretence of certain types of social play, like rough and tumble, which we share with other nonhuman animals. The latter explains why playing or watching football does not feel like it involves make-believe or pretence. Playing or watching football is something we decide to do, but the proto-pretence of some kinds of social play like rough and tumble, which is part of the basis of making football matter, operates beneath our awareness, belief and self-understanding of the activity we are engaged in.

Playing football is a human activity or practice. We invented the game and our continuous engagement in, and recognition of, it as a sport is the reason it is still around. That makes football a social kind. Unlike, for example, things we find in the natural world like mountain chains, electrons, apples, hair, and so on, being a social kind, sport exists because we will it to. In Chapter 2, we go into the details of how to understand what it means to be a social kind and which type of social kind sport turns out to be. Being a sport is partly a matter of having a set of rules that define the ensuing activity as a sport of a specific kind. You cannot score a goal in a football match unless you have decided on what counts as scoring a goal in a football match. The players must recognize these kinds of rules, which we call constitutive rules, as operative, and they must recognize that their teammates and opponents on the football pitch also recognize the rules in question. Football and other sports require collective intentionality, i.e. mutual recognition that what we are playing now is football or some other sport. However, sports are also historical kinds, and the historical dimension of the social kind of sport complicates things. When some of the ancient Greeks' rituals transitioned from being rituals to becoming sport events, the social kind of the ritual and the social kind of nascent sport shared a stage of development. The final stage of the practice of the ritual was also the first stage of the emerging sport. There is no reason to believe that at that stage those doing the sport-like ritual or the ritual-like sport had any mutual recognition that they were engaged in a sport, i.e., any collective intentionality. Still, that stage is part of the sport they ended up doing. Similar considerations hold for developments within the social historical kind of sport. Football and rugby football have the same root or origin. They share a stage in their genesis as specific sports. At that stage, there was no mutual recognition that one was playing football or rugby football, and still that stage is both part of football and rugby football as historical kinds. This gives us sport, in general, and football, in particular, as a social historical kind based on collective intentionality, which allows that at a certain stage there is no mutual recognition of being aware that one is doing any sport or a particular sport.

Having a theory of the social kind that sport and football are still leaves us with the question of what it takes to be a sport and a sportsperson. Why is football a sport, whereas bricklaying seemingly is not? In Chapter 3, we take on such questions in the dizzy heights of philosophical analysis. Our launch pad is the philosopher Bernard Suits's (in)famous analysis of games and sports. Suits's analysis is complex, but the pocket edition is that sport is the voluntary attempt to overcome unnecessary obstacles. Through a careful critique of this analysis and other philosophers' attempts to answer these questions, a novel and detailed perspective on sport and sportspersons emerges. Uncontroversially – almost – sports are unnecessary physical-skill activities or practices, where participants aim to win. Pinpointing why sports are centrally or essentially physical, why non-competitive but athletic activities or practices should not count as sports, and why being skill-based is a necessary ingredient of sport and sport engagement requires further argumentation and philosophizing. Still, these features tend to be accepted by most writers in the philosophy of sport. On the other hand, orthodoxy has it that sports need rules that limit the means by which you do your sport, and that is false. Football does put limitations on the means by which you play the game: Unless you are the goalkeeper, do not handle the ball. That is not a requirement for being a sport, however, but a rational possibility of sport. This distinction is important for understanding football and other sports. Sports are unnecessary activities or practices, and if those of us in football want to ban, say, heading the ball, tackling, or what have you, we can do it. Not because it's a requirement of sport, but because we are free to do so for no other reason than that we think it makes football a better sport. Making a good sport, you might think, involves being a good sport. Suits argued that you cannot play a sport if you break any of the constitutive rules of that sport; whereas his critics emphasized that instead players must stay within the limits of agreed-upon acceptable sport behaviour, which may involve violating the constitutive rules of the game. Both sides are mistaken, and examples from football give ample evidence to support that claim. Instead, all it takes to play a sport like football is a willingness to submit to the arbitration of the rules by a referee or referees. The notion that you need to play fair or uphold some fair play ideal is inconsequential to the game of football. Play to win and accept the rulings of the referee. The referee's role in the sport of football is not limited to interpreting and practising the rules of the game. On closer inspection, we find that the referees also take on the roles of maintaining the character of the game and minding the flow of matches. The first points back to our considerations of the fictional character of football considered in Chapter 1, whereas the latter points forwards to the aesthetics of football, which is the theme of Chapter 4.

Understanding the aesthetics of football means forging a new aesthetics, which takes the football experience seriously. We should resist pigeonholing football and other similar sports using mainstream aesthetical theories, which were primarily developed for understanding fine art and the art experience. Football is not fine art. Football is an unnecessary conflict staged for our enjoyment and pleasure. The football conflict or competition is set in a limited space and with a time limitation, which makes it well suited to being a spectator sport. The aesthetics of football and other similar sports is intrinsically tied to these being competitions, and the drama such sports create is a drama of competitive interaction. When looking at some prime examples of what is often deemed beautiful play, we find that they are competitive actions, which typically lead to the chance of scoring a goal. Scoring and winning is at the heart of the football competition. Beautiful or riveting footballing actions or interactions and functionality in the game go hand in hand. The fact that football is a constructive-destructive sport – where part of the game is to create chances and score, while at the same time breaking up and preventing the other team from doing the same – provides fertile ground for a rich social drama. You do not merely do your sport; you actively try to prevent your opponents from doing the same to the best of their ability. Watching the football conflict of the clashing, fast-moving bodies of one team against the other, together with the uncertainty of outcome – where the end result in a fairly straightforward sense does not matter for concerns outside the football context – incites and allows fans and spectators to get emotionally involved and give these emotions free rein. And even though football is staged, but not scripted, reoccurring football themes, storylines or narratives emerge as matches unfold. All these varying football themes, storylines or narratives are anchored in the basic premise of win, lose or draw – that is what drives the conflict and the drama as the clock inevitably runs down towards the final whistle of the game. Part of football's richness in dramatic possibilities is, perhaps surprisingly, the fact that it is a low-scoring sport, where matches give unfair results more often than in other sports. This adds to the unpredictability of football matches, which in turn adds to the tension once we are engaged. This tension is pleasurable for most spectators, because nothing regarding our everyday concerns is at stake in the match we are watching. We can safely engage in our favourite pastime, as there are no repercussions for our lives outside the football context. This is not to underplay the sadness, even despair, one might feel when seeing one's team lose a match or get relegated, but rather to acknowledge that it remains just that: sadness or despair at seeing one's team lose a match or get relegated.

This book is quite a long one. It includes philosophical reflections on football and sport that are illustrated with examples from football and other sports and fictitious cases. I make no apologies for that. Football and sport are complex phenomena, and when philosophizing about them we should pursue the issues at the appropriate level of detail with a keen eye to how football is actually played and could be played. We should not only try to develop theories about football and sports, but we must also put these theories to the test to see whether they fit the actual sport landscape and various fictitious cases that philosophers typically call "thought experiments". Succeeding in the first department gives us an empirically true theory, succeeding in the other gives us a conceptually sane one. Both are equally important. Yet some readers might only want to look at some of the topics addressed or otherwise read the book piecemeal. In order to accommodate such readers, each chapter is written as a more or less self-contained piece and can be read in isolation. If the reader wants to understand why we care about football and how we do it, they should head for Chapter 1. If they wonder what sort of thing, practice, tradition, activity, process, etc. sport and football are, then Chapter 2 explains what social kinds are and what type of social kind football is. If what makes your curiosity clock tick are questions about what makes football a sport and footballers sportspersons, then Chapter 3 reveals the wonders of analysis and carefully sets the stage in which all is revealed concerning those and other related issues. Finally, if you are puzzled about what people might be getting at when they talk about beautiful play or dramatic games, given that football matches are a far cry from a beautiful piece of music or a Shakespeare play, then Chapter 4 develops a new aesthetics that takes its starting point in football and other similar sports as a specific kind of competition. Enjoy!

Notes

1 See, among others, Bekoff et al. 2002, Call 2006, Clayton et al. 2003, de Waal and Tyack 2003, Matsuzawa 2001, Pepperberg 2002, Rendell and Whithead 2001, Savage-Rumbaugh et al. 1998, Smith et al. 2003, Tomasello et al. 2003 for authors who have argued that the above-mentioned features are not uniquely human. Notice that Penn et al. argue that there is a discontinuity between humans and nonhuman animals, and that the Darwinian line on this is mistaken.
2 In this book unless otherwise indicated or context makes it apparent, "art" will be interchangeable with "fine art".

1

THE CHARACTER OF FOOTBALL

This is Anfield

Introduction

In the players' tunnel, above the stairs that lead out onto Liverpool FC's home ground Anfield, there is a sign reading: "This is Anfield." The sign was originally placed there on the order of Liverpool's legendary manager Bill Shankly, to remind the Liverpool players for whom they were playing and to intimidate the visitors by reminding them who they were up against. The sign also marks a transition point. When they descend down the players' tunnel, pass underneath the sign and walk onto the pitch, the players leave the ordinary world and enter an *extra*-ordinary world.

In this chapter, I will explore and develop the idea that the extra-ordinary world of football involves some sort of make-believe or pretence. In doing so, I will build on work from the philosophy of play and sport, among others, Karl Groos, Johan Huizinga, Roger Caillois and Bernard Suits, as well as from newer philosophical aesthetics, as found in the work of, among others, Kendall Walton and Tamar Gendler. Taking my inspiration from Walton, I argue that football is fictional in character in the sense that it involves make-believe or pretence. The fictionality of football is fairly minimal. Football is not a fiction in the ordinary sense of the word. Furthermore, football is not a fiction in Walton's sense of fiction. The main fiction present in football, i.e., the essential make-believe or pretence involved in our way of playing and watching football, is that winning football matches matters. In truth, it does not. It is against a background of make-believe or pretence that winning football matches becomes important. That make-believe, I argue, is grounded in what Gendler calls aliefs, which are affect-laden and action-generating mental states that are more primitive or basic than beliefs. The purpose of these states is to ready us for action in the ordinary world. Nevertheless, both footballers and spectators understand that the aliefs that are generated when playing and watching football do not track ordinary world situations. Instead of giving rise to ordinary world behaviour, they give rise to engagement in the game. Getting exited about and acting on that which we on some level realize does not matter – in the sense of not tracking ordinary world situations – constitute the essential pretence of football. This involves a certain type of pretence, which I called proto-pretence, and that mechanism or mechanisms are also found in the kind of social rough-and-tumble play we find among human and nonhuman animals. This is the football fiction.

Preliminaries

The thesis that football is fictional in character must not be conflated with the clearly misguided idea that football is a fiction in the ordinary sense of the word. Ordinarily, calling something "a fiction" means judging it to be something that is not real, something that is made up or imagined. We can call this the naïve ordinary language account.[1] The account of the adventures of Anna Karenina, in the book of the same name written by Leo Tolstoy, is a fiction. The novel does not describe events that took place. Furthermore, the names Anna Karenina, Alexei Vronsky, etc. do not refer to anyone who ever lived (in our world). Tolstoy made it all up.[2] Unlike fictional characters and events as they are depicted in literature, fiction film, etc., footballers and football matches are real. They exist in this world and not merely in some fictional universe. Sport is, as Lev Kreft puts it, "real action" where "athletes appear and perform as themselves" and not as "dramatic personae" (Kreft 2012: 226, 228, 231).[3]

Though Kreft emphasizes that actors on a stage do pretend to be dramatic personae, while sportspeople do not, the notion of something being a fiction is not exclusively bound to art forms such as fiction film, theatre, literature, dance, computer games and painting. People readily call something a fiction when they merely want to communicate that something is untrue or made up. For example, Richard Dawkins dubbed the Christian God of the Old Testament "the most unpleasant character in all fiction" and went on to claim that the Gospels are "fabricated from start to finish: invented, made-up fiction (…) the gospels are ancient fiction" (Dawkins 2006: 51, 123). Emeritus Pope Benedict followed suit and made sure that there was no love lost between the two camps by denouncing "The Selfish Gene by Richard Dawkins [as] a classic example of science fiction" (Emeritus Pope Benedict 2013). Clearly, neither of these authors was attempting to make a contribution to the study of aesthetics, but rather using the word "fiction" to signify that which is untrue, non-existent or made up. I suggest that the naïve, ordinary language understanding of the word "fiction" minimally entails that whatever is deemed a fiction is untrue, non-existent or made up.[4] It then follows that it is uncontroversial that the content of the book *Anna Karenina* is a fiction or is fictional, whereas the status of the Old Testament, the Gospels and Dawkins's *The Selfish Gene* seems to be open to debate. The ontological status of football, however, is not controversial with regard to the fiction–non-fiction divide. The content of football – the ontological status or the nature of the game – is not a fiction in the naïve, ordinary language understanding of the word. The question of the content or nature of football concerns what it is for the activity of playing football to be a sport and a specific kind of sport. I will return to that question in the next two chapters. The question of the character of football, on the other hand, concerns how the game is played and watched. The fictionality of football pertains not to the content of the game, but to its character – the essential make-believe aspect is that winning football matches matters. Joseph Kupfer makes a similar point when he writes that "[i]n sports, we set up procedures (…) and 'pretend' that the activity and outcome are important" (Kupfer 1983: 114). The way we play and engage in watching football involves make-believe.

It is key to my line of argument that we can talk about the content or the nature of a sport like football. Without this assumption, it hardly makes sense to talk about the sport's character. Admittedly, talk about the content of football can become a bit strained, as it really amounts to talking about football as a sport. However, it is important because it brings out the contrast between the nature of football as a sport and the fact that it is a sport that can be played in various manners. Such talk about the content of football, however, does not commit me to any particular theory of sport. Rather, the only thing that follows from this assumption is that one can truly, or correctly, say about two different games of football that one "is a game of football and is played in a friendly manner", while the other "is a game of football and is played in a hostile manner". If you can grant me that, then you have granted me the distinction between the content or nature of football – that a certain activity is a game of football and a sport – and the character of the sport – how the game is played and watched. Football, I will argue, is played as if it mattered. There are games, however, where the outcome is important, like Russian roulette and ancient gladiatorial combat. Such games are not fictional in character. Football could have been more like Russian roulette. Imagine a football tournament where serious injuries were not treated, but injured players were forced to carry on no matter how detrimental it was to their health, and where the teams that lost matches were taken away and executed. In such circumstances, the players would hardly need to pretend that the activity and outcome were important. The difference between those kinds of football matches and ours does not lie in the content of the activity. Both kinds of matches are football matches. Rather, the difference lies in the manner in which the football matches are played, i.e. their character. All I assume in this book is that we can recognize an activity as football – that there is something which is properly called football – and that this activity can be played in different ways or manners.

Throughout the book, I exploit various parallels between the world of sport and the world of art. Suffice to say here that I do not conflate art and sport, and that I assume we can distinguish the aesthetic from the artistic. Football, like mountain ranges, sunsets, tiger stripes, etc., can have aesthetic value, while having no artistic function (Best 1978: 113–114). Aesthetic value is not confined to works of art. Moreover, while works of fiction, like fiction film, literature, etc., are commonly thought of as works of art, but not necessarily the other way round, there is little temptation to think of football and football matches as fine art.[5] Among the different views on artistic function, i.e. the purpose of art, the most helpful contrast to sports is the view that regards fine art as something that (at its best) teaches us important lessons about the world. Cynthia Freeland argues that "[a]rtworks stimulate cognitive activity that may teach us about the world", and Martha Nussbaum claims that the special strength of literature is that it can reveal the human condition in an illuminating fashion (Freeland 1997: 19, Nussbaum 1990, see also Nussbaum 1995). Indeed, "certain truths about human life can only be fittingly and accurately stated in the language and forms characteristic of the narrative artist" (Nussbaum 1990: 5). The Nussbaum-Freeland view is that fine art and literature can educate our emotions and contribute to our moral development. It is an open empirical question whether the Nussbaum-Freeland view on literature and fine art as a special provider or felicitator of insights into the human condition – insights that make us better persons – is correct.[6] However, I think it is uncontroversial that, on a phenomenological level, many (perhaps most) readers of great fiction writers – the likes of Tolstoy, Austen, Ibsen and others of their stature – have a sense that they are being presented with important insights into the human condition that enrich their intellectual lives.

Compared to the above-mentioned writers, I think it is safe to say that, for most of us, playing or watching football gives no similar sense of intellectual depth and importance. In line with this, Kupfer notes that:

> Where theatre presents real ends and activities in a pretend setting, the significance of even the ends and activities are pretended in sport.
> *(Kupfer 1983: 114)*

Note that, here, Kupfer explicitly endorses what I have called the Nussbaum-Freeland view on art as an activity that can help us to understand the world better, making us better persons, etc. Art matters because art has real ends, i.e., ordinary world ends. Suits has a related view on how art and sports differ. According to Suits, the subject matter of art is as follows:

> [T]he actions and passions of men: with human aspirations and frustrations, hopes and fears, triumphs and tragedies, with flaws of character, moral dilemmas, joy and sorrow.
> *(Suits 1978: 152)*

In short, fine art addresses the human condition, whereas sports have no subject matter outside the activity itself. On the latter point, David Best claims, "the very notion of a *subject* of sport makes no sense" (Best 1978: 122). Art forms such as literature, fiction film, theatre, etc., often present that which is made up, and rely on pretence, but their respective subject matters often concern the real world. Furthermore, according to the Nussbaum-Freeland view, art can also help us to deal better with that world and become better people. Sports such as football, it would seem, are not like that in any straightforward manner.[7]

Admittedly, in the philosophy of sport, claims have been made to the contrary. Stephen Mumford, for example, believes that sport "provides an aesthetic insight into the nature of our embodied existence" (Mumford 2012a: 140, see also Mumford 2014: 192). Even if Mumford may be right about this, it would also seem correct to say that football is not geared towards or set up with aesthetic insight as its main objective or purpose. Your average footballer and football spectator do not first and foremost think of football as providing aesthetic insight into the nature of our embodied existence. In contrast, one would not have to look far into the art world to find artists (fiction writers, painters, fiction filmmakers, etc.) who explicitly aim to provide us with knowledge about the world and the human condition, and to find an audience that believes artists sometimes succeed in doing just that.

On the other hand, I do not wish to suggest that you cannot learn anything about the human condition by playing or watching football matches (or sports in general). Insofar as playing and watching football are human activities, they will also be possible venues for insight into our nature and our place in the world. But again, sport does not seem geared towards gaining insights or new perspectives on the human condition or any other area (see Suits 1978: 152–153, and Wenz 2006: 238).[8] Football is an important window into the human condition, but the activity or practice as such is not about the human condition. There is a difference in ambition between the art world and the sport world in this respect. It might be difficult to draw a sharp line between fine art and sport, especially because it is notoriously difficult to define "art" and "fine art". Still, it is safe to assume that while sports can have aesthetic value, they have no artistic function and, furthermore, that the difference between making or perceiving art and playing or watching sport is immediately felt by (most of) those engaged in these activities.

Some kinds of make-believe

Football is not a fiction in the naïve, ordinary language sense or senses of the word, but there are other ways to understand fiction and fictionality. If we look at Kendall Walton's notion of fiction, which is quite different from its naïve, ordinary language counterpart or counterparts, then a football match can be a fiction. According to Walton, fictions are that which prompts games of make-believe. Let us call this a Waltonian fiction.

> *Representations* [i.e. fictions] (...) are things possessing the social function of serving as props in games of make-believe.
>
> *(Walton 1990: 69)*[9]

> Any work with the function of serving as a prop in games of make-believe, however minor or peripheral or instrumental this function might be, qualifies as "fiction".
>
> *(Walton 1990: 72)*

> [T]o be fictional is, at bottom, to possess the function of serving as a prop in games of make-believe.
>
> *(Walton 1990: 102)*

Walton adds, "representations [fictions] need not be *works*, human artifacts" (Walton 1990: 72). Take Walton's example of the child, which "comes across a stump shaped strikingly like a bear" and "imagines a bear blocking her path" (Walton 1990: 21). The stump is a prop in the child's make-believe. The stump, *qua* representing a bear in the child's make-believe, is fictional. Clearly, a football match can be fictional in this sense. Just think of children playing a game of football, while imagining that their game is the World Cup final. That game of football is fictional *qua* representing the World Cup final. On the other hand, a great many or most football matches are not used as props in these kinds of games of make-believe – they do not represent other imaginary matches or scenarios. I will ignore this category of Waltonian football fictions.

Furthermore, Walton's inclusive categorization of fiction has met resistance, and alternative views are available. Consider, for example, the intentionalist view of fiction. The intentionalist line on fiction is that for something to count as a fiction, someone must consciously present and think of that something as make-believe. Proponents of this line would take exception to both Dawkins's and Emeritus Pope Benedict's use of the word "fiction". Instead of calling the Old Testament, the Gospels and *The Selfish Gene* fictions, they should, according to the intentionalists, merely describe them as false. On the other hand, intentionalists also hold that fictions involve that which is made up and not real. That is, in the act of inviting someone to imagine that such-and-such is real, it is the such-and-such that is not actual and is meant to be imagined. According to the intentionalist view, merely being made up or not real is not enough for something to count as a fiction. This would explain why we do not generally think and talk about myths, for example the Norse myths, as fiction, even though they are all false and some perhaps inspired by natural phenomena. An example of the latter would be believing that lightning is caused by Thor throwing his hammer. The props (like the lightning) must be consciously appropriated for there to be a fiction, and in the case of mythology they were not (Lamarque and Olsen 1994: 47–49, Currie 1990: 36). Thus, according to the intentionalist view, myths do not count as fictions. One way to look at the intentionalist view of fiction is to see it as a defence of a refined naïve, ordinary language account of fiction. The intricacies of this debate, however, need not worry us, because there are sport-specific reasons for resisting the idea that football should count as a Waltonian fiction.

The intentionalist view (which includes literature, fiction films, etc.) and Waltonian fictions (which also include, among other things, child's play) define fiction restrictively, and both allow consumers of fiction (i.e., the audience) to:

> A: Fill in certain aspects of the fictional world that are not explicitly represented in the artistic vehicle providing the narrative or fictional world, but

which seem reasonable, perhaps even necessary, for understanding that fictional world or the narrative as it unfolds in that fictional world.

B: Speculate and fantasize about what happened to the fictional characters after the final page has been read or the final scene has been watched, and with regard to Waltonian fictions like child's play, add to the fiction at will.

The possibility of this sort of *filling in*, further speculation or fantasizing and *adding on* seems to be a result of or part of the nature of fictions. Peter Lamarque and Stein Haugom Olsen note that the phenomenon that consumers of fiction "often fantasize with fictive content, 'filling in' as the whim takes them" is "[a]n integral part of responding to fiction" (Lamarque and Olsen 1994: 89). There is no similar phenomenon with regard to football. We can (and will in Chapter 4) talk in a loose sense about a narrative unfolding in a football match, but there is no filling in, speculation, fantasizing or adding on to be done when watching football. A football audience might want their team to play better, wish for goals and even fantasize that their team will beat a hugely superior opponent while the game is ongoing. However, the nature and structure of a football match do not allow for the kind of filling in, speculation, fantasizing or adding on that we find in fiction appreciation. When watching a football match, you are presented with the whole of the match. There are no elements to be filled in. Furthermore, a football match, a cup run, a tournament, a season, etc., have clearly defined beginnings and ends, and thus there is no adding on to be done with regard to one's engagement in a football match, cup run, etc. This gives us reasons to withhold the label of "fiction" from football matches, if fiction is understood in the naïve, ordinary language sense, the intentionalist view of fiction or as a Waltonian fiction.[10]

Still, football matches give rise to a certain kind of make-believe – that winning football matches matters – and as will become apparent, for that reason there are similarities between football appreciation and fiction appreciation that are worth exploring. Sometimes I will write about how football is fictional in character, at other times I will condense it and write about the football fiction. The phrase "football's fictional character" will be used interchangeably with the phrase "the football fiction". One such obvious similarity between fiction and football is that neither is directly needed for fulfilling people's needs in the everyday ordinary world. They belong to the extra-ordinary side of human existence.

Sport is extra-ordinary

Even though John Austin reminded us that "ordinary language has no claim to be the last word (…) in principle it can everywhere be supplemented and improved upon and superseded", it can sometimes be useful to look at the etymology and ordinary usage of a word, because, after all, "it *is the first* word" (Austin 1956: 11). If we look at the entry on "sport" in the big *Oxford English Dictionary*, we find words like "play", "diversion", "entertainment", "recreation" and "pastime" to describe the noun, and similarly, words like "to play in a lively, energetic way", "to divert oneself", "to entertain oneself" and "to have a leisurely time" to describe the activity of doing sport. Furthermore, consult your semantic intuition on what the difference between, say, fishing and fishing for sport (sport fishing), climbing and climbing for sport (sport climbing), etc. amounts to. The latter are activities that are undertaken not as a means of survival (whether it be for economic gain or getting food) or reproduction, or that otherwise seem to be done to produce something we deem valuable, with regard to everyday concerns or as part of our quest to better our circumstances. This is in contrast to, one might suspect, doing philosophy, painting the garden shed, etc. Game playing and sport are not directly valuable for ordinary world concerns (though there might be various indirect valuable effects of such activities or practices). Rather, we engage in such activities not because we have to, but for the fun of it – as a diversion, entertainment, recreation or pastime. Games and sport are basically unnecessary activities, where unnecessary activities are understood as not directly needed (superfluous) with regard to meeting everyday, ordinary world needs. This is the sense in which games and sports are an extra with regard to the ordinary world; they are not extraordinary, but extra-ordinary.[11]

Doing something for sport, playing games and, furthermore, playing games that are sports are not everyday activities that are undertaken for specific and useful gains, but something we voluntarily engage in even though the activity *qua* that activity does not have a specific purpose outside the sport itself. The latter means that sport is not only unnecessary in the sense of not being directly valuable for ordinary world concerns, but also in the sense that doing sports does not address or is not seen to address issues or topics of that everyday world – in contrast to, based on certain conceptions, fine art, rituals, religion, etc. The basic insight that sports and games are not needed for ordinary world concerns, I suspect, was the main reason for Bernard Suits's famous analysis of games, which he summed up as follows: "playing a game is the voluntary attempt to overcome unnecessary obstacles" (Suits 1978: 55). Suits's analysis, however, is about the content of games, and, as Graham McFee has pointed out, for certain games like chess "the idea of 'unnecessary obstacles' makes no sense", because "[n]o 'obstacles' here seem explicable *independently* of the game" (McFee 2004: 25). So either talk of unnecessary obstacles is circular because in some games the so-called unnecessary obstacles only emerge as a result of the game playing itself, or it is redundant because it is the unnecessary element and not the obstacle element that is of importance. Suffice it to say here that I believe any analysis or elucidation of both sports and games would have to make this unnecessary element central.[12] Indeed, William Morgan refined and condensed Suits's definition to the basic idea of sports following a "gratuitous logic", and that involves, in effect, emphasizing sports as unnecessary activities, while omitting the part about unnecessary obstacles (Morgan 1994: 211). Similarly, Mike McNamee holds that sports are "characterized by a gratuitous logic involving, centrally, physical skills" (McNamee 2008: 19). Though many philosophers of sport reject Suits's more elaborated analysis of games and sports, most accept that sports follow a gratuitous logic. The underlying understanding of sport I will work with, until we can address the topic in detail in Chapter 3, is that sports are unnecessary and autotelic competitive, physical-skill activities involving rules.

The reason I stress that sports and games are unnecessary – both in the sense of not being directly valuable for ordinary world concerns and not seen as addressing or being about ordinary world concerns – is that some activities or practices belonging to the extra-ordinary side of human existence are seen as addressing or being about ordinary world concerns. Belonging to the extra-ordinary side of human life are artistic performances (theatre, dance, music, etc.) and art of various kinds (literature, fiction film, paintings, etc.), and these works of art differ from sport and games. Only the former has an artistic function and is conceived of by its audience as having one. Furthermore, some works of art are intended to influence and succeed in influencing the ordinary world. Harriet Beecher Stowe's *Uncle Tom's Cabin; or, Life Among the Lowly* is an example of the latter. Such works of art are extra-ordinary, but unlike sports they are not unnecessary in the sense of not addressing or being about ordinary world concerns.[13] Clearly, Stowe intended for her book to say something specific about the slave trade of her day as well as to influence her own age, i.e., the ordinary world. This is how we understand the work as a whole and its various parts. How different things look with regard to football! It hardly makes sense to think of the various parts of a football game as being anything like the parts of *Uncle Tom's Cabin*. For example, the moves Brazil's Marta pulled off when she turned USA's defence inside out and scored her famous second goal in the semi-final of the Woman's World Cup in China in 2007 (Brazil's fourth goal in their 4–0 demolition of USA) function differently. Works of art have an artistic function and can also aim to influence and succeed in influencing the ordinary world in a way that sports do not.[14] Another extra-ordinary world activity or practice, which also does not seem unnecessary in the same way as football is, is religion and religious practice, including religious rituals. I take it to be uncontroversial that (many) religious practices are believed to influence and are relevant (for their practitioners) to ordinary world concerns. Thus, religious practices do not qualify as being unnecessary in the same way sport is.

The extra-ordinary is understood as that which comes on top of or alongside the ordinary everyday world of common concerns, and which is generally conceived of as something different than everyday life. This way of delineating the extra-ordinary might seem almost trivial or vacuous. However, I am not sure if the activities or practices that come on top of or alongside the ordinary – ranging from penance to minigolf – have much more in common than being something other than the ordinary. The notion of "the extra-ordinary" proves its worth not by its definition or the delineation it provides, but by helping us to show or point to exemplars of the extra-ordinary that fit the bill of not being ordinary world activities or practices. Both the sacred and the art world are paradigmatic examples of domains that are understood by us as being something other than our everyday life. A particular bodily movement within a sacred context, such as a religious ritual, is something different and is understood differently than the same type of bodily movement carried out as part of, say, manual labour. We relate to and perceive a particular bodily movement very differently if we believe or know it is part of a religious ritual – the sacred and extra-ordinary domain – than if we believe or know it is part of a person's everyday labour – the profane and ordinary domain. The same applies to art. Take, for example, the ready-made art of Marcel Duchamp, for example, *Fountain* (1915). We behave quite differently towards a urinal from the Bedfordshire model porcelain urinal production line when it is presented as art in a gallery – the profane and extra-ordinary domain – than we do when encountering it in the men's room at the local pub – the profane and ordinary domain. Indeed, when presenting *Fountain* Duchamp exploited the fact that we conceive of things presented as art in a gallery differently than we do when encountering them in ordinary life, i.e. the ordinary world. I doubt, however, that there are many other interesting commonalities between a religious ritual like, say, communion, Duchamp's *Fountain* and a football match between, say, Plymouth Argyle and Wycombe Wanderers, than that these activities can all be marked off as things that are different from everyday, ordinary activities. These sort of activities are non-ordinary, and I call that the extra-ordinary.[15]

The fictional character of football – that it involves a type of make-believe, which I will argue is also characteristic of at least one type of play and play behaviour – gives you football as extra-ordinary. Make-believe and play are superfluous with regard to everyday needs, and that gives us reason to think of them as extra-ordinary. A similar line of thought is found in Johan Huizinga's *Homo Ludens* when he writes about "the 'extra-ordinary' nature of play" (Huizinga 1950: 13) and presents his famous definition of play:

> [A] free activity standing quite consciously outside "ordinary" life as being "not serious", but at the same time absorbing the player intensely and utterly. It is an activity connected with no material interest, and no profit can be gained by it.
>
> *(Huizinga 1950: 13)*

Whereas the tradition stemming from Huizinga often conflates the idea of play being not serious with play being playful or whimsical, Huizinga himself makes no such mistake. "[S]ome play" Huizinga tells us, "can be very serious indeed" and "football (…) [is] played in profound seriousness" (Huizinga 1950: 5, 6). Play need not be playful or whimsical. For Huizinga, the non-seriousness of play lies in the fact "that play is not 'ordinary' or 'real' life" (Huizinga 1950: 8). Similarly, when Roger Caillois discusses mimic play – arguing that it involves make-believe and as-if behaviour of a certain kind, while games and sport "are played *for real*" – he also acknowledges that, regarding games and sports, the "[r]ules [of games and sport] create fictions" and that "[t]he one who plays chess, prisoner's base, polo, or baccara, by the very fact of complying with their respective rules, is separated from real life" (Caillois 1961: 8). In this respect, games and sports are similar to play, where "play is essentially a separate occupation, carefully isolated from the rest of life" (Caillois 1961: 6). For Caillois, a sport like football does not involve mimicry, i.e.

the actions are for real within the game and are not performed by dramatic personae in an as-if-they-were-something-else fashion, nor are they used as props in games of make-believe. On the other hand, he also claims that football and other sports involve some kind of fictionality and that they are delimited from real life, i.e. as extra-ordinary.

Huizinga sees all extra-ordinary activities or practices as play. This puts sport and games on a par with other extra-ordinary practices such as religion and art. Let us consider religion. Religious practitioners often conceive of their practice as important for this life and the afterlife, believing that one can profit from religion in both realms. According to Huizinga's own lights, they should not count as play.[16] They are conceived of as having an effect on the ordinary world, while games and sport are not. At one point, Huizinga claims, "for the adult and responsible human being play is a function which he could equally well leave alone. Play is superfluous" (Huizinga 1950: 8). This accords well with games and sports as we play them, but does not hold for the committed religious practitioner, at least not from his or her perspective.[17]

We also do well to note that play is more primitive than games and sport, as "animals have not waited for man to teach them their playing" (Huizinga 1950: 1). Furthermore, "games are artifacts, conventions", and the same applies to sports like football, whereas play is loose and flexible in a way that the culturally grounded rule-governed natures of games and sport are not (Kretchmar 2007: 1).[18] If one were to hold the view that play has rules, then one might say that play's rules are player defined and dynamic, whereas game and sport rules are a priori or, perhaps better, given prior to individual gaming or sporting events. This does not mean that Huizinga is incorrect in thinking that all games and sport should count as play, even though there is play that does not count as games and sport. On the other hand, the types of games and sports that count as play in Huizinga's picture of things are very broad. They range from "[c]hildren's games, football, and chess" to "games (...) [where] duels [were] fought to the death" (Huizinga 1950: 6, 49). My inclination is to reserve the notion of "play" for the former only, and to not regard games and sports that are literally a matter of life and death as play. Indeed, I have a hard time conceiving of duels fought to the death as play, whereas I have no problem imagining scenarios in which such duels were part of a game or constituted a sport. If, however, one insists that ancient gladiatorial combat – or combat sports like pankration of the ancient Olympics and other games or sport activities in which the standard procedures include contestants being seriously injured or dying – should count as play, then there is still an important distinction to be made between play that is fictional in character and play that is not.[19]

Aliefs, football behaviour and the purpose of football

In a passing remark in his classical study *Mimesis as Make-Believe*, Kendall Walton writes that he suspects "make-believe may be crucially involved (...) in the role of sports in our culture" (Walton 1990: 7, see also Borge 2010a: 28–29, Borge 2010b:

169). Later Walton added that "[t]o participate either as a competitor or as a spectator [of sports and competitive games] is frequently to engage in pretence" (Walton 2015: 75). Also, as we saw, Kupfer believes that sports involve pretence, as we "'pretend' that the activity and outcome are important", and sports writer Heywood Hale Brown describes the basic movement of a spectator's engagement in sport as "puff[ing] up the delusion that it matter[s]" (Kupfer 1983: 114, Brown 1979: 17). However, even though make-believe is involved, football, as we have seen, is clearly not a fiction in the ordinary sense or senses of the word. Also, as argued, Waltonian fictions have properties that football does not share and should as such not be equated with football and football matches. The fictionality of football lies elsewhere. The main fiction present in football, i.e., the essential pretence (or make-believe) involved in football matches, is that winning football matches matters. But in truth it does not, or alternatively, it does not matter in the same way as ordinary world activities do. Football does not matter in itself, or alternatively, it matters due to our willingness to make it matter. It is against the background of a specific type of pretence or make-believe that winning football matches becomes important.

The suggestion that animated crowds of football fans at big matches are merely pretending to care should strike us as curious. After all, the engagement one witnesses on football's major occasions, like a Champions League final, does not have the feel of make-believe or pretence. Granted, I am not suggesting that the average football supporter makes a conscious decision to pretend to care about his or her team and how the team does during a particular match. The suggestion is rather that to view a football match as something it is important to win takes or involves a certain kind of make-believe. It is a willingness to view it as something that matters. This does not, however, preclude football supporters from genuinely caring about their teams and the actions on the pitch. An emotional reaction to something might depend on a certain kind of pretence, but that does not make the emotions any less real.[20] Once you are in the position of viewing football matches as something that matters, then you can let your emotions run free at any particular football match. In fact, I suspect that football supporters' emotional engagement in their teams is heightened by the fact that it is based on some sort of pretence. Unlike in ordinary life, you can lose yourself emotionally in the moment due to the artificiality of a situation – an unnecessary and constructed activity that does not directly serve any particular ordinary life purposes – that has no ramifications for your own life. Whether winning or losing, a particular football match normally has no material consequences for the spectator's own life, and so football does not matter – or matters in a very different way than ordinary world concerns do.

Let us take a second to contemplate the reaction of a football supporter when his or her team scores an important goal. Then imagine someone without any prior knowledge of football (or any other forms of sport) witnessing the event. What would such a person make of the supporter's reaction? A natural interpretation of the supporter's reaction would be to believe he or she just realized that something wonderful had happened – the birth of a baby in the family, winning the national lottery, an announcement that war is over, etc. The truth, however, is that the goal scored, the cup won, the relegation avoided, etc., generally have almost no actual effect on the average football supporter's life. There is a discord between the behaviour of the football supporter, i.e. his or her displayed engagement, and the importance of what happened on the pitch with regard to his or her everyday life. We can safely assume that football supporters know they will be no better off come Monday morning and another working week, even if their team won. The discordance between behaviour (wild celebrations on the terraces) and belief (knowledge that their team's win will not improve their life situation) is less puzzling if we construe football engagement as involving some kind of make-believe or pretence analogous or corresponding to that of engagement in fiction. That is, our engagement in fiction is puzzling enough, but at least engagement in football is no more puzzling. Consider the following analogy as well. We might think it is wise in ordinary life, and useful as a coping mechanism, to keep our emotions under control during difficult times. On the other hand, we allow ourselves to give these emotions free rein when watching an emotionally stirring melodrama at the cinema. Engagement in fiction is enhanced, not undermined, by the fact that it builds on a type of pretence or make-believe, and it is not far-fetched to think that something similar happens with regard to engagement in football.

This parallel between engagement in fiction and sport seems rather obvious, but has been overlooked. Whereas researchers in aesthetics readily pose the question "Why care about the fate of Anna Karenina?" philosophers of sport have not posed a question like "Why care about the fate of Manchester United FC?" in the same manner. A notable exception is Roland Barthes, who in his impressionistic comments on sport and football asks the right questions:

> What need have these men to attack? Why are men disturbed by this spectacle? Why do they commit themselves to it so completely? Why this useless combat?
>
> *(Barthes 2007: 63, 65)*

Another exception is Walton, who in a similar manner asks:

> Why should people care about the Yankees or the Red Sox? Their fortunes on the field have no obvious bearing on the welfare of most fans. Why does it matter whether the home team wins or loses? Life will go on afterwards just as it did before, regardless. (...) It is hard to resist comparing the avid sports fan to the playgoer who sheds bitter and voluminous tears over the tragic fate of Romeo and Juliet, and twenty minutes later has a jolly good time with her friends at an espresso bar.
>
> *(Walton 2015: 76–77)*[21]

Perhaps the analogy between the two questions has gone unnoticed by philosophers of sport owing to certain dissimilarities. The most glaring disanalogy, of course, is that Anna Karenina is a fictional character, while Manchester United FC is a real team with real people as players. However, once one looks past the ontological issues (fictional versus non-fictional entities) and instead asks why we care and invest emotions in matters – the fate of Anna Karenina and Manchester United – that do not in any (significant) material way positively affect our own life situation, then the two questions are more similar. Notice also that the fact that sport victories have a positive effect on supporters' emotional life does not constitute an objection to the question posed in this section (Zillmann 2013: 139–140). The question here is why care about a sport like football in the first place. Again, a comparison to everyday life serves us well. For example, the world economy does affect my life situation and that gives me reason to care about it, whereas the fate of a football team does not affect me in the same way. Once I care about a team, I can reap an emotional harvest if they win, but this does not explain why I came to feel this mattered in the first place. Moreover, recall that, based on engagement in fiction like literature and fiction film, we have uncontroversial cases of emotional engagement that build on some kind of pretence or make-believe. Thus, pretence or make-believe – under whatever guise it operates in engagement in whatever activity we are talking about – is obviously no obstacle to that emotional engagement.

Another possible reason why this similarity has eluded philosophers of sport may be that, while football teams often function as symbols of local pride and identity, fictional characters seldom serve that purpose. There are no doubt reasons to believe that part of football's success is based on the sport's potential to forge and reinforce identity, but to put it bluntly, some sort of attraction to the game of football is what made it suitable as a vessel of identity, not the other way round. Furthermore, it would seem reasonable to consider local identity part of the reason why someone would hold dear a team like Gillingham FC, though the same cannot be said of your average Manchester United supporter. Most Manchester United supporters are not from Manchester, nor do they have any connection to the region apart from the football team.[22] The same applies, to varying degrees, to a number of other football teams.[23]

The fact that football teams function as symbols of national, regional or local (or other) pride and identity does not mean that our engagement in football matches does not involve some kind of make-believe. One could argue that football teams, as symbols of identity, are made-up, artificial entities or social constructs, which, *qua* such symbols, only come to emotional life and are only upheld through a kind of make-believe, i.e., that their football team winning matters for the nation, region or local community. Unlike other social constructs such as money, football teams do not directly serve ordinary life purposes, and our emotional investment in them itself is part of the reason we care about them. On the other hand, the need or longing for a social identity, which supporting a football team can provide, is most likely an important element in understanding supporters' emotional investment in and strong responses to the fortunes of their football team. Various ritual-like elements surround football matches, especially in relation to important events like cup finals. These elements, which include playing (national) anthems, singing supporter songs, the banners, presentation of the teams, the colours of their jerseys, etc., serve as props that promote the identity-making aspect of football. These elements intensify and heighten supporters' emotional engagement in the match. But how does that engagement even come about, given my claim that football matches do not actually matter, or alternatively, that they matter in a very different manner than ordinary world activities do? Moreover, why is football generally so much more suitable as a vehicle for national or regional pride and identity making than, say, chess is? The suggested answer is that football, and other constructive-destructive contact sports, provide a less cerebral, more emotionally raw spectator experience that better fits the us-versus-them aspect of identity-making and identity-maintenance projects.[24]

The basis of our engagement in football as spectators is grounded in, I suggest, the excitement of perceiving others involved in a bodily struggle. This excitement derives from the activation of mental states involved in typical fight-or-flight situations. At the same time, however, we understand that this bodily struggle is artificial, i.e., is not an ordinary life struggle. Similarly, when we ourselves play sports like football, our excitement is grounded in the activation of mental states involved in typical fight-or-flight situations, but this excitement is tempered by the fact that sport practitioners are aware that they are not involved in a dangerous situation, merely playing a sport. The foundation upon which our emotional involvement in football is built can best be understood as an example of the phenomenon that Tamar Gendler has recently brought into focus again and that she has dubbed alief. According to Gendler, alief is a kind of belief-like state that does not quite achieve the level of belief; aliefs are more primitive and reality insensitive, though they seem to give rise to behaviour we would not consider automatic reflexes. Gendler writes:

> [A]n alief is a mental state with associatively linked content that is representational, affective, and behavioural, and that is activated – consciously or unconsciously – by features of the subject's internal or ambient environment. It is a more primitive state than either belief or imagination: it directly activates behavioural response patterns (as opposed to motivating in conjunction with desire or pretended desire).
>
> *(Gendler 2008a: 255)*

Elsewhere, Gendler gives the notion of alief a more evolutionary spin when she writes, "[a]n alief is (...) an innate or habitual propensity to respond to an apparent stimulus in a particular way" (Gendler 2008b: 282). Gendler describes aliefs as consisting of three components: "the representation of some object or concept or situation or circumstance", "the experience of some affective or emotional state" and, finally, "the readying of some motor routine" (Gendler 2008a: 263–264). "Typically", aliefs are "affect-laden and action-generating" (Gendler 2008b: 288). In general, when all is cognitive smooth sailing for creatures like us, then aliefs and beliefs travel side by side and are in accord. However, it is when there is a discord between how we react or behave and what we believe that the phenomenon of aliefs comes into focus and that justifies Gendler's introduction of the concept. Consider a key example from Gendler.

> The Grand Canyon Skywalk: When walking the horseshoe-shaped glass-floored walkway protruding 4000 feet above the Grand Canyon many visitors find themselves gripped by vertigo and anxiety, not daring to look down or struggling to walk on, but "[s]urely they *believe* that the walkway will hold (...) [so] there is something else going on" (Gendler 2008a: 256). Gendler suggests that, while such visitors "wholeheartedly *believe* that the walkway is completely safe, they also *alieve* something very different. The alief has roughly the following content: "Really high up, long, long way down. Not a safe place to be! Get off!!" (Gendler 2008a: 256).

In the *Grand Canyon Skywalk* case, the mind says "go for it" at the level of belief-desire, but the agent also seems to think "no" at a more primitive level, which Gendler calls alief. Other telling examples of this phenomenon are the disgust experiments conducted by Paul Rozin's research group (Rozin et al. 1986). For example, subjects who had eaten a piece of high-quality chocolate fudge and wanted another balked when presented with chocolate that was realistically shaped like dog faeces (Rozin et al. 1986: 705). Surely they did not believe they had dog faeces in front of them, but nonetheless, according to Gendler, they alieved "Filthy object! Contaminated! Stay away!" (Gendler 2008a: 257).

Gendler's concept of "alief" as being between mere mental and behavioural reflexes on the one side, and full-blown belief on the other, is controversial. The debated issue is whether we should credit this intermediate category with being a "fundamental mental state as opposed to an *amalgam* of several more primitive mental states" (Gendler 2012: 805). Or as Tyler Doggett puts it, "Is there a unity to alief where this goes beyond the fact that typically there is the co-activation of alief's components" (Doggett 2012: 772, see also Currie and Ichino 2012: 790–794, Egan 2011: 66–70). The issue of whether the concept should be taken at face value as a mental state *sui generis* or seen as a convenient shorthand for an explanation – which in the end will only appeal to well-known psychological categories like belief, desire, imagination, etc. – need not worry us here. The phenomenon that "alief" is meant to capture is real enough and uncontested by Gendler's critics. I am going to remain neutral on the ontological issue and treat the notion of "alief" as a convenient term to use when writing about the phenomenon, that is, the phenomenon of subdoxastic representations of objects, situations and circumstances that are resilient to countervailing beliefs the subject might have and that give rise to affects and a propensity to act, which sometimes results in belief-behaviour mismatch. Our engagement in football, I will argue, builds on such a state or amalgam of states.

Gendler touches upon sport, but her example is of the "sports fan watching a televised rerun", where "[t]he sports fan will feel the temptation to shout at the screen even if she emphatically reminds herself that she is watching a rerun", or else, whether the broadcast is live or not, must know that "the images before [her] are nothing more than patterns of pixels on a screen" (Gendler 2008b: 283, 286). As Gendler suggests, "the sports fan alieves that his team is playing right now, (...) or that his cheer will help his team win" (Gendler 2008b: 290), while Gregory Currie and Anna Ichino rather suggest "that she vividly imagines being at the match" (Currie and Ichino 2012: 793). The focus of the example is misplaced. My own experience is that, phenomenologically speaking, it makes no or little difference for engagement whether or not the broadcast of the match is live, as long as you do not know the result.[25] Furthermore, why should it be that what causes engagement in a football match seen from the terraces is fundamentally different from what causes engagement in front of the television? Explain engagement in football and you have your explanation of people on the terraces, in front of their television sets and watching reruns of matches they do not know the result of, etc. It is not essential that the event or activity be live or not, or mediated or non-mediated. Engagement in football is not the only phenomenon this would seem to apply to. Consider pornography. Watching an adult person of the opposite sex (if that is your sexual preference) undress, make sexually explicit movements, etc. in the right circumstances tends to make the onlooker sexually aroused. We might think of the alief part of this as "Potential sexual partner. Sexual arousal. Physiological reaction". Someone consuming pornography from a magazine, DVD, internet site, etc., knows that the person(s) he or she is watching is not a potential sexual partner. Still, watching pornography arouses people. Here, I submit, there is no temptation to think that the masturbating consumer of pornography is alieving, or imagining for that matter, that the event being watched is actually taking place while he or she is watching, or that he or she is on site during the event. Rather, the person – as in the case when a potential sexual partner is present – alieves "Potential sexual partner. Sexual arousal. Physiological reaction". A similar consideration holds for the sport fan example. The question is why we engage in football at all, and that question connects with the question of what type of sport football is.

Football is a constructive-destructive sport. The defining feature of constructive-destructive sports is that winning a single competition is settled with reference to conventions for counting the score, or when one of the competitors is unable to continue the competition. Another essential feature of constructive-destructive sports is that the sporting activity could not be done without the other competitor. How well you perform in a football match is partly a consequence of your opponent's performance. The reason for this is that constructive-destructive sports are dual in nature. On the constructive side, the nature of a constructive-destructive sport like football is to try to create or invent ways to score, while at the same time, on the destructive side, try to destroy, prevent or obstruct the other team's attempts to do the same. This direct-hinder criterion is what sets constructive-destructive sports apart from complex measurement sports such as running a marathon and road bicycle racing. The defining feature of measurement sports is that winning a singular competition is settled with reference to a measurement: who ran fastest, who jumped highest, who threw longest, who lifted heaviest and so on. In modern sports, the meritocratic standards for these types of competitions are typically realized by measuring a physical phenomenon numerically, such as the time it took to run a race, the length of the throw and so on.[26] Furthermore, football is a constructive-destructive contact sport, where the direct-hinder element of the sport is constituted by physical challenges between the opposing sport practitioners. In my view, the perception of physical challenges – or for the sport practitioners, the anticipation and experience of such challenges – is what initially activates our excitement and engagement in sport at the alief level.

Here the parallel between engaging in fiction and sport is useful. Consider Gendler's take on Walton's famous example: "Charles is watching a horror movie about a terrible green slime", when "Charles emits a shriek and clutches desperately at his chair" as "[t]he slime, picking up speed, oozes on a new course straight toward the viewers", while "know[ing] perfectly well that the slime is not real and that he is in no danger" (Walton 1978: 5–6). Gendler agrees with Walton that Charles believes he is sitting safely in a cinema, but in Gendler's view, at another more primitive level, Charles alieves that "Dangerous two-eyed creature heading towards me! H-e-l-p …! Activate fight-or-flight adrenaline now" (Gendler 2008a: 258). Similarly, I suggest, when watching a constructive-destructive contact sport, the spectator who perceives the physical struggle such sports involve has his or her own cognitive machinery alerted to ready him or her for a physical struggle. Constructive-destructive contact sports vary in the intensity and directness of the physical struggle they entail. This struggle ranges from the direct violence of boxing and other fight sports, where the contact is the means by which you win or score points in the contest, through the tackling and clashing of bodies seen in football, American football and ice hockey, among others, to less aggressive contact sports like basketball.[27] Still, it seems reasonable to believe that all these sports involve the same sort of alief mechanism, though the intensity may vary with the level of violence involved. The physical struggle on the pitch, which a football match is, activates the spectators' own fight-or-flight mechanisms, causing them to alieve: "Physical struggle/fight! D-a-n-g-e-r …! Activate fight-or-flight adrenaline now." At the same time, your average football spectator is clearly aware that the physical struggle on the pitch, involving physical contact and challenges between players, is not an actual (ordinary world) struggle that the spectator should be ready to participate in or flee from, but a game of football. We do not generally see fight-or-flight behaviour on the terraces, because spectators clearly know there is no real danger, even though they have readied themselves for danger at an alief level.

A further consequence of this line of reasoning is that it can explain the aggressive behaviour of sport spectators on the terraces. On the one hand, the sport spectators are merely letting loose aggressive emotions, which have been activated by or are associated with the fight-or-flight adrenaline. On the other, they know at the same time that this display of aggression will not have the same consequences it might have had if the situation had been outside the sport context. Sometimes that aggression spills over the sport context and ends up in real fighting between spectators. Note once again the parallel to fiction appreciation. As previously mentioned, when watching a stirring melodrama one might allow oneself to cry one's eyes out. This may even be a consequence of not allowing oneself or being unable to cry about troubles in one's own life. One is, after all, fully aware that the death of Catherine in Emily Brontë's *Wuthering Heights* is not sad in reality, because there is no such person (in our world). Moreover, engagement in literature can spill over from the make-believe context of fiction to reality, for instance when some young men in the grip of Johann Wolfgang von Goethe's novel *The Sorrows of Young Werther* themselves committed suicide. The so-called Werther effect, however, is controversial and has been contested (see Thorson and Öberg 2003, whereas Lester 2004 suggests that there are real cases of the Werther effect). Still, the most striking parallel between fiction appreciation and engagement in football is the opportunity they avail to let emotions flow freely. When at the football ground, one might allow oneself to let loose one's aggression, perhaps here too because one must not or cannot do so in response to troubles in one's own life, as the football game context ensures there will be no consequences to pay. There will be no actual fight-or-flight situations. The line of argument presented in this section also explains why sport spectators at football matches, boxing matches and other constructive-destructive contact sporting events behave in a much more animated way than spectators at sport competitions that do not involve similar physical challenges, such as gymnastics, figure skating, golf, etc. to mention some obvious examples.

Regarding footballers and players of other constructive-destructive contact sports, one might suspect that a very different explanation is needed for their engagement in their sport activity. After all, they experience the physical challenges directly. Obviously, at an alief level, the players experience the "Physical struggle/ fight! D-a-n-g-e-r ...! Activate fight-or-flight adrenaline now" much more intensely than the spectators do. The players experience an actual physical impact on the body, which certainly sets off various other mental mechanisms associated with that physicality.[28] However, there is also a crucial similarity between the spectators and the players. The spectators alieve fight or flight, but they also, at the level of belief, realize they are not in a genuine fight-or-flight situation – spectators do not ordinarily spill onto the pitch to fight or flee from the stadium. Similarly, the players also alieve fight or flight, while they, at the level of belief, realize they are not in any real danger – instead of starting up a fight or fleeing the pitch, they generally remain there and continue playing the game. On the pitch, fighting or fleeing players can no longer be said to be playing football. To play the game as we do requires containment of impulses at the alief level, somehow realizing this is not a genuine fight-or-flight situation, which is similar to fiction appreciation and the football spectator perspective.

There is also an important disanalogy between how footballers must deal with their alief impulses and how the spectators do it. As argued, spectators can exploit their alief impulses in order to, so to speak, let it all hang out emotionally, but players cannot. Indeed, in order for spectators to enjoy the game in this manner, the players must restrain themselves, thus preventing the game from deteriorating into an all-out fight and ceasing to be a football match. As we might expect from the general line of thought presented in this chapter, the difference between football spectators and players has an analogy in the world of fiction appreciation. Whereas the audience watching a fiction film or a stage play can fully go with the emotional flow, the actors cannot if they are to play their role properly. A method actor who plays, say, a brute and who immerses him or herself in the role to the degree he or she starts beating people up is not delivering a realistic performance of a brute, but has become one. It should be added that in football, which involves real and, at times, painful physical challenges, the likelihood of things spilling over into real violence and conflict is greater. Here, football referees play an important role, not merely as arbiters of the rules of the game, but also as match leaders charged with keeping the game within a play mode and ensuring it does not spill over into real conflict behaviour.[29]

This way of thinking about football and engagement in similar types of sports gives us a more realistic handle on how to think about the meaning, or purpose, of football than philosophers of sport have previously been able to offer. That is, this approach gives us an answer or, more likely, a partial answer to the question of why football came about in the first place and why we still engage in that sort of activity. Football is a constructive-destructive sport, and some see the constructive side of the game as beautiful, whereas the destructive side adds a darker edge. It could be that most spectators would not associate anything of beauty with preventing the opposition from flourishing in the game, though some would certainly consider a well-executed slide tackle a thing of beauty. If the creation of so-called beautiful play were the prime aim of football, then we would expect teams to make light of the darker side of the game. This is not what we find in the world of football. We can explain this using the ideas of Kupfer, who considers that sports like football have "internal purposes whose final result is scoring or the thwarting of a score" and that the activities are "aimed at winning by outscoring the opponent(s)" (Kupfer 1983: 119). Similarly, Mumford writes that "[t]he intrinsic aim or goal of sport is winning" (Mumford 2012a: 41). If a football team is to be successful, it must respect both sides of the game. The volatile mixture of trying simultaneously to excel in one's discipline and prevent one's opponent from excelling makes the unfolding of a football match a very different spectator experience than watching, say, a typical measurement sport like javelin throw. In the latter sport, each contestant tries to excel at what he or she does, and to potentially create beautiful or aesthetically pleasing throws, while allowing other contestants to do the same. The drama of football is more complex and often darker due to the sport's destructive side. Furthermore, as already argued with regard to the alief level of the football experience, on the part of both participants and spectators, it is also more aggressive.

While the internal or intrinsic purpose, aim or goal of football and other sports is winning, Kupfer argues that the scoring of goals, the jumping of hurdles, the winning of sport competitions, etc. cannot be the reason we invented sport and, thus, cannot be its external purpose. The scoring of goals, the jumping of hurdles, the winning of sport events, etc. cannot have been pre-existing needs we sought to fulfil when we invented sport, as there were no such things before sport was invented. Kupfer argues that an "activity *exists* for the sake of its purpose", and because scoring and winning are "not distinguishable from or 'external' to the game itself", scoring and winning are not the external purpose of sport (Kupfer 1983: 120). Kupfer instead favours "*how* the score/win is made" and "the aesthetic (aesthetic execution of the play)" (Kupfer 1983: 121, 123). That is the external purpose of sport. Following Kupfer, Mumford also believes that "[t]he primary goal of sport would be some other thing [than scoring and winning]" and that the primary purposes of sport are "exercise, entertainment, celebration of embodiment and so on" (Mumford 2012a: 46). Unfortunately, when thinking about football, the aesthetic execution of play, when that is understood along the lines of beautiful play as observed by a disinterested spectator, and the celebration of embodiment do not connect with or bear any resemblance to the essential internal aims of football, which are to score goals, win the match and to beat the other team, and as such, they are implausible candidates in our search for the external or primary purposes of football.[30] A more plausible story is that sports like football came about as a venue for humans to compete with and dominate each other, and for others to watch while they did so. Competition and domination are features of the human condition that existed prior to and independent of sport, in general, and football, in particular. Thus, we can imagine that as humans became organized in larger social units, the need for outlets for physical competition and domination emerged.

This latter line of reasoning resembles Norbert Elias's and Eric Dunning's work on the sociology of sport, in general, and the sociology of football, in particular. Elias and Dunning see engagement in sport and football as a quest for exciting significance. They tie this closely to Elias's theory of the civilizing process (Elias 2012). Roughly, the basic idea of Elias's theory of the civilizing process is that human societies developed in a way that demanded that their denizens exercise more self-control over feelings, emotions and behaviour. Societies became less violent and volatile, and as a consequence, our taste for violence and bloodshed as entertainment decreased. The games people play changed with the civilizing process. However, according to Elias's line of thought, sports (among other leisure activities) – as they emerged in the nineteenth and twentieth centuries – also functioned as a valve that allowed humans to let off emotional steam in "an enjoyable and controlled decontrolling of emotions" (Elias 2008: 27).

> [M]any leisure pursuits provide an imaginary setting which is meant to elicit excitement of some kind imitating that produced by real-life situations, yet without its dangers and risks. Film, dances, paintings, card-games, horse races, operas, detective stories and football matches; these and many other leisure pursuits belong in this category.
>
> *(Elias 2008: 25)*

This is the quest for excitement that releases participants and spectators from their "highly organised state societies (...) where the pressure of external and internal controls of a relatively permanent type is all-embracing" and "represents a social enclave where excitement can be enjoyed without its socially and personally dangerous implications" (Elias and Dunning 2008a: 48, 71, see also Dunning 1997).

At present, these kinds of valve theories of behaviour, which on the face of it look like a type of surplus energy theory of play, are out of favour among researchers studying human and nonhuman behaviour. However, one might view the Elias-Dunning line not as an answer to the question of why various types of leisure or pastime activities like sport came to be, but rather as an answer to why they became increasingly widespread with the emergence of industrialized societies. Whatever need or function sport, in general, and football, in particular, fulfil, the Industrial Revolution and its consequences for life in industrialized societies might have deepened that need, or otherwise opened a space for sport to fill – a need sports as they originally emerged were not designed to satisfy.[31] It is a short step from that line of thought to looking at life in such societies and asking how sports complemented it. This does not necessarily answer the question of the origins of sport, which is not surprising given that sports are found in pre-modern societies, but it might tell us something important about the success of sport, as we know the phenomenon today. In any event, the notion that competition and domination constitute the external or primary purposes of sports like football fits the Elias-Dunning picture, but is not dependent on it.

Returning to the argument from Kupfer, we see that competition and domination fit the bill of being the external or primary purposes of football. Unlike Kupfer's and Mumford's candidates, they can explain why winning over an opponent is essential in sports like football. For both players and spectators, these features of the human condition – competition and domination – are given an outlet through football. For this reason, they connect nicely with the idea that engagement in football is grounded in the type of aliefs described earlier in this section. What primarily excites us about sports like football is seeing people compete with each other, and sports involving direct physical contact or confrontation tend to have the most animated audiences. If aesthetic execution of play or celebration of embodiment were the external or primary purposes of football, then we would have no plausible explanation for why an audience watching a football match at Stamford Bridge behaves in such an utterly different fashion than, say, an audience watching a dance performance at the nearby Royal Opera House. Furthermore, we would have no theoretical resources to suggest that perhaps aesthetic sports like gymnastics (in particular floor exercise), rhythmic gymnastics, figure skating (in particular ice dance), among others, are closer to dance performances at the alief level than they are to football and other constructive-destructive contact sports.[32]

Football and proto-pretence

The fictionality of football lies in the fact that playing or watching a game of football activates certain belief-like states that cause our bodies to prepare for fight or flight, while we must somehow be aware that the game is not an actual fight-or-flight situation, because we keep on playing or watching it instead of engaging in a fight or taking flight. On the one hand, we have a physiological reaction of alieving "Physical struggle/fight! D-a-n-g-e-r …! Activate fight-or-flight adrenaline now"; on the other, the lack of the type of actions and behaviour such alieving typically generates in the ordinary everyday world. The mediating claim is that somehow, at some level, the footballers and the spectators realize the match does not matter in the same way as ordinary world concerns do – this is why we typically see no fight-or-flight behaviour – while managing to pretend that it does matter. The latter then explains why we get engaged in the game at all. How are we to understand that *somehow-at-some-level* aspect of the alleged football make-believe?

The first thing to observe when approaching this question is that it seems reasonable to distinguish between engagement in sports like football and engagement in fictional worlds with fictional characters. After all, when we as children and adults engage in games of make-believe of the kind Walton describes, or immerse ourselves emotionally in the fictional worlds presented in literature, fiction film, theatre, etc., we are normally aware that it is all make-believe. We know that the scenarios in Waltonian pretence play or those presented to us through fiction are made-up and not real. To put it bluntly, whereas the pretence of children who make-believe that a stick is a sword and that some trees are dashing, dangerous knights is very much available to the mind's eye and understood as a pretend activity, we do not find the same clear-cut awareness of the involvement of pretence in football players or spectators when they are engaging in the sport. Similar remarks apply to those who cry at the cinema, become emotionally engaged in literature, and so on and so forth. In the normal case, the make-believe involved in the latter type of engagement is also readily available for introspection and known by the agents experiencing these emotions. Moviegoers watching the hero die a violent death in the cinema do not recoil in absolute horror as close-ups show the unfolding of events. Fiction films do not depict anyone actually dying, and the what-it-is-like aspect of the movie experience includes the awareness of not watching someone die in the real world. Knowing that you are not watching the death of an actual person makes a phenomenological difference, which is immediately felt by the spectator. Phenomenologically speaking, engagement in football and similar sports does not feel like it involves make-believe or pretence in the same way.[33]

If we assume that the difference in phenomenological feel between the fictionality of literature, fiction film, theatre, Waltonian fictions, etc. and the alleged fictionality of football tracks some kind of important difference, then we need to face up to the question of how to cash in on this so-called fictionality of football. Furthermore, whereas it is easy in art forms like fiction film and theatre to discriminate between the real and the fictional – Robert de Niro performing from Travis Bickle talking to himself, etc. – football and football matches do not, in the same manner, avail themselves to being compartmentalized into the real and the fictional. Thus, if we cannot appeal to an analogy between pretence play of the Waltonian kind or involvement in the type of fiction exemplified by fiction film, theatre, etc., and our engagement in football, then how to understand the alleged make-believe or pretence aspect of that engagement? The answer is that the pretence or make-believe enters the frame through the link football and similar sports have to play and play behaviour. That is, we understand the make-believe or pretence of sport engagement by understanding how certain types of social play, like rough-and-tumble play, already involve a certain as-if aspect – as if the engagement in the social play mattered – which I will argue we should view as a type of proto-pretence. The pretence involved in certain types of engagement in sports, like engagement in football, is of the same kind as the as-if proto-pretence involved in certain kinds of social play.

Play comes in various forms – e.g., object play, pretend play, locomotor play, and social play – all of which can be social. Here I will concentrate on the social, rough-and-tumble kind of play. Among mammals, the phenomenon of rough-and-tumble play is widespread. Rough-and-tumble play can involve types of bodily contact between participants similar to those we find in football and other constructive-destructive contact sports. This makes rough and tumble the closest play parallel to football. I will argue that rough-and-tumble play, in both humans and certain nonhuman animals, involves or is underpinned by what I call proto-pretence. Proto-pretence is not itself a type of play, but a mechanism or an effect of mechanisms, which we are justified in positing based on the behaviour we find in rough-and-tumble play. The ensuing argument only seeks to establish that there is proto-pretence involved in rough-and-tumble play, and, consequently, when playing and watching football and similar constructive-destructive sports.

One of the first researchers to engage seriously with the notion of play in nonhuman animals as well as humans was Karl Groos (1898, 1919). Today, Groos's work is mostly ignored by researchers in the humanities and social sciences, while in psychology and the behavioural sciences he is still acknowledged, though dismissed as methodologically unsound (see Beach 1945, Loizos 1966). However, there are certain conceptual insights and speculations offered by Groos that are still worth considering as a starting point for thinking about play. Groos was one of the first to suggest that play has evolutionary advantages. He saw play as a sort of training for adult life (Groos 1898: 75). This evolutionary account stands in sharp contrast to the surplus energy theory of play first advocated by Friedrich Schiller (Schiller 1801). Groos credits Schiller with the view that play is "an aimless expenditure of exuberant strength, which is its own excuse for action" (Groos 1919: 362).[34] The surplus energy theory of play has been more or less left behind, whereas the evolutionary aspect of Groos's theory of play is alive and well.[35] Groos's line of reasoning is pretty much the mainstream line among developmental psychologists and animal researchers today. The details of current research along these lines are of course very different from Groos, but the basic insight is, as far as I can see, the same.

Groos's more sweeping claims about the connections between play and aesthetics, particularly art, have drawn heavy fire. According to Groos, art is founded on make-believe, and because the foundation of make-believe is play, "art belongs" to "[t]he world of play" (Groos 1898: xviii). Even more controversially, Groos connects make-believe in play with nonhuman animals. In play for nonhuman animals, "[a] consciousness of make-believe is rising" and eventually "the full-grown dog romps with his master and the make-believe is fully developed and conscious, for his bite is intentionally only a mumbling, his growl pure hypocrisy" (Groos 1898: 293–294). Groos also claims that certain types of nonhuman animal play "have the character of illusions", for instance "[d]ogs playing with a bone, treat it like prey; cats will do the same with a pebble or ball of yarn" (Groos 1898: 299–300). The general gist of the argument is as follows: If you take these alleged observations – together with the theory of evolution regarding the development of the species – and the fact that play is widespread among nonhuman animals, then surely the play impulse must be part of "the significance of conscious illusion in the enjoyment of art" (Groos 1898: 300).

> [T]he playing animal has this conscious self-deception. The origin of artistic fantasy or playful illusion is thus anchored in the firm ground of organic evolution. Play is needed for the higher development of intelligence (...) the animal, though recognising that his action is only a pretence, repeats it, raises it to the sphere of conscious self-illusion, pleasure in making believe – that is, to the threshold of artistic production.
> *(Groos 1898: 302, see also Groos 1919: 281, 334–360)*

In Groos's view, everything literally begins with play. A telling example of modern-day reactions to Groos's sweeping claims about the centrality of play as the gateway to a realm of aesthetics and art is Robert Fagen's venomous dismissal of Groos's approach to play and play behaviour as naïve, audacious and a downright embarrassment to the study of animal play (Fagen 1981: 4). Still, it is the alleged folly of Groos I wish to consider.

Admittedly, Groos overstates his case and his wording is at times unfortunate. Phrases like "conscious self-deception", "the character of illusions", "consciousness of make-believe" and "pleasure in making believe" seem to indicate that Groos sees no difference between nonhuman animal play and human pretence play. However, if we disregard such excesses and are not misled by the unfamiliar writing style, then there are important truths to be extracted from Groos's writings. Particular types of play in some nonhuman animals might give us reason to credit them with a certain capacity for pretence or make-believe. Here, our focus is on social rough-and-tumble play. Rough-and-tumble play, I argue, involves some kind of pretence or make-believe, i.e. proto-pretence. In arguing that, I will foremost consider specific nonhuman mammals of a certain level of cognitive complexity, for example, chimpanzees and dogs. If I can show that we have reason to credit such nonhuman mammals with proto-pretence, when they are involved in rough-and-tumble play, then we have a viable candidate for explaining how football somehow, at some level, involves make-believe.

I am not arguing that this alleged proto-pretence is as sophisticated as the type of pretence we see in human pretence play, where objects and behaviours are made to represent other imagined things. Similarly, humans' engagement in fiction – where we also seemingly accept imagined scenarios as they are represented in writing, on the screen, etc. – is something different than my suggested proto-pretence of social rough-and-tumble play. My suggestion is that the proto-pretence mechanism of social play as we find it in certain nonhuman animals, when engaged in rough-and-tumble play, is equivalent or similar to whatever mental mechanism it is that allows humans to get deeply engaged in football, while at the same time showing ample evidence that they are aware their engagement is in football and not in an ordinary world situation with ordinary world ramifications. The reason why the fictionality of football and similar sports does not have the same phenomenological feel as pretence play, or engagement in fiction, is that the pretence or make-believe of football belongs to the proto-pretence of social play, as found in rough-and-tumble play.

The literature on play is diverse, but most theorists in the various disciplines engaged with the topic seem to converge on certain features they consider crucial to play. These include:

- Play is autotelic, i.e. it is done for its own sake
- Play is not needed for survival or any other immediate purpose, i.e. it is unnecessary – though play might be both phylogenetically and ontogenetically very important and beneficial
- Play is non-serious, i.e. play actions are not meant to have, nor do they have, the same consequences as similar actions outside the play context

The current orthodoxy among researchers studying play is functional theories of play, which argue within the framework of evolutionary theory that play and play behaviour contribute to the fitness of the animals playing. Strip away the technical jargon of evolutionary biology and the argument is fairly simple. If play and play behaviour were merely upshots of surplus energy, then one would not expect there to be so much of it both within specific species and across species. Because play behaviour is so common, it must – from an evolutionary perspective – serve some purpose. Play behaviour would not have been selected if it did not offer advantages. The common view has been that spending time and energy on an activity that not only does not contribute to the species' fitness, but also impairs it – play takes time and energy, while there is a danger of injury – would be a disadvantage evolutionarily. Supposedly, the theory of evolution prescribes that the traits of the species that gave rise to such disadvantageous behaviour would be selected against. However, the conventional wisdom that play takes up a significant amount of time and energy has been contested (Fagen 1981, Pellegrini 2009). Gordon Burghardt tells us that "[p]lay has costs in time and energy, although *the extent of these costs has been debated* (…) Young mammals may spend 5–10 percent of their time in play and several percent of their metabolic energy (Fagen 1981, Martin 1984)" (Burghardt 2005: 122, my italics). Burghardt goes on to note that "[p]lay (…) uses metabolic resources and time that could be devoted to more 'important' or 'serious' activities", and that play has additional costs like "increased risk of predation and physical injury from performing vigorous activities" (Burghardt 2005: 122).[36]

It has turned out to be difficult to pinpoint the utility of play and there are numerous candidates, but no consensus among researchers. Note also that, despite Fagen's scathing attack on Groos in his 1981 study, today one finds biologists like Patrick Bateson who hold that "play does specially enhance physical fitness, mental well-being, and *creativity*" (Bateson 2011: 46, my italics, see also Pellegrini 2009 and Burghardt 2015a). Arguing that play enhances creativity is only one step away from Groos's position. Indeed, Fagen, in the work mentioned above, ends up entertaining the idea that play and creativity are linked (Fagen 1981: 31–32, 467–471). In later work, Fagen declares: "the heart of all play remains a mystery" (Fagen 2011: 84). Likewise, Thomas Power, in his book on children and animal play, concludes – with regard to the idea that "play contributes to the development of children and other animals" – that "the research allows for few general conclusions to be drawn" (Power 2000: 394). The mystery for Fagen is not so much what play is or how to characterize it, but the question of play's biological function; how (if at all) play enhances fitness. Also, Power's conclusion is no hindrance to thinking about how we can understand play and what being able to participate in various kinds of play behaviour involves, but rather he offers a word of warning about the difficulty of mapping various kinds of play behaviour onto specific effects on phylogenetic and ontogenetic fitness.

Setting aside the question of exactly how play contributes to a species' or an individual animal's fitness, there is the additional question of how to square the notion of play being autotelic, not needed for an animal's survival and non-serious, while at the same time contributing to a species' or individual animal's fitness. Viewing play and play behaviour as somehow autotelic and not geared towards immediate useful goals is a common stance among researchers. This is clearly expressed in Gordon Burghardt's take on things, and we also find it among proponents of the functional view of play, such as Anthony Pellegrini and Robert Fagen.

> [T]he behavior is not fully functional in the form or context in which it is expressed (...) that do not contribute to current survival (...) spontaneous, voluntary, intentional, pleasurable, rewarding, or autotelic (i.e., "done for its own sake" (...) the behavior differs from the "serious".
>
> *(Burghardt 2010: 741, see also Burghardt 2005: 70–75)*

> [I]f play is more concerned with means than ends, and not with the instrumentality of the behavior, then players are freed from constraints associated with using behaviour efficiently to get things done. Instead, the player is concerned with the activity per se, and this enables players to recombine and modify individual behaviors and sequences of behaviors (...) [Play] [d]oes not

have a "real" consequence. Behaviors are similar to functional variants. More means than ends oriented.

(Pellegrini 2009: 13–14)

Attention to means over ends and being nonfunctional are necessary for a behaviour to be categorized as play.

(Pellegrini 2013: 276)

Fagen is very careful when approaching the question of how we can think about play and opts for what looks like a fairly noncommittal understanding or definition.

I view play as behavior that functions to develop, practice, or maintain physical or cognitive abilities and social relationships, including both tactics and strategies, by varying, repeating, and/or recombining already functional subsequences of behavior outside their primary context.

(Fagen 1981: 65, see also pp. 500–508 for a survey of other definitions and characteristics of play)

However, if we unpack Fagen's view, we find that the puzzlement of play remains. At first glance, Fagen's list of functions is so broad and unspecific that it would seem to boil down to insisting that play has some sort of function that contributes to fitness – whatever it may be. Fagen's smorgasbord of functions is little less than an insistence that play has some sort of positive impact on fitness. However, in the quote above, the key to unlocking Fagen's view is the idea that the behaviour is performed "outside their primary context". Here, Fagen reiterates the idea of play being done for its own sake – not fully functional or outside that sort of behaviour's full-fledged functional context – where the latter sets the bar for when a certain type of behaviour is advantageous for the creature in question, i.e. functional, serious, or primary context. Fagen, however, insists on avoiding any talk of serious versus non-serious when addressing play, and berates philosophers for needing definitions and clarification, while doubting the usefulness of such things (Fagen 1981: 41). Still, introducing the idea that various kinds of play behaviour are outside their primary context smuggles in the distinction between serious and non-serious without owning up to it.

Furthermore, Fagen's attempts to avoid committing himself to the serious/non-serious divide have curious consequences. Instead of contrasting play fighting with fighting, Fagen introduces the notions of "nonagonistic fighting" and "agonistic fighting", where the latter is also at one point dubbed a "conventional ... fight", such as when a play fight breaks down and turns into a real fight (Fagen 1981: 21, 29, 30). This is academic newspeak. There is no phenomenon or behaviour type we call "fighting" that is neutral with regard to aggression, violence, conflict, etc., and which then can be assigned a particular mode or character – agonistic or nonagonistic – by the acting agents in question. Fighting is by its very nature agonistic. Just as a false friend is not a friend that is false in mode or character (a false friend is not a friend at all), nonagonistic fighting is not fighting that is nonagonistic in mode or character (nonagonistic fighting is not fighting at all). Nonagonistic fighting is play fighting – not the real deal. We label false friends "false friends" because there is a connection between being a false friend and friendship. A false friend pretends or otherwise behaves as if he or she were a friend. Similarly, play fighting (nonagonistic fighting) bears a behavioural resemblance to fighting and, as Fagen acknowledges, play fighting can turn into a real fight (a conventional fight). The latter is a strong indication that some of the same, similar or otherwise connected mental mechanisms may be involved in both play fighting and fighting.[37] False friends behave as if they are your friends, but they are not; play fights proceed to a certain degree as if they are fights, but they are not.[38] A bite in a play fight, which is nonagonistic, is not meant to have the same consequences as a similar action outside the play context, i.e. the bite is non-serious, whereas biting outside the play context will be fully functional, i.e. agonistic and serious. Nothing but conceptual confusion seems to follow from trying to avoid the serious/non-serious dichotomy when thinking about play, and as we saw, the distinction tends to pop up in one disguise or another even among those who try to avoid it.

The key to understanding how play can involve some kind of proto-pretence is to understand the idea of play being autotelic and non-serious. Both alleged features of play would seem to be in conflict with the idea that play has adaptive significance. Often in the literature, one finds that authors hedge their claims about play being autotelic (done for its own sake), such as when Burghardt suggests that play is "basically seemingly purposeless behavior that is enjoyable" or when Pellegrini tells us "[play] does not have a 'real' consequence" (Burghardt 2011: 10, Pellegrini 2009: 14). Presumably, Burghardt's use of the word "seemingly" is meant to indicate that play has or might have some sort of purpose, and similarly Pellegrini's quotation marks around the word "real" suggest that, from an evolutionary perspective, such behaviour must have some positive effects on the playing creatures' fitness. Other ways of expressing the apparent purposelessness of play are, as we have seen in the quotes above, to write about play behaviours as "not fully functional", "outside their primary context", "more concerned with means than ends", etc.

Consider Burghardt's claim that play is basically ostensibly purposeless behaviour that is enjoyable. Another way of expressing Burghardt's point is to say that play is the kind of behaviour that intuitively or pre-theoretically strikes us as purposeless and enjoyable. From an observer's perspective, a good heuristics for deciding whether an activity is or is not play is to determine whether it strikes the observer as purposeless and enjoyable. This applies both to laypersons and to scientists. Martin and Caro, in their widely cited definition of play, which modified an earlier version by Bekoff and Byers, even make the observer perspective part of their attempt to define what play is:

> Play is all locomotor activity performed postnatally that *appears* to an observer to have no obvious immediate benefits for the player, in which motor patterns

resembling those used in serious functional contexts may be used in modified forms.

(Martin and Caro 1985: 65, Bekoff and Byers 1981: 300)

There are good reasons for including the observer perspective. Looking at the diversity of behaviour that scientists gather under the heading of "play", the only unifying features of that behaviour seem to be that it comes across or is perceived as purposeless and enjoyable.[39] Play behaviour resembles serious behaviour in some ways, but also has novel elements such as exaggeration and does not have any immediate functions. This is how humans come to know, realize or judge something as play. Looking to nonhuman animals, we find that some of them, like dogs (and canids in general), are able both to initiate and to maintain social rough-and-tumble play like competing for objects, play fighting, tug-of-war, etc. Furthermore, dogs that are presented with, say, a play bow recognize this as an invitation to play or to maintain play (Bekoff 1995). The bow also helps other dogs recognize play, enabling them to join in. Similarly, pre-linguistic children can pick up on others' play behaviour as play (Reddy 1991, Nakano and Kanaya 1993, Legerstee 2005). Both human and nonhuman animals can fairly reliably distinguish play from non-play (for further elucidation of this claim, see Borge 2015b: 116–119).[40] I suggest that part of our ability to recognize play is perceiving the activity as one in which nothing is at stake, i.e. there are no purposes outside the activity itself, while also seeing it as an enjoyable activity.

Epistemic considerations of how we recognize and know play need not march in step with ontological concerns about what play is. On the other hand, if we allow ourselves to think they do march in step, then we should look for the features of purposelessness and enjoyableness in the lived experience of the animal playing. From the viewpoint of the animal playing, the animal does not aim at anything outside the play activity itself and enjoys it. This line of reasoning helps us reconcile the seemingly inconsistent ideas of play being autotelic, unnecessary and non-serious, on the one hand, and providing adaptive advantages – whether they be phylogenetic or ontogenetic – to the animal or species in question, on the other. From the viewpoint of the animal itself, in play the animal does not aim at anything apart from the continuation of play. Play is fun, and that is reason enough to continue with it. From the evolutionary perspective of selection, play might have all sorts of adaptive advantages, while at the same time appearing to the animal to be mere useless, non-instrumental fun. If there are benefits to be derived from play, these are deferred, not immediate. Distinguishing between the internal perspective of the animal engaging in play and the broader evolutionary perspective of natural history and selection allows us to maintain that play is both autotelic and non-serious, while having adaptive advantages. Seen from inside the animal mind (human and nonhumans alike), play is autotelic, done for its own sake, not contributing to current survival, not fully functional, concerned with means rather than ends, outside its primary context, etc. On the other hand, when seen in light of evolutionary theory, play probably simultaneously contributes to the animal's or species' phylogenetic or ontogenetic fitness. Even though a playing animal is not aiming at anything in particular outside the sphere of play, the behaviour can still be selected.

From the animal's perspective, play provides a stark contrast to a whole host of activities about which it would be natural to say that the animal itself is aiming at thus-and-thus. Consider nonhuman animals. Among our evolutionary cousins, the great apes, apart from the familiar phenomenon of play during childhood and adolescence, we also find adults playing with adults (Brueggeman 1978, de Waal 1982: 138, Pellis and Iwaniuk 2000, Palagi 2006). Take the chimpanzees, which Warneken and Tomasello call "our closest primate relatives" and "one of humans' two closest living relatives" (Warneken and Tomasello 2006: 130, see also Pellegrini and Smith 2005). Social play among chimpanzees consists of typical rough-and-tumble activities like "chasing, wrestling, sparring (...), play biting, thumping and kicking" (van Lawick-Goodall 1968: 257). Consider a chimpanzee hunting its prey. The chimpanzee aims at capturing, killing, eating, etc. that prey. From the viewpoint of the chimpanzee, from its mental interior, there is a clear goal, and we do well in bestowing cognitively sophisticated mammals like the chimpanzee the mental capacity of entertaining that goal. The chase is for real; it is serious business. However, should the same chimpanzee engage in play chasing, then from its mental interior there is no such clear-cut goal; this is not a matter of serious, ordinary or everyday chasing. Consider a case that reveals the contrast between a serious chase and an adult-adolescent play chase. Jane Goodall describes how "on two occasions the old female Flo threatened and chased the lowest-ranking male, Mr Worzle", while also "[o]n two occasions Flo joined her three older offspring in a game which consisted of chasing each other round and round the base of a tree" (van Lawick-Goodall 1968: 213, 245, see also Goodall 1971). The first chase has the clear aim of establishing or maintaining dominance, which has consequences for the chimpanzees' social world, whereas the latter has no such aims or any other aims outside the realm of play, and does not have the same sort of consequences. Certainly, it is reasonable to credit Flo with different goals when engaging in the first chase compared to the play chase. It is also reasonable to assume that, for Flo, the chase after Mr Worzle and the play chase with her three older offspring have very different phenomenological feels.

The above also applies to similar kinds of social play behaviour like play fighting. When fighting, an animal has a clear aim, which could be described in various ways as winning the fight, surviving, gaining dominance and so on. Fighting comes in a variety of gradations, and depending on the context of the fight, the goal of fighting can be described in various ways. However, if one grants the animals engaged in fighting with a mental life of a certain level of cognitive complexity, then it is reasonable to ascribe to them the mental state of aiming at some end result, such as getting the upper hand or winning. Play, on the other hand, is different, and one should expect play behaviour to differ from goal-directed behaviours. As already mentioned, the aim of play is the continuation of play. The phenomenon of self-handicapping shows this to be the case. Because play does not target any end result, but rather the continuation of play, it sometimes occurs that nonhuman animals engage in self-handicapping.

> In a play fight in nonhuman animals or children, the stronger or more dominant animal might actually use less advantageous strategies, inhibit his or her behavior, or otherwise act to keep the "opponent" in the game. This (...) can be readily seen when watching a large dog playing with a much smaller one. Here the objective of play may be to keep the interaction going rather than quickly terminating it by the larger animal "defeating" the smaller.
>
> (Burghardt 2005: 90)

Notwithstanding the above, social play sometimes also appears to be a kind of proto-contest, in that "[m]ost social play involves competition, including pinning in rats, tug-of-war in dogs, and king of the hill in goats", where it emerges which animal is the stronger and the weaker (Burghardt 2010: 742). From the inside and from the viewpoint of the playing animal in question, play is purposeless and enjoyable, and the phenomenon of self-handicapping shows that, for the player, there is no extrinsic aim of the play behaviour. This is the sense in which play is autotelic and non-serious – it is done for its own sake, and play actions are not meant to have the same consequences as similar actions outside the play context (on the intentional side of things), nor do play actions generally have the same consequences (on the uptake side of things). If humans and nonhuman animals are good at picking up on play behaviour, this would be because we are tracking the minds of the animals in question, and not tracking the evolutionary forces at work through history – the latter explaining why a type of behaviour is selected. Being able to read other creatures' minds – in the current scientific sense where mind-reading is the ability to understand other creatures' mental states – gives an adaptive advantage, and part of that mind-reading ability is humans' and nonhuman animals' capacity for recognizing play behaviour. In play recognition, the observer (humans and nonhuman animals alike) tracks the viewpoint of the observed (humans and nonhuman animals alike), and not whatever phylogenetic or ontogenetic advantages derive from such behaviour, which explains why the traits underlying the behaviour were selected. Furthermore, it might also be the case that the assumed adaptive advantages of play or certain kinds of play behaviour are preconditioned on that behaviour being recognized as non-serious. It is difficult to imagine how, say, rough-and-tumble play behaviour like play fighting could have been selected qua play, if that play behaviour was just as often, or more often than not, treated as non-play, i.e. serious behaviour, as it was treated as play. In that case, play would not, as Pellegrini put it, *not* have real consequences, in which case play would have real consequences and, of course, cease to be a playful interaction. The third-person perspective of the observer of play, the perspective of the playing creature itself and the evolutionary perspective of adaptive advantages and selection are not in conflict, but are closely linked.

We now have the pieces needed to puzzle together the notion of the proto-pretence of social play as we find it in rough-and-tumble play activities. This provides us with a viable candidate for the mechanisms underlying make-believe or pretence in engagement in sports like football. First, the perspective of the animal itself is crucial, as this is the only way we can square the idea of play being autotelic and non-serious with the widespread assumption that play also gives adaptive advantages. Regarding mammals of a certain level of cognitive complexity – dogs, the great apes, etc. – humans seem to be fairly good at recognizing their behaviour as play and judging that they enjoy it. Recent research supports the idea that nonhuman animals find play pleasurable (Trezza et al. 2010, Vanderschuren 2010). Burghardt sums up the findings as follows: "we are finding out (…) that in mammals, at least, there may be some shared neural systems underlying reward systems for social play" (Burghardt 2015b: 27). This explains why play is its own reward, and thus it makes sense that the aim of play is the continuation of play. Of course, this might not help us with claims that play and play behaviour are found in, say, reptiles or fish (Burghardt 1998, Burghardt 2005: 277–357). Given our interest in proto-pretence as it might occur in sport engagement, our interest in nonhuman animals is focused on species that are evolutionarily close to us, thus on mammals of a certain level of cognitive complexity – and not on fish, reptiles, insects, etc. It is crucial to the kind of play and play behaviour we are interested in – social rough-and-tumble play activities – that the playing animal in question have a first-person perspective (though not necessarily personhood). Furthermore, according to the line of reasoning taken here, an animal cannot play or engage in play behaviour unless that animal has a subjective viewpoint. Having a subjective viewpoint means the animal can aim or not aim at something, which is necessary if we are to square the features of play as autotelic, unnecessary and non-serious with the evolutionary considerations suggesting that play and play behaviour contribute to fitness. This has consequences, as it means that not all activities that seem not to be aimed at anything in particular are play.

Consider Konrad Lorenz's critique of what he saw as Groos's overly inclusive theory of play.

> I am of the opinion that only a relatively small number of vacuum activities earn this interpretation and that very few of them are really *distinct from the response in the vital situation*. The play-fighting of two young pups is of course quite different from serious dog-fights and is not just a lesser degree of the latter behaviour. The main difference is represented by the *maintenance of all social inhibitions **in** play*, even in the most boisterous and passionate types of play. Above all, the inhibition against genuine biting is maintained, whereas in serious fights, even in the slightest dispute, this inhibition is at once completely lifted. Similar differences between play and "serious" behaviour can be demonstrated in many cases of animal play, and in my opinion the use of the word "play" should be restricted to such cases.
>
> *(Lorenz 1970: 164–165)*

Lorenz's emphasis is on play's nature as something other than serious behaviour, and he suggests making that a requirement for something to count as play. One concern I have with Lorenz's line of thought is that he seems to indicate, with his emphasis on social inhibition in play, that only social play counts as play. That would seem to be too strict. Also, though this is far from clear from Lorenz's writings, the quote above might be seen as alluding to the notion that play must mimic or otherwise resemble an ordinary world, serious activity. Again, I suspect that is too strict a requirement for membership in the class of play. On the other hand, we are interested in finding out what it means to pretend or make-believe that a sport contest like football matters, and because sport contests are by their very nature social, the further question of whether the alleged proto-pretence of social play, as in rough-and-tumble activities, should be extended to all kinds of play need not worry us here. If there is a mental mechanism of proto-pretence that is similar in kind or shared by those engaging in sports like football and play, then social rough-and-tumble play is the clearest candidate among all play behaviour as regards exhibiting proto-pretence.

First, note that the serious/non-serious dichotomy shows up in all takes on the subject, even by authors who try to disguise their commitment to the dichotomy. If there is such a thing as non-serious behaviour and if play is non-serious, then when an animal engages in something that does not matter from the animal's perspective, i.e. something non-serious, how do we understand that engagement in play? Proto-pretence is a candidate for answering this question. However, as mentioned earlier, here we will only argue for the presence of proto-pretence in social play of the rough-and-tumble type. In rough-and-tumble play, we find behavioural evidence that the playing animals are at some level aware of the line between play and serious behaviour, and that gives us reason to posit that when animals play, some type of proto-pretence is involved. Being aware that this behaviour is not serious – that it is play behaviour – but still getting involved and deeply entrenched in the activity is to proto-pretend. That is to say, when an animal displays such behaviours, acting as if something mattered, we are justified in crediting that animal with being involved in an activity that involves, or is underpinned by, proto-pretence. This kind of social play comes with behavioural markers indicating that the animals in question are aware of the line between non-serious and serious behaviour. In rough-and-tumble social play, the maintenance of inhibition is what keeps the activity non-serious and, thus, within the sphere of play. The behavioural markers of that awareness are play signals as well as exaggerations and non-standard sequences of behaviour.

Play signals are perhaps not as prevalent in play as researchers have tended to believe (Pellis and Pellis 1996). Context – when play takes place and who the players are – is often enough to determine that something is play. This does not mean that Pellis and Pellis deny that play is behaviourally marked, only that in "most playful encounters, participants seem able to use contextual cues" (Pellis and Pellis 1996: 249). Pellis and Pellis furthermore argue, "[w]here play promoting signals do appear to exist (…) [s]uch signals are most often associated with situations where the *playful intentions* of the performer may be ambiguous to the recipient" and the signals function as a way of "avoiding escalation to *serious aggression*" (Pellis and Pellis 1996: 249, my italics). This is in line with Marc Bekoff's claim that play signals are most often used in situations of ambiguity. If there is, say, a play attack or a play chase that could be construed or conceived of as serious behaviour, then there is a need to signal that this behaviour is play if the animals are to continue playing. In his study on social play in adult and infant domestic dogs, infant wolves and infant coyotes, Bekoff found that, regarding the play bow, "bows are used to maintain social play in these canids when actions borrowed from other contexts, especially biting accompanied by rapid side-to-side shaking of the head, are likely to be misinterpreted" (Bekoff 1995: 419).[41]

> The present results from a larger data set suggest (...) that bows in some canids often are used immediately before and immediately after an action that can be misinterpreted and disrupt ongoing social play.
>
> (Bekoff 1995: 420–421)

There is an awareness of play qua play in rough-and-tumble activities – as something importantly different than a similar action carried out in a serious context – and that awareness, together with the willingness to engage in the non-serious business of play, is what I have dubbed proto-pretence.

Let us approach this from the angle of the play bite, which Bekoff mentions as a prime example of behaviour that is likely to be preceded or followed by a play signal. In eliciting a play signal either immediately before or immediately after a play bite, the animal shows its awareness that the play bite does not matter and should not have ordinary consequences. Bekoff's study shows that when play actions can be misinterpreted in a way that can turn the interaction into serious aggression, the animal compensates by using a play signal to keep the play going, while at the same time being engaged in play. Displaying awareness that the play is not a serious matter, while engaged in play, involves proto-pretence, i.e. acting as if something mattered. With regard to play bites as they emerge in rough-and-tumble play, there is a similarity relation to an ordinary world, serious activity. As already pointed out, that relation and the fact that the play activity can boil over into the activity's serious counterparts give credence to the idea that play is non-serious. With regard to the line between play and non-play, it is common to find ambiguous situations in most types of play activities with a social component. Perhaps this is amplified when the play type has a similarity relation to ordinary world, serious activities. Again, we need not make such similarity relations essential for play. It is worth noting, though, that the non-serious aspect of play is brought out very vividly when there are serious counterparts to specific play activities or patterns, and when there is a chance of play boiling over and transforming into a serious counterpart.

I have made it a requirement for play that the playing animal have a first-person perspective, and I have shown why this is needed to make sense of the serious/non-serious divide and the behavioural evidence from various nonhuman animal play, where the animals in question display awareness of the divide by patrolling and negotiating the border via play signals. Furthermore, if play is more means than ends oriented and if play is its own reward by being pleasurable, then that phenomenal conscious state of *what it is like to be* an animal in play is presumably a reason for the animal to remain in play. Based on this criterion, not all behaviour that does not seem to have an immediate function would count as play. An author like Burghardt would find the requirement of a first-person perspective too restrictive, as it might be thought of as excluding fish, reptiles and insects (Burghardt 2005: 277–379). There are two ways to respond. Whatever it is that ants do when Burghardt considers them to be play fighting, the so-called ant play fighting would probably be a very different phenomenon than play fighting among mammals (Burghardt 2005: 361–365). On that basis, one might force the issue and reject the idea that ants play. Or one might suggest some minimal definition of or criterion for play, which encompasses play fighting among both ants and mammals. The latter would most likely involve a different conceptualization of play, as our understanding of the serious/non-serious distinction involves an awareness of it, while one presumably also wants to avoid including all activities that seemingly have no apparent function or immediate purpose in the category of play. In the case where one manages to establish some sort of minimal conception of play, our approach elucidates a specific kind of play within a wider range of play. Behaviour that counts as some sort of minimal play, if it is play at all, will not concern us any further. Fish, reptiles, insects, etc. will be left to fend for themselves.[42]

Overall, for cognitive creatures with a first-person perspective that can aim or not aim at various goals, the following line of reasoning would seem to hold some promise. The ability to engage in an activity for the pleasure of it without aiming at anything other than the continuation of that activity might involve proto-pretence. One way to spin that would be to say that the playing animal proto-pretends that the activity matters, even if nothing is at stake from the animal's perspective. Clearly, playing mammals of a certain level of cognitive complexity are engaged in their play activities, even if the activities do not matter. Or, if something is at stake in play, it has a very different phenomenal feel to it. From the phenomenological perspective of the experiencing animal, engaging in play is a very different thing than engaging in a serious activity. Even if some play can have real consequences, from the animal's interior it is the continuation of play that matters. The non-seriousness of play, which as we have seen is at the heart of the phenomenon, would be understood as involving proto-pretence. To become deeply engaged in a non-serious activity is to act as if it mattered, or to proto-pretend that it matters, when in reality it does not. It does not seem much of a stretch to speculate that the pleasures of play derive from the fact that nothing is at stake, apart from the pleasures of play themselves, while the playing animal still gets deeply involved as if it did matter.

Here, we will leave the sweeping speculations of the above line of thought for a later occasion and instead settle for the idea that, with regard to social rough-and-tumble play activities, we are justified in crediting some nonhuman animals with the mental mechanism or mechanisms of proto-pretence. Proto-pretence is most easily brought into focus when there is an ordinary world, serious counterpart to the specific play activity, like play chasing versus real chasing, play fighting versus real fighting, etc. Whereas fighting and being chased are most likely stressful for the animal in question, the play counterparts of these activities are enjoyable, and that makes sense because, from the animals' perspective, no ordinary world concerns are at stake in the latter activities. How then does the animal in question engage in the activity? This is where proto-pretence comes in. By acting as if the activity matters – which is what my suggested proto-pretence mechanism does – the activity becomes enjoyable, thus giving the animal reason to engage in it and to try to continue it. The joy or pleasure of play is its own reward. Play does not target an end-result, but rather the continuation of play, which sometimes leads to self-handicapping among nonhuman animals.

This sort of role reversal of self-handicapping among nonhuman animals is only found in play. In other activities something is at stake and it is no surprise that we find no role reversal when nonhuman animals fight, chase each other, court each other, etc. All these are serious matters. In play, nonhuman animals display an awareness that the play is non-serious – where nothing in particular is at stake from the animal's perspective – and that awareness gives rise to play signals and self-handicapping. When an animal shows an awareness that a certain activity is non-serious, e.g. does not matter in the way serious activities matter, or when nothing from the animal's perspective is at stake, but the animal still engages in the activity, then the animal is proto-pretending that the activity matters and derives pleasure from the play. Importantly, with rough-and-tumble activities, when ambiguous situations occur or can occur regarding a particular action or action type, then the animal in question can negotiate the borders of play and non-play using play signals such as the play bow, thus displaying its awareness of what does not matter and what might develop into something serious.

This, then, is our response to the challenge of understanding how, in sports like football, participants and spectators alike *somehow, at some level* both realize that a football match does not matter in the same way as ordinary world concerns do and manage to pretend that it does. The pretence of football engagement is akin to the proto-pretence of social rough-and-tumble play activities – not to the pretence of Waltonian fictions or fiction appreciation. It is simpler and more primitive than the complex pretence of Waltonian fictions and other fictions. There is a difference in phenomenological feel, because the proto-pretence in question is something other than these other types of pretence or make-believe. I have argued elsewhere that play opens a social space from which sport can emerge (Borge 2015b: 116–119). Play carves out a social space that stands apart from the everyday world and everyday concerns like finding food, getting shelter, avoiding harm, etc. In this social space of play, actions are not directed towards useful ends (means of survival), nor do they have the same consequences they do in everyday life (non-play circumstances). Sports like football spring out of the social space of play. Whereas the aim of play is the continuation of play, sports like football introduce an end-state that participants seek to achieve: win the game by outscoring the opponent. Here sports and play come apart. The introduction of an end-state can fully separate a sport like football from play. That is, if an end-state is introduced as the aim of an activity, then continuation of the activity is no longer the primary goal, and this frees the participants to engage in a serious manner. If one played football in the same way Russian roulette and ancient gladiatorial combat are and were played, then something would clearly be at stake and there would be no need for the proto-pretence mechanism to make the players engage in the game. Football could have been more like Russian roulette and ancient gladiatorial combat. However, football is not played like that. Football is different in character.

Footballers and their spectators care about the outcome of the sport in a different way than they care about matters of life and death. Unlike Russian roulette and ancient gladiatorial combat, where the outcomes clearly do matter, football is played as if the outcome matters. We noted that engagement in sports like football does not have the phenomenological feel of pretence or make-believe, as we know it from, say, pretence play or fiction appreciation. Having looked at play in nonhuman animals, we have a candidate for understanding engagement in sports like football as something that is played and watched as if it matters. The make-believe or pretence of football is found in activation of the proto-pretence akin to what we find in social rough-and-tumble play. The character of football – the manner in which it is played – involves proto-pretence, i.e. the sport is fictional in character. The proto-pretence explains how animals (both humans and non-humans) – at least in certain kinds of play activities, like rough and tumble – simultaneously show awareness that the activity is non-serious and are deeply involved in it. Similarly, proto-pretence explains how there can be ample evidence, at one and the same time, that we do not believe football is a life or death matter, or otherwise important for our material everyday life, and that we are deeply engaged in the game.

Objections and replies

Objection: The solution to the problem of how to understand the fictional character of football engagement – the alleged make-believe or pretence that winning football matches matters – in terms of some kind of proto-pretence ability we share with some other mammals of a certain level of cognitive complexity is intriguing, but ultimately wrong-headed. Researchers studying nonhuman animal cognition seem to reject the idea that nonhuman animals are capable of engaging in pretence of any kind. It would be folly for philosophers to attempt to swim against the tide of current research on the topic. Here is what Power writes on the matter:

> Play-fighting in animals is not viewed as "pretend" fighting, in that there is little evidence that animals are engaging in behavior symbolic of something else; instead, they are engaged in a particular kind of play activity that has many of the same components of serious aggression but differs from aggression in its apparent goals and structure. Given the ubiquity of play-fighting among mammals across the phylogenetic spectrum, to infer that members of many species are "pretending" to fight is inconsistent with our knowledge of species

differences in symbolic abilities as demonstrated by analysis of animal behavior in other contexts (e.g., Call & Tomasello, 1996; Parker & Milbrath, 1994).

(Power 2000: 112)

Similarly, Currie has argued against the idea of nonhuman animals engaging in pretence, as "pretence involves a capacity for (...) decentring" (Currie 2006: 275). Decentring is the "ability to represent the world in some other way" than "the here and now as given from your perspective" (Currie 2006: 276). For Currie, "the pretending creature represents the world, not as it is, but as it might be" and "[a] creature that pretends is one that responds to the world as that creature imaginatively transforms it" (Currie 2006: 276, 277). When Currie addresses the evidence from the reports on behaviour among nonhuman animals, he finds that none lives up to what would count as a decentring capability and that we have no reason to think that nonhuman animals can conduct imaginative transformations of their world. Likewise, Josep Call and Michael Tomasello write about "symbolic or pretend play" and conclude that, based on the evidence, "the only serious candidates for symbolic play are all provided by home-raised apes" (Call and Tomasello 1996: 373, 376). Suffice it to say that, on the basis of the evidence on nonhuman animal behaviour, we should reject the idea of nonhuman animals engaging in pretence. If that is so, then we are back to square one with regard to what type of pretence or make-believe we can feasibly say occurs in engagement in sports like football.

Reply: Not so. All of the above-mentioned writers equate pretence or make-believe with symbolic representation. The suggestion here is that when we try to unpack the notion of play with regard to the evidence and observations of social play among mammals, especially taking into account rough-and-tumble activities like play fighting, we find the idea that such play is a non-serious activity at the centre of the phenomenon. That again, I have argued, gives us reason to posit the existence of mental mechanisms underlying of proto-pretence. The proto-pretence of social play such as rough and tumble is not symbolic pretence play or imaginative transformation of the world of the playing mammals (humans and nonhumans alike). The proto-pretence of social rough-and-tumble play refers to being engaged in an activity that the animal is aware of as being non-serious. This awareness gives rise to behaviours like eliciting play signals before or after potentially ambiguous situations. Being aware that play is a non-serious activity while engaging in play amounts to a low-level minimal pretence or make-believe, which I have dubbed proto-pretence. Similarly, the pretence or make-believe involved in football and similar sports as we play them is not the pretence or make-believe of Waltonian fictions or other kinds of fictions, where the cognizers symbolically represent one thing or activity as something else and thereby, according to Currie, conduct imaginative transformations of their world. Instead, the pretence or make-believe involved in football is the more primitive proto-pretence of social play, as we find in, for example, rough and tumble. Operating with the notion of proto-pretence in such social play facilitates the idea that play enhances creativity, an idea researchers studying play have toyed around with. Moreover, this notion is helpful if one wishes to speculate and take a step towards Groos's line of reasoning – that art and our appreciation of it are (at least in part) ultimately founded upon our nature as creatures that play.

At least for humans, when you have engagement in a non-serious activity that, among other things, involves activation of whatever mechanisms underpin proto-pretence, you can go ahead and apply symbolic representation to that. You can, for example, in tug of war or rough-and-tumble play, let participants represent more than themselves, like their street, county, country, and so on. That would look like the sort of symbolic representation at work in sport, when one pledges one's allegiance to a football team because it is seen as representing a town, region or country. There is no suggestion here that nonhuman animals do or are capable of any similar kind of imaginative transformation of play.[43]

Objection: The line of reasoning presented in this chapter only answers the question of why spectators get excited about a sport like football, but fails to make us understand why people choose to support a specific team. However, for most people, partisanship is at the core of their football engagement.

Reply: Granted. However, that was not the aim of this chapter. I have already commented on football as a vehicle for identity making and argued that first we need to understand why we engage in football at all – what explains our ability and willingness to engage in what is a game of seemingly no consequence for everyday concerns. After that, we can address the issue of why football and a fair amount of other sports have turned out to be such good vehicles for identity making and identity maintenance. Similar remarks apply to partisanship and why we have a tendency to support one team over the other when watching football. The theory of engagement in sports like football is clearly compatible with the observation that there is a tendency towards partisanship among spectators. If we assume that spectators in fact have a tendency, when watching sports like football, to align themselves with one of the teams, then the following suggestion is worth considering. It is not unreasonable to think of human beings as a kind of pack animal. Evolutionarily, we are designed to bond with and keep track of a relatively small group of people. For the type of pack animal that humans are, which cognitively thrive in and naturally form relatively small groups, we might speculate that when such a being encounters a conflict between two other packs – two football teams and their supporters – that creature, on the basis of having activated his or her fight-or-flight mode, will have a natural tendency to align him or herself with one of packs, i.e., to pick a side. For a creature that naturally belongs in a group, the arousal caused by watching a spectacle that involves struggle, like football, results in a tendency to align with one of the sides.

In practice, for the neutral football spectators the choice is often already made for them. Most neutral spectators watching football at a stadium of a certain size will sit among the home supporters. The neutrals, as I will call them, tend to fall in with whatever crowd they are sitting with. Of course, one might point out that it is also the polite thing to do. For example, in many English football stadiums, there are signs telling spectators that when they sit among the home supporters, visible support for the away team will not be tolerated. This is done not only because it is the polite thing to do, but also to prevent real conflict from breaking out among members of different packs, i.e. groups of football supporters. When emotions run high among supporters in the safe compound of the football match event, then it is reasonable to want to prevent these emotions from spilling over into real violence due to the perceived provocative behaviour of individuals sitting among these supporters but rooting for the other team. No members of the other pack should be present in our pack when we are enjoying the conflict on the football pitch.

There is also a psychological and physiological explanation for the observation that neutrals tend to align themselves with whomever the people around them are supporting. Falling in with whichever crowd you are a part of – the arousal of the crowd and its sympathies and antipathies – is part of the phenomenon known as emotional contagion. According to Elaine Hatfield, John Cacioppo and Richard Rapson, emotional contagion is "the tendency to automatically mimic and synchronize facial expressions, vocalizations, postures, and movements with those of another person and, consequently, to converge emotionally" (Hatfield, Cacioppo and Rapson 1992: 153–154). This influence and emotional convergence is generally "relatively automatic, unintentional, uncontrollable, and largely inaccessible to conversant awareness" (Hatfield, Cacioppo and Rapson 1994: 5). Emotional contagion refers to transference of emotion from one individual or individuals to another or others. Walk into a room where people are happily laughing and you will soon find yourself smiling. Something similar happens to neutrals in the context of spectator sports. Walk onto the terraces of a football match and feel how you are being swayed by the emotions of the crowd.

Furthermore, the mechanics of the game encourage or underpin partisanship. There are two packs, aka football teams, that are facing each other – not a field of participants as you would find in, for example, various track and field events. It is easy to pick sides. There are markers of tribalism – the jersey colours, the anthems, the chanting on the terraces, etc. – all of which can be seen as devices to drum up the atmosphere in the stadium, or in Waltonian lingo, as props in the make-believe or pretence that this matters. Some of these devices have obvious similarities with devices sometimes used to spark nationalistic fervour. All this is compatible with the view argued for here and does not as such represent a problem for the theory positing that constructive-destructive sports are anchored in certain alief activations of fight-or-flight states.

Objection: Games and sports do matter. Sports are not fickle activities that humans engage in at whim, but instead are deeply rooted in our human nature and meet important human needs. Play, as Clifford Geertz pointed out, might be deep (Geertz 1972). Deep play matters. Furthermore, as Mary Midgley argued, games like football "spring from the life around them, because games are, among other things, *ritualized conflict*, and the type of ritual is by no means arbitrary, but *must fit the kind of conflict which is already going forward*" (Midgley 1974: 238, second italics mine). Midgley also writes about how games like football, tennis, chess and halma are "*suitable forms for the conflicts they are designed to ritualize*" (Midgley 1974: 237).

Games and sports matter to Midgley. She goes on to note that these kinds of ritualized conflicts "are also found in a wide variety of animals" and that "throughout the animal kingdom quite elaborate rituals surround a fight" (Midgley 1974: 238). The Midgley view is that games (Midgley see sports as games) matter in an everyday or ordinary world sense, because games like football are ritualized conflicts, which stand in for the conflicts they spring out of. Midgley uses a parallel to the ritualized fights of the fallow deer – fights that determine pack order and mating rights. This is how Lorenz describes Midgley's key case of the fallow deer (quoted in Midgley 1974: 238):

> [A]mong fallow deer (…) the highly ritualized antler fight, in which the crowns are swung into collision, locked together, and then swung to and fro in a special manner, is preceded by a broadside display in which both animals goose-step beside each other, at the same time nodding their heads to make the great antlers wave up and down.
>
> *(Lorenz 1966: 111)*

The fallow deer, according to Midgley, are playing an important game – a ritualized fight – that is not discontinuous with the other spheres of fallow deer life. Indeed, this ritualized fight is a way to decide important matters in the pack, and unless the two fallow deer appear to be of equal or equal enough strength, no proper fight will erupt and no deer will get seriously hurt. The ritualized fight over status and the right to reproduction is an evolutionary solution to the problem of deciding which individual fallow deer gets to reproduce and pass on his genes, while it also serves to avoid serious injury.[44] The game the fallow deer play certainly matters, as do games like football, which also are ritualized fights. "These games" Midgley writes, "are continuous with the life around them, and their selection is not at all optional or arbitrary" (Midgley 1974: 237).

Reply: First, deeming an activity as non-serious does not necessarily imply judging it as a fickle thing that humans engage in at whim, though it may be that as well. The sense of non-serious developed in this chapter allows for deep engagement. It might be tempting to consider this "deep play" a way of indicating that the player could lose him or herself in play, and play intensely while all the same remaining in play mode. Sometimes play might be mildly engaging for the player, while at other times it might be "absorbing the player intensely and utterly", while at the same time stand "outside 'ordinary' life as being 'not serious'" (Huizinga 1950: 13). That, however, would be misleading, because the notion of "deep play" is already in use to signify a different kind of phenomenon. The notion of "deep play" was introduced by Jeremy Bentham and adopted by Clifford Geertz in his famous study of Balinese cockfights (Bentham 1894: 106, Geertz 1972). Both Bentham's and Geertz's examples of so-called deep play are cases of high-stakes gambling, where what is at stake matters, and matters a lot.[45] The betting in Geertz's study is not only a financial matter, but also a question of what "*money causes to happen*: the migration of the Balinese status hierarchy" (Geertz 1972: 17, my italics). According to the line of reasoning taken in this chapter, deep play as understood by Bentham and Geertz is not play. It is better to see deep play not as play, but as extra-ordinary high-stakes practices. High-stakes games, risk sports and similar activities would belong to the realm of the extra-ordinary, because they do not address ordinary world concerns, while they are at the same time serious because they have or can have serious, ordinary world consequences. Looking at the Geertz study, we find that he is not concerned with understanding play *qua* play. Geertz is addressing the particular cultural phenomenon of the Balinese cockfights. He contrasts deep play with "shallow games (…) in which smaller amounts of money are involved" and the "deep ones, where the amounts of money are great, much more is at stake than material gain: namely, esteem, honor, dignity, respect – in a word (…) status" (Geertz 1972: 16). Deep games are also referred to as "deep fights" or "deep cockfights" (Geertz 1972: 21, 16). It is more like a historical accident that Geertz found the term "deep play" in Bentham – Bentham as far as I know only used it once and only in passing – and decided to use it in the title of his paper, whereupon the phrase has become synonymous with risk behaviours like high-stakes gambling, risk sports, extreme games, etc.

On the one hand, this is a terminological matter and as such not that interesting. On the other, if one is not careful, terminology can cause confusion. Understanding play the way I do in this chapter, which excludes deep play, reminds us of the connection between nonhuman animal play and human play. Furthermore, to distinguishing between non-serious play and other types of serious extra-ordinary world activities is useful when thinking about when a play activity stops being play, i.e. the transition from non-serious to serious – the latter in the sense of being seen as something that matters for ordinary world concerns and that has ordinary world ramifications. When friendly bets among friends, acquaintances, colleagues, etc., on, say, football game outcomes, involving insignificant sums of money, turn into bets involving larger sums of money, their houses, fortunes, savings, etc., then the betting changes character. It transforms from a non-serious game – a type of non-seriousness we associate with play and the fictional character of sports like football – into a serious, high-stakes game. The change is not one of degree, even though there need not be sharp boundaries. With the change in character of the betting, there are also presumably major changes in how the betting is experienced. High-stakes gambling does not involve pleasurable excitement, the way shallow betting does. Or, in other words, the pleasure of deep betting is different than that of shallow betting. When then does betting go from being shallow to deep? Obviously, this depends on your economic situation and what you can afford to lose without it influencing your lifestyle. But even if we fix that and suppose Williamson-style that one penny turns a shallow bet into a deep one, I suspect that – at least from the perspective of the gamblers' own experience – there is a penumbra at which it is unclear whether the bet is shallow or deep (Williamson 1994). The same holds for sports that are fictional in character and sports that are not. There is a penumbra or, at least a perceived penumbra, with regard to the question of which sports are fictional in character and which are not. The fact that there are borderline cases between practices seen as play, fictional in character or non-serious, and practices not seen as such, is to be expected for man-made or conventional practices like playing sports. Having a clear distinction between what is play, fictional in character or non-serious and what is not makes it easier to bring into focus the key features responsible for the character of a sport and for identifying borderline cases. Football, for example, is not a risk sport, while base-jumping is. The risks involved in football are not seen as grave enough for the sport to be perceived as a risk sport, whereas they are in base-jumping. Football is fictional in character, base-jumping is not. Both are extra-ordinary. Slalom is not a risk sport, but what about downhill? One could make the argument that at times coming down the Hahnenkamm in Kitzbühel is in fact more extreme than many so-called extreme sports. Ski jumping is not a risk sport (at least not in the normal hill competition), but what about ski flying? American football is usually not considered a risk sport. Unlike, say, downhill skiing or ski flying, things are ordinarily not that dramatic when accidents occur. However, one might suspect that a collision sport like American football is dangerous, but that the dangers of a professional playing career in American football lie in the long-term effects of the collisions involved. With regard to thinking about which sports are fictional in character and which are not, the arbiter is our perception of the sport, not whether the sport in fact is dangerous and thus should not be played unless you are willing to put your health, etc., on the line. A sport that is dangerous to participants' health, perhaps through the long-term effects of the sporting actions, but which is seen as fairly harmless would be judged as fictional in character, whereas a sport that is perceived as dangerous to participants' health, but which in reality is fairly safe (perhaps certain so-called risk sport are more dramatic looking than actually dangerous) would not be. The tension when watching sports such as football and American football does not derive from one's belief that the players might die in the game, whereas it does do so when watching Russian roulette, base-jumping, someone coming down the Hahnenkamm, and so on.

Then there is the matter of loading a sport with social prestige, pride or status. This also opens up borderline cases. When we make sport matter through the pretence or make-believe that it matters, we end up caring about the activity of playing or watching football. In the same way as a moviegoer might cry, despair or rejoice while watching a movie, the football supporter might experience emotional highs and lows through his or her engagement in football. Unlike fiction, football and similar sports are competitions with winners and losers, where the outcome is undecided at the outset. The uncertainty of outcome, together with the fact that through our engagement we make this matter, enables us to invest social prestige, pride or status in the outcome of football matches and tournaments. As already mentioned, in order for us to invest social prestige, pride or status in the game of football, something about the game must already touch us. The vehicle must be suitable for investing social prestige, pride or status in. Given that we do this, investing social prestige, pride or status in the game – either as a footballer or a supporter of a specific team – functions a bit like betting money. Invest a little and it is all (more or less) fun and games; invest more and it raises the stakes; invest a lot or everything you have, and the activity is perhaps no longer non-serious because it might have serious, ordinary world consequences. Investment in a sport like football can obviously change the character of the game, i.e. the mode of engagement, for participants or spectators. However, at this point we need to pause. Looking at Geertz's study we find that cockfights do not get to be deep, i.e. matter or be serious, without a substantial amount of money riding on the result. The cockfights themselves do not feed back into the ordinary, everyday life of people. In and of themselves, the cockfights remain shallow. In the terminology of this chapter, if players manage to get involved in the cockfights without betting substantial sums of money, they are fictional in character. To make the cockfights deep – to make them matter – the players borrow a tool from the ordinary or everyday world: money. They can invest social prestige, pride or status, which makes the cockfights deeper – matter more – owing to what "money causes to happen: the migration of the Balinese status hierarchy" (Geertz 1972: 17). Geertz tells us that "[i]n genuine deep play, this is the case for both parties. They are both in over their heads" (Geertz 1972: 15).

Geertz's study of Balinese society shows that, at the time of the study, betting sums of money substantial enough to enhance or diminish your social status was needed to take a contest of no real ordinary world consequences into the deep end, i.e., to make it serious. Your average football supporters are fully aware that their social status will not change much, even if the team they are supporting wins a match or a tournament. In derby matches, players, pundits and other commentators often talk about bragging rights, and it is true that you can gain or lose bragging rights with regard to a football result, but that is the shallow end of the human social sphere. Nothing much changes in supporters' social status and material standards as the football season progresses through its various phases. I suspect that, like the Balinese with regard to cockfights *qua* cockfights and not high-stakes betting vehicles for social drama, football supporters are fully aware of the inability of football and similar sports to change their life for better or worse with regard to placement in the social hierarchy. It is generally not possible to invest enough social prestige, pride or status in the outcome of a game, a season or a tournament to change the character of the game, as one knows the social hierarchy is insensitive to the results of football matches, seasons and tournaments. Whenever one is tempted to believe the hyperboles of football supporters and sometimes players, it is useful to recall the Geertz study, which showed that the Balinese cockfights need the social consequences of winning or losing substantial sums of money to make them deep. Though statements abound about, e.g., being willing to die for the shirt and bleeding the colour of the home shirt, there is little reason to take such statements literally or as proof that football is a deep sport that matters just as much, maybe more than, ordinary world concerns. Unless you are willing to more or less gamble your life away, you cannot walk the walk of making football matter in the same way as ordinary world affairs do. But even if you cannot walk the walk, you can surely talk the talk. The hubris of various supporter statements – talking the talk of importance and commitment – becomes that much more important to enjoyment of the game when nothing much outside the game is actually at stake. Over-the-top statements, sometimes aggressive supporter songs, and other fan-related match day activities are props in the make-believe or pretence of the importance of winning football matches. The footballers play their role out on the pitch, as do the supporters in the supporter cultures surrounding the game. Both are important to the football spectacle and enjoyment of the game. In Chapter 4, I return to these issues and show that when everyday or ordinary world concerns and the value of winning a football match collide, the former generally takes precedence. Thus far, I have tried to make sense of the alleged make-believe or pretence in football and similar sports, but obviously there is more to be said about the interface between everyday world concerns and engagement in sports like football.[46]

Midgley's claim that games like football spring from life around them is true. Any human artefact or invention can by virtue of its very existence be said to spring from the life around it. Football is no exception. Furthermore, any human invention or activity that is as widespread as football and similar sports most likely serves some kind of purpose or meets some human need, thus springing from life around them. I have shown how we can square the non-seriousness of social play with the idea that social play also has adaptive advantages. A similar line can be taken with regard to sports like football. From the viewpoint of sport participants and spectators, sports generally have no material consequences, but in the wider perspective of the societies in which sports like football are played, they can very well play an important role.[47] As I have suggested, one need that drives typical constructive-destructive sports is that they allow for the elements of competition and domination, without having these elements' ordinary world consequences. This also accords well with Elias's theory of modernity as a civilizing process. Sports like football provide controlled excitement in societies that are short on the kind of excitement that the pre-modern period could provide. Midgley's claim that "games are continuous with the life around them, and their selection is not at all optional or arbitrary" can be squared with the main points made in this chapter, if her claim is understood as meaning that games and sports fulfil human needs and that, because they fulfil human needs, they are not random in form and content (Midgley 1974: 237).

The extra-ordinary is not a world of its own that is totally cut off from the ordinary everyday world. There are no Chinese walls between the different realms of human existence, but that does not mean sport is not something that is different from everyday ordinary world activities or practices. Sport in general has a certain independence from the rest of the everyday or ordinary business of life. One might say that sports are autonomous or semi-autonomous. However, we should be careful not to go so far as to claim that the sport sphere or world is a world of its own, wholly independent and self-sufficient. German philosophers of sport have provided with us the notion that sports enjoy an aspect of *Eigenweltlichkeit* (own-worldliness), which I assume basically covers much of the same territory as my notion that sports are extra-ordinary. It captures the fact that sports are different than the ordinary world and our everyday troubles and strife, while reminding us that this sport sphere or world is not in any sense fully detached from our everyday dealings. Sport is an extra with regard to the ordinary – an extra that is still connected to and dependent on that realm of the ordinary and thus not a world unto itself, while also enjoying an own-worldliness. Note as well that granting Midgley that the games and sports humans play are not arbitrary does not mean that sports do not build on conventions or are social constructs. Following David Lewis's understanding of conventions, we can note that conventions are not necessarily arbitrary, but are rather social practices that have alternatives that could serve the purposes served by current conventional activities (Lewis 1969, 1975). I am not suggesting that sports are conventional in a strictly Lewisian sense. Sports are not solutions to pure coordination problems. Rather, from Lewis we borrow the idea that, for something to be a convention or conventional, there must be an alternative activity, practice, solution, etc., that could have functioned in the same way as the current one does. However, having an alternative does not entail that selection of the current activity, practice, solution, etc., is arbitrary. A constructive-destructive sport like football could not be replaced by a randomly chosen activity, and that activity could not be expected to meet the same needs football does. However, some other alternative constructive-destructive sport surely would have met these needs had there been no football.

This leaves us with the challenge of sport being characterized as ritualized conflicts that matter in the same way that, for example, the fallow deer ritualized fight does. The analogy between the fallow deer's ritualized fight and sports like football is, however, false. The fallow deer's ritualized fight settles an ordinary world matter for the fallow deer pack: status and reproductive rights. These fights are solutions to everyday world matters.

> When an agonistic encounter is resolved without overt fighting, it is said to be *ritualized* (…) [F]lights between animals of the same species are settled without injury, taking the form of harmless, ritualized trials of strength.
>
> *(Huntingford and Turner 1987: 40, 42)*

> Ritualized behavior: Non-contact display which allows contestants to assess their opponents['] fighting ability [e.g. groaning and parallel walk, after Clutten-Brock et al., 1979].
>
> *(Bartoš et al. 2007: 8)*

> [T]he signals used to settle contests (…) can often be interpreted as ritualizations of cues used to predict the intentions or fighting ability of an opponent (…) contests were often harmless, ritualized trials of strength.
>
> *(Maynard Smith and Harper 2003: 59, 67)*

What do these contests settle? What is at stake? Bartoš et al. inform us that "[t]he hierarchy between adult fallow deer bucks is established mostly by non-contact interactions, even before the reproductive period" (Bartoš et al. 2007: 8). Something real is on the line: the buck's place in the fallow deer hierarchy and with it mating rights.

It is a question of the antler fight's connection to the non-ritualized sphere of fallow deer life, which would then be the equivalent in this setting of the ordinary or everyday world of humans. Whereas the Balinese cockfights borrow from the ordinary world, everyday life sphere of humans by introducing betting substantial sums of money into the equation, thus making the cockfights matter, no such move is available for the fallow deer. However, the connection from the ritualized sphere to the non-ritualized sphere, which makes the ritualizations matter, lies in the fact that the various behaviours of the ritualized fight are perceived as reliable indicators of how deer would manage in an actual fight. The ritualized fights of the fallow deer matter because that test of strength reflects the deer's fighting ability, and it is that fighting ability – an ability that belongs to the non-ritualized sphere – that settles matters. The ritualized fights settle matters in the non-ritual sphere of fallow deer life, i.e., they establish the hierarchy between adult fallow deer bucks, and it is this causal connection that makes the fights matter. Football and similar sports, however, do not have a similar causal link from the extra-ordinary back to the ordinary world. We do not typically settle everyday life matters by taking to the pitch. We could do, but we do not. Granted, successful footballers and other athletes might increase their chance of reproduction by finding favours among the opposite sex based on their athletic prowess, but the hierarchy of human society is determined by different mechanisms than skill at football or some other sport. Football matches and other sport competitions do not ordinarily settle conflicts on the individual level or group level in the straightforward manner that the fallow deer's ritualized fight does. If they did, the world would look very different, but unfortunately for countries like Brazil, geopolitical problems are settled by very different mechanisms than which country has the best footballers or football team.[48]

Objection: The idea that sport is extra-ordinary and unnecessary is tempting, but also curious. For many people, modern life seems to mainly or largely consist of engaging in activities that are not geared towards meeting the basic needs of life. Meeting these needs no longer takes up the greater portion of our waking lives. To think of sport and similar activities as extra-ordinary and unnecessary, surely must be misguided, if these take up most or larger parts of our everyday life.

Reply: Why? Perhaps that is exactly what one should say about modern life in certain parts of the world. First, we need to set aside the fact that a large part of the human population lives under appalling conditions, where meeting basic everyday needs takes up most of their time. Furthermore, we might consider that it is an open question whether most people in the richer parts of the world really get to indulge mostly in enjoying fine art, sport and other extra-ordinary world activities. Note here that I am not assuming that the fine arts are unnecessary in the sense of not addressing or dealing with ordinary world concerns. Understanding the human condition, if that is the goal of art, might be of the utmost importance for the survival of our species. Be that as it may. It seems clear that, in certain parts of the world, industrialization and distribution of goods within populations have freed up time for these populations, and participating in sports and especially watching sports are among the activities that have stepped in to fill up that time. Many people spend a lot of time watching sporting events. Others watch television or play computer games. I have no problem thinking about our current era as the age of leisure (in certain parts of the world). The idea that football, in particular, and sport, in general, are extra-ordinary and unnecessary, while at the same time filling large parts of many people's life, is not an objection to the line of reasoning pursued in this chapter, but rather an observation (if not an exaggeration).

Objection: The main thesis presented in this chapter sails under a false flag. It is a classical example of false advertising in philosophy. First you get the attention of your reader by stating that you are going to defend an outrageous and obviously false claim – in this case the thesis that football is fictional in character – then you moderate the view to the degree that it turns out that you did not really mean that football is some sort of fiction. The main line of thought in this chapter seems to be that football is conducted in play mode. This sort of shock value rhetoric should be discouraged in philosophy. Not all incredulous stares are good stares. Football, it seems, is not fictional in character, but rather conducted in play mode.

Reply: Guilty as charged. Almost. The argument in this chapter is that something akin to the play mode of social play, as we find it in rough-and-tumble activities, is retained in sports like football. The as-if-it-mattered aspect is the same, and I have suggested that the underlying psychological mechanisms that make this possible are also the same or similar. Still, it is not quite accurate to say that football is played in play mode. Play and sports are importantly different at one crucial junction. A distinct feature of play is that one does not aim at specific end-results or end-states. With regard to the type of rough-and-tumble social play we have looked at, which involves proto-pretence, for playing animals, whether nonhuman or human, to step out of the play mode is to stop playing. Things look different in sports like football. Episodes of football can come in various shapes such as a football match, a cup tournament, a league or more informal kick-about sessions. Football as a phenomenon consists of such episodes and is, ontologically speaking, nothing over and above them.[49] Football as a social kind does not aim at winning matches, simply because football as a social kind is not itself an episode of football. It is nevertheless correct to say that the aspect of winning is intrinsic to the social kind of football. Note, also, that what we will more abstractly call the football form in the next chapter is not itself football. Rather, the football form – when it is used – gives us football. When playing football, the players aim at winning or minimally at not losing.[50] When playing a football match, a cup tournament, a league, etc., the goal is not the continuation of playing football, but to win the football match, the cup tournament, the league, etc. The practice of football and other sports – with well-defined end-states, i.e. recognized ways of winning, the contestants are trying to achieve – differs from the practice of play as we find it in, e.g., social rough-and-tumble play.

One can *sportify* social play of the rough-and-tumble variety by substituting the goal of continuation of play with the goal of achieving a specific end-state, such as overpowering an opponent, crossing a line, etc., together with procedures for deciding who counts as best or as the winner of the contest. If you were to do that, you would no longer have a social rough-and-tumble play activity, but some kind of sport. Still, a sport can be played as if it mattered, but the introduction of end-states to aim at and ways of ranking participants liberates the sport from the sphere of play. The play mode is, so to speak, intrinsic to social play like rough and tumble. The moment an end-state goal is introduced and the subsequent ranking of participants that this enables, then the as-if-it-mattered mode is no longer intrinsic to the practice in question. As it happens, we play sports like football as if they mattered, but we did not need to play it like that. We could play it like it really mattered. It would still be football. Now contrast that to play, in general, and social play of the rough-and-tumble variety, in particular. Social rough-and-tumble play that is not conduced in a play mode is not play. To avoid confusing the practice of play with the practice of sports like football, I have chosen to call the as-if-it-mattered aspect that is common to both play and sports like football – when it is part of the latter practices – the fictional character of football and similar sports. This also brings out the commonality between sports and fiction appreciation, as the latter is also ordinarily enjoyed as if it mattered, and this connection is often overlooked in the philosophy of sport. Furthermore, there are numerous analogies between fiction appreciation and sport appreciation that can be exploited to better understand sport appreciation, and which make the label of "fictional character" appropriate. And, once again, football and similar sports are not some sort of fiction, but are fictional in character, i.e., played as if it mattered while aiming at certain end-states.

Conclusion

In the philosophy of sport, it is common to talk about the pleasure of participating in or watching sports as involving, as Warren Fraleigh put it, "a sweet tension", or following Sigmund Loland's elaboration, "the sweet tension of uncertainty of outcome" (Fraleigh 1984: 90, 91, Loland 2002: xv, 149). I have shown in this chapter why there is tension involved in participating in or watching a sport like football, and also why this tension is sweet. The tension involved both in participating and watching a sport like football derives from the activation of the aliefs associated with fight-or-flight situations. The tension is sweet because both participants and spectators alike are fully aware (though perhaps only tacitly) that this is in fact not a proper fight-or-flight situation, but an artificially created conflict that we have freely entered into or watched for our own enjoyment. Regarding the latter, we get excited when we see others involved in a bodily struggle. This struggle, I have argued, activates mental mechanisms involved in typical fight-or-flight situations. At the same time, we understand that this struggle is artificial, i.e., it is not an ordinary life struggle. It does not matter in the ordinary world. There is no real danger, and thus we can enjoy the spectacle. Similarly, for players, the activation of fight-or-flight aliefs is tempered by the fact that they are aware there is no danger; they are playing a sport. The players do not fight or take flight, but continue to play. The realm of football remains separated, though not fully closed off, from the ordinary or everyday world. And that, I believe, was what Liverpool's Bill Shankly was getting at when he talked about football not being a life-or-death matter. Shankly said, "some people believe football is a matter of life and death" and then he added, "I am very disappointed with that attitude. I can assure you it is much, much more important than that". And Shankly was right, because matters of life and death belong to the ordinary world, while football is something else. Football is an extra-ordinary, dense drama of uncertain outcome that is fictional in character.[51]

Notes

1 Though it is not easy to draw the line between fiction and non-fiction (Lamarque and Olsen 1994: chap. 2).
2 A complicating factor is that Tolstoy used his contemporary Russia as a backdrop for his narrative. This complication, however, need not worry us here.
3 Elsewhere, Kreft argues that the realness of action in sport as opposed to the scripted fictionality of the bourgeois theatre is what caused Bertolt Brecht to argue that theatre should be more like sports (Kreft 2011, Brecht 1995).
4 Another option is to argue that, in ordinary language, "fiction" is ambiguous.
5 Mumford, who emphasizes the aesthetic pleasures of watching sport, might disagree (Mumford 2012a: chap. 3). However, Mumford defends institutional theories of art (Dickie 1974, 1984) and sport, and because currently neither the art world nor the sport world recognizes sport as art, there is no temptation in light of those theories to think of sport as art. In my review of Mumford's book, I elaborate on this point and show that Mumford's institutional theory of sport lacks motivation (Borge 2012: 402–403). In later work, Mumford seems to acknowledge this point, as when he writes that "[a]rt and sport are clearly different forms of social practices, occupying different spaces in human social history" (Mumford 2014: 192).
6 See Carroll on the view that "literature and art can impart knowledge of virtue and vice" (Carroll 2002: 3–4). Currie has argued against this view (Currie 2013). The Nussbaum-Freeland line, which insists on epistemic value as the aim of artists or great artists, fiction writers or great fiction writers, is only one among many theories of art and the value of art. One might suspect that, with regard to the fine arts, the insistence on epistemic value as a (necessary) aim of the artists (in all instances) is a bit of a dogma.
7 The Nussbaum-Freeland line of thought on art as a venue for insights into the human condition, together with the Kupfer-Suits-Best way of contrasting art and sport, sits most easily with representational art and art practices, whereas non-representational art and art practices, like certain types of music, do not provide a clear-cut contrast to sport in the same way. However, one might suspect that the arguments in the next section – that art and sport differ in ambition and that sports have no artistic function, whereas art does – also hold with regard to non-representational art and art practices versus sport and sport practices.
8 McFee argues that some, but not all, sports can play a special role in moral education (McFee 2004: chap. 8). McFee mentions boxing, synchronized swimming and basketball as sports that have no potential value in the development of one's moral compass (McFee 2004: 146–147). It is unclear where McFee would place football. McFee refers to cricket as "an especially suitable model of the moral", it "illustrates [morality] in some distinct way" (McFee 2004: 186). McFee acknowledges that even in cricket we might find morally dubious behaviour. McFee views sledging as "reprehensible" (McFee 2004:

120), but as cricket represents, in the words of Neville Cardus, "the eternal Englishness" (quoted with approval in McFee 2004: 186), "[i]t cannot be an accident that Australian cricketers are prime purveyors of both practices [sledging and spoiling gestures]" (McFee 2004: 120). I suspect that, for McFee, football would represent the wrong sort of Englishness or Englishness from the wrong side of the tracks.

9 "'Fiction' (...) will be interchangeable with 'representation'" (Walton 1990: 3).

10 One might worry that when I, say, go to a philosophy talk I, for example, assume that the speaker got there by fairly standard means of transportation like an aeroplane, train, bus, taxi, etc., and not by a spaceship or teletransportation. I fill in what it is reasonable to assume is true about the speaker in order to understand how he or she ended up behind a lectern at that particular time. Furthermore, I might also use counterfactual reasoning in order to explain what I observe. When I watch my plumber fixing the pipes in the basement, I might have the following stream of thought: "It's funny she didn't just connect this pipe to that one. Oh, I see why she didn't do that: it would have meant sewerage being pumped into my neighbour's yard. That would have been bad – good thing she didn't do it." That can be part of appreciating the plumber's skill in plumbing, but it does not make plumbing into a fiction or the counterfactual thinking on a par with the sort of filling in we find in fiction appreciation. This sort of filling in also happens when watching football. I assume that the away team got there by ordinary means of transportation, etc. Furthermore, the sort of counterfactual thinking we find in the plumber case can also happen with regard to football. When I watch a football match, I might have the following stream of thought. "It's funny the striker didn't just run straight towards the opposition's goal but instead curved her run. Oh, I see why she didn't do that: it would have meant she would have been in an offside position, when the pass was made. That would have been bad – good thing she didn't do it." That can be part of appreciating the footballer's skill in football, but it does not make football into a fiction or the counterfactual thinking on a par with the sort of filling in we find in fiction appreciation. Importantly, in thinking about the football match *qua* football match there is no such filling in – what you see is what you get – the whole of the match takes place in front of you. Basically, the point about fictions like literature being filled in by the readers or listeners is the point about fictions being incomplete or indeterminate with regard to the background assumptions being filled in (Lamarque and Olsen 1994: 91). In football one might talk about a type of filling in on the basis of knowledge of the game, the teams, etc. with regard to, say, team tactics, aspects of an understanding of the perceived behaviour of the footballers, etc. For example, spectators might draw the conclusion, i.e. fill in, on the basis of how a team lines up, organize themselves on the pitch or play that, say, the players have been told to aim for a draw by their manager, to fear the opposition's star player, etc. The assumptions of the kind we find in the philosophy talk type cases answer to the world, there is a fact of the matter of whether they are true or not and the same goes for the spectators' filling in about what must have been said to the team before the match, players' behaviour on the pitch on the basis of what one assumes they think, etc., whereas there are no such alethic constraints in the filling in that works of fiction allow. Or else, if one subscribes to David Lewis's view on truth and fiction, then one would say that any filling in regarding assumptions about footballers' behaviour on the pitch, football tactics, and any other this-worldly phenomena gets settled in this world, while truth in fiction takes us to other worlds and in the case of Lewis's theory, to counterparts (Lewis 1978, see also, among others, Currie 1990). Regarding football matches, there is no adding on at will. The latter point also holds with regard to the philosophy talk case – we do not add on at will in the same way as fictional settings allow. Note that one might argue that there are other constraints in fiction cases, viz. "authorized by the content itself and its presentation, where the relevant authority resides not only with the author but with the genre, literary tradition, historic context, and so on" (Lamarque and Olsen 1994: 89). Be that as it may. On the other hand, football fans can daydream about how matches are going to end or should have ended, and engage in counterfactual thinking about specific matches,

seasons, etc., but these phenomena are different from the type of filling in and adding on that fictions allow for. The daydreaming or wishful-thinking case I take as uncontroversially different than the filling in and adding on that fictions allow, while the case of counterfactual thinking needs some further elucidation. There are several types of cases to consider. First consider the case of your average football supporter lamenting all those could-have-beens and should-have-beens that did not go his or her team's way. If only the referee had not mistakenly disallowed Spain's Fernando Morienties's goal in the first half of extra time against South Korea in the 2002 World Cup quarter-final, then Spain would have won the match and booked their place in the semi-final. If only John Terry's standing foot had not slid when he took the potentially deciding penalty for Chelsea in the penalty shoot-out against Manchester United in the 2008 Champions League final, then big ears, aka the Champions League trophy, would have ended up in London that year, not Manchester. Contemplating such a what-if scenario is not the type of adding on that fiction appreciation allows, as it does not concern what happened after the match under consideration. As noted, it is all on display in football matches. Nor does it count as a filling in in the sense of trying to make sense of what happens or happened in a fiction, as the football supporters in question are not trying to make sense of how the match took place or ended – they know that all too well – they are lamenting injustices, bad luck, or what we didn't do in the match that happened and speculating about how things could or should have been. The addition of non-actual facts does not feed into our understanding of the football match in the way it does with fiction appreciation (what is actual in fiction appreciation is what is written, spoken or shown in the presentation of the fiction), where, in the case of fiction, or so the observation goes, it is needed to form a coherent or reasonable picture of the fiction under consideration. However, there is a type of thinking in football regarding both players and spectators where non-factual scenarios are being considered and where these considerations feed into how the game is understood as it takes place. The above-mentioned curved run of a striker in a football match is a typical example. Furthermore, in Chapter 4, I argue that we could imagine a football aesthete who favours low-scoring games over high-scoring games, when the former consists of high-quality offensive moves by the attacking team, which are then brilliantly countered by defenders who grasp how these attacking moves – if the defenders do not position themselves appropriately to close down certain venues of opportunity – will lead to goal-scoring chances and subsequent goals. Similarly, I point out that the best defenders in the game are not necessarily those who make the most tackles, but those who know how to position themselves in such a way that the opposing team is not given chances that require tackling. The imagined football aesthete enjoys games, which for untrained eyes might seem boring with little action, because he or she sees the possibilities that did not come to fruition due to the diligence of the defenders, i.e., contemplates non-actual facts and what could or would have happened if the defenders had not acted as they did. The consideration of such non-actual facts about the game then feeds into the enjoyment of the game for such a football spectator. Similarly, football players who position themselves well do so on the basis of considering non-actual facts about the game – if I do not position myself in such-and-such a manner, then this-and-this space on the pitch will be left open for the attacking team to exploit and such-and-such goal-scoring chances can occur, and we might possibly concede a goal and lose the match – and that feeds back into the game behaviour of the players as they position themselves to prevent such possibilities (non-actual facts about the game) from becoming actualities (something that happens in the game). Obviously, these considerations by spectators and players do not count as adding on, as they are not about what happens after a particular game has come to completion. Moreover, strictly speaking, with regard to the players planning their moves on the pitch, the considerations in question are not examples of counterfactual thinking, as they are not about what could have been (contrary to what is actual or factual), but about what can be. They are not about alternatives to past events, but about alternative future events. In fiction appreciation, one fills in the fiction to make sense of that very same fiction qua fiction, but that is not what happens with regard to football matches in the case of players positioning themselves with an eye towards what might happen in the matches. However, the imagined football aesthete spectator seems to be involved in genuine counterfactual thinking in his or her appreciation of the game. Such a spectator might reason as follows: Player X is having a great game because if he or she had not done thus-and-thus on such-and-such occasions, then this-and-this would have happened. That appreciation of contrary-to-what-actually-happened non-actual facts enhances such a spectator's appreciation of the game. Does this then count as the sort of filling in we find in fiction appreciation? No. They are still significantly different. The type of filling in we do in the actual world, which influences our appreciation, evaluation or understanding of how things actually panned out is still about what could have happened in order to understand what actually happened in the actual world. There is no incompleteness or indeterminacy regarding the actual world that gets filled in when we make choices on the basis of how we think the world might turn out and act accordingly, all depending on how we think we can actualize one or more of these possibilities, or else appreciate, evaluate or understand the current state of affairs on the basis of a similar sort of thinking. In fiction, or so the basic pre-theoretic insight or intuition would have it, the filling in is a filling in of such an incompleteness or indeterminacy with regard the fictional world. We do well to notice that this line of thought does not accord well with Lewis's approach to truth in fiction. In Lewis's theory of truth in fiction, there is no good way to make sense of filling in. After all, for any p, and any fiction F, there is a fact of the matter for Lewis concerning whether or not p is true in the fiction. Now it is possible that p is not true in the fiction, and ~p is not true in the fiction. (Let F be an ordinary realistic fiction, and p be the proposition that a minor character has more than ten second cousins; the story is just neutral on that.) But there is still a (possibly unknowable) fact of the matter about whether p is true, depending on whether the counterfactual T > p (where T is roughly the text of the fiction) is true. This is why Lamarque and Olsen, when commenting on the Lewis picture, complain that "[t]he trouble with possible worlds is that they bear *too much content*. They are 'complete', not only closed under deduction but determinate in detail. Fictional 'worlds' or fictional settings, in contrast, are incomplete; they leave a large number of details indeterminate (...) we cannot infer that in the fiction these details are determinate *in this way or that*" (Lamarque and Olsen 1994: 91). Fortunately, it is not our task in this section to provide a plausible theory of why it is fine to talk as if there is a fact of the matter in fiction when there is good reason to think that there is no fact of the matter, and so we will leave that for others to solve.

11 This is in line with Kreft's view that "aesthetics of sport covers an activity which is not an ordinary aesthetics of everyday" and that "[t]he place of sport is a place under suspension of everyday reality, but still part of life" (Kreft 2012: 228–229). Kreft and I draw our distinctions somewhat differently. I emphasize how football and sport belong to the extra-ordinary side of existence together with fine art, rituals, religion, etc. and contrast it with the ordinary everyday world, whereas Kreft positions sport as a "specially constructed part of everyday life" (Kreft 2012: 231). In my view, a suspension of ordinary life brings you to the extra-ordinary, while Kreft wishes to emphasize that, even though sport is extra-ordinary, it is still "*a real life drama*" – unlike, say, theatre (Kreft 2012: 232). I do not think the difference between Kreft's and my take on this issue is philosophically significant.
12 A mistaken reading of Suits and the idea of sports being unnecessary is that sports are not worth doing. Unnecessary should not be read as not worth doing, but as not directly needed to meet everyday ordinary world needs.
13 Notice that fine art and sport are both unnecessary in the sense that they are not directly required to meet everyday ordinary world needs. If you need food to survive, writing a novel is not going to help you right away. However, fine art might help indirectly with meeting everyday ordinary world needs, because it can – as the example shows – address ordinary world topics, and this can be valuable in remedying ordinary world concerns.

14 This does not mean that one cannot exploit sporting events like football matches and tournaments to aim and perhaps succeed at influencing the ordinary everyday world. However, even though football and sports are not beyond good and evil, they *qua* sports remain neutral as regards further good or bad consequences, and can be exploited either way. Football and sport can unite, but also divide. Regarding the former, see Black and Nauright 1998, Grundlingh 1998, and Steenveld and Strelitz 1998; regarding the latter, see Mills 2009, and Sack and Suster 2000. Sport is, as John Sugden writes, "a social construct and its role and function depends largely on what we make of it and how it is consumed" (Sugden 2005: 251). Unlike works of art, football matches themselves cannot be seen as encouraging or discouraging people from doing anything.

15 Brian Sutton-Smith writes that "[e]ven in modern society, in the past one hundred years, there has been a constant association made between games, sports, and moral development. It is possible to speculate that the primordial association of the two, play and religion, is due to the power of alterity, or otherness, that they both share" in the sense that "[r]eligion and sport are ways of going beyond the restrictions of everyday life" (Sutton-Smith 1997: 85–86).

16 Huizinga grapples with this aspect of his theory. He acknowledges that religious rituals and practices are geared towards influencing the ordinary world when he writes of "[a] sacred space (…) with the end of the play its effect is not lost; rather it continues to shed its radiance on the ordinary world outside, a wholesome influence working security, order and prosperity for the whole community" (Huizinga 1950: 14). So, it seems that religious play is connected with material interests. The next words in the sentence quoted above are "until the sacred play-season comes around again", and one suspects that Huizinga conflates the extra-ordinary activity of religious rituals and practices with other extra-ordinary activities, like play, as the practitioners of both types of activities can lose themselves in the activities – the activities can absorb the player intensely and utterly.

17 Caillois argues that Huizinga's understanding of play is too broad, because, according to Caillois, the affinities we find between play and the secret or mysterious "cannot be part of the definition of play" and that "when the secret, the mask, or the costume fulfils a sacramental function one can be sure that not play, but an institution is involved" (Caillois 1961: 4). Caillois also complains that Huizinga's definition is too narrow, as it excludes "gambling houses, casinos, racetracks, and lotteries" (Caillois 1961: 5).

18 Play simpliciter should be understood as the type of play behaviour, which we find in nonhuman animals and humans alike, that is non-conventional and without explicit rules. There are affinities between Kretchmar's view that games are "first cousins of art, literature, and other forms of culture" (Kretchmar 2007: 1) and the view presented here, but there are also differences. Whereas Kretchmar emphasizes the dissimilarities between play simpliciter and games, I emphasize that games, sport and play simpliciter all reside on the side of the extra-ordinary, and in that respect games and sport are more similar to play than they are to a cultural institution like a legal system, the latter residing on the ordinary world side of things.

19 In the sixth section of this chapter, I will present an understanding of play that excludes the latter types of activities from the category play. I will not return to this part of Huizinga's theory.

20 The dialectical background for this clarification is that, in Walton's theory of fiction and his solution of the paradox of fictional attitudes, Walton argues that works of fiction do not give rise to genuine emotions, but to quasi-emotions (Walton 1990: 240–255). Nothing like the Walton line of thinking on quasi-emotions regarding the emotional impact of fiction and representational artwork is assumed in this book.

21 Critchley notes that "[w]e can watch the most exiting, thrilling, pity-and-fear-inducing match, and then – peep, peep – it is full-time and we return to our lives, go back to work, mow the lawn, make a cup of tea and check Facebook. Nothing is fundamentally changed. Life goes on" (Critchley 2017: 80–81).

22 In 2012, Manchester United FC was ranked by *Forbes* magazine as the world's most valuable sport team. Greater Manchester has a population of fewer than 3 million people and had at the end of the 2011–2012 season no fewer than four top-tier teams: Bolton Wanderers, Manchester City, Manchester United and Wigan Athletic. You do not become the most valuable club in the world by only or mostly having supporters from the Greater Manchester area. However, supporters of a team like Manchester United – who have no geographic ties to the team, but still build up an identification with the club – might for that very reason develop a connection to and pride in the Manchester region as such.

23 Similar remarks apply to nationalism of various kinds. After all, millions of football fans adore both the Brazilian national team and FC Barcelona without having any connection to Brazil or Catalonia other than the football teams.

24 Part of an identity-making and identity-maintenance project can be to work football matches, cup tournaments or league campaigns into a broader or larger narrative. This seems especially prevalent in international football with regard to the identity-making and identity-maintenance projects of nations and nationalism. For example, supporters and the media might cast an England versus Germany game as a continuation of World War I and II, or an England versus Argentina game as a continuation of the Falklands/Malvinas conflict or war, etc. Obviously, football matches are not continuous with, or even comparable in importance to, the actual wars. Recalling our discussion of filling in and adding on in fiction appreciation, the co-opting of football proceedings into larger contexts or narratives is better seen as a kind of *extending* of the football phenomenon. One extends the significance of the match, tournament or campaign beyond its sport perimeters, thus making it be about something more than the staged, artificial sport contest of the football match, tournament or campaign. It is not like the football match, tournament or campaign tells a story about, say, the ongoing disagreement about the Falklands/Malvinas between the United Kingdom and Argentina. Sporting events like football matches are not communicative vehicles by which humans tell stories about themselves and the world around them and their understanding of that world. However, a football match between two countries can be drafted into a story that is spun of, say, a conflict between the two countries, but, of course, the basis or source of that narrative is something different from and independent of the sport proceedings themselves. On the latter example of the phenomenon of extending the football proceedings, see Tamburrini 2000: 28, Downing 2003: 162–172, Maradona with Arcucci and Bialo 2007: 127–128, and Wilson 2016: 354–356. No doubt, the possibility of extending – steering especially international sports into a larger narrative – is part of the reason why football in particular, but also other sports, enjoys such worldwide success as a spectator sport.

25 Here the analogy between watching football and fiction appreciation holds up quite well, as many consumers of, say, fiction film and serialized fiction television think that knowing what is going to happen in a fictional story detracts from the excitement of watching it – hence so-called spoiler alerts.

26 Another feature of measurement sports is that the sport activity could, in principle, be done independent of other competitors. However, some complex measurement sports like running a marathon and bicycle racing often involve a lot of tactics. Here it must be admitted that the performances of others in the competition do influence each competitor's game plan. So there is an aspect of the latter types of measurement sports that involves considering how the other competitors behave, though there are no direct obstructive actions. See Borge 2010a: 24–25.

27 Following the American Academy of Pediatrics in their "Medical Conditions Affecting Sport Participation", one could also distinguish between collision sports such as "boxing, ice hockey, football [American football], and rodeo" where "athletes purposely hit or collide with each other or inanimate objects, including the ground, with great force", and contact sports such as "basketball and soccer", where "athletes routinely make contact with each other or inanimate objects but usually with less force than in collision sports", though the committee admits that "there is no clear dividing line between

them" (American Academy of Pediatrics, Committee on Sports Medicine and Fitness, 2001: 1205).
28 Though the spectator might (to some degree) mimic other such mental reactions that players have to a physical challenge. Currently, we tend to think of this under the headings empathy or emotional contagion, explaining it in reference to mirror neurons. See, among others, Gallese, Fadiga, Fogassi and Rizzolatti 1996, Rizzolatti, Fadiga, Gallese and Fogassi 1996, Rizzolatti and Craighero 2004, and Iacoboni 2008.
29 I will return to and expand on the latter point in Chapter 3.
30 I am happy to grant that exercise can (often) be one of the (external) purposes of playing football, though it fails to explain why we instead of merely exercising, also make competitions out of our exercise. As for entertainment (as already mentioned), it is clear that one would not bother to participate in (notwithstanding the complication that professional football and professional footballers bring to this equation) or to watch a sport unless one found it interesting, engaging, etc., i.e., entertaining on some level. That tells us that one would not engage in an unnecessary extra-ordinary activity, unless one got something out of it. It does not tell us what exactly it is we get out of it that makes it worthwhile.
31 Whereas the original surplus energy theory of play has more or less been abandoned, Burghardt's version of it, called the surplus resource theory of play, is very much in play (Burghardt 2005: 172–180). Burghardt argues that for play to develop in a species, there must be a surplus of resources. Among the processes underlying play, Burghardt suggests four main factors: "sufficient metabolic energy (...) [t]he animals are buffered from serious stress and food shortages (...) [t]here is a need for stimulation to elicit species-typical behavioral systems or to reach an optimal level of arousal for physiological functioning [and] [t]here is a life-style that involves complex sequences of behavior in varying conditions, including diverse and unpredictable environmental and/or social resources" (Burghardt 2005: 172). Interestingly, with regard to the above suggested modification of the Elias-Dunning line, Pellegrini writes that "[i]n most modern industrial societies where resources are generally abundant, juveniles have extended and protective childhoods (...) Correspondingly, and consistent with Burghardt's (2005) Surplus Resource Theory, children in this sort of rich environment should spend a substantial portion of their time and energy budgets in play" (Pellegrini 2009: 61–62).
32 In a previous work, I compared dance performance and boxing, and argued that Mumford's "celebration of embodiment" cannot explain why such audiences behave so differently, while concluding "that your average sport spectator's reason for engaging in sport is based on a primitive, almost brutish, impulse; we like to see people beat people" (Borge 2012: 405). This line, however, falls prey to the same problem. Audiences that watch floor exercise and ice dance do not behave like your average football or boxing audience. Furthermore, the quote above seems misguided as a description of the audiences that watch floor exercise and ice dance. Domination as a prime purpose of some sports sits well with sports like football, boxing, etc., which are grounded in alief types like "Physical struggle/fight! D-a-n-g-e-r ...! Activate fight or flight adrenaline now". I suspect that more aesthetically driven sports like floor exercise, ice dance, rhythmic gymnastics, etc., are grounded in other sorts of aliefs, suggesting that something other than domination is the external purpose of those sports. What we need in the philosophy of sport is sport-specific reasons – grounded in human psychology and sociality – for why a particular candidate fits, as the primary (or external) purpose of a specific sport or a cluster of sports. Note that competition seems like a candidate that will fit all sports, as one of the external purposes of the sport in question, and one could argue that in any competitive engagement there is an element of dominance. It could, for example, be used to explain the difference between floor exercise and dance performances.
33 Orthodoxy in aesthetics has it that engagement in fiction involves imagination. Matravers argues, "the consensus view is hopeless" (Matravers 2014: 3, see also Friend 2011, 2012).

34 Caillois gets close to Schiller's view when he writes, "[p]lay is an occasion of pure waste: waste of time, energy, ingenuity, skill, and often money" (Caillois 1961: 5–6).
35 Though, again, see Burghardt's surplus resource theory of play (Burghardt 2005: 172–180).
36 Assuming that there is a correlation between the costs of an activity and its adaptive advantages, and on the basis of what they see as a relative low cost of play, Martin and Caro as well as Sharpe doubt that play has a biological function (Martin and Caro 1985, Sharpe 2005).
37 The reason for this careful formulation is Power's claim "that play-fighting and serious aggression are independent behavior patterns, each under the control of separate neurophysiological mechanisms" (Power 2000: 111–112). My claim is merely that as it is well documented that play fighting sometimes leads to fighting, then there must be some sort of reason for that, either because play fighting involves the same or similar mental mechanisms as the real thing, or because it provides a segue into the mental mechanisms that trigger fights.
38 Being a false friend will normally entail deceit and that the as-if aspect is hidden – false friends behave like other friends. In contrast, play fights are meant to be conceived of by all involved parties as as-if fights.
39 The observer perspective is best seen as a methodological principle. Philosophically, regarding the Martin, Caro, Bekoff and Byers line of reasoning, the immediate ontological question is whether there is never any unobserved play behaviour. One would at least need to conditionalize their line: what the informed, well-placed observer would observe were he or she to exist, or maybe the playing animal itself is sufficient to satisfy the observer condition. If the observer perspective is interpreted as a behaviouristic theory of play and play behaviour, then standard Putnamian worries of the super-Spartans kind come into play (Putnam 1975).
40 Sometimes observers have difficulty distinguishing between rough-and-tumble play and aggression. Pellegrini tells us that "[i]n a study among young primary school children in Sheffield, England, Rebecca Smees, Peter Smith, and I (…) observed children's playground behaviors and videotaped children's R&T [rough-and-tumble play] and aggression", and when later showing these videotapes to participants and nonparticipants to see if they would spot the rough-and-tumble play, they found that there "was a participant versus nonparticipant difference. That is, children who played or fought with each other each agreed on what they saw, both on the same day and two weeks later" (Pellegrini 2009: 11).
41 Palagi et al. argue that play signals are more important than these authors indicate (Palagi et al. 2016).
42 Burghardt favours a more behaviouristic approach to play. The motivation might be some sort of scepticism about the scientific viability of thinking about systems as having a subjective viewpoint – who is to say who has such a viewpoint and how would you determine it – perhaps going so far as to consider any crediting of nonhuman animals with a viewpoint as an anthropocentric or anthropomorphic approach. I have no sympathy with these sorts of behaviouristic worries, and I will not spend time rehearsing all the arguments that can and have been launched against behaviourism. The furniture of the world is to be reckoned with and not to be discounted or ignored on the basis of methodological straightjackets when it is reasonable to credit certain nonhuman animals with a subjective viewpoint, given that humans have one.
43 As a description of the state of the current research, this objection gets it wrong. Whiten writes that "[t]he evidence for pretence in primates, although it appears quite convincing in some cases for great apes, is thus still fragile" (Whiten 1996: 307). Similarly, Pellegrini informs us that "[t]here is some evidence, admittedly controversial, that nonhuman primates also engage in pretend play" (Pellegrini 2009: 180).
44 Notice that an appeal to group selection is controversial in evolutionary theory; see Maynard Smith and Price 1973.
45 Ackerman and Kretchmar's usage of the phrase "deep play" is closer to Huizinga's description (Ackerman 1999: 3–26, Kretchmar 2005: 150–158). This is unfortunate, as

Huizinga did not coin the phrase "deep play", Bentham did and Geertz brought it into academic prominence.
46 Consider UK betting companies' current practice of offering customers the chance to cash in on their bet before the bet has come to a completion, and the case of Leicester City's 2015–2016 Premier League campaign. At the outset of the season, betting on Leicester winning the league gave odds of 5,000 to 1. The character of the bet, which at the beginning of the season had a just-for-the-hell-of-it feel, changed as Leicester, come early March with nine matches to go, had a five-point lead and looked like they could win the title. Punters were then offered the chance to cash in their bet for a reduced sum. Suddenly there were substantial sums of money to be lost. The bet had gone from being shallow – a shallow bet of not much consequence – to becoming deep or deeper. For some, the transformation of a shallow bet to a deep or deeper bet was detrimental to their enjoyment of Leicester's wonder season. "For lifelong fan John Pryke the money at stake was all getting a bit too much (…) He cashed out his £20 bet, taking home a useful £29,000 (…) 'It was ruining the game, to be honest,' he said. 'I just want to enjoy the time when Leicester actually win the Premiership'" (Truslove 2016). Ladbrokes spokesperson Alex Donohue told the BBC that "[a]round half of the 5000–1 backers have cashed in their chips (…) Record sums have already been paid out on a bet yet to be a winner and for many fans the lure of a life-changing sum of money is too much with several difficult games still to go" (Truslove 2016). One might want to reserve the term deep play for gambling that could be catastrophic for the gamblers' place in society, which is how Geertz reports the Balinese deep play case. Obviously, a gambler like Pryke in the Leicester case is not in danger of slipping down the social ladder by losing a £20 bet. Pryke is not in over his head. On the other hand, gambling on the bet becoming a winner came at the price of forfeiting the £29,000 that was on offer. When a life-changing sum of money is at stake, it is a very different proposition than the fun of putting £20 on a ridiculously unlikely outcome. Deep or deeper, the terminology does not matter much here. The game of betting on Leicester winning the 2015–2016 English Premier League had changed its character. Suddenly, it had become a serious business – a betting question not to be taken lightly.
47 Professional footballers and other professional athletes are a counterexample to this general line. I deal with the question of professional athletes in Chapter 4.
48 The nationalistic fervour sometimes surrounding sport spectacles like the World Cup in football might tempt one to think of sport as ritualized conflict or war. Also, the politicization of sport and viewing the practitioners of sport as representatives of states, political parties, races, etc. is nothing new. Nielsen tells us that the Panhellenic games at Olympia in ancient Greece had "a highly politicized atmosphere rife with tensions" (Nielsen 2014: 142). "[A]thletes were thought of as representing not only themselves, but also their city-states. Perceived offenses against individual athletes, accordingly, often ended up as the concern of their home states. The flogging of Lichas is a case in point and provided Sparta with a *casus belli* against Elis" (Nielsen 2014: 141). What happened at Olympia did not necessarily stay at Olympia. However, Nielsen does not suggest that underlying conflicts and rivalries were actually settled at Olympia. There, as elsewhere, *Realpolitik* ruled the day. Winning at Olympia might be the highest athletic honour of the Panhellenic world, but that is not going to help you when your local rivals' army marches on your city.
49 However, I am not going to argue this, as it will take us too deep into metaphysics and entail the real possibility of not being able to surface again.
50 In the next chapter, I will address the question of how we can understand activities that look like football playing, but where the participants do not aim primarily or at all at winning.
51 Occasionally one finds writers who exploit this often-quoted line from Shankly to maintain that the line of argument taken in this chapter is wrong and that football is not just a game, but so much more than that. Midgley enrols Shankly in the ranks of those who think that football is an ordinary world or everyday life matter. I am, to mimic

Shankly, disappointed with that attitude. I think it shows or indicates that these thinkers somehow regard games and sports that are not the same as or of the same importance as ordinary world or everyday matters, as uninteresting or unworthy of our attention. That I find disappointing, when it is in fact the relative unimportance of an activity with such a widespread following that makes it so interesting as a window into the human condition. I think Midgley and others are showing their unfamiliarity with Shankly's sense of humour and Scottish wit. This is brisk and deadpan Scottish humour and should not be read straightforwardly, as a literal statement about the status of football. Note that Shankly does not repeat the line in his autobiography. Of course, there is the occasional hyperbole like "if I'm fighting for my life or fighting to win a football match – I would die for that!" or describing Don Revie's job as England manager as being "at war", but Shankly also complains about players taking things too far, such as when England's Wilf Copping clattered Shankly in an international match between England and Scotland, and Shankly notes that "while we were fighting for Scotland that day, we didn't go round trying to cripple people (...) I said to him, 'Oh, you're making the game a little more important'" (Shankly 1977: 29, 152, 48–49).

2
THE NATURE OF FOOTBALL
A game of two halves

Introduction

It does not take much to get a kick-about going: a street, a back garden, a little clearing in the woods, whatever space provides an opening that allows you to stand upright. You do not need a ball. Anything that can halfway roll will do. Something to mark a goal is always nice – or two goals, if you have the space. Some shirts, or stones, or sticks will do. That is all. Then you can play. If you have feet and can move them, you can also kick the ball or ball-like object towards a goal. It does not take much. It is a simple game. Take it from Johan Cruyff, who should know. Playing simple football, on the other hand, is the hardest thing. At least, Cruyff thought so, when he told us that "[v]oetballen is simpel, maar het moeilijkste wat er is, is simpel voetballen" (Winsemius 2004). Football. A game you can learn to play in an afternoon, but spend a lifetime trying to master. The threshold for participation is low, while the canvas for development is vast. Simple to play, hard to play in a simple way.[1]

Football is a multifunctional and multidimensional phenomenon that is deeply embedded in the cultures in which it takes place, but also transnational with its Football World Cup and other international tournaments. Football is a competitive sport that, as a social activity, involves multiple dimensions. Football can be played for a variety of reasons: love for and excitement about the game, for exercise, for money, for the joy of movement, as a means to hurt other people, for education, and so on and so forth. Similarly, though football authorities and supporters alike have fallen in love with the overused catchphrase of the beautiful game, football can exhibit all sorts of aesthetic qualities from beauty to ugliness; the sport can sometimes be downright disgusting. Furthermore, football can be exiting and exhilarating, but also boring and tedious, aggressive, but sometimes slow and passive, and anything in between. From an ethical perspective, football encompasses fair play, respectful sportsmanship, friendliness, good will, etc., but also cheating, shameless gamesmanship, anger, dominance, and other not particularly high-brow qualities.

Before we can make further considerations about the aesthetics of football, in particular, and sport, in general – or the ethics of it for that matter – the question of how to understand football as a sport needs addressing. The traditional starting point for such an inquiry has been Bernard Suits's classic definition of games and sport. Suits's position on the nature of sports is a formalist one. Here we will follow suit by beginning with the question of formalism, but then veer from traditional approaches by addressing the question of sport and football as social kinds. Suits's own analysis will be the topic of the next chapter. Instead, we will try to achieve some clarity on what social kind sports are and, in particular, on how to understand the social kind of football. Subsequently, I introduce a distinction between the football form and the football function, showing how that distinction helps us to make sense of a variety of activities that are often gathered under the unqualified heading of football, but which are also different in important ways.

The variety of formalism and social kinds

In Chapter 1, I argued that when looking for a functionalist theory of constructive-destructive sports one does well to think along the lines of competition and domination and – as will become apparent in Chapter 4 – to consider the dark drama brought on by sports that cater to the darker part of our nature. However, before we can proceed to investigate the agon aesthetics of football and its dramatic potential, there is the question of understanding football *qua* sport.

In the philosophy of sport, it is fair to say that Suits's work has served as a more or less obligatory starting point for those interested in the question of what a game and, subsequently, what a sport is. Suits's position on games and sport is often dubbed formalism and is understood as the view that games and sports are defined by their constitutive rules. In other words, to be a game or a sport is to instantiate specific constitutive rules. An activity is the sport that its constitutive rules prescribe it to be. The following is Scott Kretchmar's opening gambit when approaching the topic of formalism:

> Formalism is [the] position (…) that games are a product of their constitutive rules. That is, these rules jointly create and define the game.
>
> *(Kretchmar 2015: 11)*

This points towards a base-camp formalism that can be subsumed under the banner of *foundational formalism*. From the foundational formalism perspective on sports, for an activity to be considered a sport, certain types of constitutive rules must be essentially or centrally involved in the activity. Sports are founded on their constitutive rules. Take away the constitutive rules of a sport and you no longer have a sport or that particular sport, but something else. The second sentence in the quote above indicates a more specific and substantial form of formalism, and when Kretchmar goes on to write that "many formalists" regarded "[t]he work [constitutive rules] accomplish (...) as sufficient", he is describing something stronger (Kretchmar 2015: 11).

> [A] game at any point in time is nothing more or less than what its constitutive rules say it is.
>
> *(Kretchmar 2015: 11)*

The question of what it is to be a sport is reduced to a question about constitutive rules. The question of what sport an activity is, is reduced to a question of what constitutive rules it has. Sports *qua* sports are nothing but their constitutive rules. Let us call this *reductive formalism*. Reductive formalism is the view that sports are fully defined by their constitutive rules. Take away one constitutive rule and you no longer have a sport or that particular sport, but something else. Whereas reductive formalism is highly controversial, foundational formalism is more or less generally accepted across the board, though often not acknowledged as a type of formalism. Suits's analysis of games and sports in many ways fits the mould of reductive formalism. However, before taking a closer look at that in the next chapter, we will explore foundational formalism to achieve some clarity on sports as a social phenomenon or practice. One way to accomplish this is to examine the idea of sport as a social kind.

In scholarly circles, it seems that everyone, in some way or another, subscribes to the idea that "sport is a social kind rather than a natural kind" (Morgan 1994: 213). Natural kinds reflect the structure and reality of the natural world as described by sciences like physics, chemistry, biology, etc.; they are not the result of human activities and interests. Social kinds, on the other hand, are the result of human activities and interests. The traditional view of natural kinds is that they come readymade from nature. Nature itself comes with a natural kind typology. One task of the sciences is to reveal or discover these divisions in nature. The borders between natural kinds are drawn by nature and not by us. "The kinds mark true joints in nature" (Armstrong 1997: 67). The philosophy of natural kinds need not worry us here, notwithstanding that the distinction between natural and social kinds is perhaps not as watertight as the orthodox view would have it (Khalidi 2013, 2015).[2] The social kind of sport is not in contention for a position in the penumbra between natural and social kinds.

> Something can be a mountain even if no one believes it is a mountain (...) But for social facts, the attitude that we take toward the phenomenon is partly constitutive of the phenomenon (...) Part of being a cocktail party is being thought to be a cocktail party; part of being a war is being thought to be a war. This is a remarkable feature of social facts; it has no analogue among physical facts.
>
> *(Searle 1995: 33–34)*

Social facts or kinds are "things that exist only because we believe them to exist" (Searle 1995: 1). They are constructed out of, or result from, human attitudes or beliefs, making them social constructions. However, the category of social kinds is a mixed bag that requires some specification, if it is to serve as an aid in understanding sports.

Searle's favourite example of a social kind, social fact or socially constructed entity is money (Searle 1969: 51, Searle 1995: 37–51, Searle 1998: 112–115, Searle 2010: 17). Money is easily recognized as a human invention that emerged in various historical periods at various geographical locations, making it uncontroversially a social kind. By believing that certain pieces of metal or paper have value – i.e., count as money – a function is transferred onto these entities that they did not have in the first place.[3]

> [W]e collectively impose a function on a phenomenon whose physical composition is insufficient to guarantee the performance of that function, and therefore the function can only be performed as a matter of collective acceptance or recognition.
>
> *(Searle 1995: 124)*

What is the function that is transferred onto these physical things? Before the monetary system, we had a system of barter or a gift economy. Here goods and services perceived as valuable were traded or exchanged. Money is inserted into this process and becomes a middleman, and because we impose a function on money – the function of being a means to obtain goods and services – it becomes valuable. We are aware that we impose this function on the entities that count as money, and they function the way they do in part because we believe or act as if they do.

> [T]he very definition of the word "money" is self-referential, because in order that a type of thing should satisfy the definition, in order that it should fall under the concept of money, it must be believed to be, or used as, or regarded as, etc., satisfying the definition.
>
> *(Searle 1995: 32)*

Searle's way of understanding this collective acceptance or recognition of social facts or kinds like money is to think of it along the lines of acceptance or recognition of certain constitutive rules. These constitutive rules define the social kind in question. The rules create the social kinds and take the form of "'X counts as Y' or 'X counts as Y in context C'" (Searle 1995: 28). Call this *the constitutive rule formula*. Accepting that this piece of paper (X) counts as money (Y) in such-and-such community, cultural circle, etc. (C), is the theoretical underpinning of how that social kind came to be.[4] Pre-theoretically, it is easy to see that money enjoys some sort of objective reality – aka social reality – as most of us have felt the causal impact of having or not having money in the bank, in our pockets, etc. Searle's project is to understand how to reconcile the seemingly conflicting aspects of social kinds as both being constructed or dependent on our belief and attitudes, and being part of the furniture of the world.

> How is it possible that human beings, through their social interactions, can create an objective social reality of money, property, marriage, government, games, etc. when such entities, in some sense, exist only in virtue of a collective agreement or a belief that they exist?
>
> *(Searle 2008: 19–20)*

We will not consider the larger question of tallying social kinds' objective reality, which is subjectively grounded in human attitudes, beliefs and agreement, with their also being part of the physical world, but instead focus on the question of what type of social kind sports like football are.[5]

In Searle's view, three distinct types of entities are constitutively responsible for the construction of social kinds: attitudes, beliefs and agreement. The paradigmatic social kind of money probably relies on all three (at least attitude and belief), but other social kinds need not. Furthermore, we would not want to say that mere mind-dependency is sufficient for something to be a social kind. Human emotions like fear, joy, disgust, love, etc. are trivially mind-dependent, as are the various attitudes we can take towards the world. If one believes that our psychological make-up is not something that is wholly amendable to various historical or social contexts, i.e. we can sensibly speak of a human nature, then being mind-dependent is not sufficient for something to be a social kind. Moreover, activities like walking, as opposed to things that merely happen to us like oxygen uptake while walking, are mind-dependent, but not candidates for being social kinds. However, a social phenomenon resulting from the attitudes or beliefs of two or more cognizers might do the trick.

Amie Thomasson, in her critique of Searle, argues that the existence of some social kinds is not dependent on being believed to exist; instead they emerge without such self-referentiality. "[S]omething or someone", Thomasson argues, "can be racist without anyone regarding anything as racist – racism clearly existed long before anyone took any activity or pattern of behavior to be racist" (Thomasson 2003a: 276, see also Thomasson 2003b: 585). Recession is another example.

> Recessions (…) certainly depend on collective intentionality (and thus qualify as social facts by Searle's criterion), for they depend on collective acceptance of certain monetary systems. But a given economic state can be a recession even if no one thinks it is, and even if no one regards *anything* as a recession or any conditions as sufficient for counting as a recession.
>
> *(Thomasson 2003a: 276)*

Commenting on Thomasson, Muhammad Ali Khalidi concludes, "there are social kinds whose nature is such that human beings need not have any propositional attitudes towards them for them to exist (e.g. *recession, racism*)" (Khalidi 2015: 99).

That is, "members of that society need not have any propositional attitudes that involve the category *racism* itself. They may never have consciously formulated such a category or concept" (Khalidi 2015: 99).

This is not a rejection of the Searlean picture of social reality and its kinds, where social kinds ultimately depend on collective intentionality. Thomasson writes that "Searle's basic picture of social reality as (...) dependent on collective intentionality (...) seems exactly right" (Thomasson 2003a: 277). There are no social kinds that do not have collective intentionality at their base. Thomasson suggests that the problematic cases "arise as byproducts of our collective beliefs, practices, and existing institutions", and "that social facts and entities may be generated as by-products of collective intentionality" (Thomasson 2003a: 278, 289). Searle concurs.

> [I]nstitutional facts (...) require recognition or acceptance by the community in question in some form or other. Cases that do not seem to meet this condition are systematic fallouts, or consequences, of ground-floor institutional facts.
>
> *(Searle 2010: 116)*

Searle adds, "you can have intentionality-independent facts about intentionality-relative phenomena" (Searle 2010: 117). Recessions, though independent of belief in there being recessions, still rely on a social kind that is self-referentially existent, namely, the monetary system. Racism, though independent of belief in there being racism (or racists), still relies on a social kind that is self-referentially existent, namely race.[6]

However, some social kinds do not even rely on having collective intentionality at their base. Consider fashion and fashionableness.

> Jussi Haukioja (...) argues that to be fashionable is nothing more than being taken to be fashionable; "some *x* is fashionable, at least roughly, *because* we take *x* to be fashionable" (Haukioja 2013, 167). Fashionableness, Haukioja tells us, is nothing but the attitude we take towards it, i.e. what we take to be fashionable.
>
> *(Borge 2015a: 356)*

If we replace "take x to be" and "the attitude we take towards it" with belief, then this treatment of fashionableness echoes Searle's theory of social kinds. Just as with money, to be fashionable is to be believed to be fashionable. If enough people think something is fashionable, then it is. Certainly, part of the phenomenon of fashion or fashionableness fits this. At the high end of fashion, we have institutions and institution-like organizations such as Central Saint Martins, London College of Fashion, Milan fashion week, *Vogue* magazine, etc. One might say that whatever comes out of these counts as fashion or fashionable, because it is believed to be fashion or fashionable. The high end of fashion fits the depiction of social kinds as self-referentially dependent on being recognized as being the social kind they are.

However, like racism and recessions, fashion or fashionableness does not need self-referential belief of collective intentionality for its existence. Certain types of garments could be preferred and sought after in (a certain stratum of) a population without anyone thinking of him or herself as following a fashion or being fashionable. We can correctly judge something to be racism, a recession or a fashion without crediting anyone in the society we are considering with having propositional attitudes that involve the category or concept of racism, recession or fashion. Unlike recession and racism, fashion and fashionableness can emerge even without collective intentionality at the base of the phenomenon. Consider the following case, taken from the high end of fashion, of the emergence of similar taste without prior agreement or acceptance.

> At a seasonal opening of a major Parisian fashion house there may be presented a hundred or more designs of woman's evening wear before an audience of from one to two hundred buyers. (...) [U]sually about six to eight designs (...) are chosen by the buyers. (...) Now, these choices are made by the buyers – a highly competitive and secretive lot – independently of each other and without knowledge of each other's selections. Why should their choices converge on a few designs as they do?
>
> (Blumer 1969: 278–279)

Individual choices from a large set of options – choices that may even be made with the intent to make different choices than the others – end up converging on a few designs. The fact that this is from high-end fashion is inessential. What is important here is that these buyers – the tastemakers – converge on a few designs without any collective intentionality.

Now consider the emergence of a teen fashion fad. For the uninitiated, it looks like a large number of individuals in a social group have decided, almost overnight, on something new being the cool, in, done-thing, etc. to wear. Take Blumer's example above and replace the buyers with certain teenage girls with high social standing among their peers and the clothing designs with whatever choice of clothing is available in that teen community.[7] The Blumer example shows that it is possible for certain key members to converge on some styles or one style. These individuals are the tastemakers. If their choices influence other members of the community, then one might fairly quickly have the outline of a teenage fashion fad. Because certain individuals favour a particular garment, the garment becomes fashionable – many teenage girls wear it, while they could have worn alternative clothing – and the garment's very fashionableness reinforces its fashionableness. That is, the very fact that the garment goes rapidly from being worn by few to being worn by many will cause – through various sociological mechanisms – even more members of that social group to wear the garment in question. We can furthermore imagine that these girls, when asked why they wear the garment, will all claim that their choice is based in their individual taste and that none will mention the garment's fashionableness as a reason for wearing it. We have a case of fashion without collective intentionality. Individuals' convergence on the idea that a certain style is desirable makes the garment itself fashionable or count as fashion in that social setting, and at this point its fashionableness functions in part to make it fashionable. All this occurs without being founded on collective intentionality, and compared to, say, recessions, this looks like as good a social kind as any. We have no collective intentionality, as the convergence of style or taste is done individually. At the same time, this convergence of style or taste – due to those tastemakers' place in the social hierarchy – influences others and can propel the convergence of style or taste into a teenage fashion fad. I suspect that similar considerations sometimes hold for other types of cultural and artistic fashions and fads, ranging from music, literature and various other art forms to the spheres of academia.

This then gives us the first two types of social kinds to consider with regard to sport.

1. Social kinds without collective intentionality.
2. Social kinds without direct collective intentionality, but with collective intentionality at their base.

Are sports like the social kinds of cultural and artistic fads and fashions, or like racism and recessions? Consider the following two contrasting cases:

> The Human Stampede: A crowd of humans, spooked by something in their environment, suddenly starts running in one direction following a straight path until they at some point calm down.

> The Running Race: A crowd of humans, set off by the sound of the starting gun, suddenly starts running in one direction following a straight path until they at some point reach the finishing line.

Let us assume that, from the perspective of a third-person physical description of the moving bodies, the two events are indistinguishable. That would take some stage setting, but surely a good novelist would be able to tell a story about the *Human Stampede* where that was the case.

The human stampede is not a sporting event. The reason is simple. Neither the participants in the human stampede nor anyone else believes the running people are participating in a competition. This fact prevents it from being a sporting event. Unlike fashion and fashionableness, a sporting event involving running a race cannot emerge out of individual choices and influence of these choices on others in the absence of collective intentionality. If human stampedes were fairly common events, then I suppose the phenomenon would be a candidate for a social kind without collective intentionality at its base. The human stampede falls short of being a sport. One can imagine cases where something that looks like a sporting event emerges more or less spontaneously. Consider the following case:

The Shoreline Runners: Along a shoreline, middle-aged men who are concerned with being fit frequent a running path. At one point, one of the runners starts racing the others, feeling triumphant whenever he overtakes other runners. The others runners are unaware that this runner is racing. Imagine furthermore that not only one, but all of the runners start behaving in this manner, frantically racing along the shoreline.

Do we have a race and a sport event here? No. In the case of only one man racing the others, he is, at best, pretending to participate in a running race. The second part of the case is more interesting. Imagine that the other middle-aged men notice the first man's behaviour and respond in kind by trying to keep up with or overtake him and each other. Quite quickly, this might develop into a spontaneous running race and a sporting event would be in place. However, for mere running to develop into a sporting event we need acceptance or recognition among the participants that their running along the shoreline has turned into a race. This understanding need not be stated, but could and most likely would be implied or tacit. Imagine then another scenario, where one runner starts pretending to be in a race and that this pretence causes the others to also start pretending to be running a race until finally every single runner is pretending to run a race. Still, we do not have a sporting event. It would be inappropriate for one of the runners to claim he won the race or beat one of the other runners because he has not recognized them nor been recognized by them as a runner in a race. It is difficult to see how a sport or sporting event could possibly come about as a by-product, consequence or the systematic fallout of another social activity regardless of whether that social activity counts as a social kind. Exercisers on a running path do not accidentally create the social kind of sport as a by-product or fallout of what they are doing.

Sports are a social kind with collective intentionality at the centre, where this is cashed in as a certain type of self-referential we-belief or we-intention. Consider again the case of the *Shoreline Runners*, in which all of our competitive runners are individually doing their running as a race, resulting in collective sprinting along the shoreline. Each of them might tell himself that this is a race or that this should count as a race. However, because these type-identical self-referential beliefs fail to make contact with each other, the intention for this to be a race or the belief that this is a race fail to create a race and a sporting event. Consider the following analogy. Two people who are in love with each other – but who have no recognition or awareness of the fact that the other person has the same feelings – do not constitute a couple in love. Similarly, a group of runners who are racing does not constitute a running race. Not only must a runner in this scenario recognize that this running is now a race, but he must also recognize that the others recognize his willingness to let this running count as a race, and that his recognition of the others' recognition of his willingness to let this running count as a race is part of his reason for letting this running count as a race and so on and so forth, in the more or less obvious Gricean or Lewisian fashion.[8] It need not concern us whether the process of transforming running along a shoreline for exercise into a running race involves the Gricean mechanism, a Lewis understanding of convention, or some other way of establishing common ground. Suffice to say, here, that it takes collective intentionality, understood loosely as a type of we-intentionality or we-belief, creating common ground to make this happen.

Part of this common ground is an understanding of the type of constitutive rule or rules the social kind is founded on. The constitutive rule formula – X counts as Y or X counts as Y in context C – is itself not enough for distinguishing social kinds with collective intentionality at their centre from the more minimal conceptions of social kinds. A sociologist lecturing on the fashions of philosophy in the twentieth century might say that a topic in philosophy (X) counts as fashionable (Y) in twentieth-century western philosophy (C), when so-and-so many journal articles have been published in a certain time span in particular journals. Or, a historian giving a talk on the history of discrimination could say that a society (X) counts as racist (Y) in a certain historical period (C), if such-and-such laws were enforced with regard to various racial perceptions, such as skin colour. If the agents in these cases – fashions of philosophy and racism in a society – do not think of themselves as following a fashion or being racist, then perhaps those social groups do not even have a concept of fashion in philosophy or racism – in which case it would be labouring the point to talk as if they adhere to or follow the constitutive rules of fashion in philosophy or racism in a society. It would be better to say that they instantiate the rule. Adhering to or following a constitutive rule takes more than instantiation. It is still perfectly sensible for a sociologist or historian to apply the constitutive rule formula to pinpoint fashions of philosophy or racism in a society, thus allowing researchers to discover such phenomena independent of the research subjects' own self-understanding and conceptual resources (Thomasson 2003a: 269, 270, Thomasson 2003b: 606–607). The social scientists using such a constitutive rule formula must know, accept or somehow recognize the rule in question, but those participating in the phenomenon considered by scholars to instantiate the formula need not.

In social kinds with collective intentionally at their centre, some sort of knowledge, acceptance or recognition of the constitutive rule or rules (upon which the phenomena are founded) exists among the agents participating in the social kinds. Two distinct social kinds with collective intentionality at their centre can be identified:

3. Social kinds based on direct collective intentionality, which allow for token exceptions.
4. Social kinds based on direct collective intentionality, which do not allow for token exceptions.

Social kinds of the third type include money. For an entity to count as money there must be an acceptance or recognition of it counting as money – i.e., direct collective intentionality. With regard to collective intentionality, this type of social kind allows for token exceptions. There can be instances of money – a particular piece of money – that have not been the object of any attitudes, let alone collective intentionality, but which nevertheless count as money. Imagine the following scenario.

> The Coin Minting Machine: A coin minting machine is set in motion due to a mechanical error and spews out coins without anyone witnessing the event. One of the coins produced in this event falls off the production line. The coin gets swept up in the morning by the cleaner, taken out with the garbage, dumped in a landfill and is never seen by any human being, until it at some point decomposes.

Was the coin money? Searle writes that "[f]or some institutional phenomena, such as money, what I say applies more to types than tokens", and Khalidi concurs that if a ten-dollar bill "drops straight from the printing press into a crack in the floorboards (…) it would still be a ten-dollar bill" (Searle 1995: 33, Khalidi 2013: 152). Some social kinds demand that we regard them as belonging to that social kind, thereby bestowing upon them certain functions, but allow that membership of the social kind can be granted by being a token of that kind, even when no one regarded that specific token as belonging to that social kind. Does a sport like football allow for a similar type of token exception, where the excepted token still counts as, say, a game of football?

How could that be? It is not like you can accidentally lose a sporting event such as a football match in the same way a wayward coin might fly under the radar of collective intentionality. It looks as if the token exception case only works for money, because the tokens of money are artefacts and not activities. An artefact might not be recognized as a token of a social kind by way of the collective intentionality of the group in which that social kind is grounded and nevertheless remain a member of that social kind. An activity that is a practice of a sport, on the other hand, seems intrinsically linked to recognition of the sport as a sport. Furthermore, I have elsewhere argued that if someone, when encountering a sport like football, does not recognize it as a competitive activity, then that person does not know football. On the observer side, we find that failure to recognize a sport as competitive is a failure to recognize it as a sport.

> [S]omeone who knows of football (who has heard of it or even seen it) but mistakenly believes that it is some sort of art performance, or, say, an elaborated, but mostly unsuccessful rainmaking ritual; that is, does not recognize it as a sport, does not know football.
>
> *(Borge 2015b: 120)*

Consider the following scenario:

> Football and the Natives: A tribe of native Norwegians coming to the British Isles oversees a football match. Not having any conception of sport, the natives quickly conclude that this is some form of elaborated ritual. Imagine the natives' amazement when, courtesy of the British weather, it starts pouring down just before the

end of the match. Highly impressed, the natives acquire a rule book and bring home what they take to be an elaborated rainmaking ritual; they then start acting in accordance with their understanding of the rule book of football.

Are the natives playing football? No. The activity or practice has changed. The function of the movements with a ball on the pitch, and so on, has changed. The natives are doing something else. They are not playing a sport. They are performing a ritual. We can say that they are adhering to or following the rules of the rule book in a mere formal sense. They are, so to speak, executing the syntax of football, and this formal aspect of football – when considered in isolation – points towards a minimal conception of formalism. In the hands of the natives, football's constitutive rules, such as the rule that prescribes the conditions and circumstances for something to count as a goal, can still be executed in this minimal sense. The natives' rainmaking ritual fulfils the formal aspect of football. On the other hand, in the natives' mouths the word "goal" means something different than it does in the mouths of the British. You have the form of football, but the semantics have changed. The external or primary purpose and internal or intrinsic aim, goal or purpose of what the natives are doing does not match up with the external or primary purpose and internal or intrinsic aim, goal or purpose of football. Should the British at some later stage come to Norway and encounter what we can call *the native football rainmaking ritual*, they would be mistaken if they concluded that the natives are playing football. The natives are not playing football; they are performing a rainmaking ritual. Unlike wayward coins that throughout their existence fail to be accepted or recognized as money and at no point serve the purpose of their social kind, while still retaining their status as tokens of that social type, formal tokens of football, like the native football rainmaking ritual, cannot retain their status as tokens of the social kind of football. That would seem to push football and sports towards being social kinds of the fourth type – social kinds that do not allow for token exceptions.

What do the social kinds that do not allow for token exceptions look like? Searle claims that cocktail parties and wars are social kinds that do not exist unless the particular instances are subject to a collective awareness of them as cocktail parties and wars. Consider *Searle's Cocktail Party*:

> If, for example, we give a big cocktail party, and invite everyone in Paris, and if things get out of hand, and it turns out that the casualty rate is greater than the Battle of Austerlitz – all the same, it is not a war; it is just one amazing cocktail party; part of being a war is being thought to be a war.
>
> *(Searle 1995: 33–34)*

This is not very convincing. It seems like the cocktail party at one point has turned into a war-like state. There is nothing queer about saying that "this is no longer a cocktail party, but a war". A token of a social kind like a cocktail party can stop being one without any explicit declaration of it ending, before anyone has thought about it no longer being a cocktail party. Is it inconceivable, bordering on a category mistake, to describe as war some types of armed conflicts between social groups that do not include declaration of war conventions in their social repertoire? Or, is it unthinkable to describe as the beginning of a war episodes of violent conflict when the participants in the episodes did not understand or conceptualize them as war? I would be surprised if we fail to find that historians do just that. Khalidi argues, "individual tokens of war are dependent not solely on the attitudes of members of society but also partly on certain causal properties" (Khalidi 2015: 100). Khalidi also writes, "[w]ar (…) is organized, planned, and conducted according to certain rules (…) it is not clear that the practice could get off the ground without some propositional attitudes involving the category itself" (Khalidi 2015: 101). This makes war a social kind that, in the same way as money, allows for token exceptions within a social kind that otherwise depends on direct collective intentionality.

Instead of cocktail parties and wars, Khalidi suggests that social kinds that do not allow token exceptions are best understood as those where membership or inclusion in the social kind in question can be accomplished by fiat. These social kinds "are more strictly institutional or conventional in character" (Khalidi 2015: 102). Examples of this type of social kind are the social kind of being a permanent resident or the social kind of being a prime minister (Khalidi 2015: 102). You cannot be a permanent resident or a prime minister of a country unless someone believes you are a permanent resident or the prime minister of that country. Belonging to social kinds that involve direct collective intentionality – and that do not allow for token exceptions – is a matter of having a certain status endowed upon or transferred to the token of the social kind in question. Properties that come with the status of permanent resident or prime minister of a country are "associated with a kind on the basis of logical or conventional links" and "we do not have the impression that this marks a real grouping of things in the world" (Khalidi 2013: 209). Consider becoming the prime minister of the United Kingdom. When David Cameron was endowed with the property of being prime minister of the United Kingdom, Cameron himself did not change, but his status did. When Cameron stepped down, he did not change back into his old self or became something new, but remained the same entity with a change in status. There is nothing ontologically interesting about the persons meeting as political heads of state at the G8 meetings. They do not, in this sense, mark a real grouping in the world. This does not mean there are no limitations with regard to membership in a social kind such as permanent resident, prime minister, etc. There can be a whole host of conditions or requirements that need to be fulfilled, while the status of membership in the social kind is still conferred by fiat. Take the process of becoming a citizen of a country. In order to belong to the domain of eligible candidates for citizenship, there are conditions or requirements that need to be met. One condition or requirement is that you are human. Cats and dogs may be welcome to stay in a country, but they are not in the domain of eligible candidates for citizenship. The fourth type of social kind can reflect real groupings in the world, but not mark them. Once something is deemed eligible to be part of social kind of the fourth type – like a permanent resident, prime minister, citizen, married person, etc. – then actually acquiring the status of belonging to the social kind in question is done by fiat. To be a citizen of some national state you must be recognized as a citizen by the appropriate institutional representative of the state.

Unfortunately, this fourth category of social kinds is ill suited to understanding sports like football. There are aspects of football matches that can be subsumed under the banner of this fourth social kind – and that do not allow for token exceptions – but nothing much interesting results from considering them. For example, being a World Cup qualifier is a question of having the status of being a World Cup qualifier endowed upon the football match by FIFA's (the Fédération Internationale de Football Association) governing bodies. To be a World Cup qualifier, the match must be recognized as a World Cup qualifier by the appropriate or chosen representative organ of FIFA. To be eligible for this status, the event must belong to the domain of football matches, but membership in or the status of World Cup qualifier is given by fiat. This does not constitute a philosophically interesting grouping in the sport world. It might tell us something interesting about the institutional set-up of football and the balance of power between FIFA, the six continental confederations, and the various football associations. However, it does not tell us anything important about football *qua* sport or about football and sport as social kinds.

Could something become a sport through the sort of fiat this fourth category of social kinds allows for? We saw that being a World Cup qualifier does not constitute something ontologically deep in the sport world, whereas eligibility for being a World Cup qualifier does, since that is the domain of football matches. When trying to figure out what sort of social kind football is, we cannot inherit the domain of eligibility for being a World Cup qualifier without begging the question. Similar remarks apply to sport in general. We need a domain that includes activities or practices that we do not already pre-theoretically consider football or sport. Only then can we ask whether we can, by fiat, turn some of these activities or practices into football or sport. Let us consider the domain of skill-based physical activities, which have a beginning and an end-state. According to our working definition of sport, this domain will include sports, but not pre-theoretically be exclusive to sports. This is our domain of eligible candidates for becoming sport by fiat. The domain rules out certain things, such as being alive, breathing, etc., but includes activities that pre-theoretically are not considered sport, like building houses. Building houses is a suitable test case. Can we make it a sport by fiat? No. Why? Simply because sports are not the types of activities that are nothing but being seen as sports. You cannot turn house building into a sport by seeing it as a sport, when there is no change in the structure of the activity itself. There is more to the phenomenon of sport than is allowed in the social kind of the fourth type. This accounts for the impression that being part of the social kind of World Cup qualifiers does not mark a philosophically interesting grouping in the sport world, when our interest is in understanding football *qua* sport. That kind marks no true joints in the sphere of sport. Unlike citizenship, prime ministership and similar phenomena, inclusion in a social kind by fiat is not applicable to the social kind of sport. Declaring that house building is a sport does not make it so. House building is not the sort of activity that can be turned into a sport by fiat. Or, better, sport is not a social kind that allows for membership by fiat.

This does not mean that we cannot turn house building into a sport. You can 'sport up' your world whenever you want to. However, you cannot make any old activity a sport just by saying that it is a sport. Making house building into a sport is different than attempting to make it a sport by fiat. In our discussion of the aims and functions of sport in Chapter 1, we followed Kupfer in thinking that the internal or intrinsic and external or primary purposes of sports are not the same. The internal aim, which is intrinsic to sport, is to win, but this cannot be the external aim, function or purpose of sport, because in order to win in a sport the sport itself must already be established. The internal aim of sport serves no ordinary or everyday purpose, whereas the external purposes serve other broader needs. In house building, which is an ordinary world activity, the internal and external aims, functions or purposes of the activity coincide. The reason for the phenomenon of house building is that creatures like us need shelter. Our need for shelter explains why people build houses. That is the external reason. The internal reason for building a house is also to provide shelter. Generally speaking, the aim of every single builder is to help to produce a shelter; when builders are not building their own house, they will be rewarded with some kind of salary. Talking about the external and internal aims of building a house is in some sense odd, as everyday or ordinary world activities tend not to have a distinguishable outside (external aim, goal or purpose) and inside (internal aim, goal or purpose). Extra-ordinary activities or practices, on the other hand, often do. In order to turn house building into a sport, you must change its internal aim or goal – or, alternatively, introduce the internal aim or goal of winning the sport of house building. That is a structural change. Someone who sports up house building in this manner has changed the activity. This is not a matter of bestowing the status of sport by fiat onto an already existing, unchanged activity, but of appropriating the activity of house building for sporting purposes. As such, it is a converse case of *Football and the Natives*. Furthermore, a sport like football is a matter of convention in the sense that a sport can be created by agreement. It is not difficult to make a new sport. Sit down and agree on some rules and regulations, and you have yourself a brand-new sport. Creating a sport that catches on might be difficult, but making a new sport is not. But, again, there are limitations. If there were not, then it should have been possible to make house building into a sport by fiat, but it is not. The fact that you at will can create a new sport shows that sports are a social kind and, furthermore, indicates that they most likely belong among the social kinds that have collective intentionality at their centre, but not much more.

The social kind of sport

The last section ended with the discouraging claim that the sport phenomenon, including football, escapes the theorizing that, thus far, has been done on social kinds. But all is not lost. The fact that sports like football do not fit the first two types of social kinds shows that there is some type of transparency with regard to sports and their constitutive rules. Whereas social kinds like recession and racism are "opaque kinds" that can "remain unknown even to those within the relevant society", sports are not (Thomasson 2003b: 606). It will turn out that the transparency relation between sport and those doing sport is more complex than one might expect, but suffice to say for now that sports are not opaque in the sense that their constitutive rules can be wholly obscured for the relevant society or social group.

Sports like football belong in the vicinity of social kinds of the third type, but addressing these sorts of social kinds only along the line of token exceptions has led us astray. Talk of types and tokens is not the problem. The sport of football has a type – what football is as a sport; the blueprint of the sport, so to speak – and tokens – among which the individual football match is perhaps the most basic or natural unit.[9] The primary football tokens are the football matches played around the world. The key to understanding football and similar sports' place in the pantheon of social kinds is to introduce the idea that, besides tokens of a type, we should also think about the stages of both tokens and types. Talk of tokens indicates discrete objects and events, which acquire their status as a specific social kind through their connection to the type. This works fine for social kinds like money that use physical objects onto which a designated function has been endowed, but for practices and processes such talk blurs the fact that we can also talk about the stages of social kinds. Perhaps a coin is not money until it is fully formed. If our minting machine breaks down, then the unfinished coins inside the machine are not money. They are unfinished coins, but not money. In order to count as tokens of this type, there seems to be a requirement that tokens be fully formed versions of the social kind in question. Things are not necessarily so clean cut with regard to social kinds like war and football.

Consider, once again, *Searle's Cocktail Party*. One might suppose that the reason for rejecting this as a war is that, according to the type standards of war, the warlike party is not fully formed as a token of that type. Certain features intrinsic to war as a type are lacking and that excludes the party from counting as a token of that type. This would account for the justification for Searle's view that regardless of the death toll or what the cocktail party leads to, it will still not count as war. Khalidi, who thinks that it should count as war, argues as follows:

> [T]okens of war are dependent not solely on the attitudes of members of society but also partly on certain causal properties. There may be no hard and fast conditions that a series of events needs to satisfy to be correctly considered a war, but there are certain criteria that historians, journalists, and others might employ. They might, for example, attend to the number of troops deployed, casualty figures, duration of hostilities, and other features to judge whether a conflict can indeed be deemed a war.
>
> *(Khalidi 2015: 100)*

That is exactly the right thing to say about war as a social kind. Unfortunately, Khalidi goes on to write that *"war* as well as kinds like *money"* allow that "tokens of these kinds may be instantiated even though no one considers them to be such", while also arguing that it "seems implausible" that there could be "war without beliefs involving the concept of *war*" (Khalidi 2015: 100). How? We have already explained the coin counting as money without collective intentionality. Is there anything similar in the realm of war? Certainly not. Battles and wars do not go astray (in the manner money might) in the process of doing battles and wars. Stages of social kinds are the key to unlocking social kinds like war and sport.

Instead of thinking in terms of types and tokens, we should frame the discussion of such practices and processes in terms of types and stages of types, and tokens and stages of tokens. Stages of a social kind, on both the type and token level, have less strict requirements with regard to what features are demanded of a stage of a type or token of a social kind to count as part of that social kind. This theoretical move permits a reinterpretation of *Searle's Cocktail Party*. The Searle-Khalidi debate centres on the question of whether the cocktail party is a token of the war type. Searle says that the cocktail party is not war because it lacks collective intentionality, while Khalidi suggests that it is, but given his appeal to an analogy to money, he fails to convince. Introducing the idea that a token of a social kind like war has stages opens up the possibility that there can be stages of the token that are not seen by participants as a stage of that token. What does that mean? First, let us grant Searle and Khalidi that war is a social kind that demands some level of collective intentionality. War is not an opaque social kind, but a transparent one. War is, in this sense, more like money than like racism and recession. Allowing for the stage exception of a token of a type permits one to say that the question of whether the war-like cocktail party is war depends on the further consequences of that episode. If the cocktail party is the beginning of a chain of events that at one point is seen as a war, then that stage, i.e. the cocktail party, can be war without collective intentionality. The cocktail party would be a stage exception with regard to the collective intentionality of a token of war, i.e. a specific war. We have stage exception at the token level of war. If that particular stage were the beginning of a specific war, then it would get to be war because it is connected to or part of a token of war. This means that Searle's warring cocktail drinkers missed something when they failed to see it as war. For the same reason, the partygoer who exclaimed that the cocktail party has turned into a war would be mistaken should it turn out that the brutal episode was nothing more than that. In the latter case, it would be natural to describe the cocktail party as a war-like state. This would indicate that the episode had the potential to be the beginning of a war, though it was not. Last, the question of when a war started is not only a question of when the warring parties started seeing the hostilities as war, but also something that can be discovered by historians. This is the right result. The latter points towards the possibility of also allowing for a social kind like war to have stage type exceptions with regard to collective intentionality.

Consider doing work on the history of war and warfare. Presumably, the first step would be to think about whether or not one wants to think of any conflict between social groups as war. If one follows the Searle-Khalidi line, there is more to war than violent conflict. Perhaps war and warfare only demand that the conflict be between societies, which could include fairly low-scale conflicts, depending on how you define society. Maybe the involvement of organized armies is needed for something to count as war. Perhaps one wishes to include the practice or convention of declaring war before calling a violent conflict between societies a war. Another way to proceed would be to give various labels, such as pre-historic war, ancient war, medieval war, modern war, etc., to whatever it is one wants to study. Take the case of war as armed conflict between societies. It is reasonable to think of historical development as gradual – to consider that before a social group or society has self-awareness of being at war with another social group or society, it could be in violent conflict with another social group or society. We would then have a situation of a war-like state or war between two groups without belief involving the concept of war – i.e., no collective intentionality of being at war. If one only wants to admit that this stage, seen synchronically, is merely a war-like state, but diachronic studies show that this stage is part and parcel of a development that led to a self-understanding of being a society at war (including the formation of a concept of war), then that war-like state, I submit, is part of the social kind of war. One could imagine that the social kind of war emerged in this manner, in which case we have the stage exception of collective intentionality with regard to the kind itself. Similarly, assume that we instead think of war as a social kind that requires a whole host of codified conventions of war to be in place for a violent conflict to count as war. Codified conventions of war demand collective intentionality. Before conventions of war were codified at least some of them were probably already in place, in which case it seems reasonable to assume that there has been a stage of the social kind of war (given this understanding of the kind) without collective intentionality of being at war. Cut the conceptual cake any way you want to and you get the same result. If historic change is predominately gradual, then there will often be a case for thinking that there have been stages of the social kind at which the parties involved have yet to come to any self-awareness that they are part of that social kind, i.e. without collective intentionality. We have stage exception at the type level.

This gives us an additional two types of social kinds, which belong in the same ballpark as the type of social kind based on direct collective intentionality with token exceptions.

5. Social kinds based on direct collective intentionality, which allow for stage exceptions regarding tokens of the social kind.
6. Social kinds based on direct collective intentionality, which allow for stage exceptions regarding the social kind itself, i.e. the type.

Do sports like football belong to either or both of these types of social kinds?

Given our treatment of the *Human Stampede* and the *Shoreline Runners*, it is safe to say that sports do not fall into category five. This is not to say that an event like the sprinting men in the *Shoreline Runners* cannot come very close to being a sport, but without some sort of understanding among the participants that this is now to count as a sporting event, it falls short of being such an event. The shoreline runners are not involved in a sporting event until there is at least a dawning understanding among the runners that their running is to be seen as running a race. Once such collective intentionality is in place, the running can become a sporting event, but not before. This marks the transition point between non-sport running and running a race with regard to tokens of a sport: with collective intentionality (including a dawning of collective intentionality), a possible sporting event and a token of a sport; without it, not. Unlike the case of war, sporting events do not allow for stage token exception. Note also that these considerations are only relevant at a stage in human development – be that a social circle, a cultural area, a historical period, etc.— when some sort of concept of sport already exists. Stage exceptions of a token of sport entail that there is a type in place – i.e., that there is a functioning concept of sport in place for the relevant domain of activities. This makes a difference. Without collective intentionality about something being or not being a sport available for potential sport participants, any case or example that is suggested to be a sport without collective intentionality will belong to the sixth category of social kinds.

Why does sport not allow for stage token exceptions when another practice or process like war does? I suspect the answer lies in the fact that mere violent conflict and war are on a continuum of conflict, whereas jogging and a running race are not on a continuum of physical activity. A violent conflict that fulfils enough of the criteria for being a war or otherwise is deemed similar enough to be thought of as a war-like state – that is, as the first stage or stages of a war, thus being part of that war – counts as war. War runs the gamut from some level of large-scale violent conflict to codified violent conflict. A peculiarity with the social kind of war is that once your have certain institutions of war in place, including the convention of declaration of war, then a nation can declare war on another in the absence of existing hostilities. One can then imagine a situation in which a peace is brokered before any hostilities take place. In that case, we have had a war without hostilities, casualties, etc. In ordinary language, we single out the oddity of such wars by dubbing them "phoney wars". Here, war is started by fiat.[10] There is no similar convention of declaration of sport and the possibility of there being phoney sporting events. You might line yourself up with your football team outside Estadio Azteca and declare a football match with Club América, Cruz Azul or Mexico. However, without some actual football playing between two teams taking place, you do not have a football match that is phoney – you do not have a football match at all. Similarly, if one year the Olympic Games were declared open, but no sporting events took place – say, due to the outbreak of war or some terrible disaster – one would not say that we had a phoney Olympics, but instead that the Olympics that year were cancelled or did not take place. Phoney wars are possible because wars serve direct purposes in the ordinary world. Ordinarily, you do not go to war just because you enjoy the killing part; you go to war because there is some material or ideological goal you wish to achieve. Perhaps you go to war because you want to get part of your neighbour's land: the part you believe should belong to you. A mere declaration of war might just do the trick. Wars are not autotelic in the way that sports are. This brings us back to the observation that violent conflicts and wars exist on a continuum, while jogging and running a race do not. A running race is not merely, say, large-scale running or a form of codified jogging. A footrace is something else. The fact that sports are extra-ordinary and unnecessary makes an important difference with regard to the possibility of stage token exceptions. Sport not being continuous with ordinary life explains why there is no temptation to say that the early stages of building a house were the early stages of a sporting event, even if, as it happens, the builders turn their activity into such an event. Sporting up house building means turning the activity into something different. In such a case, the pre-sport stages of house building would be something different and thus not candidates for being stages of the sporting event. You do not get stages of tokens of sport unguided by collective intentionality.

Unlike some neighbouring phenomena in the sphere of the extra-ordinary – for example rites and rituals and, in some conceptions, art – sports are unnecessary with regard to ordinary world concerns, in the sense of both not being directly valuable for and not addressing or being about such concerns. Does that make a difference with regard to not allowing stage token exceptions? I am uncertain. Rites and rituals are (at times) perceived as being concerned with ordinary world concerns. It seems to me that rites and rituals do not easily lend themselves to being thought of as having stage token exceptions. In this respect, sports, on the one hand, and rites and rituals, on the other, do not seem to differ. Art raises other, but related concerns. Let us assume that art is a social kind that in part requires being recognized as art, i.e. collective intentionality. Consider art that involves ordinary world artefacts or objects. If we agree with the commonly accepted view of the art world that, say, Duchamp's infamous urinal *Fountain* is art, then a key question is whether the urinal was already art before it was relocated to an art gallery. If you say yes, then you have a token of art with stage token exception. If you say no, then art in this respect is like sport.[11] You might push the question further and challenge the assumption that art is a social kind which requires some sort of collective intentionality. Is any urinal from the Bedfordshire model porcelain urinal production line (perhaps all sanitary equipment) also art on a par with *Fountain*? An affirmative answer to that question would make art a very unruly social kind. One solution with regard to fringe cases concerning social kinds like art, but also sport, would be to borrow a methodological principle applied by Lewis in the realm of metaphysics.

> When common sense delivers a firm and uncontroversial answer about a not-too-far-fetched case, theory had better agree. (...) But when common sense falls into indecision or controversy, or when it is reasonable to suspect that far-fetched cases are being judged by false analogy to commonplace ones, then theory may safely say what it likes. Such cases can be left as spoils to the victor,

in D.M. Armstrong's phrase. We can reasonably accept as true whatever answer comes from the analysis that does best on the clearer cases.

(Lewis 1986a: 194)

With regard to art, we need to change "common sense" with "the art-world". Lewis's methodological prescription is that you must first get the uncontroversial cases right, that which the art world deems to be art. This means, among other things, providing a theory that explains or encompasses *Duchamp's urinal in the gallery* as art. The advice is that whichever theory best explains the uncontroversial and commonly accepted cases of art gets to dictate how to deal with fringe cases like *Fountain's* pre-Duchamp, pre-gallery existence. Is all sanitary equipment art? That depends on what Armstrong's victor tells us art is. You extrapolate from the most successful theory about art and see what it says about *Fountain's* pre-Duchamp, pre-gallery existence and other sanitary equipment. Whereas *Fountain* is a work of art and its stages before being included in the art world constitute a fringe case that is open for being considered a stage token exception with regard to collective intentionality, the phenomenon of sport does not present similar challenging and problematic fringe cases.[12] The latter is the suggested take-home lesson from thinking about the case of sporting up house building. That leaves us with social kinds with collective intentionality at their centre that allow for stage exceptions of the kind itself with regard to collective intentionality. And that is exactly the type of social kind I believe sport should be subsumed under.

Before we proceed, let us recap our understanding of sport so far. The assumption was that sports are unnecessary, autotelic, competitive, physical-skill activities involving rules. When looking at possible stage type exceptions of sport with regard to collective intentionality, we rely on this conception of sport. The conception will not rake up the spoils – not without some arguments for why this conception of sport is the right one – but it will be important when thinking about sport-like stages that might count as stage type exceptions for the social kind of sport. When do activities that look like they are fulfilling most or enough of the criteria of sport show up in history? A quite common take on the genesis or origin of sport is to argue that sports grew out of cultic or ritual activities. Another take is that activities that have a shape comparable to our modern sports, and are recognizable as sports, first show up in ancient Greece.[13] We are not going to evaluate these claims so much as students of history, but rather examine them with a view to understanding the social kind of sport. We will limit much of our discussion to the ancient Panhellenic world. The reasons are pragmatic. We have the benefit of a decent amount of archaeological and historical sources on the emergence of sport and sport-like activities during this period in that area and a fair amount of research that draws on those sources. When we reach the ancient Olympics taking place at Olympia and organized by the city-state of Elis, which Donald Kyle describes as hosting "the earliest, greatest, and longest-enduring Greek athletic festival", we find activities deserving of the label of sport (Kyle 2014: 23). This is a good place to look, when thinking about possible stage type exceptions of a social kind of sport with regard to collective intentionality.

Allen Guttmann tells us that "Carl Diem's monumental world history of sports begins with the bold assertion, 'All physical exercises were originally cultic'" (Guttmann 2004a: 16). Historians tend to avoid such sweeping claims, but the Greek case lends itself to thinking about sports in the Panhellenic world as having a cultic or ritualistic beginning.

> The earliest literary account of Greek athletics comes from Homer's *Iliad* (23.262–897), which describes how Achilles organized funeral games consisting of eight events (starting with a chariot race and ending with a spear-throwing contest) for his dead friend Patroklos. (…) Competitions could apparently include traditions from sources as varied as funeral games, initiation rituals, and hero cults, but there was a pattern: most formal public athletic competitions were held as components of religious festivals. Games were seen as an appropriate way to honor gods and heroes, and a fundamental tie between religion, sanctuaries, and games endured for centuries.
>
> *(Kyle 2014: 22)*

There are various ways in which the extra-ordinary and sacred domain of religion could have spawned what became the extra-ordinary and secular activity of sport. Sarah Murray lists quite a few possibilities, and we will look at her first two: "[t]hat athletic competitions in Greek sanctuaries originated as a form of reiterated funeral games for local heroes" and "that at least some religious festivals had their roots in initiation rites that included a footrace and that these religious festivals, as a result, had an athletic component from the outset" (Murray 2014: 311).

Assuming that this line of thinking concerning the emergence of sports in Greek antiquity is correct (no doubt it could have happened that way), then what does it tell us about sport as a social kind? It tells us that a social kind can emerge out of another social kind, while its outward manifestations remain or mostly remain the same. Consider the footraces mentioned by Murray and her further elucidation:

> Rites of passage involving a physical trial of some kind and a standard cycle of separation, liminality, and reintegration are widespread in ancient cultures throughout the world, and ancient Greece was no exception. Scholars, such as David Sansone, who trace the origins of Greek athletic competitions to initiation rites, cite the early existence at Olympia of a race for young girls (the Heraia) that had overt initiatory aspects (Sansone 1988). Footraces as initiation rites are themselves quite common in ancient Greece, and the original program of the Olympics was thought to have consisted of a single foot race, the *stadion*. Very little is known about when and how the Heraia and the original Olympic *stadion* race came into being, and no single feature of the Olympics can be definitely identified as being derived from an initiation rite.
>
> *(Murray 2015: 437)*

Recall *Football and the Natives*. There we found that if something – the outward physical manifestations of the game of football – gets appropriated into a new context with a new function and meaning, it does not stay the same. The English in our example were playing a sport called football. The natives – even though they produced the same movements when acting out the rule book – were doing something else; they were performing a ritual. Outwardly the same, but with a different function.

We can tell a reverse story regarding the kind of initiation ritual footrace described by Murray.

> Footrace and the Professors: An ancient Greek city-state leaves behind only one document. The document is a carefully written description of how to correctly and successfully carry out an initiation rite called footrace. *The Book of Footrace* is like a manual or rule book for the initiation rite of footrace, but it is silent with regard to footrace's ritualistic and religious meaning. Centuries later, a group of Oxford professors, incensed by the rise of the unhealthy, brutal plebeian sport of football, discover *The Book of Footrace* from the ancient Greeks. Delighted by what they take to be a formula for a sport, they agree that this is an activity worthy of the British ruling class. The sport is a success, and soon an annual footrace takes place between students from Oxford and Cambridge.

In the same way as the natives were not doing sport, but performing a ritual, the Oxonians are not performing a rite or ritual, but engaging in a sport. Considerations similar to those applied to *Football and the Natives* also apply to *Footrace and the Professors*.

The important take-home lesson is that the outwardly observable parts of a practice need not change even though the practice as a whole changes, possibly becoming something different. Both of our thought experiments are striking given the abrupt change of context – from the British Isles to Norway, or from ancient Greece to Oxford – but gradual change can yield the same result. Consider again the footraces described by Murray and her observation that the first Olympics featured only the footrace *stadion*. In ancient Greece, foot-racing as a form of initiation seems to have generally been a part of liminal ceremonies geared towards advancing from childhood to adulthood. Regarding the Olympics, Paul Christesen informs us that:

> What would ultimately become perhaps the world's most famous sporting event, the Olympics, were probably founded at some point during the eighth century as part of a religious festival. (...) Excavations at Olympia have shown that it became a religious sanctuary around 1000 (...) There is, however, no clear physical evidence that helps fix the date for the beginning of athletic contests there.
>
> *(Christesen 2012: 127–128)*

Keeping in mind Mark Golden's warning that ancient Greece was "a society in which every part of life was pervaded by cult activity and invocation of the gods", the evidence as relayed by Murray and Christesen invites us to consider that Greek sport emerged out of rites and rituals (Golden 1998: 23). Our sources on exactly how and why, in the ancient Greek culture, an intensive sport-focused culture of religious festivals was formed are inconclusive and at times problematic. However, in the context of thinking about sport as a social kind, which might allow stage type exceptions with regard to collective intentionality, the sources suffice.

Consider the possibility that the footrace that we find in the first Olympics – the *stadion* – was originally solely an initiation rite. Imagine a time traveller observing that event and reporting back that the ancient Greeks were staging sporting events with running races just like we do in our track and field events. Like the Oxonians in *Footrace and the Professors*, the time traveller would be wrong. The Greeks at this point were not participating in a sporting event, but performing an initiation rite. Say then that the athletic part of *stadion*, which was part of the rite from the beginning, starts to take on an importance or significance of its own. This is in keeping with the sources available to us. Golden, who we saw wanted to tone down the cult-sport connection, informs us that "there does seem to be one objective criterion by which a diagnosis of early secularization might be reached" and this criterion is the "telling evidence [of] increasing separation of the areas of competition and cult" (Golden 1998: 21). In the days of early secularization of footraces like *stadion* in the Olympics, we might find that even though the event had started taking on all the hallmarks of a sporting event, it was still also an initiation rite. At that stage, we would have a sport-like rite, or a rite with a sport-like element. Lastly, following the previously mentioned scholars, the secularization process is at one point completed, and we no longer have an initiation rite whenever a footrace like *stadion* is taking place, but a sport. This does not mean that sporting events at Olympia had fully shed their religious cloak (cf. Golden's warning). Some events like the Heraia Games at Olympia were perhaps never fully secularized. That, however, is no reason for us not to think that the Panhellenic athletics at Olympia displayed "ancient Greek culture['s] (...) extraordinary devotion to sport" (Nielsen 2014: 133).

This suggests the following delineation of the developmental periods of a footrace like *stadion*.

I: Footrace as initiation rite.
II: Footrace as a rite, but also as a sport-like activity.
III: Footrace as athletic competition that counts as a sport.

During Period I, the footrace belongs to the sphere of the extra-ordinary and sacred. There is a physical movement aspect of the activity, which is also integral to the later sport version of the activity, but otherwise there is no temptation to say that the footrace during this period is a sport. In Period III, following the classicists, archaeologists and historians, we deem the footrace to be a sport. Note again that, for the footrace to be a sport, it need not shed all its rite-like features. In fact, ancient Greek sports never fully do. What about Period II: Is it a rite or a sport? The suggestion here is that it can be both, or that it is a rite with a sport-like element. If the sport-like part develops into a full-blooded sport, then that sport-like part is deemed a sport by virtue of being the first or an early stage of a sport. If enough of the criteria for being a sport are fulfilled to allow us to judge the stage as sport-like and if there is a historical and causal connection to what later became a sport, then we have a stage of that sport without collective intentionality. The stage can be part of a sport, even though the participants and spectators at the time did not view it as a sport or had no concept of sport, or an equivalent concept or understanding that would cause us to judge them as viewing the activity as a sport. We now have a sport example of stage type exception with regard to collective intentionality. Should the sport-like period of the footrace fail to yield a sport, then by the very same token it does not get to be part of a sport. If we think of some social kinds as having stages, then there is no reason why two social kinds cannot share a stage. I suspect that this might often be the case with regard to more secular activities or practices in the sphere of the extra-ordinary in relation to the sacred. The dusk of one social kind can be the dawn of another.

In a previous work, when addressing the possibility of being mistaken about an activity being a sport, I introduced the example of *danza de los voladores*.

> When the Spanish conquistadors invaded what is today known as Mexico, they encountered "a religious ritual (…) *danza de los voladores* (dance of the flyers) (…) that survived remarkably intact because the Spaniards took it for an acrobatic display of skill" (Harris 2000: 113, see also Leal 1982). If we allow ourselves to distinguish between doing something for sport and something being a sport, where the former is understood as an unnecessary activity undertaken as diversion, entertainment, recreation or pastime, then it seems reasonable to say that the Spaniards mistook that which was a religious ritual for sport.
>
> *(Borge 2015b: 116)*

The social kind of *danza de los voladores* presumably started its life as a religious ritual, but ended up as something done for sport with no religious connotations. There is no reason to believe that there was a sharp transition between *danza de los voladores* being done as a religious ritual and *danza de los voladores* being done for sport. Again, we find the possibility of two social kinds sharing a stage – this time on a token level of ritual and being done for sport, and simultaneously at the type level of *danza de los voladores* as ritual and being done for sport. Returning to sport, we find that the task of discovering when a social kind like sport or a specific sport emerged is not merely a question of the self-understanding of those partaking in that social kind, i.e. collective intentionality, but also something researchers can discover. The rise of a social kind and the self-understanding of the agents partaking in the social kind need not march in step. Sport is a social kind that allows stage type exceptions with regard to collective intentionality and football qua sport also allows for this.

The social kind of football

Football as a historical phenomenon – or association football as we will call it in this section – has, like many social kinds do, a blooming, buzzing and confusing origin. Historians tend to trace the origin of association football to mediaeval ball games in the British Isles sometimes referred to as traditional football, other times as folk football. One of the first references to a game called football in this part of the world dates back to a proclamation in the name of King Edward II made by the Lord Mayor of London in 1314 – a proclamation banning the activity due to "great uproar in the City, through certain tumult arising from great footballs in the fields of the public, from which many evils perchance may arise" (cited in Elias and Dunning 2008b: 174). Throughout the mediaeval era, we find references to football games and footballs, perhaps none more scathing than Thomas Elyot's description of it as "beastely fury" and Philip Stubbes's argument that the game might lead to "fighting, brawling, contention, quarrel picking, murther, homicide, and great effusion of blood" (Elyot, *The Boke of the Governour* (1573) and Stubbes, *Anatomy of Abuses* (1583), both cited in Guttmann 2004b: 65). British folk football consisted of a cluster of local variants – like hurling, bottle-kicking, knappan, camp-ball, etc. – of an activity, where kicking, carrying and throwing the ball were allowed. The teams did not need to be even and could consist of up to whole villages pitted against each other. The playing fields were equally varied and could be vast. The aim of the game often seemed to be to get the ball through some sort of portal, which could be located in front of the two participating villages' churches. The games have been described as "contests of brute strength and collective violence" (Holt 1989: 14), "wild and riotous" (Elias and Dunning 2008b: 175), and "relatively simple, wild and unruly" (Dunning and Sheard 2005: 2).[14] The games bear some resemblance to our current association football, but also to other types of ball game activities or practices involving the feet and found elsewhere in world, such as the French *soule*, the Italian *gioco del calcio*, the Aboriginal Australasian *Marn Gook*, the ancient Chinese *Tsu Chu*, the Japanese *kemari*, the Roman *harpastum*, and the Greek *episkyros*. None of these games is close enough in their sport set-up to be considered association football. Furthermore, they do not stand in a causal historical connection to association football as it first emerged in Britain, so they are not candidates for being considered association football-like practices that might constitute early stages of association football. Only the British folk football practices are causally connected to the emergence of association football.[15]

The origin of association football has traditionally been understood in the following manner.

> Traditional histories of football have been fairly clear about its basic origins and chronological development in Britain. An orthodox viewpoint has emerged

which holds that the modern game as we know it is the product of the rationalisation and civilisation of a traditional folk activity in the nation's elite public schools and universities. The codified game that emerged then gained ground among working-class players and spectators and in time was transformed into a genuinely popular recreational activity.

(Taylor 2008: 20)

A prominent champion of the orthodox view has been Dunning. Dunning, together with Kenneth Sheard, uses five stages to describe the development of football, but for our purposes we will simplify this into three stages (Dunning 1971: 133–134, Dunning and Sheard 2005: 2–3):

1. Folk football: 1314–1750
2. Proto-football: 1750–1863
3. Association football: 1863–present

The year 1314 is chosen because this is the first time folk football is mentioned. Obviously, the practice of folk football is older than that, but 1314 is the year it shows up in our sources. The year 1750 is taken from Dunning and Sheard, who use it to demarcate when the public schools get in on the football action (Dunning and Sheard 2005: 2). The year 1863 is chosen as it was the year of the fifth meeting of what was to become the ruling body of association football in England – the Football Association (FA) – where a code of the game resembling association football rules was introduced and "[t]he supporters of the Rugby code were heavily defeated in a vote and the contentious rules [hacking and carrying] were struck out" (Curry and Dunning 2015: 132). On the other hand, according to Adrian Harvey, these rules did not take hold in many parts of proto-football-playing England, and Tony Collins argues that it was not until the 1870s that the difference between association football and rugby football was established (Harvey 2005: 144–166, Collins 2005: 295–296, Collins 2019: 31–37). Dave Russell argues that "[t]he rules of 1863 went only a modest way towards the production of a genuinely new game" (Russell 2013: 17). Still, the date is chosen because it marks a year in relation to which we can talk about association football. Matthew Taylor tells us, "the foundation of the FA in 1863 remains a major landmark in the development of the game" (Taylor 2008: 30). Furthermore, we can, as Curry and Dunning do, sensibly talk about association football before that date, such as seeing "the Eton field game as a prototype of association football" (Curry and Dunning 2015: 58). However, in 1863 we have a set of association football rules or association football-like rules in place, allowing that year to serve as a convenient cut-off point between proto-football and association football.

The origin of folk football is in many ways beyond us. Some writers have speculated that folk football started as "a fertility rite" (Guttmann 2004b: 64), others have argued for the game's tribal origins (Young 1968), or emphasized both its ritualistic and tribal background (Morris 1981). Many of the folk football contests we know about took place on various festival occasions connected to pagan and Christian traditions. But as Curry and Dunning sum it up, "there is no way of determining conclusively whether football had a ritual origin or not" (Curry and Dunning 2015: 28). Following orthodoxy, there is a causal historical link between British folk football and association football. This does not mean, however, that folk football counts as association football or that they share stages. When looking at the descriptions of folk football, it is fair to say that it is neither association football nor association football-like. When we compare British folk football with the blueprint of association football – its constitutive rules and the manners in which the game has been played both when the sport emerged and today – there is simply not enough overlap to warrant any such conclusion. Folk football does not belong to the social kind of association football. This is in line with Russell's description of these folk games as "precursors of association football rather than true ancestors" (Russell 2013: 13).

If we follow orthodoxy and the Dunning school of thought, the next step towards association football begins with the "cultural marginalization of folk football" and folk football being "taken up by boys in the public schools, elaborated in certain respects and adapted" (Dunning 1999: 90, Dunning and Sheard 2005: 2). The transition from folk football to the proto-football played at these public schools is under-described in the literature. Dunning and Sheard tell us that the folk game represented "the 'common matrix' from which Rugby and soccer are descended" (Dunning and Sheard 2005: 2). This is not an unreasonable claim, but it does not tell us how the game transitioned from being a folk game to being central in the life of public schools. Unlike the writing on later developments of football, there seem to be no sources that track individuals engaged in both activities, and the sources from public schools on the proto-football played there do not seem to mention folk football. The next key element in Dunning's theory of the development of football towards association football is "Dunning's 'status rivalry hypothesis', looking at the juxtaposed rules of Rugby School football and the Eton Field Game" (Curry and Dunning 2015: 8). According to Dunning and collaborators, the local variants of proto-football played at various public schools moved towards codification due to the rivalry between Rugby and Eton. In the period between the 1820s and the 1840s, Rugby developed the game so that you could run with the ball and score by kicking it between goalposts and over a bar, and Eton followed contra suit by making their field game one that prohibited handling the ball and where goals were scored getting the ball between goalposts and under the bar (Dunning and Sheard 2005: 86, Curry and Dunning 2015: 27–61). After that, as public school boys from various schools went on to the universities, the need for codification of the game deepened, the end result being the split between rugby football and association football with the formation of the FA in 1863.

The traditional view of the emergence of association football has been challenged both with regard to the so-called marginalization of the folk football game and the dominant role of the public schools. Historian Richard Holt raises the question of continuity versus invention when he notes the following:

> Perhaps we have taken on board too eagerly the heroic accounts of the public school men, who founded the Football Association in 1863, and assumed in consequence that traditional football was suppressed lock, stock and barrel during the first half of the nineteenth century to be re-invented and re-popularized in the second.
>
> *(Holt 1988: 70)*

The leading advocates for a revision of the orthodoxy have been John Goulstone and Adrian Harvey (Goulstone 2001, Harvey 2005, but see also, among others, Tranter 1998: 8, and Vamplew 1988: 10). Harvey has aimed to show that football outside the realm of the public schools continued to exist and that public house-related football matches involving gambling were arranged. Moreover, he has detailed the football culture in Sheffield that, independent of the public schools, produced the Sheffield rules: the Sheffield FC codification of 1858 (Harvey 1999, 2001, 2002, 2004a, 2004b, 2005, 2013).[16]

> While the rules of soccer have always been credited to the public schools, in actual fact they sprang from many sources and were modified significantly. One of the major sources of these transformations was the football culture that emerged in Sheffield during the 1850s.
>
> *(Harvey 2005: xxiii–xxiv)*

One interesting feature of the revisionist line of thought on the emergence of association football is that it at least allows us to bridge the gap between the folk football and proto-football predecessors of association football. It also promises to solve another puzzling feature of the rise and spread of association football.

> Certainly, if evidence of the continued popularity of football on any scale can be found before the arrival of the association system, the rapidity with which the northern working-class teams took over the sport and their proprietary attitude towards it becomes more readily comprehensible. In their own eyes they may simply have been asserting ownership over what had been theirs all along.
>
> *(Holt 1988: 72)*

Harvey suggests that he has in fact provided that evidence (Harvey 2005: 51–125). Defenders of the orthodox view in many ways concur, though Collins argues that the so-called influence of Sheffield football and rules amounts to myth-making and invented tradition (Collins 2019: 25–29, 33, 43, 93–94). Curry and Dunning write, "[t]he modern form of the game of football (Association football) developed from the matrix of 'folk' and public house-related games that existed in England before the beginning of the nineteenth century", and further that there is "no doubt (...) that early Sheffield football can be described as an embryonic Association form of the game" (Curry and Dunning 2015: 173, 92). The disagreement between defenders of the orthodox view and the revisionists is about who and what were most influential in the development of association football. Curry and Dunning believe the evidence favours the orthodox view of "the public schools and universities (particularly Cambridge) as having formed the principal institutional *loci* where, not only the incipient modernisation of football but also (...) the bifurcation into the Association and Rugby forms took place" (Curry and Dunning 2015: 37). Defenders of the revisionist line hold that a "'mixture of influences' (...) helped to create the association game (...) football should no longer be regarded as having been made solely in the environment of the leading public schools and universities" (Taylor 2008: 31).

When addressing the emergence and formation of association football as a social kind, one does well to keep in mind the almost platitudinous saying that every generation writes its own history – not as an uncritical endorsement of some sort of crude form of historicism or relativism, but as an acknowledgement that as the world changes and moves forward (linearly or circularly), the questions asked by historians also change. The historical sources might be the same, but the threads we are looking for in those sources will be different, reflecting new circumstances of the present. This also holds when we think about social kinds. Social kinds do not have natural borders. That is what it is to be a social kind. Furthermore, some social kinds are also historical kinds that change and evolve. The social kind of sport is a historical kind, as is association football. The social historical kind of association football is still evolving. There are at least two important lessons to be learnt from the above-mentioned platitude. The first is the uncontroversial observation that as new concerns emerge in the present, we ask new questions of history. For example, currently there is a new awareness in academic circles about issues of diversity, including questions of implicit biases in methods of conducting research. In football studies, this new awareness has given rise to work tracing the previously unaddressed topics of the history of female and black footballers in the early stages of the game (see Lee 2008, Newsham 1994, Vasili 1996, 1998, 2000, Williams 2003, 2007, 2014, Williamson 1991). The other lesson is that diachronic studies of social historical kinds like sport and association football start with a synchronic understanding of the kind in question. Whether one performs a synchronic study or analysis of the kind under scrutiny is another question. Nevertheless, one will rely on one's own concept of sport and association football when thinking about the emergence and history of these kinds. Guttmann writes that "[y]ou can't study sports if you aren't clear about what you want to study" (Guttmann 2004b: 1). The point of departure for our inquiry is indexed to the present and our understanding of what counts as sport and association football, and it is on that basis we ask whether the social kind of association football includes – in part, fully or not at all – the proto-football of 1750–1863.

The historical roots of association football lie in British folk football, but these are not candidates for being considered as belonging to the social kind of association football. Regarding the phase of proto-football and its relation to association football, the picture is multifaceted and, quite frankly, messy. This should not come as a surprise. Given that social kinds do not have natural borders and that at least some of them are also evolving historical products, it is no wonder their roots, origins as well as current states do not come in clear-cut, neat ontological packages. Taking the starting point in our own conception of association football, then following Dunning and collaborators, it might be tempting to pick out only the Eton field game as the first stage of association football, as it fulfils the criteria of being association football-like in its set-up and has a causal historical link to the formation of association football as a social sport kind (Dunning and Sheard 2005: 69–112, Curry and Dunning 2015: 27–61). On the other hand, Collins has argued, "the similarities between the various codes of football in the mid-nineteenth century were far greater than their differences" (Collins 2005: 294). Curry and Dunning's own account – of how the public school boys, upon entering universities and still wanting to play the football game they knew but meeting others from other schools, were forced towards codification of the game – might suggest that they saw themselves as playing variants of the same game (Curry and Dunning 2015: 62–86). Let us simplify and allow ourselves to think that the proto-football played in Britain was seen by the participating agents as variants of the same game and let us follow Collins's assessment that these codes were more similar than dissimilar, while ignoring the complicating factor of proto-football played outside the public school system, which, for example, gave rise to the Sheffield rules of 1858. If we do so, we can tell the following story of the social historical sport kind of football. Proto-football, or the latter part or parts of it, is the first stage of association football. Obviously, there was at that time no awareness of playing association football, i.e. collective intentionality, as the kind is only fully formed at a later stage. In this picture, proto-football gets to be part of the sport kind of association football because it is association football-like and has an immediate causal historical relation to association football. By the very same line of reasoning, proto-football also gets to be part of the social sport kind of rugby football. Two social sport kinds, i.e. two sports, can share a stage, and based on the picture presented here, association football and rugby football both spring out of and share proto-football as their first stage of existence.

> Regarding variations in the use of hands – i.e. the biggest difference between the Association and Rugby forms of football – it is, we think, useful to view the various school football games in this period as differentially located on a continuum stretching, at one end, between an imaginary game with no handling at all, and, at the other, an imaginary game with no restrictions whatever on the use of hands.
>
> *(Curry and Dunning 2015: 40)*

> In fact, all forms of football that were played in the 1850s and 1860s had far more in common than that which set them apart. Kicking and handling the ball differed only by degree. Rather than being two distinct codes, there was one football with a spectrum of views about how it could be played.
>
> *(Collins 2019: 21)*

Or, rewritten somewhat, we can view the various proto-football games of this period as being on a continuum of the two games – association football and rugby football – that proto-football split into. Social kinds like sport can undergo both fission and fusion.[17] When a social kind like sport undergoes fission and spawns two different sports, then there is a theoretical choice of either seeing the two new branches as something completely new or viewing the two branches as encompassing and sharing the stage or stages that preceded them. On the basis of the sources available and the general gist of history writing, which is to emphasize both continuation and change when describing and explaining historical processes, I find it reasonable to think of at least the late part or parts of proto-football as part of both association football and rugby football. Neither the historical sources available nor theory forces one's hand on this, but, again, it seems to me the best way to think about these matters.

When a social sport kind splits, it is not a given that we will end up regarding the two branches as new sports instead of variations on each other and their origin. When comparing association football and rugby football, it is clear that we are dealing with two distinct sports that should not be grouped or subsumed under a common kind. The mechanics of the games are very different, and practitioners and audiences in the sport world view them as different kinds. However, both association football and rugby football have also spawned variations, the latter quite quickly split into rugby union football and rugby league football, also giving rise to at least American football. Association football has produced five-a-side football, futsal, beach football and others. New offshoots of a sport can be seen as variations on the mother sport, as constituting new sports, or otherwise, as distinct enough to be specific social sport kinds in their own right, while remaining close enough to the mother sport and possible sibling sports to warrant them as being regarded as branches of the same overarching kind. Synchronically, this is a question of similarities and dissimilarities in sporting mechanics and conduct of play, together with the practitioners' and sport audiences' own self-understanding, i.e. collective intentionality. Diachronically, however, this is a matter of origin and influence. This is a reasonable result. Sports are the sort of social kinds that can both share stages and partake in various social kinds all at once. Also, given our understanding of social kinds like sport, association football can and most likely will give rise to still new variants to come and possibly one day morph into yet another sport kind. This is as it should be. When we think about social kinds like sport, there is no vantage point at which we can freeze the research topic under consideration. The world is a work in progress and so is the social historical sport kind of association football.

The football form and functions

Before stepping back from the messy, but important historical considerations of the roots of association football (from now on again called football) and into the realm of abstraction, let us be clear on some ontological concerns. We are not assuming that there is anything in the final ontology of sport, when thinking about the phenomenon of sport, other than the actual sporting events taking place. Everything else is considered abstractions and theorizations. This should not be read as a shortcut to reductionism or eliminativism about sport. That would only follow if one added further assumptions and arguments about what is real and allowed into the final ontology. However, it is a rejection of any kind of Platonism about sport and football. Such a Platonism would have it that the sporting events and football matches one can participate in and watch are real only insofar as they partake in the idea of sport or a sporting event, or football or a football match. One might furthermore argue, along Platonic lines, that the aim of sport and sporting events, including football and football matches, is to fulfil their Platonic forms. This is not how I think about sports like football in this book.[18] Embracing the ontological stand introduced at the beginning of this section only entails a rejection of Platonism about sport. Nothing more. Nothing particularly exciting follows from adhering to that line of thought, and I am generally quite happy to keep an open ontological house, but I draw the line at Platonism about sport. This should be uncontroversial. I know of no one in the philosophy of sport who defends any kind of Platonism with regard to sport and sporting events. Having revealed our ontological colours, we should now be able to proceed to doing a bit of abstracting and theorizing about sport without fear of being branded as Platonists when it comes to sport.

At the beginning of this chapter, I identified two types of formalism in the philosophy of sport: foundational and reductive formalism. We have thus far been exploring the foundational formalism side of things and with it questions of how we can understand sport as a social kind. Reductive formalism has been put on hold and will remain there for a little while. In my treatment of *Football and the Natives*, I touched upon what might be seen as a third kind of formalism: *Bare-bones formalism*. Taking our inspiration from speech act theory, we can distinguish between the formal aspect of a sport and the functional aspect of a sport. Let me explain. Consider the speech act of asking a question. We can distinguish between functional and formal questions. Information questions are paradigmatic or prototypical functional questions. By asking a question, the speaker indicates his or her ignorance of some topic in question and the illocutionary point of the speech act, i.e. the speaker's (assumed) main purpose in making that type of utterance, is to elicit information. A speech act that is performed with the aim of eliciting an answer is a functional question. Formal questions have interrogative morphology, syntax or prosody, but need not be functional questions. Rhetorical questions and so-called out-loud questions are interrogatively formatted, but do not function as a way to elicit information. Rhetoric and out-loud questions are formal, but not functional questions. When analysing a specific performance of a rhetorical question, a researcher will distinguish between the formal aspects of the speech act – how it is formally formatted – and the functional aspect – the illocutionary point of this type of speech act. Note as well that functional questions need not be interrogatively formatted, as shown by the existence of so-called declarative questions that are not interrogatively marked by rising intonation. More often than not, a question is both a formal and a functional question. In the latter cases, we can still distinguish between the formal and the functional aspects of the speech act. Strictly speaking, the only thing actually existing and available as a research subject is the performed speech acts. Talk of form and function should be understood as no more than ways of abstracting away from the speech acts as they occur in order to understand the very same thing (see Borge 2013 for a full review of the speech act of asking questions). The take-home lesson here is that we can distinguish between the form and the function of a phenomenon without making any dubious ontological commitments. We can apply this sort of tool, in an adapted form, to the phenomenon of sport and football.

Bare-bones formalism involves considering a sport's form in isolation from its function, or better, considering how the form can partake in various functions. Bare-bones formalism is not in contention for replacing either foundational or reductive formalism. Bare-bones formalism is entailed or included in both alternatives. Bare-bones formalism earns its keep in our inquiry not as a position, but as a method by which we can gain some clarity on the actual phenomenon of football. The bare bones of football, the form of football, or the football form, is the sport's constitutive rules. It is the rule book or the blueprint of the sport. The function in question is the reason for doing the sport, i.e., the internal purposes, the intrinsic aim or goal of the sport. The purpose of football for the practitioners and supporting spectators – its equivalent to the illocutionary point of speech acts – is to win football matches, or minimally not to lose them, or to stay in a tournament. Social historical kinds like football have a surface, an inside and a context. The context of sport is the psychological and social setting in which the sport takes place, which will explain why the sport survives and thrives, or else is abandoned and dies. The social setting of a sport is what we thus far have called the outside of the sport. This topic has already been addressed in our discussion, in Chapter 1, of what we called the external or primary purpose of sport. The suggestion was that physical competition and domination fit the bill for being the primary purpose of football. This is part of the sport's external function; another function might be, as briefly mentioned in Chapter 1, the sport's potential as a vehicle for identity. The psychological setting of the sport is what we discussed as the character of football. Football's inside – internal or intrinsic aim, goal or purpose of football – is what the people engaged in the sport aim at and see themselves as aiming at. Scoring goals, avoiding conceding goals and in the end winning the match, or at least not losing it, make up the internal aim of football. Football's surface is its formal rules, its rule book, or the blueprint of the game. This is the football form. Bare-bones formalism is when we allow ourselves to think of the football form in isolation from the internal aim of football. Unlike speech acts in which speakers can pull off their illocutionary point without using the corresponding speech act format – you can ask a question without interrogatively formatting your utterance – you cannot achieve the aim of the sport of football without using the football form, football's formal aspect, the football formula, the rule book of the game, with its constitutive rules, or the blueprint of the game. The reason for this is that, from the perspective of the practitioners, speech acts have aims that are not intrinsic to the usage of a speech act formula, whereas with unnecessary activities like football, the use of the football form has no such aims. Football is autotelic; speech acts are not. Furthermore, the dependency between form and function in football is not symmetrical. Though you need the football form to play football and fulfil the game's internal function or intrinsic aim, the football form can partake in other relations.

We can evaluate the football form and other sport forms with regard to bare-bones formalism using the following five parameters:

- Use
- Abuse
- Application
- Appropriation
- Parroting

To use the football form is to play football. When someone reports that they themselves played a game of football or saw someone else play a game of football, then the default position – what you will assume that they have done, unless they tell you otherwise or the context makes it apparent – is that they used the football form and played football.

> Use: Usage of the football form (the formula for the sport) in accordance with the sport's internal aim. Playing the sport of football fulfilling the internal aim of the sport, i.e. aiming to achieve the internal purpose of the sport.

In order to play football, you have to use the football form. This is the paradigmatic or prototypical manner in which the football form partakes in a relation to a function, and without it there would not be a sport of football. Had there not been use of the football form, then there would not have been football as the sport we know. There could have been something else like a native football rainmaking ritual; but that is, as argued, a ritual, not a sport. The football form as far as we know emerged in tandem with the sport function, i.e. the internal or intrinsic aim of the sport. Currently, as long as the sport function is still in effect and widely recognized, all other functions that the football form partakes in are parasitic on or derivative of the usage of the football form.[19]

> Abuse: Covert or deceptive usage of the football form (the formula for the sport) for some other purpose than the sport's internal aim. Playing the sport as if fulfilling its internal aim, while covertly or deceptively seeking to realize some other aim or function.

The most obvious case of abuse of the football form is match fixing. Ordinarily, a match-fixing case would be one where a player or a minority of players seek not to win the match, but instead, for gambling purposes, aim at the match ending in a specific outcome. However, to make our example even clearer, consider the following case:

> The Fully Fixed Match: A football match where every single player on the pitch pretends to want to win the match, while they all instead seek to achieve – contrary to the intrinsic aim of football – some pre-arranged result.

The reason for forfeiting the intrinsic aim of football can be manifold, but in reality, it is most often done for gambling reasons. The abuse lies in the fact that the participants pretend to use to football form, while they covertly or deceptively aim at something else. Unlike the clear-cut case of the *Fully Fixed Match*, real-life cases of match fixing usually consist of some players using the football form while others abuse it.[20] Abuse could also be motivated by sheer spite. A case reported by Phil Ball as exemplifying the *morbo* between two local Spanish football rivals, Sevilla and Real Betis, shows this.[21]

> Sevilla, already relegated, took on Oviedo at home and were 3–0 down by half-time. Oviedo were involved, coincidentally enough, in the struggle to avoid the third relegation place with Betis. Sevilla even took off their best player, the Norwegian goalkeeper Frode Olsen, at half-time, because he had clearly misunderstood instructions and was manfully keeping the score down. Sevilla made a token comeback in the second half and the game ended 3–2, but the result as good as relegated Betis.
>
> *(Ball 2003: 27–28)*

In keeping with our speech act analogy, we can say that match fixing stands in a same relationship to usage of the football form as lies do to assertions. If Ball is right, then the case of Sevilla's conduct in the match against Oviedo at the end of the 1999/2000 season looks like the football version of what, in the literature on assertion, is known as a barefaced lie. Furthermore, notice that our speech act analysis holds up with regard to abuse of the football formula. Someone who abuses the speech act formula of assertion in order to make someone else believe something that the utterer holds to be false counts as having asserted that (assumed) falsehood. Similarly, someone who takes a bribe in order to lose a football match still counts as playing football, courtesy of the match being a case of usage of the football formula. The same holds for the case of the fully fixed match. The players count as playing football in the fully fixed match, courtesy of the match being embedded in the practice or tradition of usage of the football form, which might or might not involve various institutions.

There is no assumption here that abuse is necessarily morally wrong. Additional arguments are needed to reach that conclusion. Such arguments can be easily provided in most cases of match fixing, but there is no intrinsic normative element in my notion of abuse of the football form, as the following case shows.

> Football and the Bust: A counter-counterfeit wristwatch unit of the Metropolitan Police Service has tracked down a ruthless Swiss gang known to sell counterfeit Rolexes in public schools and has located their headquarters. The headquarters is next to a local football ground, and the only way to do surveillance for the bust is to be on the football pitch. Consequently, the Met stages football matches so that they can do surveillance for setting up the bust. Though all the police officers on the pitch know football and its rules, no one is playing to win or otherwise cares about the result of the match.

I suspect that many, probably most, find the Metropolitan Police Service's abuse of the football form in *Football and the Bust* perfectly legitimate and unproblematic. The notion of abuse, as understood here, is descriptive, not normative.

> Application: Overt or honest usage of the football form (the formula for the sport) for some other purpose than the sport's internal aim. Playing the sport pretending to fulfil its internal aim, while overtly or honestly seeking to fulfil some other aim or function.

As is apparent, application of the football form and abuse of the football form differ only in that the former is done overtly or honestly, while the latter is done covertly and deceptively. As with the notion of abuse of the football form, the notion of application should also be understood as descriptive, not normative.

Real-life examples of application of the football form are somewhat harder to come by than abuses of the football form. If someone staged a football match as part of a work of art, then that would be a potential case of applying the football form. This would only count as a case of application if the players in the football match infused in a work of art had no intention of winning the match. However, there is nothing in the football form that prevents usage of the form within a work of art. One can easily imagine a conceptual artist hiring two football teams to play a match as part of an art installation, in which case we have a football match and usage of the football form as part of a work of art. The world of sport, however, does provide proper cases of application of a sport form. The exhibition basketball team the Harlem Globetrotters, at least when they put on matches with their business partners the Washington Generals and the San Francisco Chinese Basketeers, played basketball not to win matches, but primarily to entertain their audiences through dazzling displays of basketball skills paired with slapstick humour. Such matches played by the Harlem Globetrotters are not sporting events, but rather a sport spectacle or a kind of improvised sport theatre. In the world of football, there has never been and still is no team cast in the exhibition mould of the Harlem Globetrotters. However, testimonial matches in honour of specific players in many respects fit the bill of being applications of the football form and not competitive football matches in which the football form is used. In testimonials, it is generally understood by both teams that the match is not fully competitive and that it is important that whomever the match is played in honour of should not end up on the losing side. These events are tribute matches and not your ordinary competitive football match in which players aim to win.

> Appropriation: Usage of the football form (the formula for the sport) for some other purpose than the sport's internal aim and in disregard or ignorance of that internal aim, thereby creating a new internal aim and a new activity or practice.

The examples of *Football and the Natives* and *Footrace and the Professors* are cases of appropriation. One can appropriate a practice while being fully aware of the practice's original internal aim and consciously swap that aim with a new one, though I am not aware of any sport examples of such a dramatic and immediate appropriation process. I suspect that more often than not when a practice changes its internal aim or purpose, there is a more gradual transition taking place, like that in the cases of the ancient Greek *stadion* and the Mexican *danza de los voladores*. In these two cases, it would be odd to say that someone changed the practices' internal functions, though the internal aims did change. In the case of *danza de los voladores*, it seems perhaps correct to talk about a cultural appropriation of the practice, even though no one in particular appropriated it. Any simple-minded question about whether the practice of *danza de los voladores* – as it is performed for sport and as a spectacle for tourists in present-day Mexico – is the same as the pre-Spanish practice should be rejected as ill-formed. The form of *danza de los voladores* might have survived intact, whereas the internal aim and cultural meaning of the practice have changed. Similarly, it would be correct to say that the natives are playing football when considered from a bare-bones-formalism perspective, while they are not when considered from a football-the-sport perspective. Questions concerning the present-day flyers of Mexico must be evaluated according to both its form and its internal function. They might fulfil the form of the pre-Spanish practice, but otherwise we have two practices: *danza de los voladores* for sport and *danza de los voladores* the religious ritual.

Our notion of appropriation is somewhat different than the ordinary language usage of the word. In ordinary usage, the word can also be applied to cases where someone takes over someone else's cultural practice without changing either form or internal function. In the case of football, several authors have suggested that folk football was appropriated, in the latter ordinary language sense of the word, and then changed into what I have called proto-football. In my way of laying out the conceptual landscape, this kind of appropriation amounts to an adoption of the football form. Taylor writes that the Dunning group's take on the transition from folk football to proto-football involves "the adoption and adaptation by the public schools of the folk game", and Guttmann calls football in its modern form an "adaptation of folk-football" (Taylor 2008: 20, Guttmann 2004b: 106, see Dunning 1971, Dunning and Sheard 2005, Curry and Dunning 2015). Adoption in the sense used by Taylor only means that a new social group has begun engaging in the same practice, with form and function intact.

> Parroting: Mimicking, replication or simulation of usage of the football form (the formula for the sport).

In the case of football parroting, there is mimicking, replication or simulation of the movements seen in others' instantiations of the football form, but otherwise the performance of those movements need not be connected to the internal aim or function of football, or any aim at all. The following is a case that would count as parroting football.

> Robot Football: Mindless self-programming robots, after having observed or registered football matches, program themselves to replicate what they have observed and play out a football match.

Are the robots in *Robot Football* playing football? Again, what bare-bones formalism does for you is to make it clear that this question as it stands is ill-formed. Do the robots instantiate the football form? Yes. Considered along the parameter of the bare bones of the sport – the football form – the robots in *Robot Football* are playing football. Do the robots aim to achieve the internal aim of football or can they otherwise be said to use the football form (the latter entailing that usage is something conscious and intending systems do)? No. By stipulation the robots are self-programming, but mindless, so usage is ruled out. The lights are on, but there is no one home. Currently, there are no robots that are close to replicating football in its full complexity. However, with regard to considering games and sports and potential cases of parroting, the case of chess-playing computers is interesting. Does a chess-playing computer like Deep Blue play chess? Obviously, the answer cannot be a simple refusal of chess-playing status to Deep Blue. Instead one should say that it is beyond doubt that Deep Blue fulfils the chess form and that, evaluated along the lines of bare-bones formalism for chess, Deep Blue plays chess. If one believes there is more to playing chess than merely fulfilling the chess form (the formula for the game), then perhaps the status of playing chess evaluated along these other parameters should be denied chess-playing computers like Deep Blue. Further arguments would be needed to establish that. The question of whether machines can think will not worry us in this book.[22] Our concern is with the human game.

Objections and replies

Objection: The author somewhat inconspicuously introduces the distinction between something being done for sport and something being a sport. It is not clear that this way of delineating sports from non-sports is as innocent as the author might think. It not only favours sports that are also competitions, but it makes being a competition a requirement for being a sport. The author is no doubt clearing the way for Bernard Suits's analysis of sport, which he has flagged will take centre stage in the next chapter. Suits thought of games and sports as being geared towards end-results or end-states – specific states of affairs, which Suits dubbed prelusory goals – and this is echoed in the author's understanding of the transition between play and sport, presented in Chapter 1. However, that picture fails to accommodate sports, where the purpose or the meaning of the activity or practice might lie in the performance of it and not the end-results or end-states of a win or a loss. Indeed, in Chapter 1, the author has already brought up field sports like mountain climbing and sport fishing, and there is a host of other activities like surfing, sailing, etc., as well as the quite recent phenomenon of parkour, all of which defy the idea of sports being intrinsically linked to competition. Why should activities or practices like climbing, sport fishing, surfing, sailing, parkour, and others not count as sports?

Reply: Why indeed? The short answer is that they do not get to count as sports, but are something being done for sport, simply because they are not competitions. Of course, that is the bone of contention and as such it is not much of an answer. Though I think that, in philosophy, it is fair game to appeal to intuition, one might argue that when they clash with others' intuition on the same matter, they do not count. Let me try to do better. First, I do think that the distinction between what is done for sport and sports is fairly innocent. I tend to think of mountain climbing, sport fishing, parkour, etc. as not being sports, but I do not mind if any of my readers insist on them being non-competitive sports. If this is your inclination, then whenever I write "sports" and "for sport", you might substitute that with "competitive sports" and "non-competitive sports". Nothing in the arguments about sports, in general, and football, in particular, changes. I will argue that there are important differences between activities or practices of doing something for sport and those that I regard as sports, which justifies this distinction, but one can also take these differences as reasons for thinking that there are non-competitive sports. Furthermore, I think the distinction earns its keep by coming in handy when we think about the differences between these before-mentioned activities or practices and what I call sports, and the various transitions that can be made from everyday or ordinary world activities or practices to that which is done for sport, from everyday or ordinary world activities or practices to that which is sport and, importantly, from that which is done for sport and to sports. This is perhaps most apparent when thinking about everyday or ordinary world activities or practices and how they can be transported into the realm of the extra-ordinary.

Consider our previous example of house building. Building houses is an everyday ordinary world activity. We build houses because we need shelter. We can sport up house building both to be done for sport and to become a sport. If someone discovered that they really just liked building houses, even though none were needed at that time or would be in the foreseeable future, and went ahead and built houses for fun, perhaps only to dismantle them afterwards and start over again, those builders would be building houses for sport. Such house building is a *for-sport activity or practice*. Here, I submit, I have no inclination to think of the sport house builders as doing a sport that is on a par with, for example, football or the 100-metre dash. Those who reject the distinction between being done for sport and being a sport had better be prepared to defend this as a sport. The analogy to, say, sport fishing or mountaineering is clear. Fishing and overcoming mountain ranges are both activities that at one point belonged solely to the ordinary world, but which later also became something done for the pleasure of doing it. What goes for sport fishing and mountaineering also goes for sport house building. When a type of activity or practice travels from the ordinary world to the extra-ordinary world, there is a structural change to the inside of the activity or practice, i.e., its internal aims or goals. Similarly, when extra-ordinary activities or practices done for sport like sport fishing, mountaineering and sport house building are made into competitions with the elements of winning-losing and ranking of competitors, another structural change happens to the inside of the activity or practice. Now the aims of the activities or practices are not just to catch fish, overcome mountains or build houses for the pleasure, the excitement, the challenge, etc., of catching fish, overcoming mountains or building houses, but also to beat the other competitor or competitors. It is this structural change of the inside of the activities or practices that justifies our making a distinction between something being done for sport and something being a sport.

In practice, I also think the distinction comes in handy when looking at the genesis and history of various sports. Especially concerning sports that are sport counterparts to ordinary world activities or practices like javelin throwing, archery, various running events, swimming, etc., researchers would do well to ask themselves whether the activity or practice, on its path from being an ordinary world activity to becoming a sport, did a detour through being done for sport.[23] If a sport has taken that route in becoming a fully formed sport, then that opens up interesting questions about the psychological and social mechanics involved when an activity or practice done for sport transitions into becoming a sport. My speculation is that when something that is done for sport becomes loaded with highly skilled practitioners, who also start comparing themselves to each other along the parameters of best and better, then there is a basis for, perhaps even a pull towards, turning the practice into a sport, which provides a way of ranking the competitors. The for-sport activity or practice of parkour provides us with an interesting case in this respect.

Signe Højbjerre Larsen informs us that currently "[p]ractitioners (...) take exception from the categorization of parkour as an extreme sport", and she goes on to note that "[p]arkour is not a sport, but closer to an art of movement" (Larsen 2015: 8, my translation). In another work, Larsen describes parkour as "more playful than competitive and in this respect sport-like" (Larsen 2016: 298).

> [P]ractitioners can cultivate an expansive relationship between body and space without necessarily turning each other into competitors. (...) In this process, practitioners relate to each other as resources not as competitors. The practitioners' comparisons are to a larger extent a measure of *the individual's struggle against the body's limitations of movement* than an expression of any competition between them.
>
> *(Larsen 2015: 243, my italics and translation)*

The first thing to observe is that any appeal to, say, any sanctimony of self-description of what does or does not count as a sport, i.e. how the practitioners view themselves, should be resisted. It might be that those involved in climbing outside a competitive setting self-ascribe that they are doing a sport, but practitioners of parkour serve as a good antidote to any such move. Consistency in theorizing demands that we, when addressing the sport or for-sport question, treat climbing and parkour similarly. The parkour community does not view themselves as doing a non-competitive sport, but something else.

As identified by Larsen, parkour is sport-like, while at the very same time being closer to the art world than the sport world. This makes parkour interesting and provides us with a good example of how our notion of for-sport activities or practices earns its theoretical keep. On the one hand, there is athleticism involved in parkour, which definitely pushes it towards being sport-like. In the next chapter, I will argue that sports involve physical skills, but that does not entail athleticism. However, prototypical sports involve athleticism, and thus athleticism is one factor that can make a non-sport sport-like. Furthermore, such prototypical sports represent physical challenges of an athletic kind to practitioners, and so does parkour (see Aggerholm and Larsen 2017: 75–78). One could quite easily turn parkour into a sport. If one were to model a sport version of parkour on some of the snowboard disciplines, then one could easily envisage parkour as a sport that combines time-taking with acrobatic elements being awarded style points for tricks performed while navigating and negotiating the parkour track environment. Like ski jumping, the sport would be a combination of measurement, i.e. how fast you get through the parkour track, and style points, how well you perform tricks along the track. However, its internal aim would change from what Larsen describes as the individual's struggle against the body's limitations of movement to winning the competition, thus making the two activities not different in degree, but in kind.[24] In this respect, Larsen is right to point out that parkour is closer to an art of movement. And though it is not part of the art world, one can, once again, easily envisage it moving closer to that realm of the extra-ordinary. If parkour were to develop towards becoming primarily a spectator activity or practice, where the emphasis is on spectators enjoying the aesthetics of the moves, then in the same way as professional wrestling and *lucha libre* are closer to theatre than sport, parkour would share more with variety art acrobatics and dance than with sports. Operating with a distinction between what is done for sport and what is a sport brings such lines and questions into sharper focus.

Objection: In Chapter 1 we were told that social play opens up a space from which sport can emerge. In this chapter, on the other hand, it is suggested that sports instead have cultic or ritualistic beginnings. When talking about sports as having roots in play, the emphasis was on the non-seriousness of social play, whereas rites, rituals and other religious practices are, in many cases, clearly designed to influence or be valuable with regard to ordinary world concerns. Something has to give.

Reply: Not at all. Sport as a social kind can have several ancestors, and the cult-sport connection and the play-sport connection are not incompatible in this respect. Note also that even though researchers are largely in agreement about the cultic background of sports as they emerged in ancient Greece, though they vary on the question of how close the connection remained throughout antiquity, there is no such agreement concerning football. On the question of whether folk football has a cultic origin, it is not as if the jury is out, rather it looks like it will not be in at all. We do not have enough sources to reasonably rule this option either in or out. Having said that, one should also note that our detour through the ancient Greeks was primarily done for the purpose of understanding the social kind of sport and how it might arise from another social kind with which the kind could share a stage. There is no argument here that proto-football was cultic or ritualistic in kind, though as mentioned, folk football might be. In Chapter 1, we were primarily concerned with synchronic observations concerning what to say about the sport of football as we find it today. It was argued that football, as we find it today, involves the proto-pretence of social play. This does not preclude us from entertaining the idea that sports, in a diachronic perspective, involve more than the proto-pretence of social play. Moreover, we have touched upon sports' identity-making potential and how various ritual-like elements surround football matches. Thus from a synchronic perspective, we have already allowed more elements than the proto-pretence of social play to come into the equation when trying to understand our engagement in sports like football.

One advantage of the approached taken in Chapter 1 is that both rites and religion, together with sport and art, belong to the extra-ordinary realm of human life. This carries over to this chapter. When we look at the line of thinking that sees the sports of antiquity as growing out of cult activity, we have the theoretical resources for understanding why such a transition need not be sharp, but is most likely gradual, because both activities or practices, despite their differences, belong to the extra-ordinary. At this point we should tip our theoretical hat to Groos and Huizinga. Groos, one might recall, claimed that the capacity for play is a key element of the higher development of thinking and with it the creation of art and artistic expression. Huizinga went further and viewed as play all that belonged to the realm of the extra-ordinary. Present-day biologists, when discussing play, avoid such sweeping claims, but do not shy away from suggesting that play, at the very least, enhances the human capacity for creativity. It is not much of a stretch to assume that activities belonging to the extra-ordinary all involve human creativity. If that is the case, then cultic and ritualistic practices might also already involve play or elements from our play capacity – or, at least, such practices do not exclude play, which, in many ways, takes the wind out of this objection.

Objection: The treatment of the social kind of sport in this chapter is problematic. The author's usage of cases from ancient Greece and the Panhellenic athletics at Olympia relies on a dubious assumption that pre-modern sports and modern sports like football are two of a kind, but that is not the commonly held belief among researchers in this field. Paul Christesen reports:

> [It is] a commonly held belief, perhaps most evident in the influential work of Allen Guttmann, that ancient and modern sport were fundamentally different,

not just with respect to the sports that were played, but also with respect to the very nature of sport.

(Christesen 2012: xv).

Following the orthodoxy of Guttmann, we should reject the anachronism of the approach now under consideration. In light of that rejection, we should also seriously question whether the so-called proto-football of the seventeenth and eighteenth centuries and the early years of what the author identifies as association football, with its amateur ethos, really belong to the concept of sport we would use to understand present-day football.

Reply: This objection might instead be seen as friendly advice to be careful when using a unifying concept of sport to compare practices that belong to very different historical periods.[25] The most glaring example of anachronism is, perhaps, how the invention of the modern Olympics, with its original amateur ethos, was portrayed as a direct ancestor of the ancient Panhellenic athletics of Olympia. "An ancient amateur is", according to Mark Golden, "an anachronism" (Golden 1998: 142).

> The popular picture of ancient Greek amateurism is quite fictitious. I refer to the usual image of the highly trained and idealistic athlete who competed for a mere olive crown and some glory. This myth (…) was conceived by partisans of the 19th-century Anglo-American amateur movement. They wished to legitimize with an ancient precedent their own athletic system, which sought to restrict participation to a wealthy, leisured class.
>
> *(Young 1988: 27)*

No such crude mistakes are being made here (see also Young 1984, Parry 1988).

Moreover, as argued in the previous objection-reply pair, we used the sports of the ancient Greeks to show how a social kind can transition into another social kind, which then gave us a clearer understanding of what sort of social kind sport is. At no point was it claimed that the sports of the ancient Greeks were just like the sports of the twentieth and twenty-first centuries. However, like all other researchers in this field, I write about the ancient Greek sports as sports.

In fact, I think orthodoxy gets Guttmann wrong. Or, at the very least, it is not clear that we need to go with the commonly held belief that ancient and modern sport were fundamentally different when considering Guttmann's ideas. In the beginning of his *Sports: The First Five Millennia*, Guttmann lays down some of the basics of his outlook, which guide his treatment of sports through the ages.

> [M]uch of what follows consists of narration explicitly or implicitly organized within a comprehensive historical framework derived, in part, from Max Weber and from Norbert Elias. Basic to this framework [is that] [t]he formal-structural characteristics of modern sports are *strikingly different* from those of pre-modern sports.
>
> *(Guttmann 2004b: 4, my italics)*

They are strikingly different, not strictly different. The latter would have looked like the view that pre-modern and modern sport were completely different kinds of practices. The former, on the other hand, explicitly brings the readers' attention to how the sports of those historical periods strike one as different, emphasizing the perceptions of the onlooker. It is almost as if to direct, advise, or even invite the reader to pause and, perhaps, consider or entertain the idea that underneath the eye-catching differences, you might also find commonalities. It is not clear how Guttmann would want us to read the phrase "strikingly different". Guttmann goes on to tell us that "[m]odern (as opposed to pre-modern) sports can be defined by a set of seven interrelated formal-structural characteristics", where one of them is "quantification" (Guttmann 2004b: 4, 5). However, it turns out, according to Guttmann, that "the achievements of ancient Roman charioteers and seventeenth-century Japanese archers *were* quantified" (Guttmann 2004b: 6). Guttmann correctly argues that such exceptions do not invalidate his list of defining features of modern sports, but they do invite us to think that pre-modern and modern sports are not perhaps fundamentally different in nature. Another of Guttmann's defining features of modern sport, which is closely linked to quantification, is modernity's obsession with records in sports. These two features of the sport world, as we find it today, certainly provide a striking contrast to what we know about pre-modern sports. However, upon reflection, we will also find commonalities between pre-modern and modern sports even with regard to these two features, which seem so quintessentially modern.

Quantification is in fact part of the very fabric of sport. According to the picture presented in this book, sport by its very nature is concerned with ranking – its most basic parameter being win-lose – and ranking requires some way of either counting or measuring with regard to some end-state state of affairs towards which the sport competition is geared. Sports are competitions that yield winners and losers. Winning or losing depends on ranking, and ranking entails quantification, whether that is in the form of counting or measuring. In Chapter 1, it was argued that the introduction of such an end-state state of affairs and ways of ranking is what can unshackle play and enable it to become or be a sport. In this chapter, our focus has been on understanding the social kind of sport, and in doing that we have addressed historical practices. Whatever else we know about the transition from rites and rituals to sports in ancient Greece, we know that their sport practices – as recorded, e.g., at the Panhellenic athletics at Olympia – involved ranking of the competitors. They quantified various aspects of sports, such as:

- Speed: Fastest/faster/slower/slowest. For example, the various footraces, *stadion, diaulos, dolichos,* etc.
- Length: Longest/longer/shorter/shortest. For example, *diskos* (discus throw), *akon* (javelin throw) and *halma* (broad jump), which were all part of the *pentathlon.*
- Endurance: Standing/not-standing or submitting. For example, the various combat sports, wrestling (*pale*), boxing (*pyx, pygmachia, pygme*) and *pankration,*

which all lasted until one of the competitors could no longer go on either by being knocked out or dead, or else declared himself incapable by raising a finger.

With regard to the *pentathlon*, Donald Kyle tells us that there is still a debate about the "operation, and scoring of the pentathlon" (Kyle 2014: 27). There seems to be some sort of agreement among historians that wrestling was the last event in the *pentathlon*, but that does not exclude the operation of some sort of point system or method of counting a score throughout the events, leading up to the final competition. After all, knowing the ancient Greeks' fiercely competitive nature, it is hard to imagine that they would merely go through the motions of discus throw (*diskos*), javelin throw (*akon*), broad jump (*halma*) and footrace (a *stadion* race), before the outcome was solely decided by a wrestling competition. That does not look like the Greeks of antiquity who shine through from our various historical sources. It is more than possible that they were at ease with a method of counting a score, if nothing else by, say, some system of elimination. Kyle, who is somewhat dismissive of the pentathlon problem, agrees that "the pentathlon is unusual in combining sub-events" and that "[o]bviously the ancient Greeks knew how to decide the victory without controversy" (Kyle 1990: 295, see also Kyle 1995, and Golden 1998: 69–73 on the pentathlon problem). In other words, the structure of sport competitions yields winners and losers by some conventionally agreed-upon way of ranking the competitors and, strikingly, but not surprisingly, the pre-modern sports of the ancient Greeks and our modern sports are similar in that respect.

Looking at the ancient Greek sports makes clear that pre-modern sports had quantification of performance with regard to speed, length and endurance, which yielded a ranking of the competitors. I do not think this invalidates what I take to be one of Guttmann's main points regarding modern sports, nor does it show that his theory of modern sports is incorrect, though there is no space here to critically evaluate the latter. However, I do think it serves as a word of warning. Just as one should be careful not to read too much of a modern conception of sport into pre-modern sports, one should also be careful not to err on the side of safety by depicting pre-modern sports as *das ganz andere* (to borrow a phrase from Rudolf Otto). Assuming that pre-modern sports are something completely and utterly different from modern sports might lead one astray. The differences between pre-modern and modern sports under consideration, and those brought to our attention by Guttmann, are not a question of quantification, but rather partly a question of the manner in which it is done and, subsequently, of comparison classes. In Chapter 1, we noted that, in modern measurement sports, the meritocratic standards for winning – who ran fastest, who jumped highest, who threw longest, who lifted heaviest and so on – are typically realized by measuring a physical phenomenon numerically, like the time of running, the length of the throw and so on. The ancient Greeks did not use numbers in that way, but they used formal structures like ranking and comparisons and that is also to measure, thus being a species of quantification. The ways in which we measure in modern measurement sports are standardized and the results transferable for purposes of comparison, at least at the top level of various sports, where performance records are made.[26] This impetus for standardization carries over to the sport arenas and sport equipment, especially with regard to sport equipment that is integral to the mechanics of the sport itself, like the javelin or the discus. One runs on standardized tracks, uses standardized sport equipment (e.g., there are defined standards of size, shape, minimum weight and centre of gravity for the javelin), etc. The net effect of such standardization is that the comparison class of each measured sport performance in a sport competition broadens. Where the quantification of pre-modern sport events like the Panhellenic athletics at Olympia remained local and anchored in or indexed to the particular, the quantification of modern measurement sport events becomes global, reaching towards the universal. This is a striking difference between pre-modern and modern sports.[27]

Football, on the other hand, is not a measurement sport, but as previously argued in Chapter 1, a constructive-destructive sport grounded in the particular match and the two teams facing off. How well a team performs and what result it gets out of a match are ultimately also consequences of the other team and its performance. Football's dual nature – to construct chances and goals, while preventing the opposition from doing the same – ensures this. Football remains anchored in the particular.

> [T]he footballer is *not primarily interested* in the statistics of the game (…) he or she is interested in the qualities of the performance of the individuals and of the team as a whole. Such an interest is conditioned by the fact that such qualities produce the result (…) [C]oncern of footballers with "world records" is minimal. Scarcely any meaningful ones exist (…) apart from the primitive counting of national victories in the World Cup.
>
> *(Parry 2006: 199, my italics)*

Football is, without question, currently awash with counting of league titles, cup wins, and various statistics on individual players' performances: goals scored, assists, metres run during a match, etc. Furthermore, you will find that pundits, journalists and football supporters gladly engage in comparisons of players either from the same time period, like Lionel Messi vs. Cristiano Ronaldo, or from different time periods, like Pelé vs. Diego Maradona. Another comparison could involve determining the greatest European club side to have graced a football pitch, where the candidates tend to be Real Madrid 1955–60, Ajax 1971–73, Bayern München 1974–76, Liverpool 1977–84, AC Milan 1989–94, and Real Madrid 2014–2018, and so on and so forth *ad nauseam*. Still, Parry's point is well taken and in agreement with the general direction of this reply. All talk of records or comparisons outside the particular – this match, this league season, this tournament, etc. – remains inessential to the general conception of the game. The mechanics of the game ground it in the particular. Notice also that more often than not when such conversations come up, they are not centred around any clearly defined and undisputable measurement of the performance of footballers and football teams, but rather focused on the relative dominance of a player or a team indexed to a given time period.

Returning to the general theme of this objection, one is ill advised to ask the polar question of whether or not pre-modern and modern sports are the same. Instead, we should ask about where they differ and where, possibly, they do not. There are various parameters that can be used to address such issues. In Chapter 1, I argued that we can distinguish between the character of a sport and its content. It was argued that football is fictional in character, but there was no argument that this holds for all sports at all times. How sports are played varies both diachronically and synchronically. It is unproblematic to think of part of the football culture and practice in its early days as having an amateur ethos, which you do not find in the modern game at its top level. But again, we need to attend to the details and not settle for simple either-or views. First, as we have seen in this chapter, new research on the origin of association football suggests that the orthodox view that football solely springs out of public schools is not the whole story. Perhaps the idea of early football being enshrined in an amateur ethos is not the full description of the way football was played in its formative years. Furthermore, looking at the current practice of football, one does well to remind oneself that most football matches are in fact played out at fairly low levels and not at the shining top, the latter having a tendency to draw the attention of researchers in the field. The atmosphere surrounding low-level football matches is often quite different than what one encounters at high-profile games at the more elite levels of the sport. The character of a sport like football comes in degrees, and it can vary within a football culture, depending on the level at which the match takes place, and between football cultures. The thesis that football is fictional in character stands on solid ground and provides for variety in the intensity with which the game is enacted, encompassing professional ethos, amateur ethos, and anything in between.

Another parameter we considered in Chapter 1 was the distinction between the internal or intrinsic purpose, aim or goal of a sport – that of winning the sport competition, which depending on the mechanisms of the sports will take various forms and shapes – and the external goal or primary purpose of the sports – the reason why a sport or sports were created, invented or came about in this first place. As for the external purpose or purposes, I argued that, with regard to a constructive-destructive contact sport like football, competition and domination fit the bill, while admitting that domination might not sit as easily with some other sports. The latter observation should be taken as a call for sport-specific considerations, where one takes seriously the mechanisms of the sport under study and how they connect with what one takes to be the sport's external purpose or purposes. Furthermore, I have suggested that identity-making could be yet another external or primary purpose of the game, one that, as the game took hold, helped it spread and established its status. Identity-making connects nicely with domination and competition and the raw emotional, us-against-them spectator engagement that the mechanics and execution of the game allow. In Chapter 1 I showed how football as a venue for competition and domination, while also being fictional in character, sits well with the alief theory we took up from Gendler. It is hard to see how competition will not be part of the external purpose of sports as we know them, that is, how having a venue for competing is not part of the reason a sport came to be. As for other features identified as external aims of sports, these might not only vary from sport to sport synchronically, but also diachronically with regard to the very same sport. We might not have enough sources to reasonably track which features should be considered the external aims of a pre-modern sport. The way I paint the picture of sport in this chapter enables us to speculate that cultic or religious goals might be part of it, or remain part of a sport after a certain activity or practice has transitioned into a sport from the cultic. This, of course, would make the transition from the cultic or ritual to sports a gradual one. Again, the bottom line is not to settle the polar question of whether it is or is not a sport *simpliciter* – agreeing in all aspects of sport – but to have enough tools to be able to pinpoint both differences and commonalities.

We have connected the idea of competition and domination as external purposes of football with Elias and Dunning's sociological approach to sport, which builds on Elias's theory of the civilizing process of human societies, where sports can "elicit excitement (...) without its dangers and risks", and we have argued that they sit well together (Elias 2008: 25). This kind of externalist approach is, as is apparent from the quote above, Guttmann's approach. Note, however, that I have not put my stamp of approval on Elias and Dunning's overall theory as a theory of all existing sports, but pointed out that it is well suited to football. It is not clear to me that either Elias and Dunning's or Guttmann's theories of modern sports fully fit all present-day sports. Or, at least, it is worth considering the idea that what binds sports together as a well enough defined category is, in fact, the internal perspective, the defining features of which are to be physical skill competition and subsequent ranking – aimed at winning the competition. The inside matters. In Chapter 1, working from a biological and evolutionary perspective, we squared the seemingly incompatible features of social play being autotelic, not needed for survival or any other immediate purposes, while at the same time being thought of as enhancing fitness, by appealing to the inside and the outside of the activity with regard to human or non-human animals. A similar move is needed in this area. Paying careful attention to the inside of sports and the various mechanics of how they are done, whether they be pre-modern or modern sports, as well as to their accompanying psychological realities might serve as a corrective or modification to the grand theories of sport and society. This is especially pertinent with regard to what is done for sport. Many of the for-sport practices, like parkour, are looser and freer in their organization and execution, sometimes even representing a reaction to the type of modern sports identified by Guttmann. These need also to be accounted for in our mapping of the conceptual landscape of sport and its surrounding areas. In any event, when looking at the various sports we have around today and how they vary in character, mood, execution, etc., I would be surprised if they could be easily identified as serving all the same external purposes, and be lumped together as pulling in the same historical direction or fully exposing the same historical tendency or tendencies. That does not rule out theorizing about overarching historical tendencies, for instance the urge for quantification to reach for the universal so aptly pointed out by Guttmann, but it does call for sensitivity for the sport practices themselves and the mechanics by which they are done. We can use the theories of Elias and Dunning, Guttmann and others on modernity and modern sports to identify features of present-day sports and for-sport practices that satisfy one, some or all of the defining features of modern sports as laid out by these authors, while also identifying non-modern or pre-modern features of the sports we play today. In which case, we will not be so concerned with the dichotomy of pre-modern sports vs. modern sports, but with the modern, non-modern and pre-modern features of sports. It is not clear that Elias and Dunning or Guttmann must necessarily resist such a move. For example, Dunning, when writing about the configurations underpinning sports, along with its defining idea of a quest for exciting significance, tells us that in modern boxing, "[p]unching 'below the belt' is taboo and, unlike fighters in French *savate* or Thai kick-boxing, boxers are not allowed to kick. Modern boxing can thus be said to be *more* 'civilized' – but not 'civilized' *tout court*" (Dunning 1997: 480–481). Dunning allows many features of French *savate*, Thai kick-boxing – and today we would probably want to add the sport of mixed martial arts – to fall outside the identified modernity of sports, whereas modern boxing gets closer in many respects, while still also containing non-modern, perhaps even pre-modern, elements.

In this chapter, we have addressed the social kind of sport and argued that it allows for stage type exceptions, which would also permit us to think about the transition between pre-modern and modern stages of a sport as gradual – which might have been the case with regard to the transition between folk football and proto-football. That would be helpful, if it were the case, in explaining how and why certain residual pre-modern elements of a sport, which has transitioned into a modern sport, are still part of that sport. When comparing a pre-modern version of a sport with its modern counterpart, considerations about continuous causal connections matter. When thinking about a particular sport in this regard, like the social kind of football, javelin throwing, footraces, etc., a continuous causal connection between stages of a practice would make us *ceteris paribus* think of some stage or stages on each side of the pre-modern–modern sport divide as belonging to the same social kind of football, javelin throwing, footraces, etc. One might still argue that the difference between the social setting of the pre-modern version of a sport and its accompanying primary purpose or purposes and the on-the-surface similar sport in modern time is too large for them to be regarded as the same sport. Nothing in this chapter decides any particular case as such, but it is made clear which questions are pertinent to ask. Imagine a case where one revives a pre-modern sport that has not been practised for centuries. Let us envisage that the modern revival of the sport gets the surface of the pre-modern sport right, i.e. the sport form is revived correctly. Is it the same sport? If your theoretical interest lies in the sport's external or primary purpose, and how the sport functioned in interplay with the wider social setting, then you would be prone to think that they are not members of the same kind. If your focus is solely on the sport form, then certainly they look to be of the same kind, but the lack of a continuous causal connection might warrant reservations, together with the question of the inside of the pre-modern and modern versions of the sport. Moreover, if you have two sports that happen to be isomorphic with regard to both surface and inside, but which emerged completely independent of and with no causal influence on each other, then perhaps you would want to say that we are dealing with two different sports that happen to have identical surfaces, i.e. sport forms, and insides. This will be a question of how much emphasis you, in your theoretical outlook, put on origin, continuous practice and causal connection. No doubt, in the latter case, should these two sports come in causal contact with each other, they might merge to become one practice, and at this point one might want to say that up until they merged, there were two sports – two sports that became one sport with two different historical ancestors with identical sport forms and insides.

Overall, besides the above-mentioned parameters and considerations, our discussion of form, and the various functions the sport form can partake in, makes it clear that in order to play a sport, the sport form in question must be used to achieve the internal aim of sports, which is to win, or minimally to not lose. This aspect is the core of sports in the current approach. Having that core enables us to see how we should think about cases where the sport form is involved in other types of activities with different internal aims as well as about to which degree, or which part of, such other activities might still be regarded as sport. This final piece of the puzzle, which we spent larger parts of Chapter 1 discussing with regard to football, is the character of a sport. Again, there are various ways sport can be played, and changes in character do not entail that the activity or practice stops being a sport, which I think is a welcome result. The net effect is that we have numerous methods to address questions of sport – methods that hopefully do justice to the complexity of the sport landscape, while at the same time identifying common treads and tendencies. I have shown how to use these methods with regard to the phenomenon of football and at various junctions drawn on other sports as well.

Conclusion

The social kind of sport, in general, and football, in particular, is founded on constitutive rules and involves centrally collective intentionality, while allowing stage type exceptions with regard to collective intentionality. Football is not an opaque, but a transparent social kind. Social historical kinds like football evolve, but once the sport form of football is in place, then for there to be football *qua* sport, the form of football must be used. The form of a social kind like football can migrate through various social kinds, but once the inside of the social kind has changed, it is no longer the same social kind. The surface of the activity or practice would look the same, but the practice has become something different. The inside of football – what people engaged in football aim at and see themselves as aiming at, i.e. according to collective intentionality – is what makes football a sport and the kind of sport it is. Scoring goals, avoiding conceding goals and in the end winning the match, or at least not losing it, constitute the intrinsic or internal aim or purpose of football. Footballers *qua* sportsmen and -women use the football form and play football to achieve the internal aim of the sport.

Notes

1. This Cruyffism expresses the idea that the most effective football is often not fanciful or complicated, but consists of simple passes or moves strung together in a consistent manner, with an eye for the opposition's goal. The hardest thing is not executing some complex dazzling trick on the pitch, but rather to consistently find the right move or pass, which according to Cryuff, is often the simple or simpler move or pass. Identifying the right football action on the pitch, not necessarily the most difficult one, is the hardest thing. A good example of this line of thought is the development of Portugal's Cristiano Ronaldo, at the time of writing at Juventus in Italian Serie A. It was when Ronaldo went from being a mere amazing footballer with dazzling footballing skills to consistently choosing the right move or pass, and yes, sometimes that would still be the dizzy display of step overs, that he became stellar. Notwithstanding the fact that for most footballers in the world, there is most of the time nothing simple about anything a player of Ronaldo's stature does, Cruyff's point is well taken and serves as a good indication of the complexity of the game of football.
2. The natural versus social kinds divide does not necessarily exhaust the landscape of kinds. See Funkhouser 2014: 8.
3. Friedman writes, "[t]he pieces of green paper have value because everybody thinks they have value. Everybody thinks they have value because in everybody's experience they have had value – as is equally true for the stone money of chapter 1 (…) our whole monetary system owes its existence to the mutual acceptance of what, from one point of view, is no more than a fiction" (Friedman 1994: 10).
4. On the history of the emergence of monetary systems, see, among others, Davies 1994, Chown 1994, Weatherford 1997, and Seabright 2010.
5. Searle argues that social kinds are ontologically subjective and epistemologically objective (Searle 1995: 8, 63, Searle 2010: 18). Ontologically speaking, social kinds depend on our minds and that makes them ontologically subjective. Epistemologically speaking, social kinds are objective as they impose and create constraints on our lives as well as offering possibilities. These constraints and possibilities are independent of individual cognizers' thoughts about and attitudes towards these social kinds.
6. For a discussion of race as a social kind, see among others, Appiah 1995, 1996, Haslanger 2000, Mallon 2006, 2016, Zack 1993, 2002.
7. Any worries that clothing shops in the imagined teen fashion fad example smuggle in collective intentionality at its base can be met by rewriting the example without these.
8. Grice 1957, 1968, 1969, 1982, 1991, Lewis 1969, 1975.
9. The football tokens include all units of football that can be won, lost or drawn like football matches, cup tournaments, leagues, park games, etc.
10. Phoney wars are the result of the convention of declaring war, which in turn is dependent on or derivative of the social kind of war as understood here.
11. If you chose to argue that *Fountain* pre-Duchamp, pre-gallery is not art, you can still credit it with having aesthetic qualities or value before it appeared in the gallery and the art world.
12. There is no equivalent to Marcel Duchamp's *Fountain* (1915), Andy Warhol's *Brillo Box* (1964), Carl André's *Equivalent VIII*, aka *The Bricks* (1966), etc. in the sport world (Borge 2012: 402–403).

13 Ingomar Weiler notes that, according to recent research "[t]he traditional notion that Greeks had a unique agonistic spirit has been reevaluated and qualified by scholars" (Weiler 2014: 113). See also Bignasca 2009, Wacker 2006, Ulf 2006, 2008, 2011, Decker 2004, 2010, Scanlon 2009, Kyle 2007, and Rutter 2014.
14 The full quote from Holt reads "[t]hese games were not just the contests of brute strength and collective violence that they were assumed to have been by the inventors of 'new' games in the mid-nineteenth century" (Holt 1989: 14). That entails that they were contests of brute strength and collective violence, only that there was more to them, as exemplified by the Norfolk practice of camp-ball encompassing "the idea of balancing up sides carefully", which "assumes a fairly sophisticated concept of play" (Holt 1989: 14).
15 For a diverging view, see Gessmann 2011: 45–51.
16 Curry and Dunning, and Collins have contested the independence of the Sheffield rules from public school influence (Curry and Dunning 2015: 91–92, 113–116, Collins 2019: 24–26).
17 Chess boxing is a candidate for being considered the result of a fusion of social kinds – the sport of boxing and the game of chess.
18 See Borge 2010a for an argument for why Platonism about sport cannot handle or make sense of constructive-destructive sports (Borge 2010a: 24–25).
19 The word "parasitic" is used here because philosophers tend to use it to mean exploiting someone else's effort, and not the way biologists use it in evolutionary theory, where it instead denotes impairment of another species' or individual's fitness.
20 I am ignoring the type of match-fixing case where the referee is bribed to influence the outcome, as the role of the referee is different than that of a player.
21 "Morbo (…) it's one [the word] of those awkward ones that defies easy translation. (…) It's not merely that they [Real Madrid and Barcelona] hate each other with an intensity that can truly shock the outsider, but that each encounter between them always has a new ingredient. This is the essence of morbo. It feeds off itself and keeps growing until it becomes a self-regulating and self-perpetuating organism" (Ball 2003: 17). On the rivalry between Real Madrid and Barcelona, see Lowe 2013.
22 I have elsewhere argued that the question of whether artificial systems like computers could remain mindless no matter the complexity of the systems' performance – or else that the material that computers are made of could give rise to intrinsic intentionality and with it the same causal powers as our brains have – is a question of what sort of world we inhabit, i.e. our modal address. For the Modal Address Argument, see Borge 2007: 130–131.
23 The phrase "done for sport" does not enjoy the same intuitive ring for activities or practices that do not have ordinary world counterparts. On the other hand, one can tweak the expression and use it, for example, to distinguish football from activities that are done for football, and by doing so a whole genre of counter-examples to attempts to analyse sport evaporates.
24 An activity or practice that has made the journey from for-sport with certain internal aims, a character and psychological reality to becoming a sport with subsequent change of its inside, is surfing with its transition from being countercultural chill-out recreation to being scheduled to debut as an Olympic sport in 2020.
25 Christesen does not himself hold the commonly held belief, which he has identified; instead he emphasizes that his thesis is that both ancient and modern sports function as schools for democratization (Christesen 2012: xvii).
26 On performance records and other types of records in sport, see Loland 2000, 2001, Parry 2006, Hämäläinen 2013, and Borge 2015a.
27 Commenting on the ancient Greeks, Guttmann seems to get this right, apart from his unfortunate use of the word "quantification", when he writes, "[c]omparability beyond the circle of athletes gathered together for the event was never sought and quantification of the result was unnecessary" (Guttmann 2004a: 49–50).

3
THE ANALYSIS OF FOOTBALL
Four four two

Introduction

Football matches begin with a touch of the ball. Perhaps a referee blows his or her whistle to signal that the match can begin. You are in the mid-circle with the ball. The opposition awaits your first move and so do the spectators, if there is anyone watching your game. There is a quiet before that first touch, then your foot touches the ball, it rolls and your game is on. You know what to do – you should score goals, avoid conceding goals, and win the match – but not yet how or if that will happen. Soon you find your place on the pitch as the two teams fall into familiar formations and, all according to their tactical acumen, adapt to each other's ways of lining up. If you are a defender, you seek out the striker you are most likely to mark, or, if you're a striker, your counterpart defender on the pitch will find you, and so on for the other positions on the pitch. Now it is up to you and your teammates. To achieve that aim of winning the match, you must put your footballing skills to the test and apply your knowledge of the game, so that your skills – to the best of your knowledge – fit the frame of the game. In brief, your skills in and understanding of the game are what will, if anything, get you there. "[F]ootball is all about winning" Ruud Gullit tells us, it is "how you play, how you train, how you coach, how you watch"; however, "that's not how it begins. It begins with the ball" (Gullit 2016: 1).

In Chapter 2, we reached an understanding of what sort of social phenomenon, i.e. social kind, sports, in general, and football, in particular, are. With this theoretical groundwork in place, it is time to address Suits's analysis of games and sports. This will give us a chance to further explore the social kind of football and shed light on some of the knowledge of the game that most footballers, at least tacitly, possess when playing the game. I will present Suits's analysis and provide a detailed critique of it. The analysis fits the phenomenon of football quite well, but needs to be modified fairly extensively with regard to sports in general. After having given

Suits's analysis a thorough going over and presented my own amendments and alternative views, I end the chapter by looking at how we should understand the role of the referee in sports like football. Exploring the role of the referee and refereeing in the game of football finalizes the emerging picture of football that comes out of considerations of football as a social historical kind. This picture largely fits the Suitsian analysis of sport, although our own analysis of sport and what constitutes playing a sport is more minimalistic than that of Suits.

An outline of Suits's analysis of sport

Through a series of works, Suits put forward the perhaps most-discussed definition of games and sport in the literature. Our concern will be with the definition of sport, not games. In his main work – *The Grasshopper: Games, Life and Utopia* – Suits borrowed the character of the Grasshopper from *Aesop's Fables* and turned him from a sad protagonist of a cautionary tale about the vices of too much leisure and play into a hero of the human play spirit, where "the life of the Grasshopper is the only life worth living" (Suits 1978: 26). Though the Grasshopper is quick to point out that "they are the principles of Grasshoppers" and thus not necessarily suited to everybody and definitely not to ants, there is a strong normative undercurrent in this work (Suits 1978: 26). We will not address that side of *The Grasshopper*.[1] We will be much more ant-like than grasshopperesque in this chapter. We will labour through Suits's celebrated, but also berated, definition of games and sport. This will be done through sport-specific considerations of football, but it will also serve as a springboard for general considerations about sport.

Suits argued that for something to count as a game, it must meet the following clauses, each specifying a separate criterion.

1. That the activity has a prelusory goal – that is a goal that is specified prior to a contest
2. That the activity has a set of means that limits the ways in which the prelusory goal could be legitimately achieved
3. That the activity has rules that define the activity and specify permissible and impermissible means in the achievement of the prelusory goal
4. That the game players adopt a certain attitude or disposition in their attempt to achieve the prelusory goal
   (Suits 1973b: 49–55, Suits 1978: 50–54, McNamee 2008: 13)[2]

Here is how Suits puts it in *The Grasshopper*:

> [T]o play a game is to engage in activity directed towards bringing about a specific state of affairs, using only means permitted by the rules, where the rules prohibit more efficient in favour of less efficient means, and where such rules are accepted just because they make possible such activity.
>
> (Suits 1978: 48–49)

> To play a game is to attempt to achieve a specific state of affairs [prelusory goal], using only means permitted by rules [lusory means], where the rules prohibit use of more efficient in favour of less efficient means [constitutive rules], and where the rules are accepted just because they make possible such activity [lusory attitude].
>
> *(Suits 1978: 54–55, see also Suits 1973a: 203)*

Suits sums up this view by saying that "playing a game is the voluntary attempt to overcome unnecessary obstacles" (Suits 1978: 55).

To make a game a sport, Suits claims that the activity must also meet the following criteria.

5. That the game be a game of skill
6. That the skill be physical
7. That the game have a wide following
8. That the following achieve a wide level of stability

(Suits 1973b: 56–60, McNamee 2008: 15)

This definition of sport is by far the most discussed and criticized attempt to define sports in the philosophy of sport. Before diving into this analysis, we will mention a sticky issue, only to then ignore it. According to Suits, sports constitute a sub-set of games. All sports are games, but not all games are sports. This is not a given. However, in this chapter, I am not going to consider the difference between games and sports, but treat Suits's analysis as an analysis of sport and not worry about whether it is correct to call, say, the 100-metre sprint a game. Furthermore, I am not going to consider whether Suits's definition of games is correct or not. Again, our concern is with sports. With that in mind, we are in a position to address the various clauses in Suits's analysis of sport and how they relate to football and other sports.

Football and prelusory goals

Sports, according to Suits, have *prelusory goals*. What does it mean to have a prelusory goal – a goal prior (pre-) to playing a sport (lusory)? Presumably, it is something that is specified prior to a sport contest. One way to approach the question is to contrast prelusory goals with the lusory goals of sports. A lusory goal of a sport is what you aim at in playing that sport. In the case of football, that lusory goal may be stated in negative or positive terms according to the sport's dual nature. Positively, it is to win the match by scoring more goals than the opposing team; negatively, it is not to lose by not conceding more goals than the opposing team. The lusory goal of a football match is to win the game by outscoring the opponent or, minimally, not to lose by conceding more goals than the opponent. This is precisely what we identified as the internal or intrinsic aim of a sport like football. However, according to Suits, prelusory goals should not be identified with what we called the external or primary purpose of sport. This brings out the puzzling status of prelusory goals. They are presented as something different than the internal or intrinsic aim, goal or purpose of sport, while clearly not falling into the category of the external or primary aim, goal or purpose of sport.

Prelusory goals are to be understood as aiming at some state of affairs before the playing starts. The goal specified prior to doing sport. The problem is how that goal is to be described. With regard to football and similar sports, two alternatives readily present themselves. First, as a goal that is there to be achieved before we invented the game of football, or else, as a goal that is there to be achieved before every single competition, i.e. football match. The intuitive answer is the latter. The goal of the football team before a football match is to score more goals than the other team or, at least, not concede more goals than the other team, i.e. to win, minimally not to lose. However, that makes the prelusory and the lusory goals of football the same. Instead, the prelusory goal must be described in sport-neutral terms, that is, without mentioning anything belonging to the game of football, such as scoring goals, the goal line, and so on and so forth.

> This kind of goal may be described generally as *a specific achievable state of affairs*. (…) [T]he *pre-lusory* goal of a game (…) can be described before, or independently of, any game of which it may be, or come to be, a part.
>
> (Suits 1973b: 50)

What you will get is a fairly long, convoluted and somewhat odd description of the physical facts involved in bringing a football over the opposing team's goal line, between the goalposts and under the crossbar, and in preventing the opposing team from bringing a football over one's own goal line, between the goalposts and under the crossbar.

In Chapter 1, we followed McFee's lead and complained that analysing games and sports in terms of how they overcome unnecessary obstacles is problematic, because in some sports like football, the obstacles to be overcome are not explicable independent of the sport. The same holds for the prelusory goals of football. The goal of making the football cross the goal line, between the goalposts, etc., is not explicable without having a pre-existing institution of football already in place. Furthermore, if the lusory goal is to win the game, or minimally not to lose, then having an opposing team to play is a logical requirement for having a game of football. Without the opposing team, there is no contest. Without them, we do not have the game of football, even if we do have the pitch, the markings, the ball, the goalposts, and so on. If the alleged state of affairs or obstacles are suppose to somehow exist prior to and independent of the game, then talk of bringing about or attempting to achieve a specific state of affairs or voluntary attempts to overcome unnecessary obstacles gets it wrong. The emphasis should be on football being an unnecessary activity and not on football being an attempt to overcome unnecessary obstacles (in the favoured sense of the latter). In other words, one can keep the part about unnecessary obstacles, but it is trivial. If playing football is an unnecessary activity in the sense that it is not something you normally need to do for survival, reproduction, etc., or that does not address or relate to ordinary world concerns, then any obstacles you encounter within that activity – like brutal defenders, tricky wingers, slippery pitches, half-blind referees' assistants, and so on – are also unnecessary.

Suits airs McFee's worry through the voice of one of the Grasshopper's interlocutors, whom he calls Skepticus. Skepticus complains, "chess and a host of other games as well do not appear to have such goals" that "can be accomplished independently of the rules" (Suits 1978: 57). Suits's Grasshopper replies that rules can both be used to describe actions in order to achieve checkmate, but also "to *describe* a state of affairs", and regarding the prelusory state of affairs of checkmate, "it is possible to achieve it aside from a game of chess" (Suits 1978: 58). However, Suits acknowledges that, in the latter case where you assemble the chess pieces in a checkmate configuration independent of any game, it "is in some sense dependent upon *chess*", i.e., "an *institution* of chess which can be distinguished from any individual game of chess" (Suits 1978: 58). Thus "it is not possible to achieve the prelusory goal of chess (...) aside from the institution of chess" (Suits 1978: 58). This move of distinguishing between the institution of a sport and specific instances of it, i.e. a sport type and its tokens, and admission that the idea of the independence of prelusory goals of a sport from the sport itself only makes sense on a token level is admirable, but damaging. It takes the wind out of the notion that prelusory goals are illuminating in an analysis of sport, i.e. the social kind of sport. What you are left with after Suits's admission is the trivial observation that sports, like any other activity, can be described independent of the social kind itself. The latter might be put to good pedagogical effect – though when teaching someone to play a sport like football, perhaps demonstrating how to score goals would be more effective – but it does not add anything to our understanding of football qua sport. The ball arriving over a goal line, between goalposts and under a crossbar only counts as a goal when it is part of a football match. Suits's institution move when trying to save the notion of prelusory goals in an analysis of sport shows that this way of understanding prelusory goals either assumes that which it was meant to explain or else is of mere pedagogical value.[3]

Furthermore, Suits's way of thinking about sports as aiming at prelusory goals precludes gymnastics and other aesthetic sports from counting as sports.[4] In these sports, there are no aimed-at end-states like reaching a goal line, throwing something as far away from a given line as possible, lifting the heaviest weights, etc., but instead there are ways of ranking competitors according to how they performed certain moves within certain set parameters of accepted sport-specific moves. Suits admits that his view that "sports (...) *were* the same as athletic games" was "wrong" (Suits 1988: 2). However, Suits makes no concessions to these types of sports in his analysis of sport, instead he merely adds on the idea that there is a different kind of sports, which he classifies as judged sports that are not games.[5] This is born out of Suits's failure to see that his institution move, made in support of his notion of "prelusory goals", renders Clause 1 obsolete. When considering diving, Suits suggests that "the identification of constitutive rules is logically dependent upon the identification of a prelusory goal" and that this is where the notion of prelusory goals earns its keep (Suits 1989: 1). There are two problems with this line of reasoning. First, it does not help us deal with the observation that you do not get a sport's prelusory goal without the institution of that sport, so prelusory goals enjoy no primacy over constitutive rules. Second, it is false, if it is meant to show prelusory goals' independence of or primacy over constitutive rules. Suits unwittingly concedes this when he tells us that understanding the end-states of sports that are also games, i.e. prelusory goals, is needed if we are to understand constitutive rules, "since it is precisely limitations upon means for achieving the latter [prelusory goals] that constitutive rules specify" (Suits 1989: 1). In effect, Suits is saying that in order to grasp prelusory goals, you must understand how they came to be, i.e. how certain constitutive rules put limitations on how such states of affairs should come about. According to Suits, without identification of prelusory goals, no identification of constitutive rules. But it is the other way round. If understanding prelusory goals is identified with understanding limitations on the means of achieving prelusory goals, then constitutive rules are primary. If you understand or know the constitutive rules of a sport, then you can calculate or figure out what sort of state of affairs constitutes the state of affairs that leads to a competitor winning the sport in question.

One can speculate that Suits's mistake was influenced by the sort of examples where you have some sort of challenge or test that already exists prior to any sport competition – like a mountain to cross or a long distance to cover – and that can be sported up. This is a tempting line to take, as many sports have specific end-states towards which the activities are geared. Consider Kretchmar's distinction between tests and contests (Kretchmar 1975, Kretchmar and Elcombe 2007). A test is an unnecessary voluntary undertaking of a specific task, which involves some kind of difficulty. Contests are shared tests, where the test-taking involves recognizing that the other(s) is participating in the same test and having a procedure to decide which contestant was better or whether they were equally good. Tests produce achievements and failures, while contests produce winners and losers. The ordinary language usage of the word "test" is not limited to tasks that are unnecessary and voluntary, i.e., that belong to the extra-ordinary side of things. Let us call tests that take place in everyday ordinary life *ordinary world challenges*. Anything that contains a specific task, which for humans involves some kind of physical difficulty, is a *physical ordinary world challenge*. A physical ordinary world challenge might be to reach the top of a mountain, run the distance between Marathon and Athens, cross the Alps, build a house, and so on and so forth. Physical ordinary world challenges are independent of the sport world, can be described without mentioning any sport, and can be overcome outside any sport context. You can take any physical ordinary world challenge and turn it into a test. Undertaking any activity of this type – when there is no need for it – amounts to a test. Challenging oneself to climb a mountain – when there is no ordinary world need for it – amounts to climbing the mountain as a test and doing it for sport. Furthermore, when you have a test, you can turn it into a contest by having two and more persons take the same test, recognizing that the other or others are taking the same test, i.e. collective intentionality, as well as having a procedure for ranking the test takers as better and worse. Now you have a sport.

You do not need to go through a test stage to get from physical ordinary world challenges to sports. One famous example is that of the marathon. The sport's origin lies in a physical ordinary world challenge. According to legend, after the Battle of Marathon in the ancient Greco–Persian wars, the Greek soldier Phillippides ran from Marathon to Athens to report that the Athenians had been victorious. One of the routes between Marathon and Athens that Phillippides could have taken is around 40 kilometres long. When the modern Olympic Games were invented, this physical ordinary world challenge – running approximately 40 kilometres nonstop – was sported up, giving us the sport of the marathon. The legend of the run from Marathon to Athens during the ancient Greco–Persian wars was used to turn that physical ordinary world challenge into a sport, and the discipline of the marathon was born. It should not be difficult to find other examples. When you take a physical ordinary world challenge and sport it up, then it is natural to describe the sport result, i.e. the sport you created, as having had a goal prior to the sport contest. The prelusory goal will more or less be a description of the goal of the physical ordinary world challenge you sported up. However, the insides of a physical ordinary world challenge and its for-sport and sport counterparts are different; Phillippides's aim was to deliver a message, a marathon test-taker runner aims at completing, whereas the goal of the marathon race runner is not merely to run the whole distance, but to compete and win by running the distance faster than the other competitors. The latter aims at completing the marathon distance, but only within the context of a sport competition contest, thus the prelusory goal is independent neither of individual races nor of the institution of marathon running. Furthermore, the irrelevance of prelusory goals, as Suits understands them, is even clearer for sports like football, which have no physical ordinary world challenge counterpart. The goals of football and similar sports are only specifiable within the sport context of the activity or practice. There will exist descriptions of those goals that do not mention or rely on the sport perspective, because all sports take place in physical space and that space exists and is describable independently of doing sports. Still, such descriptions are irrelevant for understanding sports.

This does not mean that there should be a wholesale rejection of the idea of there being goals prior to sport contests. We should think of goals prior to sport activities as simply being the goal of bringing about the playing of a sport. Prior to a game of football, you want to cause a game of football to happen. This prelusory goal guides action; you find a pitch, you decide on a time, you get a certain amount of willing players together and, perhaps, even draft in a referee. This picture manages to maintain the distinction between the prelusory goal of sports and their lusory goals. The prelusory goal is to realize a sport or sporting event, while the lusory goal is to win that sporting event. The fact that the prelusory goal of a sport like football, when the institution or practice has been created or instigated, is not as such independent of the sport itself is a consequence of football and similar sports being social kinds that are based on direct collective intentionality. Furthermore, it explains why it might be debatable whether domination counts as an external or primary purpose of all sports, though it fits football, whereas competition as an external or primary purpose of sports is not debatable, because the latter coincides with the prelusory goal of sports. Sport is a type of unnecessary activity, where the mentioning of unnecessary obstacles and aiming at a state of affairs are harmless enough, if read the right way. Football does have unnecessary obstacles that are to be overcome – the opposing team trying to prevent you from scoring goals and winning the match, etc. – and the end-states of goals can be described as states of affairs through a long description, one that need not mention that these states of affairs also happen to be part of a football match, where they count as goals. Still, the bottom line is that football qua sport is a type of unnecessary activity.

Football and limited means

Sports, according to Suits, involve *limited means* for legitimately achieving or reaching the types of state-of-affairs end-states that Suits called prelusory goals. In football, a typical intended state-of-affairs end-state is bringing a football over a goal line, between goalposts and under a crossbar. Part of something being a sport is that it rules out more efficient means of achieving or reaching such state-of-affairs end-states, i.e. the various sport-specific goals of the activities. Suits tells us that:

> Let us now baldly characterize work as "technical activity", by which I mean activity in which an agent seeks to employ the most efficient available means for reaching a desired goal. [G]ames differ (...) in that the means employed in games are not the most efficient. Let us say, then, that games are goal-directed activities in which inefficient means are intentionally chosen. For example, in racing games one voluntarily goes all around the track in an effort to arrive at the finish line instead of "sensibly" cutting straight across the infield.
>
> (Suits 1978: 37)

Suits's notion of technical activity would include all ordinary world or everyday life activities. Take the ordinary world or everyday life activity of escaping tigers. If you were trying to escape a tiger and the goal line in a standard setup for an 800-metre race was also where safety from the animal could be found, then you would, if you were sensible, cut across the infield to reach it. In the ordinary world, you would normally choose the most efficient means if the sole aim of the activity was to reach a certain state-of-affairs end-state, like safety from tigers. Sometimes other ordinary world or everyday life concerns, such as moral considerations, might trump the most efficient means of reaching a goal, but Suits's general point about his so-called technical activities is well taken.

Looking at various sports, we find that Suits's requirement of not doing it the most efficient way permeates the sport world. Football provides a fine example.

The most natural way for humans to deal with and manipulate objects is by using our hands. To base a sport on not being allowed to use your hands when trying to reach the sport-specific aim of scoring goals is very much about opting for inefficient means regarding that goal-directed behaviour. Take the sport of golf. If your aim were merely to get that tiny ball into that tiny hole, then occasionally handling the ball would certainly be more efficient than only using golf clubs. Yet golf is not an everyday life or ordinary world activity, but a sport, and thus there are all sorts of rules in place that exclude more efficient means in favour of less efficient ones, like the rule saying you can only use a tee on the first shot of every hole; it would be more efficient to tee it up in the fairway as well, but that is not allowed. And the list goes on for other sports. However, Suits's requirement of making inefficient means a necessary condition for something to be a sport is too strong. Talk of means that limit, though true of a great many sports, is not necessary for something to be a sport. Like the Clause 1, the heart of the matter is the observation that sports are unnecessary activities. One way this manifests itself is through the possibility, within *the sport rationale*, of creating rules for the sport that prescribe inefficient means as the way of achieving or reaching the goals of the sport. However, that does not mean you could not design a sport in such a way as to allow the sport activity to be performed in the most efficient manner possible with regard to the sport-specific aims. For ordinary world or everyday life activities and the goals of such activities, assuming standard instrumental rationality, it would be *prima facie* irrational to make it a requirement of the acting agents that they not use the most efficient means for reaching their goals. Sports are different. Instrumental rationality does not demand the most efficient way of solving sport-specific problems, but instead allows for inefficient means. The aim of sport is not to reach certain state-of-affairs end-states *simpliciter*, but to reach them within the sport context. Inefficient means is not a necessary condition for something to be a sport, but a *rational possibility* within the sport logic of such unnecessary activities. In sports, there is no point in insisting on necessarily doing what there is no need for you to do in the most efficient way possible. However, if you like to do your sport in the most efficient way possible, you can.

Consider the 100-metre footrace. The runners are lined up, and on the cue of a starting pistol they are to run in a straight line until they reach the goal line. No need to cut through the infield. The most efficient way to reach the goal line is also the best way to run the 100 metres. A Suitsian will complain that this does not show that runners use the most efficient way to reach the goal line. To be confined to only using one's legs is in fact already to opt for inefficient means. They could go blade runner Oscar Pistorius style, use a motorbike or a rocket, or what have you. Sure. Let us allow for that. Our open-style 100-metre race now looks like some kind of drag race. Let us stipulate that experience has shown that trying to destroy the other competitors is not the most effective way to win the open-style 100-metre race. It looks like we have a sport where the most efficient means of getting from the starting line to the finishing line is allowed. If you think motor sports are sports, like I do, then the open-style 100-metre race is a sport where the most efficient means of doing the sport activity are allowed.

At this point, a Suitsian will probably argue that we have failed to heed the lesson from Suits's story of the game-playing generals Ivan and Abdul. The gist of the Ivan and Abdul story is that the two have grown tired of the "outrageously arbitrary restrictions" that games impose on them. As the story unfolds, both Ivan and Abdul up the ante of rule breaking and additions in the games they play using, for example, "self-propelling radar-controlled golf balls (...) hallucinogenic drugs as an offensive weapon [in chess]", and so on and so forth (Suits 1978: 67–68). Eventually, they agree that they are in a situation where "we can no longer play any game, for games require that we impose artificial restraints upon ourselves in seeking victory, and we refuse to do that" (Suits 1978: 69). There seems to be only one game left for them to play: "A fight to the finish" (Suits 1978: 70). Call this case *Ivan and Abdul's Ultimate Game*. However, even this ultimate game is not available to them, when they refuse to accept limitations on the means employed in the service of playing games. Why? According to Suits, to get the ultimate game up and running, the contestants must agree to start the fight at some specified time, and herein lies the problem. The very act of committing to a starting time means adhering to a limitation on the means at one's disposal for reaching the game-specific state-of-affairs end-state aimed at – in this case, the demise of the other. Thus, any game or sport involves not seeking the most efficient means for reaching the intended game- or sport-specific state-of-affairs end-state (Suits 1978: 73–76).

That does not follow. Ivan tells the Grasshopper, in the disguise of the Voice of Logic, that he has "no interest in destroying Abdul *per se*", to which the Grasshopper responds that this constitutes "a rule which forbids you to make a move in the game before a certain agreed upon time" concluding that "a starting time is such an artificial limitation [on the means at your disposal for achieving victory]" (Suits 1978: 73–74). Again, I suspect that Suits is led astray in his reasoning by the fact that the game-specific state-of-affairs end-state aimed at in the ultimate game – the demise of the opponent – happens to also be a possible goal of ordinary world or everyday life activities like duels, wars, etc. Thus, it is easy to think of this game-specific state-of-affairs end-state as being achievable independent of the game in question. We have already shown that this reasoning is wanting. Ivan in fact gets it right when he wants Abdul's demise in the game, and from there it follows that you need a game to fulfil that game-specific goal. The latter does not limit the means by which you can play the game, but enables there to be a game. The two are importantly different. To decide to play a game or a sport at a certain point in time x does pose limitations on what you can do in the ordinary world or everyday life. If you are to play the ultimate game in a fight to death at 2 pm, you cannot at the same time pick up the kids from school. Moreover, you cannot destroy your intended game opponent before the game starts, because your intention to play the ultimate game depends on there being an opponent to play against. However, deciding to play a game or sport at a certain point in time x does not necessarily pose limitations on the manner in which you play that game or sport, because prior to x there is no such game or sport, whether that be on the type or token level. This has consequences with regard to the ultimate game as envisaged by Ivan and

Abdul in Suits's *Grasshopper*. Should you choose to start a fight to the death prior to the time set for the game action by ambushing your opponent, you have *de facto* forfeited the game event in favour of plain old murder. This gives us the conclusion that, prior to games and sports, there is the prelusory goal of having a game or sport to play, whether that be on the type or token level. The prelusory goal is independent of the game or sport itself and does not constitute a limitation on the means the players have at their disposal when playing games or sports.

Suits got it wrong when he argued that games and sports must have a set of means that limits the ways in which the game or sport is played. However, it is a near miss. First, recall Suits's argument that an agreed-upon starting time is an artificial limitation. The starting time of games and sports is artificial in a fairly clear sense, for the simple reason that games and sports themselves are artificial or unnecessary. The fact that sports are unnecessary activities means that the intended sport-specific state-of-affairs end-states in sporting events do not meet any ordinary world or everyday life needs, address these needs or even concern them. Nothing outside the sport event is gained directly by getting a ball over a line, between two goalposts and under a cross bar, and so on for other sports. That is, people can clearly make money out of sport, but sport itself does not produce solutions to ordinary world or everyday life problems.[6] This indicates that if you want to introduce elements into a sport that make achieving those sport-specific state-of-affairs end-states more difficult, i.e. means or manners that limit the way in which the sport can be played, then you can do so, without offering any other rationale than that you think the change makes for a better sport. How different things look in the ordinary world.

Consider the following case:

> The Cancer Game: At the cancer research centre at the *University of Research Excellency*, the research group decides to pretend that they are playing a game instead of doing research. Rather than having any focus on the instrumental value of their research, they think of their research as a game of outwitting the cancer cells. The specific state-of-affairs end-state being targeted is to defeat the cancer cells. In reality, this as-if-the-research-is-a-game approach makes no practical difference to the running of the lab. One day, a dim-witted research assistant suggests that they could make the cancer game even more interesting if they conducted all their experiments with one arm behind their back. Obviously, that is not going to happen and the research assistant might ever so gently be told: "This isn't really a game, you know."

And it is not. Why? Not because there are no means to limit the way they play the cancer game. We have already established that there could be sports without such limiting means. Rather, the cancer game reveals itself to not be a game because introducing an unnecessary obstacle or limitation on the way they do this activity so as to make the practice more interesting or fun is unacceptable. The actual intended state-of-affairs end-state of curing cancer takes precedence over the fun of doing the research. Suits was on the right track when he emphasized the idea of having less efficient means in games and sport, but failed when he made that a necessary requirement for being a game or sport instead of making it *a rational possibility* of any game or sport.

Looking back at *Ivan and Abdul's Ultimate Game*, we can say that they are playing a game only if had they been persuaded that the introduction of an unnecessary obstacle or a limitation on the way they played the game would result in a better game, then they would have accepted it. The important observation is not whether two old war horses like Ivan and Abdul would abandon the no-limitations-on-available-means feature of their ultimate game, but whether they counterfactually could accept the introduction of such changes, if they thought that made for a better, more enjoyable game. If they could not, then that shows they were never playing a game in the first place, but rather using the cloak of game to hide the fact that they were involved in an ordinary world or everyday life duel. The gratuitous part of what Morgan so aptly called the gratuitous logic of sport is not the presence of unnecessary obstacles or means that limit the ways in which the intended sport-specific state-of-affairs end-state could be legitimately achieved, but rather that such elements can be introduced in sports at will without changing the nature of the practice. The gratuitous logic dictates that you are free to make your games and sports as hard or easy as you wish. Whether you do so is another question, but you can. The hand of the game and sport logic is not going to stop you.

Football and constitutive rules

At the foundation of sports we find *constitutive rules*. Acknowledging the important role of constitutive rules entails giving one's approval of what we, in Chapter 2, dubbed foundational formalism. Whereas Suits's Clause 2 was a near miss, because sports need not have limitations on the means of reaching the sport-specific state-of-affairs end-states aimed at, Clause 3 stands on solid ground. However, regarding Clause 2, I suspect that all sports involve ways of limiting the means of action, or at least that most do. As an empirical generalization over sports, Suits got it right, or else he got it right for the vast majority of sports. We like our sports setups to have a variety of limitations on the means by which we perform the sports. That makes them more interesting and more passable for us, as limitations often keep the sports relatively safe to play, i.e., allows them to have a fictional character.

The constitutive rules of sports typically put limitations on the means by which we play. However, before we address the issue of sport-specific constitutive rules, we do well to return to the topic of social kinds and remind ourselves of what I called the constitutive rule formula. Constitutive rules are often presented by way of examples showing that the rules make certain actions possible by prescribing that, in a certain context, x is to count as y. Often writers opt for examples from games and sports. Jacob Mey tells us:

> A *constitutive* rule, in the case of chess, is one that makes up, "constitutes" the game of chess, as that particular game (...) The constitutive rules of chess determine what counts as a move for the individual chess pieces.
>
> (Mey 2007: 101–102)

Searle's favoured examples are chess and American football.

> The rules for checkmate or touchdown must "define" *checkmate in chess* or *touchdown in American football* in the same way that the rules of football define "football" or the rules of chess define "chess".
>
> (Searle 1969: 34)

Constitutive rules establish sports like football, thus enabling sport actions such as scoring a goal, taking a throw in, committing a foul, and so on and so forth. Besides this *enabling aspect* of constitutive rules, there is also an important *framing aspect*. Recall our example of the *Shoreline Runners* from Chapter 2. When the emergence of a collective intentionality turns the jogging into a race, it frames the ongoing activity, i.e. the running, in a sport context, while turning the joggers into competitors in a sporting event and enabling them to have a race. In this case, it is reasonable to assume that there is some sort of tacit understanding of some kind of rules of running a race, like not being allowed to tackle other runners. Such a tacit understanding will be dependent on there already being in place a practice of running races, and thus the framing aspect of constitutive rules is not independent of the enabling aspect. However, looking back at the social kinds of type one and two, it seems reasonable to say that when historians or social scientists discover such social kinds, they frame the social phenomenon by applying a constitutive rule formula to it. With regard to opaque social kinds, it would seem best to think of them as being framed by whatever constitutive rule formula they instantiate. With regard to social historical kinds like football, it is based on direct collective intentionality, while allowing for stage exceptions regarding the social kind itself. The early stage of a social kind like football might not involve collective intentionality, thus remaining opaque at that stage. Such a stage might lead to a transparent social kind, while partaking in the latter kind, and the transparent social kind involves having a grasp or understanding of the constitutive rules that enable there to be a sport of that kind. In that case, the early stage or stages of a social kind of the sixth type like football are framed as belonging to that kind by the constitutive rules, which only show up fully formed at a later stage in the life of the social kind in question. In football, the early stage or stages are framed as belonging to that social kind by the constitutive rules of football.

Returning to constitutive rules' more familiar aspect of making a certain activity or practice possible, the gratuitous logic of football gives specifications as to the means allowed when playing football. One way of illuminating constitutive rules is to contrast them with regulative rules. The distinction between constitutive and regulative rules is closely associated with Searle. Searle claims that the distinction was "foreshadowed by Kant's distinction between regulative and constitutive principles", while acknowledging John Rawls's "discussion of a related distinction" (Searle, 1964: 55, see also Searle 1965: 224, Searle 1969, 1995, Rawls 1955). However, a paper by Geoffrey Midgley stands out as the closest and most obvious predecessor of Searle's way of handling the topic (Midgley 1959). Regulative rules regulate behaviour, activities or practices that exist independent of and prior to such rules. For example, rules of etiquette regulate human behaviour, but are not constitutive of those behaviours. In the *FIFA Laws of the Game* in parts of *Law 4 – The Players' Equipment*, we find regulative rules telling players to wear shin guards as parts of their basic equipment and that "[t]he basic compulsory equipment must not have any political, religious or personal slogans, statements or images" (FIFA (Fédération Internationale de Football Association) 2014: 23). These rules regulate the already existing practice of playing football. Constitutive rules, on the other hand, do not regulate already existing pre-established behaviours, activities or practices, but instead make these possible. They enable us to play football. Football is defined and made possible by its constitutive rules, which is why such rules often take the form X counts as Y in context C. The part of the *FIFA Laws of the Game* called *Goal Scored* under the *Law 10 – The Method of Scoring* is a constitutive rule:

> A goal is scored when the whole of the ball passes over the goal line, between the goalposts and under the crossbar, provided that no infringement of the Laws of the Game has been committed previously by the team scoring the goal.
> (FIFA 2014: 34)

X (the whole of the ball passes over the goal line, between the goalposts and under the crossbar) counts as Y (a goal) in context C (no infringement of the Laws of the Game has been committed previously by the team scoring the goal, the latter entailing that the action takes place within a game of football). If you want to score a goal in football you must fulfil or be seen as fulfilling this rule of the game. Constitutive rules can also be negative, in which case they do not state when something counts as something in the game, but rather prescribe what is not part of the game. These are specified in the *FIFA Laws of the Game* under *Law 12 – Fouls and Misconduct* (FIFA 2014: 36–39). These constitutive rules limit the ways in which the aim of scoring a goal in football can be legitimately achieved. Constitutive rules such as the Goal Scored rule have the feel of a definition to them, and that is only natural as it is the constitutive Goal Scored rule that enables scoring in football. Without some such rule that stipulates what counts as scoring a goal in football, there would be no scoring of goals in football. With no constitutive rules of football, there would be no football. Games are, as Kretchmar points out, "the product of their constitutive rules" and that also applies to sports like football (Kretchmar 2007: 2, see also Kretchmar 2001).

This is all in keeping with our discussion of social kinds in Chapter 2, where we concluded that sports do not belong to the opaque social kinds. There is a transparency to the social kind of sport – and with it football – that demands collective intentionality both as enabling and framing the activity as sport. However, the transparency relation between participants or practitioners of a sport in a sporting event and the sport's constitutive rules is not as straightforward as one might expect. Consider someone with a concept of sport overlooking a football match without knowing the rules of the game. Knowing that someone plays a sport minimally involves framing it as a sport according to a generic or general constitutive rule formula along the line of that activity counting as sport in this context. Our spectator does not know the specific constitutive rules of football and does not know how it is that what he or she is observing counts as football and not, say, as basketball. However, he or she is aware that the proceedings on the football pitch in front of him or her count as a sport called football. Moving on from the audience to the footballers themselves, it is natural to assume that they know not only what they are doing, i.e. playing a football match, but also know to a certain extent or have a certain grasp of the sport's constitutive rules (at least the most important ones). Nevertheless, this is not necessarily the case. Many young children have been thrown into the activity of playing football without having much, if any, knowledge of the rules of the game. They might not even be aware of the fact that they are playing a sport. Still, they are playing football. How can we square that with the argument that sports like football are transparent social historical kinds?

First, we should remind ourselves that asking the question of whether something is football without qualification is ill-formed, because we can distinguish between the football form and the football function. One might be tempted to say that clueless children are not using the football form to play football, but are doing something else. This is not the right solution for the simple reason that it is not clear what else exactly they are doing. If the children in question had been copying the movements of grown-ups playing football, we would say they were mimicking the adults playing football and subsume that under the category of parroting, mimicking being a subset of parroting. However, in many cases where children are relatively clueless with regard to the rules of football, they have been instructed by someone on what to do and that makes an important difference. The instructor knows the rules and that is enough transparency for the activity to count as usage of the football form. For an activity to be the sport of football, someone connected to a particular training session or match must know the rules, even if, in the case of young children learning the game, the only one who knows the rules is the instructor overseeing or officiating the training session or football match. With regard to the usage of a sport form, we can distinguish between being *a sport participant* and *a sport practitioner*. Both sport participants and practitioners are using a sport form and doing a sport. Both are *sport performers*. Being a sport participant demands that someone connected to the sport event knows that the activity counts as doing a sport and knows the sport's constitutive rules. Being a sport practitioner requires that the sport performer him- or herself possess that knowledge. For adults, learning a sport like football is a question of being told its constitutive rules and then attempting to implement and follow these rules. For young children, it is equally a question of transitioning from being a participant to becoming a practitioner by way of football performances (like being on the pitch in training sessions and football matches), habituation, and finally understanding the sport and its constitutive rules.

This is the correct solution, not only because it makes sense of young children's football playing and how they learn to become practitioners of the game, but also because it offers a tool for understanding how and why we should allow certain animal sports into the sport pantheon. I take it for granted that some sports involving animals, like various types of horse racing and equestrian sports, are unproblematic qua sports because humans are an integral part of the sport performances. An animal sport like dog racing, on the other hand, represents a problem for the general line of reasoning on sports taken in this book. The dogs participating in dog races are devoid of any understanding of their activity as a sport, and thus the criterion of sports involving collective intentionality looks dubious. However, with a better understanding of the complexity of the transparency relation with regard to the constitutive rules of sports and collective intentionality, we see how, say, hound racing can be accommodated in our theory of sport. The greyhounds are participants and performers in the sport of greyhound racing, but not practitioners. The greyhounds get to compete in a sporting event, because someone else – the organizers, the dog owners, etc. – has set things up in such a way that we have a type of sport and these actors are aware of the constitutive rules of greyhound racing. If clueless young children being induced into the practice of playing football, with a view to making the transition from participant to practitioner, count as playing football by courtesy of someone else knowing football's constitutive rules, then, by the very same token, greyhounds in greyhound races are also sport participants. The hounds will never make the transition from mere sport participants to practitioners, so our claim in the introduction that only humans are a sporting animal stands on solid ground, as long as we add the specification of that meaning a practitioner of sport or else an organizer of sports without practitioners. The sport phenomenon belongs to the human sphere. How we divide the conceptual cake between sport and non-sport activities will, in this case, be a question of what goes into the context under consideration. If context C from the constitutive rule formula applied to dog races only includes the perspective of the canines themselves – the dogs' perceptual and cognitive world – then the statement that the dogs' running after an artificial lure around a track, etc., counts as a sporting event is false. From the perspective of the racing dogs, there is no awareness, i.e. collective intentionality, of being involved in a sport.[7] However, when considering dog races, we do not normally limit ourselves to only considering the hounds' perspective. Instead, we consider the whole event setup, including the reasons for arranging such events, how they are organized, etc. – this being our context C – and when we do so, the statement that the dogs' running after an artificial lure around a track, etc., counts as a sporting event is true.

The fact that the transparency relation with regard to constitutive rules and collective intentionality in the realm of sport need not actually involve the collective intentionality of the sport participants themselves creates an interesting possibility. In the *Cancer Game*, we showed that doing some activity as if it were a game or sport does not turn it into a game or sport. When we claim that ordinary world or everyday life activities like cancer research, raising our children, tying our shoes, visiting relatives and so on, are not a game or sport, our starting point is the perspective of humans – our own perceptual and cognitive world. If this is our context C, it is true that life in general is not a game or sport. Presumably, seeing our lives as not being part of a game or sporting event reflects an objective truth, but it does not constitute a metaphysical truth. For all we know, the gods at Mount Olympus overseeing the world might have us all involved in one big sporting event. If they have designed human existence as part of one of their sporting events, then we are in the same position as the dogs in the greyhound races. As far as the greyhounds are concerned, they are chasing prey. On the other hand, those of us who have set up and organized the races know that they are not involved in a chase per se, but in a type of sport competition. Just as the dogs are blissfully unaware of their status as participants in an animal sporting event and cognitively closed to grasping that they are, we too might be unaware of and cognitively closed to the sport of human life that the gods of Mount Olympus have made us part of. It is not very likely, but it is possible.[8]

Football and the lusory attitude needed for playing the sport

Suits tells us that the necessary *lusory attitude* for playing a game or a sport is "the knowing *acceptance* of constitutive rules just so the activity made possible by such acceptance can occur" (Suits 1973b: 55, my italics). Or, that "games require *obedience* to rules (…) where such rules are *obeyed*" (Suits 1978: 47, my italics). A minimal interpretation of this more or less gives the line of thought on lusory attitude defended in this section.

> The lusory attitude needed for playing a sport is a willingness to enter and remain in the sport sphere of an unnecessary activity or practice like football until completion of a particular sporting event of that type, therein accepting the rules of the sport, where this attitude is required for the constitutive rules of the sport to take effect, premised one's prelusory goal of having a sport to play.

Because sports are unnecessary activities, the lusory goal of winning whichever sport one is playing by reaching the intended sport-specific state-of-affairs end-states will not come about in any ordinary everyday world course of events. It requires a decision to play. You must enter the sport sphere. To get your game going, you must be willing to accept from the outset that such-and-such actions and events will count as these actions and events in the sport. You cannot reach your sport-specific state-of-affairs end-states, like scoring a goal, unless there is acceptance of or obedience to some sort of rule prescribing what counts as a scored goal in the sport you are participating in. Continuous acceptance of or obedience to the constitutive rules is needed for your match not to break down, but to come to completion, where an end result, which involves a ranking of the competitors, is reached. You cannot be a footballer unless you are in some sense committed to the constitutive rules of the game. You cannot have a football match unless you have footballers. When the football form is being used, the participants have entered the football sphere freely to have a game to play, thereby accepting or obeying the constitutive rules of the sport, which enables and regulates the various football-specific state-of-affairs end-states aimed at. In other words, we have a match on our hands that can conclude with a win, draw or loss for the participating teams.

Suits, however, wanted a more substantial reading of the required lusory attitude, which led him to argue that "to break a game rule is to render impossible the attainment of an end (…) one cannot (really) win the game unless one plays it, and one cannot (really) play the game unless one obeys the rules of the game" (Suits 1978: 39). If you break the rules of a sport, then logically speaking you are no longer playing that sport, and subsequently you cannot win the competition you seemingly are part of. You cannot cheat, i.e. wilfully violate the rules of a sport, and at the same time play that sport. Morgan calls this the "logical incompatibility thesis" (Morgan 1987: 1). One could perhaps make a case for the logical incompatibility thesis with regard to games like chess. If you move your knight three squares horizontally and one square vertically, you are simply not playing chess anymore. However, with regard to football and similar sports, the Suits line of argument flies in the face of facts. The *FIFA Laws of the Game* under *Law 12 – Fouls and Misconduct* state: "[a] direct free kick is also awarded to the opposing team if a player commits any of the following three offences" where the first one is "holds an opponent" (FIFA 2014: 36). Consider the following case.

> A Fistful of Fouls: On a corner kick in the knock-out stages of a tournament between two football teams, in the dying minutes with the defending team leading 1–0, all players on the pitch, except the one taking the corner, find themselves in the penalty box of the defending team. As the corner is struck, every player in the box grabs hold of an opposing player's shirt, i.e. committing a foul, while the ball is in mid-air. 21 out of 22 players simultaneously, intentionally commit a foul.

According to Suits, in this case 21 out of 22 players would not be playing football, as they are all intentionally violating a rule of the game. *A Fistful of Fouls* might feel like a bit of a parody of football for the uninitiated, but the truth is that it is not far from the truth. The following interchange between the BBC's Steve Wilson and former footballer Danny Murphy commenting on Italia vs. Spain in the Euro 2016, when the Spaniards were defending a corner in the 28th minute, is telling:

WILSON: Jordi Alba had a big fistful of De Rossi's shirt there
    (…)

MURPHY: Just a little tug. I suppose on every corner really you can pick someone out that's having a little nibble with someone, it's –
WILSON: Every corner, every country, every league
MURPHY: Yeah exactly
WILSON: Any level. Sadly, probably any age group as well
MURPHY: Yeah

Football is *that kind of sport.* Wilson's statement of every corner, every country, every league, any level and any age group is surely hyperbolic. But as hyperbole goes, the point is that shirt tugging on corners at that point in football was a constant occurrence, at least at the upper levels of the game, and the matter-of-fact manner in which these comments were delivered, free from moral outrage, shows that Wilson and Murphy did not except this to be news to their audience. But surely, corners are a part of football and football is a sport. The Suitsian map, i.e., this part of the analysis as understood by Suits himself, does not fit the football landscape.[9]

How could a Suitsian deal with the mismatch between theory and phenomenon? Going normative will not do, as Suits is not arguing that players who break the rules of football should not be counted among the footballers, but that they cannot. The logical incompatibility thesis holds that being a player of a sport and a rule-breaker in that sport are incompatible. Intentionally or unintentionally breaking a rule of a sport deprives you of the status of playing that sport. Suits's analysis of games and sport is meant to track how things are, not how they ought to be.

> It is impossible for me to win the game and at the same time to break one of its rules.
>
> *(Suits 1967b: 150, and Suits 1978: 40)*

Given how football is actually played, an error theory of sports like football is an option for a Suitsian. The 21 players in *A Fistful of Fouls* tugging each others' shirts to gain a sport advantage are all conceptually confused, because through that very action they stop being players in the sport of football, thus disqualifying themselves from being able to gain a sport advantage. Their audience, whose members continue to treat them as though they were playing football, is equally misguided. Still, rule violations are widespread in football, and in this connection, the Wilson line about every country, every league, any level and any age group is probably very close to the truth. The footballing world does not share Suits's view on this matter, and we are all wrong and in error. This is what an error theory of football looks like.

Should we accept an error theory of football? No. In any field of research, opting for an error theory comes at a theoretical cost. The cost is the theory's counterintuitiveness. Sometimes that loss of intuitiveness is not very or at all serious. No physicist would worry about his or her theory not matching up with folk physics. However, things look different with regard to social kinds that are based on direct collective intentionality. Football is a transparent social kind, and that does not sit easily with the error theory entailed in Suits's view on lusory attitude.

In an overall consideration of theoretical virtues, our theory of the social kind of football commends us to jettison this Suitsian error theory. In the philosophy of sport, Suits's incompatibility thesis has typically been seen as a consequence of his reductive formalism. McFee notes that "some rule-breaking is explicitly allowed for, when rules of a sport incorporate penalties for that kind of rule breaking" and "[i]f formalism is not simply to *define away* counter-cases, it must offer some account of the difference between these two kinds of rule-related situations" (McFee 2004: 34, 34–35). You can play football in accordance with the rules of the game, like scoring a goal in a rule-prescribed manner, but you can also play football not in accordance with the rules of the game, like tugging an opponent's shirt on a corner. *Positive rules of conduct* define the former, and *negative rules of conduct* are in place to identify the latter. However, positive and negative rules of conduct do not reflect a deep difference between the two types of rules with regard to these rule-related situations. I suppose that the reason for having these two types of rules is pragmatic or practical. All rules of conduct in a sport can either be formulated positively by having a set of rules stating that "In sport X you are *only* allowed to do thus-and-thus", or negatively by stating that "In sport X you are *only* prohibited from doing thus-and-thus". The net effect would be that in the positive version, play continues as long as only such-and-such things happen on the pitch, or else, in the negative version, play continues as long as none of the such-and-such things happen on the pitch.[10]

There is a type of rules in football, and similar sports, that differs from the two types mentioned above, and that is the *rules of penalties*. When an action in the playing field has been spotted by a referee and determined not to fall inside the scope of positive rules of conduct or inside the scope of negative rules of conduct, then if the sport in question has rules of penalties, they will be meted out to the offending party. The first thing to observe is that, theoretically, a sport like football does not need these rules. One can envisage that if a referee spotted an action not falling within the scope of allowed football actions, or inside the scope of disallowed football actions, he or she would stop play and that whatever happened after or as a consequence of the rule-breaking action would be discounted before play again resumed. Such an approach to handling rule-breaking actions in football would be in line with the ethos found in parts of the football community during the sport's formative years. When the English Football Association (FA) introduced the penalty kick in 1890, it was met with opposition from many amateur teams consisting mainly of southern-based players with Oxbridge and public-school ties.

> Working-class professionals, they reasoned, motivated by money or fear of losing their place, might foul an opponent intentionally (...) "Considerable exception was taken to it at the outset by the 'better' class of players", noted an early history of the game. It was "somewhat of an insult to their dignity to have to play under such a rule" [Gibson and Pickford 1906: 108–109] (...) "Wag" Greenland, a referee and later AFA secretary, recalled awarding a

> penalty only to be informed by the Corinthians' captain that "they never attempted to profit from such kicks" [Greenland 1965: 14–15].
>
> *(Porter 2006: 411)*

Had the Corinthian culture won the day, then there would not be a penalty rule or penalties, and, perhaps, no similar rules awarding free kicks, handing out yellow and red cards, etc. Still, we would be playing football without such rules. Given this observation, it is tempting to think of the penalty kick rule and similar rules as regulative rules. There is something to this line of reasoning. The introduction of the penalty kick rule modified the game of football. Rules of penalties can correct, like when the ball is given back to the team that was fouled. This feature could exist in football without such rules, if rule violations were only treated by resuming play from where in the play the rule violation took place. However, penalty rules do not merely modify the practice of football and the behaviours within it. They are also corrective, creating new behaviours by rewarding and penalizing, thus making substantial additions to the practice itself. They are *reaction rules*.

Consider the following rule of football:

> Where a player denies the opposing team a goal or an obvious goal-scoring opportunity by a deliberate handball offence the player is sent off wherever the offence occurs.
>
> *(FIFA 2016: 87)*

If such an offence happens outside the penalty box, then the ball is placed where the offence took place. Play is corrected. The sending off of the offending player is a corrective penalty, which is meant to compensate for the loss of the obvious goal-scoring opportunity. These are hybrid rules. They modify the game of football because play is corrected. Furthermore, footballers will take into account the possibility of creating a free kick, a penalty kick, incurring a warning (yellow card) or a sending off (red card), etc., when entering into a football interaction. This is the regulative aspect of the rules. At the same time, these types of rules create the free kick, the penalty kick, the sending off, etc. and make possible the behaviours of taking a free kick, taking a penalty kick, being sent off, etc. This is the constitutive aspect of the rules. The rules of football consist of constitutive rules, regulative rules and reaction rules, though only the first set is needed for having a sport of football.

Suits could have accommodated reaction rules within his reductive formalism, but instead he takes the following route:

> There is a third kind of rule (...) This is the kind of rule for which there is a fixed penalty, such that violating the rule is neither to fail to play the game nor [necessarily] to fail to play the game well, since it is sometimes tactically correct to incur such a penalty [e.g. in hockey] for the sake of the advantage

gained. But these rules and the lusory consequences of their violation are established by the constitutive rules, and are simply extensions of them.

(Suits 1973b: 52)

Given Suits's incompatibility thesis, he does not have the theoretical resources to make these claims. If a player violates a constitutive rule of football, then according to Suits's incompatibility thesis, he or she is no longer part of the game when the rule-breaking incident takes place and cannot be punished by the rules of the game *qua* a footballer.

Suits could have accommodated reaction rules by arguing that, in football, there are no rule violations or penalties for these, only constitutive rules and their effects. For example, awarding a free kick is not a reaction to a rule violation functioning correctively, but instead it is just another example of a case of a constitutive rule, where X (this and this action) counts as Y (creating a free kick) in C (a football match). The making of free kicks is on a par with the making of goals, corner kicks, throw-ins, dropped balls, etc. No one in the footballing world thinks this way. FIFA's rule book *Laws of the Game 2016/17* freely mentions fouls, that an action is against/breaks/infringes/violates the rules of the game, offences, misconduct, infringement, etc. and carefully describes how to penalize or sanction such actions. This is another error view. Furthermore, the interplay between football's constitutive rules and footballers' violations of them is often what drives changes in the football blueprint, i.e., the rule book or laws of the game, or the way the blueprint is used, i.e., interpretations of the rule book or laws of the game. Consider so-called professional fouls, which often occur when the other team is prevented from scoring. At one point in the history of football, denying the opponent an obvious goal-scoring opportunity by intentionally fouling outside the penalty box only led to conceding a free kick. In such cases, it was clearly advantageous to commit a foul, and footballers exploited this part of the rule book. Due to the widespread occurrences of professional fouls and some high-profile cases, prior to the 1982–1983 season the English FA decided to reinterpret such episodes as serious foul play, for which the penalty was a sending off. Later the rules of the game were amended. In 1991, the *Denial of an obvious goal-scoring opportunity* offence was written into the rule book and with it details on the penalization of this offence. The reaction of the FA and later FIFA was designed to penalize professional fouls as a means of deterring such conduct. The error view under consideration fails to capture how such changes in interpretation of the rules and later amendments came about. The view should be rejected.

Alternatively, Suits could have argued that when a referee seemingly deems something a rule violation, what he or she does is to point out that the apparent offender is no longer playing, thus the stop in play. In fact, play has already stopped and the referee is just making sure everyone is aware of that. The referee in such cases is not making decisions within the game, but rather on what is and is not part of the game. In this picture, footballers *qua* footballers pop in and out of existence. The players take themselves out of the game by violating a rule and can only be reinstated into the game when play resumes after a referee's decision that play has already stopped. This explains why referees stop the interactions on the pitch. In this picture, the red card can be explained, not as a sending off, but as a denial of re-entrance into the game. However, other types of meting out of punishment, which create events in the game, cannot be accommodated. How can someone create what in the rule book is acknowledged as part of the game, like free kicks, penalty kicks, etc., by not being part of the game? That makes non-sporting events part of the sport itself, which they supposedly are not. This error view can safely be set aside. There is no viable way out for Suits, and the conclusion is to reject the incompatibility thesis.

In the philosophy of sport, giving up Suitsian formalism, i.e. reductive formalism, due to the indefensibility of the incompatibility thesis usually leads to endorsement of *the ethos view of sport*. The lusory attitude is not to be found in strict adherence to the formal rules of the game, but rather in endorsement of a sport's ethos, i.e. interpretation of the rules of a game. The first to introduce this line of reasoning was Fred D'Agostino. D'Agostino observed that, with regard to several sports, the way a sport was played did not always strictly reflect the formal rules of the game.

> According to the formal rules of basketball, basketball is a "noncontact" sport: in general, physical contact between players is prohibited by the rules of basketball. But any game of American professional basketball is filled with (one might almost say consists of) incidents in which players (accidentally or deliberately) make contact with one another. Of course, only some of these incidents are observed by game officials. But only some even of these observed incidents actually result in the invocation of penalties. Why is this so? This is so because the players and game officials have, in effect, conspired to ignore certain of the rules of basketball, at least in certain situations, in order to promote certain interests, which they share, for instance, with team owners and spectators – e.g., to make the game more exciting than it would be if the rules were more strictly enforced.
>
> *(D'Agostino 1981: 14)*

D'Agostino advises philosophers of sport "to recognize that any particular game has an ethos as well as a set of formal rules", where the ethos comprises "those conventions determining how the formal rules of that game are applied in concrete circumstances" (D'Agostino 1981: 7). "The ethos of a game G is that set of conventions which determines how the rules of G are to be applied" (D'Agostino 1981: 15). As a matter of observation, D'Agostino is clearly correct. Furthermore, the basketball case described by D'Agostino is not a one-off. We find similar cases in other sports, and in football one such case would be the already discussed phenomenon of tugging the opponents' shirt. Call this the *interpretation view of refereeing*. Rules are not merely mechanically applied, but subject to the interpretation and judgement of the arbiter or arbiters of the rules. Not surprisingly, Suits holds what looks like a *mechanical view of refereeing*, when he writes that "referees see to it that the rules are followed and impose penalties when they are not" (Suits 1988: 5). Again, Suits's reductive formalism betrays him, leaving him without tools to explain what goes on in sport competitions like basketball, football and similar sports.

At this point, a Suitsian might argue that the examples of how the ethos of a game differs from its formal rules merely demonstrate that some formal rules are implicit. The history of the professional foul and how a rule interpretation was later turned into a formal rule show that. But this is of no help. Calling interpretations of a set of formal rules implicit rules is merely acknowledging the failings of reductive formalism, i.e. that sports are more than their formal or explicit rules and the mechanical implementation of them. Second, this line only works if you deem any rule interpretation to be an example of an implicit rule, which seems question begging. Instead, what the example shows is that "no rule-formulation can capture all the cases that a rule might come up against" (McFee 2004: 70). Up to a certain point, the rules of football had not faced a situation with widespread professional fouling, and the rule of serious foul play had been interpreted as not including professional fouls. No rule implementation without rule interpretation. The idea that rules demand interpretation can be extracted from Nelson Goodman's new riddle of induction and Ludwig Wittgenstein's problem of rule following (Goodman 1955, Wittgenstein 1967: § 183–243). How things have behaved, have been done or been in the past is no guarantee for how things will pan out in the future. In our sport context, this means that knowing how a rule of football has been instantiated up to a certain point does not dictate how it will go on being implemented. In mainstream philosophy, Goodman's new riddle of induction and Wittgenstein's problem of rule following are often seen as issues that need solving or dissolving. No such worries arise with regard to rule following in social kinds like football. Social historical kinds evolve. They are not static entities. Knowing the interpretation of a rule in such a kind at a stage in that kind's existence is no guarantee for how the rule will be interpreted at a later stage of that kind.

The ethos view of sport, including the interpretation view of refereeing, sits well with foundational formalism and the theory of sports as social historical kinds that allow for stage type exception with regard to collective intentionality. Proto-football evolved into association football and rugby football, and these again have spawned five-a-side football, futsal, beach football, etc. on the association football side of things, whereas rugby football, at least, gave us rugby league, rugby union, and American football. Furthermore, association football and its various side-branches have also evolved internally. The question of whether our football stays the same sport as rules change and ethos changes is foremost a question of how footballers and their audience view it, i.e., a question of collective intentionality. However, this is not exclusively a question of collective intentionality. A rule change might, unbeknown to the sport participants, practitioners and audiences, mark the last stage of one sport and the first stage of another. Or conflicting interpretation of a rule, i.e. conflicting ethos, might mark the first stage of a fission into two distinct sports or two distinct versions of the same type of sport. On other occasions, what in effect marks the first stage of what became two distinct sports or two distinct versions of the same type of sport can be something other than disagreement over rules or rule interpretations. The latter applies to the development of rugby football, which split into different organizations in the sport's formative years, marking the beginning of what became rugby union and rugby league (the Northern union) (Delaney 1984, Dunning and Sheard 2005: 142–149, Holt 1989: 105). This should not surprise us given our understanding of social historical kinds. With the split into two organizations both handling the same sport, we can also get a split in collective intentionality in the sense that the two sport cultures playing the same sport no longer refer to or take into consideration the other culture's understanding of the game. We then find that they develop along different trajectories eventually turning out two distinct sports or two distinct versions of the same type of sport. The sport communities might not be aware of when such processes begin, these being transitions for historians to investigate, though the end results of such processes – new sports or new versions of old sports – are anchored in collective intentionality.

However, the ethos view in fact does not solve the problem of rule violations in sport, but merely pushes it back one step. D'Agostino tells us that:

> [T]he ethos of a game distinguishes between behavior that is permissible, behavior that is impermissible but acceptable, and behavior that is unacceptable. Permissible behavior is, on this nonformalist account of games, either in accordance with the formal rules of a game or violates those rules only in a way which, according to the ethos of that game, does not require the invocation of penalties. Impermissible but acceptable behavior, on this account, violates the rules of the game in a way which, according to the ethos of the game, does require the invocation of penalties. And unacceptable behavior violates the rules of the game in a way which, according to the ethos of that game, *disqualifies its perpetrator as a player of that game*. According to this nonformalist account of games, only such unacceptable behavior is not game-behavior; only a player engaging in such behavior ipso facto *ceases to be a player*.
> (D'Agostino 1981: 15, my italics)

The ethos view suffers from a flaw akin to that of reductive formalism. Whereas reductive formalism got into trouble by arguing that you cannot play the game unless you adhere to the rules, the ethos view suggests that you cannot play the game unless you adhere to the ethos of the sport. In Suits's view, it is impossible to win a sporting event while breaking the rules of the sport. In D'Agostino's view, players who behave unacceptably ipso facto cease to be players, and it follows that it is impossible to win a sporting event while violating the ethos of the sport. Rule breaking or ethos violation in effect excludes you from being a participant or practitioner of a sport. We have already shown why the Suitsian line of argument has to be given up, and we will show that D'Agostino's view is equally misguided.

The first thing to note is the emergence of the familiar problem of holding someone to a certain conventionally set standard of action, whether that be rules of the game or their interpretation, when by violating that standard he or she is directly transported outside the scope of the standard. How can you penalize someone within a football match for an ethos violation when he or she has ipso facto ceased to be a footballer? The ethos view is in no better shape on this issue than the Suitsian view was. The ethos view fares better with regard to how a game like football is played. While the Suitsian line was obviously false, the ethos view as laid out by D'Agostino is merely false. That is, rule breaking in football happens all the time and it is the consensus of the football world that the players who break rules do not stop being footballers. Unacceptable behaviour that passes under the radar of referees, on the other hand, is rarer, but when it happens, the player in question still counts as a footballer, and what he or she did is an action in a game of football made by a footballer. Unacceptable footballing conduct does not automatically make you a non-footballer. You remain a participant or practitioner of football in a football match until a referee rules that you are no longer to be part of that game. Consider the following case. When Liverpool's Graeme Souness, in the first leg of the European Cup semi-final in 1984 at Anfield against Dinamo București, decided to teach Lică Movilă a lesson off the ball by breaking his jaw, that was an act done by a footballer in a football match. Souness tells us that "I let loose with the best punch I have delivered in my life" (Souness with Harris 1985: 107). The game advantage of injuring the opposing team's captain, while not being sent off, is clear for all to see. We agree that it is an infernal shame and so on and so forth – that sort of thing should not happen in football matches – but it did. Furthermore, Souness remained a part of the rest of the match, the return match, and the subsequent European Cup final in Rome, which Liverpool won on penalties against AS Roma, allowing Souness to lift the European Cup trophy as Liverpool captain. Breaking opponents' jaws has never been part of any football ethos, but that did not prevent a footballer, while being a footballer, from doing just that. The Souness-Movilă incident is in no way unique, which leaves the ethos view at odds with the football landscape.[11]

There is another problem for the ethos view that runs deeper. With regard to what it takes to be a practitioner of a sport, i.e. the required lusory attitude, the view entails that in order for there to be a sport like football, a shared ethos must be in place. Step outside the conventions that determine how the formal rules of that game are applied in concrete circumstances and acceptable behaviour, i.e. the ethos of the sport, and ipso facto you cease to be a player of the game. That is false. A shared ethos is not necessary for playing the same sport. D'Agostino's American professional basketball case can mislead us, because it is a monocultural case. Here we would perhaps expect there to be a shared ethos, not because sport necessitates it, but because sport competitions favour convergence towards a shared understanding of the rules, i.e. an ethos. Also, I suspect that it is harder to detect tensions in interpretations of the rules in monocultural practices. Football is different. The social historical kind of football fairly quickly outgrew its monocultural English origin to become a multicultural phenomenon. Football is an international sport encompassing a variety of football cultures and with it possible conflicting ethos, i.e. rule interpretations and views on what counts as acceptable and unacceptable behaviour. By far the most prestigious competition to win in football is the FIFA World Cup. This tournament, from its very inception, included teams from more than one continent. Uruguay 1930 included teams from three continents: South America (Argentina, Bolivia, Brazil, Chile, Paraguay, Peru and Uruguay), Central and North America (Mexico and United States), and Europe (Belgium, France, Romania and Yugoslavia). Italy 1934 saw the inclusion of Africa (Egypt); Switzerland 1954 saw Asia join the fold (South Korea); and finally West Germany 1974 had a team from Oceania in the tournament (Australia). Can two teams that do not share the same ethos play against each other? Logic is not going to prevent it from happening and the history of football, especially World Cup tournaments throughout the twentieth century, has given us a multitude of examples of such occurrences.

Consider the following observation from Iranian footballer Ghafoor Jahani, commenting on how the Iranian national team in the 1978 World Cup in Argentina committed too many fouls (four penalties in three matches and numerous free kicks):

> Ghafoor Jahani: In Iran none of the challenges we made would have led to penalties. It was the first time we realised what was considered a penalty in the outside world. It wasn't because we were weak in defence or were nervous. We were used to playing in this way. Iranian referees lacked the training to communicate the rules used by foreign referees to us the players.
>
> *(Shout Factory 2001)*

The Iranian team of 1978 suffered from not being in line with how the referees of the games they played interpreted the rules. The Iranians played with a different or differing ethos, i.e. different or differing rule interpretations. However, there is no temptation to say that they were not playing football or not participating in a football match.

The football World Cups in which the different continents clashed have been marred by or blessed with volatile episodes that at times have got out of hand, often partly due to conflicting understandings of the way the rules were to be interpreted and put into practice, i.e., the way you are allowed to play the game. Not surprisingly, these matches have often involved teams from the two dominant football continents – Europe and South America. The World Cup of 1962 in Chile with its many undisciplined matches including the infamous Battle of Santiago between Chile and Italy, and the sending off of Argentina's captain Antonio Rattín in the quarter-final against England in the 1966 World Cup are only two examples that spring to mind. The South America–Europe rivalry is ripe with fraught but completed matches, such as those early clashes between the winner of the European Cup (later named Champions League) and the winner of the Copa

America in the Intercontinental Cup (later named the FIFA Club World Cup). From inside Europe, the so-called Battle of Highbury between England and Italy in 1934 provides a telling example. Historians Mike Huggins and Jack Williams report:

> The *Daily Express* (...) [o]n an inside page it acknowledged the Italians' "individual cleverness, speed, thoroughness, and deft manipulation of the ball" but did not want to see them again "until they have acquired a newer knowledge of the original rules of football and of traditions that, unless, respected, will push all sportsmanship to the wall" (...) the *Daily Herald* wrote that the Italians seemed to "disregard the rules, as we read them". Another *Daily Herald* columnist argued that "the Italians, and every other European country for that matter, should know that dangerous fouling ... cannot be tolerated in football".
>
> *(Huggins and Williams 2006: 124)*

Conflicting ethos does not preclude a football match from taking place or the participants from being footballers, i.e. playing the game.[12] The lusory attitude required to play football can neither be strict adherence to the rules of the game nor observance of a shared ethos of the game. Instead, we should opt for something more basic.

To be a player of a sport is to enter an activity in which that sport form is used. When discussing football, I have previously made this point in terms of social contracts:

> The social contract players enter into when playing competitive matches is rather an obligation to play to win, or at least not to lose, while the task of making the game fair is entrusted to a referee. Entrusting a referee to decide which events or actions within a match are rightful or which not, entails an agreement not to interfere with (even to the extent of influencing) the referee's decision-making.
>
> *(Borge 2010b: 155)*

This idea, though basically on the right track, is not quite correct. First, claims about social contracts can be difficult to evaluate, and it is not clear that we need to appeal to them when defining the lusory attitude needed in order for someone to count as playing a sport. Most importantly, in my attempt above, I made it a requirement that the footballer adhere to the internal or intrinsic aim of football, and that is false. I have already argued that you can be a sport participant without having the faintest idea that you are part of a sporting event (young children and nonhuman animals). Furthermore, even a sport performer who is fully aware that he or she is entering a sport competition with various rules need not be motivated by achieving the internal or intrinsic aim of sport. He or she might be entering the pitch with the sole intent of impressing the opposite or same sex (for further obvious reasons), carrying out aesthetically pleasing bodily movements with or without the ball, performing health-promoting movements, and so on and so forth. Today, with the institution of football well established, i.e. the social historical sport kind of football, all it takes for someone to be a footballer is to enter the pitch as a sport performer in a football match, i.e., be part of a football match. Our understanding of the lusory attitude required for playing the game should reflect that. Or, taking a better approach, we first address *the lusory state* required for playing the game.

The lusory state required to play football should be described as follows:

> To be a participant in football requires that one endure, obey or accept the arbitration of the rules of football through which the football form is implemented.

This requirement should be minimal enough to allow us to consider various implementations of the football form – use, abuse, application, appropriation and parroting – with a view to acquiring a more sophisticated understanding of what it is to take part in a sport than the understanding mere intuitions about various cases can deliver. As I previously argued, what holds the sport of football together is "the players' decision to defer to the referee and to respect his decisions" (Borge 2010b: 164).[13] The various ways one can be part of football are bound together by the minimal requirement of being subjected to arbitration of the rules of football. This allows us to include mere sport participants. Small children placed together on a football pitch in an organized game or training session aimed at inducing and habituating them into the practice do not obey or accept the rules of football, as they most likely have no or very little understanding of the practice they are engaged in. Still, they are playing football and thus count as footballers. According to our definition above, these children find themselves in a lusory state because they are being subjected to arbitration of the rules of football through which the football form is implemented, and that is enough to make them footballers.

Usage of the sport form enjoys primacy, because without usage of the football form the sport of football would not exist, but something else (under the assumption that the bare bones of the football form existed). Diachronically, a lusory attitude is required for football to emerge as a social historical sport kind, as it is based on direct collective intentionality. The lusory attitude requires more than the mere state, though it is part of this state. It requires an understanding that one is entering a sport competition with certain internal or intrinsic aims, which is captured by the phrase "accepting arbitration of the rules of football". Obeying is meant to capture cases where the sport performer might have other reasons for participating, whereas accepting is supposed to entail adherence to the game's internal or intrinsic aims. Someone merely obeying the rules – while, say, only caring about making aesthetically pleasing bodily movements with or without the ball – would not mind if everyone else also adopted that stance, as long as that did not prevent the aesthetic motivation from being pursued. If that were to happen, we would either have an abuse or appropriation of the football form situation. This leaves us with acceptance of arbitration of the rules of a sport as a foundation for understanding sport, in general, and football, in particular. Acceptance should not be read as entailing a commitment to not violate the rules of the game. Rather, it should be read as a commitment to accepting the rulings of an arbiter or arbiters of the game's rules within the sport context – rulings on what counts as what within the game and when these rules have not or have been violated in such a manner that play should stop.

The lusory attitude of practitioners of football required for there to be football *qua* sport, i.e. football matches in which the football form is used, can be formulated as follows:

> To be a practitioner of football who uses the football form requires that one aim at fulfilling the internal or intrinsic purpose, aim or goal of football and accept arbitration of the rules of football.

The lusory attitude also covers how players are perceived *qua* footballers and how they perceive others *qua* players of the sport. The lusory attitude required for playing football, and subsequently a sport, is best viewed as a *sincerity condition* for playing football and sport. In the case of abuse, a player makes as if he or she aims at fulfilling the internal or intrinsic purpose, aim or goal of football, i.e. makes as if he or she has a lusory attitude when entering the game.

When the football form is used or abused, we can talk about football being played as a sport. Consider an abuse case where every player independent of each other, but with no knowledge of the other players' deceit, behaves as if they are using the football form. I am perfectly happy to say that the game was played as a sport. If every as-if player knew that all the other players were as-if players and knew that these players knew that all the other players were as-if players, while wanting to be seen by onlookers as playing a football match, we would have the abuse situation described in *Football and the Bust* in Chapter 2. However, in this latter type of case, if there is no intention to dupe onlookers, then it seems to me it would count as application or appropriation of the football form.[14] And finally, in a scenario where every as-if player knew that all the other players were as-if players, but did not know that the other as-if players knew that all the other players were as-if players, we also have an abuse of the football form situation. In the latter scenario, every player can truly be said to behave as if he or she is using the football form and intends to be seen as using the football form, this being part of the deceit. These cases are theoretical fringe cases. It is hard to imagine how sport, in general, and football, in particular, could have evolved historically to become sports or continued to be sports if abuse of the sport form was the most widespread or only type of instantiation of the sport form. However, these sorts of sceptical scenario-like situations regarding the lusory attitude are theoretical possibilities and they should be acknowledged as such.

The fringe cases serve the purpose of showing that, when we have the theoretical apparatus to deal with them, other cases closer to the way things actually are fall more easily into place. Take the case of match fixing. If a footballer who is on the take is bribed to lose matches partakes in a football match, does he or she count as being a footballer and playing a football match? The answer is not a simplistic yes or no. Rather, we have the resources to say that, courtesy of the football form being used, the corrupt player is a footballer and is playing football, while acknowledging that something is amiss when the player violates the sincerity condition of football – play to win or minimally not to lose. The corrupt player is a type of free rider on usage of the football form. A further and natural follow-up question is to ask how many of this type of free riders usage of the football form can bear before it no longer counts as a sporting event – before the practice breaks down and becomes something else. One-off abuse cases like *Football and the Bust* do not threaten the practice of football, but if they became widespread, they might. Again, the right move is to resist the temptation to force a definite answer to such a question. When considering specific cases, we have the resources to instead identify features of a given case that would count towards seeing it as usage of the football form, features that would count towards seeing it as abuse of the football form, and so on and so forth. Furthermore, there is more to such considerations than merely counting heads with regard to the question of usage of the football form and fulfilling the sincerity condition of football. Questions of social position, power, hierarchy, hegemony, institutions, etc. with regard to players, managers, owners, audiences, and others connected to a specific game or a period of the sport's existence might come to bear on such considerations. Synchronically, the question of whether the football form is used, abused, applied, appropriated, etc. need not yield a definite answer with regard to specific cases under consideration. Mixed cases are to be expected. Diachronically, one would have to know something about which part of a social kind's life is under consideration, and there will be mixed cases where two social kinds share a stage. One can imagine a case where historians, when considering a certain period of the sport of football, argue that a given period, due to widespread abuse of the football form among the sport performers, counts both as the last stage of football *qua* sport and the first stage of football *qua* something else. All of the above are welcome consequences of thinking about football as a social historical kind and of making a distinction between the football form and the various relations it can partake in.

Having settled for a less demanding conception of lusory attitude, we are now in the position to return to the question of ethos and how to better incorporate talk of ethos into our model of football and sport. Acknowledging that rule implementation requires rule interpretation together with the lusory attitude of accepting the rule arbitration of a referee or referees, while seeking to win, minimally not to lose, predicts convergence towards a shared rule interpretation, which we can sensibly talk about as a shared ethos. If a player or players aim at winning a football match, while accepting that a match referee has the final say in what counts as what in the game based an interpretation of the sport's rules, such as when a goal is scored, then the players are motivated to adopt the same rule understanding as the referee in question. This convergence towards a shared ethos, i.e. shared understanding of the rules, does not necessarily happen because it is the right thing to do, for the good of the game, etc. It might be that the main motivation is that being in line with the referee's understanding of rule implementation gives the various sport practitioners a better chance of fulfilling the internal or intrinsic aim of football or similar sports, i.e. winning football matches or other sport competitions. A certain adherence to the sport's rules and their interpretation is also needed in order to fulfil the prelusory goal of having a game to play. For example, something as simple as both teams lining up in the manner prescribed by the game's rules is a prerequisite for getting the match started. Furthermore, enough continuous and sustained adherences to the rule interpretation of the chosen arbiter of the rules of the game are probably needed for the activity to remain a sport of a specific kind and not change or deteriorate into something else. This does not mean that two teams in a more loosely organized match could not conspire to ignore the rulings of an appointed referee, but that would probably mean that one needs somewhat stricter adherence to the rules of the game, as such a match would in effect be self-refereed. If a game is refereed, then given the lusory goal of winning, players will do well to coordinate their game behaviour with the prevailing ethos of the game, i.e. rule interpretation. If the game is self-refereed, then the players face a more demanding task. In the latter case, there will not only be a question of coordinating their game behaviour and game ethos with an eye to winning the match, but also coordinating and correlating that with their own role as arbiters of the rules of the game, while reaching and maintaining a workable consensus on rule interpretation with the other players *qua* co-referees.

A shared ethos, i.e. rule interpretation, should not be thought of as something akin to conventions as understood by Lewis, where there is supposed to be a high degree of conformity with the conventions, which are seen as solutions to pure coordination problems (Lewis 1969, 1975). Rather, we should look at the shared ethos as a congruence of rule interpretation that is great enough to be workable, i.e. the game gets started, is maintained and does not break down. This operational understanding of how much overlap in rule interpretation is needed for a shared ethos to enable and maintain the game has the advantage of being appropriately context sensitive. Consider again the Iranian team's experience in the 1978 World Cup. This was Iran's first appearance in a World Cup. Obviously, they were not going to walk out of such a prestigious tournament, even when they suffered from not being able to change the way they tackled in accordance with the dominant ethos of the tournament. The Iranians soldiered on in a manner that they would perhaps not have done had the clash between football cultures, with their different or differing rule interpretations, taken place in a park game. The question concerning the status of a match comes into play when we think about what overlap of rule interpretation is practicable for a football match to proceed as a football match. Various other sociological factors might also influence what is needed in terms of shared ethos for a sport competition to be maintained. I will not labour through them here. It is important to understand that coordination between the players' game behaviour and the rule interpretation on display by a referee is not (to stick with the game theoretical terminology) a problem of pure coordination. As a matter of fact, many or most players, at least at certain higher levels of football, will consciously seek to overstep the boundaries of the ethos of the game in order to gain a game advantage. One does not only want a game of football to be in place, one also wants to win the game. These rule and ethos violations are balanced with the knowledge of possible reactions from the referee should he or she spot the violation in question and of further possible reactions from the relevant football authorities. Still, players seek advantages over and above playing within the confines of a shared ethos, i.e., shared rule interpretation and understanding of acceptable and unacceptable behaviour. The matrix of player behaviour on the pitch and the rules and their interpretation do not necessarily reach any kind of equilibrium. Instead, one finds a constant push and pull between the players' game behaviour and interpretation of the rules. This instability might be part of the attraction of the game, and it points to a salient feature of the social historical sport kind of football.

On the one hand, football is a cooperative effort. People get together to do an unnecessary activity that in most cases serves no other direct purpose than having a football match of some kind to play. On the other, one cooperates to set up a conflict situation – win, lose or draw – and given our competitive nature, which is brought out even more starkly when identity, prestige, etc. are invested in the proceedings, the commitment to having a game is supplemented with, and sometimes gives way to, the commitment to win the game. Setting up the football frame is a cooperative enterprise, while the content of that frame or practice is to have a conflict, i.e., an uncooperative enterprise. Prelusorily, we cooperate to have a match: lusorily, we aim at defeating each other. Much of the dynamics in the game and game development are found in the interplay between these juxtapositions. The cooperative nature of football finds its way into the game through the various efforts made at different levels of the game to ensure that referees react to players' behaviour in a uniform and predictable manner, i.e., using a shared ethos or rule interpretation. The uncooperative nature of the game is the fact that the football match is an artificial conflict, which furthermore might or might not be enacted in a cooperative manner. In the latter case, the uncooperative character of football finds its way into the game through the various efforts made by players, at least at the upper levels of the game, to seek game advantages by bending, breaking or violating the game's various rules and ethos requirements, when trying to win the match.[15]

The *A Fistful of Fouls* case serves as a good entry point for exploring the dynamics between the game's cooperative nature and its, at times, uncooperative character. At its upper levels, football is a niggling game in which players seek to understand the ethos of the game only to try to stay on its edges and go slightly beyond them, the aim being to gain game advantages over the opposition. In the game's modern era, grabbing hold of the shirt of an opposition player who has possession of the ball and dragging him or her down almost always draws a foul. However, because part of the game's attraction is that it has a certain flow and is not perpetually punctuated by referees calling fouls and stopping the game, at some point footballers discovered that a little shirt tugging here and there would not be called out by referees. When the shirt tugging avant-garde gained a game advantage, the rest of the players followed suit. This was not due to any distain for the rules of football, but because the prelusory goal of having a match to play and the lusory goal of aiming at winning the match, while accepting the referees' rulings on the rules and actions of the game, allow or provide for such behaviour. Then throw into the mix that in football the rules tend to be practised differently for fouls outside and inside the penalty box, owing to the widespread understanding that awarding a penalty to a team more often than not results in a goal, thus greatly affecting the outcome of matches. The refereeing practice is to place the bar higher for rule violations inside the penalty box. So football ended up in a situation so aptly described by Wilson and Murphy. That summer after the European championship, the English FA decided that the rule of no shirt tugging should be applied more strictly. Sky Sports' Peter Smith offered the following report on the opening weeks of the 2016–2017 Premier League campaign in England.

> Referees have been in the headlines in the opening weeks of the Premier League season after enforcing – and then failing to consistently enforce – laws around grappling in the penalty area. Following a pre-season directive to referees to get tough on shirt-pulling and blocking in the penalty box at corners and free-kicks, Stoke City's Ryan Shawcross and Manchester City's Raheem Sterling were both penalised in the same game in the second round of fixtures, while Bournemouth's Charlie Daniels was punished on Saturday for a challenge on Crystal Palace's Christian Benteke. However, also this weekend, Tottenham's Jan Vertonghen escaped with a warning when he hauled down Liverpool's Joel Matip, while Swansea City's Federico Fernandez and Leicester City's Daniel Amartey also escaped punishment for similar offences.
>
> *(Smith 2016)*

And as the season proceeded, it was clear that there was overall less pulling of shirts in the box at set pieces, but also that the players had sized up the new rule interpretation of which they had been informed, only to push back on the new line by making their rule violations less conspicuous, less obvious and harder to crack down on. Footballers at this level have a tendency to manoeuvre on and over the edges of the sport ethos, i.e. rule interpretation, both when entering the game with a preconception of a shared ethos (on the background of rule interpretation congruence that justifies such a preconception) and when observing in specific matches how individual referees manifest their conception of the shared ethos. Should a type of trespassing of a rule like holding the opponents' shirts or blocking them at set pieces be deemed out of hand, football's ruling bodies can and do come together to give direction to their game officials to crack down on the unwanted behaviour by modifying their implementation of the rules of the game. In turn, those modifications will be subjected to the same sort of manoeuvring and exploitation on the part of the players. There is no reason to believe that any kind of equilibrium will be achieved with regard to handling shirt pulling and blocking in the penalty box at corners and free kicks, while allowing the duels between players in the box at set pieces to have a certain physicality and maintaining the overall flow of the game. All this is to be expected and is a natural consequence of a sport like football, which at this level is played in an uncooperative manner.

If we look at football's key constitutive rule of not handling the ball, we find the very same dynamics showing up. The handball rule in football tells players that they are not allowed to handle the ball, while it is in play. When learning to play the game, this rule, if any, is key to becoming a practitioner of the sport. The way the rule is interpreted is telling as regards the game's potential for being played uncooperatively and provides us with further evidence for why we should stick to a fairly minimal requirement for the lusory attitude of practitioners of the game. The handball rule, as it is practised in football, is an eternal source of confused delight and frustration in footballing circles. In light of how much debate interpretation of the rule engenders, the rule itself is infuriatingly simple and clear. Here is what we find under *Law 12 – Fouls and Misconduct*:

> A direct free kick is also awarded to the opposing team if a player commits any of the following three offences (...) handles the ball deliberately (except for the goalkeeper within his own penalty area).
>
> *(FIFA 2015: 37)*

This is not the way it is practised. Commenting on this law with regard to yet another controversial handball penalty decision, Premier League referee David Elleray told the BBC that "[r]eferees look at two specifics – did the hand or arm go towards the ball or in a manner which would block the ball, or is the hand in a position where it would not normally be" (Bakowski 2016). But why not stick to the deliberate handball, which I assumed is covered by the phrase of "did the hand or arm go towards the ball or in a manner which would block the ball" – this being an epistemic device for deciding when we have deliberation? Or else, why not go with an interpretation of the no-handling-of-the-ball rule in football, which simply states that whenever a hand or arm touches the ball it counts as a handball foul? The latter would make the task much easier for referees around the globe.

Practitioners of the sport of football, I am certain, have a good grasp of what the handball rule is suppose to achieve in our game. Football is supposed to be a sport played with your feet, where hands and arms are given no active role, with the obvious exception of the goalkeeper. Had footballers in general been prone to be cooperative – playing the game in the spirit of the handball rule as they understood it – then certainly either making it a requirement to not intentionally touch the ball or just not touch the ball could have served equally well as a way of implementing a handball rule in football. However, footballers are not like that. It is easy to predict that if the deliberate handball rule were practised as close to the letter as possible, then defenders would at some point or another discover that approaching tackles and blocks with arms flapping and waving could give them a game advantage. They would be speculating that a disorderly style of play might be seen as non-deliberate. After all, allowing oneself to be hit by the ball is not quite the same as handling the ball deliberately, and spreading oneself out as much as possible when defending certainly gives a game advantage. Swinging the pendulum to the other side and instead applying a handball rule interpretation that only takes into account whether the ball touches the arm or hand would probably fare no better. If such a practice were put in place, I predict we would quickly find attacking players speculating in trying to hit defenders' arms and hands with the ball in the penalty box, when that seemed like a more likely way to earn a penalty and score than doing so through open play. This trick has already been performed with great success, for example, when Italy's Roberto Baggio aimed at and hit Chilean defender Ronaldo Fuentes's hand at close range to earn Italy a penalty; Baggio scored and salvaged a draw for Italy in their opening match in the 1998 World Cup in France. One reason why the practice of calling the handball foul is interpreted fairly openly – deliberate when the arms and hands are moved towards the ball, or when the hands and arms are in an unnatural position – is that, given the uncooperative manner in which the game is played, the other alternatives would most likely have game consequences that are deemed undesirable.[16] Again, we find that the less substantial reading or formulation of the lusory attitude requirement argued for in this chapter fits the bill of how the game is actually played.

Football and physical skills

Clauses 5 and 6 in Suits's analysis of sport distinguish sports from games of chance, such as lottery, roulette, and so on, and mere games, such as chess. Football fulfils both requirements of being an activity of *physical skill*. The requirement of skills being involved for an activity or practice to count as a sport is uncontroversial. However, we might elaborate on why skills pave the way for engagement, and one way to do that is to contrast the skill requirement with certain animal sports and games of chance. In Chapter 1, we noted that, according to Geertz, money is what turns cockfights into deep play. With the addition of money, Geertz noted, something important and with real ramifications for the players is at stake. The same applies to games of chance. Sports and games, I submit, generally need to reflect back on the players if they are to engender engagement. There are two ways in which sports and games can do that. Either the game or sport has ordinary world consequences for the players, or the game or sport performances and outcomes are considered connected to abilities and skills that are held in some degree of esteem. The six-numbers game of Lotto without prizes hardly makes sense, Russian roulette with no bullets in the chamber is not much fun, and so on and so forth, in the more or less obvious manner for other games of chance. The abilities needed to play games of chance are not held in high enough esteem to be engaging for humans, making it a requirement for human engagement to have other mechanisms that connect the players to the game. When players make something of ordinary world importance depend of the result of a game of chance, that connection is secured. With regard to animal sports like cockfighting and dog racing, I suggest that human involvement is perhaps not substantial enough for these activities or practices per se to engage us, thus the general tendency towards betting and prizes being key elements in making them matter to us.[17] Looking at animal sports where the human element is central to sport performance, like dog and horse agility, show jumping, dressage and others, the human factor in the success or failure of sport performances is significant enough for these activities to catch the imagination of people without the aid of, for example, betting. Obviously, betting can be part of an animal sport, i.e. the culture of the sport, even if human abilities and skills are crucial. The argument here is not that sports that reflect back on the abilities and skills of the participants cannot attract betting – football is a big betting business – but that humans find such sports interesting and engaging in their own right. In games of chance, you invest money and the outcome reflects back on you either by making you richer or poorer. In non-chance games and sports, you invest effort and the outcome reflects back on your abilities and skills. In competitive activities like sport, this reflection will also include a ranking of your displayed abilities and skills in comparison to those of the other competitors. This does not exclude chance playing a role in sports. In the next chapter, I will argue that due to the mechanics of football, i.e. the way the sport is designed, chance plays a greater role in football than in similar sports and that this is part of the game's attraction. However, activities or practices that are wholly determined by chance, like roulette and lotteries, are not sports. There are no skills involved in these activities or practices, and the results of games of chance do not, in this respect, reflect back on the players. Moreover, even in lower leagues, skills play a big enough role for football to meet the requirement unproblematically. With regard to the ratio between skills and chance, there might be intermediate cases where it is not clear whether or not an activity should count as a sport. Concerning such intermediate cases, there need not be any fact of the matter regarding the chanciness involved in an activity or practice for deciding whether or not it counts as a sport. This is to be expected. Sports are social, not natural kinds. In football, physical skills are centrally involved in the sport, rendering it in this respect a typical or paradigmatic sport.

Clause 6, on the other hand, is more controversial. It, for example, rules out chess as a sport. However, among philosophers of sport, Suits's Clause 6 has been well received. Klaus Meier considers "the demonstration of physical skill to be a necessary component of all sports" (Meier 1989: 16). McNamee tells us that sports are activities "involving, centrally, physical skills" (McNamee 2008: 19). According to McFee, "Suits's account seems correct in recognizing sport's *physical* requirement" (McFee 2004: 19). Morgan muses that sports share the "delight in gratuitous difficulties with games, differing perhaps only in the physical sorts of challenges it poses" (Morgan 1994: 211). More recently, Andrew Edgar considers "sport as a test of physical skill", and Jesús Ilundáin-Agurruza tells us that, in sports, "movement plays a key role to how they accomplish their ends (Edgar 2013: 3, Ilundáin-Agurruza 2014: 230). Looking to more sociologically minded writers, we also find the idea of sports being physical. McPherson and collaborators call sport "a structured, goal-oriented, competitive, contest-based, ludic physical activity" (McPherson et al. 1989: 15). Furthermore, Jean-Marie Brohm thinks of sport as follows:

> [S]port is an institutionalised system of competitive, delimited, codified and conventionally governed physical practices which have the avowed aim of selecting the best competitor.
>
> *(Brohm 1978: 68–69)*

These are only a select few formulations of endorsement of Suits's Clause 6, but they indicate how well ingrained in the literature the idea of the physicality of sport is:

- The demonstration of physical skill
- Involving, centrally, physical skills
- Physical requirement
- The physical sorts of challenges it poses
- A test of physical skill
- Movement plays a key role
- Ludic physical activity
- Physical practices

How then are we to understand the physical in physical activity? There is an argument to be made that the physicality of football – that bodies move in time and space – is essential to football and other sports, but not to games like chess (see Tamboer 1992 for another way to address this problem).

Consider the thought experiment of *Mind Games*:

> Mind Games: Consider a competitive game of some sort where the physical manifestations of the game, whether they be the game player's movements of his or her body or the tools of the game, are inessential or accidental to the game itself. We can imagine such a game being played by two clairvoyants without moving their bodies or having physical game tools. We can call such games mind games.

Let us apply this thought experiment to various practices. Consider chess. We can envisage two clairvoyants playing chess with each other. They would not need to move either their bodies or the physical chess pieces. Still, they would be playing chess. Mind chess is recognizable *as* chess. Contrast this with activities typically thought of as sports. Try to imagine similar mind versions of these activities. Do the exercise for activities like the 100-metre dash, ice hockey, archery, football and so on and so forth. You will find that it hardly makes sense to think of mind versions of these competitive activities, and even if it did, they would be different than the original activities. Mind archery is not archery, mind ice hockey is not ice hockey, the mind 100-metre dash is not the 100-metre dash, and *mind football is not football*. Imagine two teams of 22 clairvoyants who undertake to play mind football. The first thing to note is that there is a question of whether mind football would even be possible, as there would be no physical limitations to constrain the mind actions on the mind pitch. Be that as it may. Now ask the following questions: How can we decide who wins the header, the tackle, and so on, in mind football? And even if it were possible, which I doubt it would be, unlike chess where there is no principled difference between actions in the mind and physical movement of bodies and chess pieces, mind football simply is not football. Mind kicking a mind football is different from kicking a football. Mind football is something different in kind, if at all possible, given football's nature as a constructive-destructive sport where how well you do is in part determined by how well your opponent does. The skills of football are essentially physical. The thought experiment gives us a method for delineating sports, which are essentially physical, from games like chess, where the physicality of the game is inessential.

Football and wide following with a wide level of stability

Suits's last two requirements for something to be a sport are fulfilled by football, in that football clearly enjoys *a wide following with a wide level of stability*. However, even though "Suits makes it clear that what he is ruling out are mere fads", there is nothing "logically improper about imagining a sport that does not persist substantially over time" (McNamee 2008: 15). Philosophically speaking, Clauses 7 and 8, the final clauses, are ill-conceived. The notion that football has a wide following with a wide level of stability is a historically, psychologically and sociologically significant fact, but it is philosophically irrelevant for understanding what a sport is and why football is one of these sports. Why could not a sport be a mere fad? There is nothing conceptually impossible about that, and there is nothing odd or queer about judging a sport to be a mere fad and nevertheless recognizing it as a sport. As argued, one can easily invent a sport, but whether it will catch on is an entirely different question. In fact, failed sports – sports that came, were played, but did not conquer the world or any significant part of it for any substantial period of time – are also historically, psychologically and sociologically interesting. They too open a window into human engagement in sport and the human condition. Why did they fail to gain a wide following, or if they did have a wide following, why did they fail to subsequently achieve a wide level of stability? In this respect, mere sport fads can also be made subject to philosophical considerations.

Refereeing and match minding and maintenance

The key element of the lusory state required for playing football and similar sports was to endure, obey or accept arbitration of the rules of the game, and the lusory attitude required aligning oneself with the internal or intrinsic aim, goal or purpose of the sport. This places arbitration of the rules of the game at the centre when considering what it is to be a football participant or practitioner. This should come as no surprise given our endorsement of foundational formalism. Footballers play the game, while a referee or referees tend to rule arbitration. If a match is self-refereed, then that changes the dynamic of how players can act on the pitch. This is not because it changes the lusory state or attitude needed for playing the game, but it is due to the role of co-referee that self-refereeing bestows upon each player. Furthermore, referees do not merely apply the rules of the game, they also interpret them. This interpretation view of refereeing is an ethos view of sport, albeit a minimal one. Sports like football can in principle be played without any other sort of shared ethos, but in practice – due to the internal or intrinsic aim, goal or purpose of the sport – we find a convergence of rule interpretation. Insofar as philosophers of sport pay attention to the role of the referee, it is typically the role of either applier or interpreter of the rules that is dealt with. From a conceptual or metaphysical point of view, that is perfectly fine. But if one is also interested in understanding the human game of football, then the picture is incomplete. What is lacking is the understanding that football referees are not only interpreters of the rules of the game, but also minders and maintainers of match development and game character.

One observation we enlisted when rejecting the mechanical view of refereeing was that referees do not always call a foul when they see shirt tugging, even if the rules prescribe it. Barring playing the advantage, there is no reasonable interpretation of the rule of awarding a direct free kick when a player holds an opponent that would justify referees sometimes deliberately ignoring episodes of players holding opponents. Still, this is what you find in football. Something else must be going on. Taking a leaf out of D'Agostino's work on sport ethos and applying it to football, one reason for this is that we expect and want a certain flow to football games, and referees are part of the equation for achieving flow by refraining from stopping the game to call every foul, even when there is no advantage for the team being fouled. Of course, football has a rule for playing the advantage, which is partly founded on considerations of not rewarding fouling, when it can be avoided (*FIFA Laws of the Game 2016–17. Law 05: The Referee. 3. Powers and Duties*). However, playing the advantage also makes for a better game to watch. If the referee knows when to ignore certain rule-breaking incidents and not break up the game for officiating reasons, when chances can be created and goals can be scored, then all the better for the game's watchability. Similarly, minor rule infringements are quite frequently ignored with a view to making the game more appealing. This is old news for anyone familiar with football. However, it is important to understand that this role of the referee goes beyond merely interpreting the rules of the game. It is a role of *minding or managing the game* according to how we want the game to be enacted, i.e. our aesthetic expectations and likings. In the next chapter, I will elaborate on the aesthetics of football and what I call its *agon aesthetics*. One of the features I will focus on is the action-reaction patterns of play in football and the dramas they create. A good referee, who minds or handles the game well, plays an important role in making such action-reaction patterns of play possible. Nothing in the rules of football, or the idea that all rules must be interpreted, necessitates that this is how the game will be officiated. It could have been different. This part of the referees' unofficial or unspecified job description of aiding and abetting a certain flow of play in football matches is something different, or something more, than just interpreting the rules in a match situation. In the philosophy of sport, this aspect of football refereeing and its connection to the aesthetics of the sport have not received much attention.[18]

Furthermore, having a good game of football with the desired flow of action-reaction patterns might also require a certain level of *game character maintenance*. In Chapter 1, I argued that football is fictional in character in the sense that it involves the proto-pretence of social play, with the basis for our engagement in the game including activation of the alief state of "physical struggle/fight! D-a-n-g-er ...! Activate flight or flight adrenaline now". As we can safely assume that tackles and other physical challenges in football result in many of the same psychological reactions and inclinations they would trigger in non-sporting circumstances – remember that unlike beliefs, aliefs are more primitive and reality insensitive – there is always a danger that the football conflict will spill over into a real conflict. As the tackles fly in the heat of the match, tempers might flare and fighting break out. The physicality of a constructive-destructive contact sport like football imparts a higher intensity to the staged artificial conflict of football, but also the danger of real conflict. The latter point is made vivid if we compare football with sports like volleyball, archery, ski jumping, etc., where there is no physical contact or challenges, and where fisticuffs seldom erupt or threaten to erupt as a result of playing the sport. When discussing nonhuman social play like tug of war, rough-and-tumble play, play fighting, etc., we found that, at times, part of the play behaviour of nonhuman animals includes play maintenance. Nonhuman animals have play signals in their behavioural repertoire, by which they can defuse ambiguous situations and make sure they remain in play. If football is fictional in character and involves proto-pretence, then we might expect to find something similar in football – and we do. In particular, we find that referees function not only as interpreters of the rules of the game and minders of the game, they also, at times, perform the task of maintaining the game's fictional character, i.e. ensuring that it does not spill over into a real conflict.

Consider the case of the *Strategic Yellow Card*.

> The Strategic Yellow Card: A yellow card in football is a caution, where the next step is a red card and a sending off. There are various cautionable offences in football, but one is of particular interest to us: "Persistent infringement of the Laws of the Game" (*FIFA Laws of the Game 2016–17, Law 12 Fouls and Misconduct*, FIFA 2016: 85). What this means is that a foul, which in isolation would perhaps not merit a yellow card, can still draw one if the player in question is a serial offender. In such a situation, the player receiving the card is in effect told to calm down his or her game, or risk being sent off. However, the football rule book gives no indication that referees also occasionally give a

yellow card because, in the match over a certain period of time, there have been persistent infringements of the Laws of the Game, even if the particular player receiving the yellow card is a first-time offender. In such a situation, the whole set of players on the pitch are warned to calm down their game. This sort of yellow card is a strategic device referees use to control and maintain the character of the game within the limits of the fictionality of football.

When we talk about referees losing control of a match, it is precisely the task of game character maintenance we think that the referee in question failed to perform. Maintenance of game character depends on referees' judgement of game development. How referees maintain game character has probably changed over time. For example, it is my impression that if we went back 30 or 40 years in time, we would more often than today find referees issuing a yellow card early in the match to assert their authority over the game. I suspect that today – due to lower tolerance for rough play and referees' other task of contributing to a good game, i.e. minding the game for aesthetic reasons, which in part might be seen as avoiding unnecessary sending offs – early *yellow card of authority signalling* is rarer.[19] Still, the latter case, insofar as such cases occur or occurred, counts as a case of game character maintenance.

There are further examples of refereeing that only make sense if they are considered to involve game character maintenance. Consider the following case.

> Hardman's Referee: The phenomenon of corner flagging is when a player decides to take the ball towards one of the opposition's corner flags in order to protect the ball and run down the clock. Philosopher Alun Hardman reports that a top-level referee told him that in corner-flagging situations, the referee would generally, when the situation demanded a decision from him, award the ball (throw-in, goal kick or free kick) to the defending team.[20]

If the task of football referees were merely to interpret the rules to the best of their knowledge, then Hardman's report would be quite astonishing. However, if we think of *Hardman's Referee* as a case of game character maintenance, then the pieces fall into place.

Corner flagging most often occurs at the tail end of matches when the corner-flagging team has a slim-margin result they wish to preserve, while the other team is desperately looking to change the outcome. The player from the time-wasting team will try to protect and keep the ball, or attempt to get a throw-in, a corner or a free kick, and if he or she gets the latter, then he or she can embark on the same routine once more. This, understandably, tends to frustrate the opposing team, which at that point in the match needs to score a goal, allowing them to salvage a point or three, get extra time, the score line they need, and so on and so forth. Corner flagging creates a volatile situation in which temper flair-ups are not infrequent. The match is in danger of spilling over. The rationale behind *Hardman's Referee* must surely be that, at such a junction in the match development, game character maintenance trumps rules and rule interpretation. There is, of course, the possibility that Hardman's informant's practice is entirely idiosyncratic, but an episode that took place in a Premier League match between Liverpool and Chelsea in February 2009 at Anfield shows that this is not the case. As that match entered stoppage time, Liverpool, who led the match 1–0, took a short corner, upon which Liverpool's Yossi Benayoun went corner flagging. While Chelsea's Didier Drogba was trying to take the ball off Benayoun, José Bosingwa came to Drogba's aid, stamped on Benayoun's lower back and literally kicked him off the pitch. According to the rules of the game, it should have been a free kick to Liverpool and a sending off for Boswinga. Assistant referee Mo Matadar, who was right next to the situation, waved his flag frantically to signal an infringement of the laws of the game, but referee Mike Riley instead decided to award the ball to Chelsea, while telling the Liverpool players to calm down. There is no way a seasoned referee like Riley could have failed to register the blatant foul on Benayoun, or at least Matadar's signalling for a foul, but he decided not to act on it. The only way to make sense of Riley's decision is to think of him as one of Hardman's referees, who was looking to break up the volatile corner-flagging situation instead of implementing the rules of the game. The role of game character maintenance, in this case, took precedence over other concerns like interpreting the rules of the game.

You need not look far for other examples from the footballing world that show a clear understanding of the referee's role as more than that of mere arbiter and interpreter of the rules of the game, where one of those additional roles is maintaining the game's character. Consider Ian McCourt's match report from an Arsenal vs. Tottenham derby in 2013:

> A derby of any kind is always difficult to officiate. *The blood boils*, the crowds cry and it is rare that one will pass without a controversial incident. However, Mark Clattenburg's refereeing of the north London love-in managed to do just that on Sunday. He was consistently in the right place and he consistently made *the right decisions, keeping all around him in check*. His handling of the early card for Emmanuel Adebayor is the perfect example. (…) Adebayor could have walked and could have had few complaints if he had. Instead Clattenburg *sized up the situation* and just booked him, *successfully defusing a potentially tricky situation*. It was an excellent and eminently *sensible example of officiating*.
>
> (McCourt 2013, my italics)

In short, McCourt is describing how well Clattenburg maintained the game character of this derby, when it so easily could have got out of control. The match is described as a high-pressure match for the referee ("the blood boils"), one in which play might easily spill over into real fighting. So even though the rules of the game might have predicated Tottenham's Adebayor being sent off ("could have had few complaints if he had"), the referee considered the match development in a broader context than mere rule interpretation ("sized up the situation") and chose a venue of action that also took into account his role as maintainer of the game's character ("successfully defusing a potentially tricky situation"). Clattenburg did well balancing the various tasks of a referee – interpreting the rules, minding the game development and maintaining game character – that day at White Hart Lane ("excellent and eminently sensible example of officiating"). These referee roles obviously overlap, but it is important to acknowledge their distinctness. Doing so helps us deepen our understanding of the sport of football and ties our exposition of the nature and analysis of the game in with its character, as laid out in Chapter 1, as well as its aesthetics (match minding being an aesthetic concern with the watchability of the game), which will be our topic in the upcoming chapter.

Objections and replies

Objection: The approach taken in this chapter prides itself in having bypassed or solved the incompatibility problem – how to account for a rule violation in a sport when the perpetrator, by that very act, rules him- or herself out as a participant or practitioner of that sport – but something is lost. The author no longer has any theoretical tools with which to deem something a non-sport action, if that action was done while playing a sport. Commenting on the views of D'Agostino 1981 and Morgan 1987, McFee makes the following observation.

> [B]oth might agree on the reprehensible character of such-and-such behaviour (say, shooting a member of the opposing team) (...) such that it *cannot* be part of the game.
>
> (McFee 2004: 69)

The line argued for in this chapter cannot explain or even admit that, by shooting a member of the opposing team, the shooter stopped playing football. That just seems wrong. It is back to the drawing board for the author. Clearly, there is something right about having some kind of incompatibility thesis of playing a sport and certain kinds of actions.

Reply: No, there is nothing correct about any of the incompatibility lines of argument on offer. The reason why there is an intuitive pull towards an incompatibility thesis when considering McFee's example is because the question of whether someone is a sport participant or practitioner is offered one-dimensionally as an either-or question. The question of whether someone is a sport participant or practitioner when undertaking a certain action without further specification is ill-formed. To bring some clarity to this, let us consider an actual and well-known incident of assault and grievous bodily harm perpetrated on a football pitch by a footballer. Here is how the perpetrator himself described the attack that occurred during a Premier League match between Manchester United and Manchester City at Old Trafford on April 21, 2001:

> Few days passed when I didn't think about Alfie Haaland (...) I hadn't forgotten Alfie. Bryan Robson told me to take my time. You'll get your chance,

> Roy. Wait (…) I'd waited almost 180 minutes for Alfie, three years if you looked at it another way. Now he had the ball on the far touchline. Alfie was taking the piss. I'd waited long enough. I fucking hit him hard. The ball was there (I think). Take that, you cunt.
>
> *(Keane with Dunphy 2002: 175, 231)*

Manchester United player Roy Keane in effect ended Manchester City's Alf-Inge Håland's playing career that day and was initially given a three-match ban for his trouble (with an additional match for picking up his second red card of the season). Legal scholar Mark James assesses the gravity of the assault as follows:

> Roy Keane will almost undoubtedly not be prosecuted for his challenge. However, if he had committed such a challenge in a parks game, he would probably be looking at a term of imprisonment of about six months.
>
> *(James 2002: 90)*

Was Keane still playing football when he attacked Håland? Considered along the lines of whether the football form was in usage that evening, Keane was most certainly participating in a football match. According to that parameter, Keane was participating in a football match and, by courtesy of that, whatever he did during the match was something done by a footballer playing a football match. Did Keane fulfil the lusory state requirement for playing football? Did he endure, obey or accept the arbitration of the rules of football by which the football form was implemented? Absolutely. As Keane informs us, "I didn't wait for Mr Elleray to show the card. I turned and walked to the dressing room" (Keane with Dunphy 2002: 231). Referee David Elleray does not appear shocked by the tackle and, in his autobiography, he is more concerned with the fact that he got the decision right.

> It is among the worse three or four tackles certainly, but more crucially for me it was a moment where I was tested to the full (…) felt that I had my career precariously balanced in the palm of my hand.
>
> *(Elleray 2004: 243)*

In fact, the only thing Elleray takes exception to is that "Keane confuses the sequence of events", since according to Elleray, Keane did see the red card before he walked off (Elleray 2004: 241).

On the other hand, one might argue that Keane, when taking on Håland, violated the sincerity condition of playing football – play to win, minimally not to lose – because, even by his own description, it looks as though he was meting out personal revenge and settling an old score, thus not trying to win the game or minimally not to lose. What jars us is not that Keane deliberately committed a foul, but that the foul seemed unnecessary, even contrary to the internal or intrinsic aim, goal or purpose of football. If this is the correct interpretation, then Keane abused the football form in order to assault Håland. Keane made as if to play football to settle an old score, or he barefaced made as if to play football, while meting out revenge. That, however, does not cast doubt on his status as a footballer or the tackle as a footballing action, because clearly the match in which it took place was a case of usage of the football form. In the theory argued for in this chapter, we can explain what is amiss in the Keane-Håland incident without resorting to endorsing the either-or picture of the various incompatibility views. If we up the ante and instead consider the footballer who shoots a member of the opposing team and the same explanation is readily available to you. This is because tackling as revenge and shooting a member of the opposing team are on a continuum and the difference between them is one of degree. Both actions will rightfully result in a sending off. What is not a difference of degree are the effects such actions most likely would have on the game after the incidences. After tackles like Keane's tackle on Håland, play resumes and the match continues. However, it is hard to imagine that, in football as it is played today and has been played earlier, play would resume after a player pulled a gun on an opponent and shot him or her. Such an action would be what I have previously called "a game- or sport-destroying event or action" (Borge 2010b: 169). On the other hand, it is not difficult to imagine a case in which, after a shooting incident on the pitch, players would dust themselves down, carry the casualty or casualties off the pitch and continue to play the game in the same way as the Manchester United and Manchester City players continued their match after Keane had been sent off. Logic or sport logic does not block or prevent that possibility. The manner in which we today and previously have played the game, i.e. the character of the sport, predicts that an incident of a player shooting a member of the opposing team on the pitch would end our willingness to continue to play and watch the football match. This explains why one might have the urge to think that Keane's tackle and the shooting of the opponent are two different things with regard to the question of whether someone is still playing football and why any such temptation to endorse some sort of incompatibility thesis should be resisted. Football is fictional in character, and that provides us with the theoretical resources needed to deal with the example McFee offers. I will elaborate on this phenomenon of aesthetic engagement resistance in the next chapter. For now, suffice it to say that McFee's example falls neatly in line with the general take on football presented here.

Consider another infamous episode from the football pitch, which pre-theoretically might come across as one where the footballer in question has stopped playing football and instead is engaging in something different.

> The Curious Incident of Mwepu Ilunga Kicking the Ball Away: In a 1974 last group stage World Cup match between Brazil and Zaire, the Brazilians, who were 3–0 up with only five minutes remaining of the match, had been awarded a free kick. As the Brazilians prepared and the Zairians were organizing the wall, suddenly Zairian player Mwepu Ilunga broke away from the wall, sprinted towards where the free kick was to be taken and kicked the football

away. A puzzled footballing world was taken aback, wondering what on earth Ilunga was up to.

If your intuition tells you that Ilunga lost the plot when he launched the ball upfield in what has later often been depicted as a bit of a comedy act, you would do well to note that it is not because he broke a rule, but because his rule violation seems purposeless. This is telling. The football world does not ridicule good old-fashioned professional fouls, like an Ole Gunnar Solskjær hunting down Newcastle United's Rob Lee in a Manchester United Premier League home game on April 18, 1998, only to viciously hack him down from behind to the applause of the Old Trafford faithful. Solskjær's rule violation served a purpose and kept Manchester United in contention for the title, even though they would eventually lose out to Arsenal by one point. Solskjær took one for the team, got sent off and the home crowd recognized that. It is the seeming senselessness of Ilunga's professional foul that has earned the move its claim to fame and which would account for any inclination to dismiss Ilunga as no longer playing football when he hoofed the ball away.

Unfortunately, there was in fact nothing funny about the *Curious Incident of Mwepu Ilunga Kicking the Ball Away*. The Zaire team had lost 2–0 to Scotland, were then humiliated in a 9–0 hiding by Yugoslavia and were out of the tournament before their last match. In the last game Brazil beckoned. Ian Hawkey reports.

> Could the World Cup turn any more humiliating? For one man, it could. (...) Ilunga (...) whacking the dead ball as a bemused Jairzinho and Roberto Rivelino prepared to address it. He had broken the rules embarrassingly. (...) He collected a caution. But, he felt and would later explain, he had wasted some valuable seconds. Why? Because it had been made clear, from the very, very top, to the players that a greater margin than three goals would be deemed unacceptable back home.
>
> (Hawkey 2010: 85–86)

Of course, the very, very top in this case meant military dictator and president Mobutu Sese Seko, as "Zairian football (...) was in the grip of the iron fist of General Mobutu" (Dietschy 2012: 222). Ilunga recalls that the team was given a message from Mobutu: "[t]he great leader says that if you concede more than three goals against Brazil in the final match, you will never see Zaire or your families again" (Spurling 2010: 28). The man breaking off from Zaire's defensive wall heading towards the ball was a man in fear for his own and his family's lives and futures back in Zaire – a man who wanted the match to end at a mere 3–0 defeat for the Zairian team against Brazil.

The line of reasoning taken in this book has the theoretical resources to make sense of both Solskjær running the lion's share of the pitch cutting down his opponent before he can score and Ilunga merely kicking the ball away. Furthermore, we can understand the difference between the two incidents while still regarding both players as playing football, when they did what they did. The Solskjær incident, of course, needs no further elaboration, because we have already explained how to deal with fouls in football. An ethos view theorist can incorporate the Solskjær incident into his or her theory, but would have to deem Ilunga a non-player when he kicked the ball away. Still, it was Solskjær who was given his marching orders, while Ilunga was only cautioned and remained on the pitch for the rest of the match. How then can we understand the *Curious Incident of Mwepu Ilunga Kicking the Ball Away*? First, let us remind ourselves that giving the ball a little nudge, or perhaps more than just a nudge, when play has stopped is a well-known time-wasting tactic in football. Doing it the way Ilunga did, however, was unheard of and has not been repeated at a senior level of any stature, as far as I know. It is not to be expected in football matches and certainly not part of the game's ethos. What then is amiss with what Ilunga did? To the audience watching this match, Ilunga's professional foul seems to have no functionality within the sport contest context, leaving one with the impression that something else is going on. Ilunga does not seem to heed football's internal or intrinsic aim, goal or purpose of winning the match, minimally not losing or, in this case, not conceding more goals. Ilunga, according to Hawkey, saw it as a time-wasting action to keep the score down for reasons already made apparent. In Ilunga's own words, "I thought I could waste some time if I kicked the ball away before the referee instructed Brazil to take the kick. So I kicked it away" (Spurling 2010: 29). This then would fall neatly in line with similar footballing actions. Unorthodox in the manner it was done, but not as such unique. However, we might doubt Ilunga's own explanation of his action.

The manner in which this alleged time wasting was done suggests that, in the quote above, Ilunga has touched up the incident by making it look like just another time-wasting footballing action. Doing what Ilunga did is not a very effective time-wasting tactic, as a referee certainly would add time and, perhaps most importantly, there was a real possibility of Ilunga being sent off for his trouble, which certainly is not the way to go if you are trying to keep the score down. It seems just as likely that Ilunga buckled under the extreme external pressure of the dangers posed by losing by more than three goals and in desperation whacked the ball in the feeble hope that the match would just end. Ilunga admits that "I panicked" because "we were playing for our lives" (Spurling 2010: 29–30). If that is what happened, how do we fit it into our theory of football and sport? Whereas reductive formalism and various ethos views will be silent on this question, not having the resources to explain Ilunga *qua* a footballer kicking the ball away, we can accommodate and explain the *Curious Incident of Mwepu Ilunga Kicking the Ball Away*. First, Ilunga counted as a footballer when he kicked the ball away courtesy of the same line of argument we used to show how Keane counted as a footballer when he exercised his vengeance on Håland. A further question is how we can explain the oddness of the episode within a theory of football, and the answer is that we can do so by appealing to the distinction, introduced in Chapter 1, between the content and the character of football. The content of a sport is the nature of the sport, and the question of whether someone counts as a player of a sport is related to the content of the sport. Keane, Solskjær and Ilunga were all playing football. The character of a sport is the manner in which it is played, and the very same sport can be played in different manners. Football is a sport that involves the essential make-believe that winning football matches matters. I will address the question of professionalism and the fictional character of football in the next chapter, but it is safe to say that, in football, the players are not putting their life on the line. My suggestion is that, for the Zairian players in the *Curious Incident of Mwepu Ilunga Kicking the Ball Away*, the character of the game changed with the score 3–0 to Brazil given the background of General Mobutu's threat. Certainly, the Zairian players coming into the World Cup may have been playing for the opportunity to play abroad and a better future for themselves and their families, but they were as such not literally playing for their lives and a liveable future. Against Brazil, being 3–0 down, it might just have felt like they were, and it is this change in character that best explains what happened when Ilunga kicked the ball away. As I see it, the new character of the game for the Zairian players, when heading into those last five minutes with the Brazilians having been awarded a free kick in a good position, got the better of Ilunga. If football actually had a different character, where players' lives were truly at stake in matches and terrible consequences awaited players and their families if they lost matches, then incidences akin to Ilunga kicking the ball away might be commonplace in football. In such a world, they would still be playing football – the nature of the game remaining the same – but in a very different manner than we do. Furthermore, the possibility of seeing players coming unscrewed in the face of defeat might, perversely enough, be part of the viewing attraction for spectators. It is the unfamiliarity with this sort of situation in our game and with a reaction like Ilunga's that accounts for any temptation to view Ilunga as no longer playing football. With the distinction between the content and the character of football, together with our view of what it takes to be a footballer, the *Curious Incident of Mwepu Ilunga Kicking the Ball Away* can be accommodated and explained within our overall theory of football and how it is currently played.

Objection: The author makes a case for the physicality requirement of sports by using a thought experiment called *Mind Games* to argue that whereas mind chess is chess, mind football is not football. From this it follows that the sport of football is essentially physical, but not necessarily that chess is excluded from being a sport. Perhaps chess is a sport that fails to meet the physicality requirement. Others have been happy to bestow the status of sport onto chess. For example, since 1997 the Mind Sports Organisation has arranged the Mind Sports Olympiad which includes chess, the International Olympics Committee has granted the World Chess Federation status as a Recognized International Sports Federation, Bobby Fischer insisted that "[c]hess is a sport", McNamee has brought to our attention that "in Cuba, for example, chess is considered a sport", and Tamboer mentions the Netherlands where "the union of chess players is a full and respected member of the National Sports Federation" (Blecker 1984: 143, McNamee 2008: 15,

Tamboer 1992: 32). The author rules out mind games as sports by the fiat of his own favoured definition.

This is what Wittgenstein warned us about. This is the poverty of analysis and definition. Regarding games, Wittgenstein's advice was to "[d]on't say: 'There *must* be something common, or they would not be called "games"' – but *look and see* whether there is anything common to all" (Wittgenstein 1967: § 66). Foundational formalism fails to capture the phenomenon of sport, because it forces sports into a straightjacket of analysis or definition, but "if you look at them [games] you will not see something that is common to *all*, but similarities, relationships, and a whole series of them at that" (Wittgenstein 1967: § 66). Some sports are essentially physical, others are not, some are competitive, others are not, some aesthetically pleasing, others are not, some are athletic, others are not, and so on and so forth. The various activities or practices falling under the heading of sport are so varied and multifaceted that no analysis or definition, no matter how minimal, can expect to capture the phenomenon at hand. Instead we should expect a loosely connected web of activities or practices that share some features while also displaying dissimilarities. The fallacy of analysis and definition should give way to describing the world and the phenomena within it along the lines of resemblance, without any presuppositions of hidden commonalities or essences.

> I can think of no better expression to characterize these similarities than "family resemblance"; for the various resemblances between members of a family: build, features, colour of eyes, gait, temperament, etc. etc. overlap and criss-cross in the same way. – And I shall say: "games" form a family.
>
> (*Wittgenstein 1967: § 67*)

Looking at various sports, the conclusion to be drawn is: "these phenomena have no one thing in common which makes us use the same word for all, — but that they are *related* to one another in many different ways" (Wittgenstein 1967: § 65). Sports hang together as a category not by some minimal core or essence, but by a continuous overlapping of features or qualities of activities or practices.

Consider the following standard way of illustrating Wittgenstein's family resemblance line, taken from McNamee (2008: 11). The numerals below stand for various sports and the letters for features or qualities of each individual sport.

1. a, b, c, d
2. b, c, d, e
3. c, d, e, f
4. d, e, f, g
5. e, f, g, h

There cannot be an analysis of 1 to 5 in terms of necessary and sufficient conditions, with regard to which features or qualities are needed for something to be a sport, because there are no such conditions to be had. Sport 1 and Sport 5 do not share any features or qualities, but instead we find a thread of similarity running thought the various sports tying them together. We should follow Wittgenstein's thread out of the labyrinth of analysis and call it a day with regard to providing any definition of sport.

Reply: Let us first address, only to dismiss, the idea that something is a sport because it is called or labelled a sport. That something is called or labelled a sport might be a good indicator of that activity or practice being a sport, but it is not the reason why something is a sport. In Chapter 2 we saw that sports are not a social kind that allows membership inclusion in the kind by fiat, and this is echoed in the observation that calling any old activity or practice a sport does not make it one. Determining whether or not something is a sport is not merely a question of finding out whether someone or other calls the activity or practice in question a sport. In the case of chess, I have given an argument for why chess is importantly different than typical sports like football, track and field, etc. – the physicality of chess is inessential to the game as such – and I have suggested that this gives us reason to exclude chess from the category of sport. However, in the same way as you can choose to call that which is done for sport a non-competitive sport, you might also insist on chess being a non-physical sport. In that case, this book is about competitive physical sports. I think the arguments presented for not applying the notion or concept of sport to activities or practices that are done for sport or are not essentially physical activities or practices are sound. However, one can insist on retaining the title of sport for those activities or practices, given one makes the appropriate adjustment of categorizing them as non-competitive or non-physical sports.

The Wittgensteinian line of family resemblance appealed to in this objection is flawed, if taken in isolation. The reason is simple. Uncontrolled or unchecked usage of the method will connect everything with everything else. Certainly, there must be some things that are not sport, but no doubt any object or phenomenon is connectable to an uncontroversial case of a sport by way of a family resemblance lineage. Does that make them sports? Hardly. What then is the job description of the family resemblance idea? If we had already established the domain of sport, then we could see whether the family resemblance idea held true with regard to sports. It is hard to imagine that it would not, given that it is hard to imagine how everything is not connected through family-style resemblance to everything else. However, the question of which activities or practices fall within the domain of sport is part of the question of what sport is. Here our dismissal of the idea that a sport is that which is called or labelled sport earns its keep. The domain of sport will not be settled without further theorizing.

On the other hand, there is something appealing about the family resemblance line of thought with regard to social kinds like games and sports. As argued in Chapter 2, we should expect blurry lines and intermediate cases for a social historical kind like sport. Still, if viewed globally the result of the family resemblance line is the interconnectedness of everything. We need some way of bringing some manner of theoretical discipline into the proceedings. One way to do this is to use prototype theory, as introduced by Eleanor Rosch, in tandem with the methodological insights of Lewis, which we introduced in Chapter 2. Inspired by Wittgenstein, Rosch's work on the internal structure of categories jettisoned the idea of searching for necessary and sufficient conditions in favour of finding typical or representative members of a category, from which one can draw similarity lines to allow gradual membership in a category on the basis of resemblance (Rosch 1973, 1975, 1977, 1978, Rosch, Simpson and Miller 1976, Rosch et al. 1976).

> [W]hen describing categories analytically, most traditions of thought have treated category membership as a digital, all-or-none phenomenon. That is, much work in philosophy, psychology, linguistics, and anthropology assumes that categories are logical bounded entities, membership in which is defined by an item's possession of a simple set of criterial features, in which all instances possessing the criterial attributes have a full and equal degree of membership. In contrast to such a view, it has been recently argued (...) that some natural categories are analog and must be represented logically in a manner which reflects their analog structure. Rosch (...) has further characterized some natural analog categories as internally structured into a prototype (clearest cases, best examples of the category) and nonprototype members.
>
> *(Rosch and Mervis 1975: 573–574)*

The prototype members of a class exemplifying a concept are those that are seen by users of a word or concept as typical of that class. Prototypical members or central exemplars of, say, the concept of sport are considered more representative of sports than are non-prototypical or non-central members. Taking your starting point in the prototypical exemplars of sport, you can map membership of the category sport from the features or qualities of the representative sports to the less typical sports using various resemblance relations. This gives you degrees of membership in the class of sports. James Hampton tells us the following:

> According to prototype theory, the prototype for many natural object classes is a set of attributes that defines the central tendency of membership of the class, based on the family resemblance of members. Items may vary in their similarity to the central prototype, according to the relative number of matching attributes that they posses. To define membership in the class, one places a flexible criterion on the scale of similarity to the prototype, so that membership can be a matter of degree and depends on the degree of similarity of an item to the class as a whole.
>
> *(Hampton 1987: 55)*

Prototype theory is concerned not only with mapping membership of a class, but, importantly, also with providing a theory of what concepts are. The latter will not be our concern here, as we are dealing with the concept or notion of sport and not with a theory of concepts in general. Consider the natural objects class of birds. If you want to find out how we think about birds and their features or qualities, you find prototypical birds, for example robins or seagulls, and based on the features or qualities associated with the typicality of such exemplars, you can explore resemblance relations to non-central members of the class of birds, for example penguins and ostriches. If you already know the various members of the class of birds, then this way of thinking provides a good method for checking whether our understanding of membership in the class of birds consists of a set of features or qualities they all share or is more loosely connected by similarity relations. Representative members of the family of birds can fly, but being able to fly is not a make-or-break feature or quality of birds, because various flightless birds like penguins and ostriches exist. However, if there are controversial cases with regard to membership of the class of birds, the method described by Hampton is not going to help, because the controversial fringe cases up for consideration for category membership will most certainly have resemblance or similarity relations either directly or indirectly to prototypical members of that class. One way out of this conundrum with regard to the class of birds is to think of them as a natural kind and argue that the borders of membership in such classes are established or settled by nature itself. Nature controls and establishes the borders for natural kinds and that provides the all-important restrictions on class membership.

However, the move of appealing to natural borders of membership in a category is not going to work for the concept or notion of sport, as there are no natural borders to be had for social historical kinds like sport, in general, and football, in particular. How then can we control membership inclusion by resemblance or similarity when there are no natural borders for a category like sport? This is where we combine prototype theory with analysis or a reasoned description of sport using the Lewis methodology. The first step is to establish which sports are the prototypical sports. Instead of the researcher in question merely giving what he or she regards as typical sports, we have empirical research on the prototypicality of various categories. Empirical research tells us that football is a prototypical sport. In a study from Hampton and Gardiner, football tops the table for typicality (Hampton and Gardiner 1983: 512). Likewise, a study by Armstrong, Gleitman and Gleitman corroborates the prototypicality of football (Armstrong, Gleitman and Gleitman 1983: 276). Finding and identifying prototype sports like football does not answer the question of what sport is or what it takes to be a sport. However, it provides you with exemplars of sport, which you as a theorist must get right, if your analysis or description of sport is to count as an analysis or description of our current concept of sport. Common sense, as Lewis would have it, or categorization judgements, as the prototype researchers would write, give us the core, central or standard cases of sport with which our theory better agree. Suits's analysis of sport largely fits football, but as argued, it must be amended at quite a few junctions. Our current theory of what sport is fits not only football, but also other prototypical sports. The other top-five prototypical sports in the Hampton-Gardiner study are rugby, tennis, badminton and basketball (Hampton and Gardiner 1983: 512). The results from Armstrong, Gleitman and Gleitman give us American football, baseball, hockey and soccer as clearly prototypical sports (Armstrong, Gleitman and Gleitman 1983: 276). Two studies from Eleanor Rosch give American football and hockey, and American football, baseball, basketball, tennis and softball as undoubtedly prototypical sports (Rosch 1973: 133, Rosch 1975: 232).[21] For the sake of argument, we will consider these as our starting point and see how the suggested way of thinking about this proceeds.

Our analysis of sport as it has emerged in this book fits these prototypical sports. Furthermore, we have gone through various philosophical arguments for the theoretical choices we have made with regard to our understanding of sport, so we stand on solid philosophical ground. We now have a tool to impose limitations on membership in the category of sport. It is this analysis or description that brings discipline to the notion of sport and establishes the borders of membership inclusion. Our analysis or description gets the core or central cases of sport right. When common sense or, in our usage of prototype theory, categorization judgements deem an activity to be low on prototypicality, then the Lewis suggestion is that such fringe cases be determined to fall in or outside the category in question based solely on whether they fit the analysis or description given. Our analysis or description of what it is to be a sport would not count, for example, hiking, mountaineering, fishing and hunting among the sports. In this picture of things, they are not sports because they are not competitive activities or practices. Looking at empirical studies, we find that when these activities or practices are evaluated with regard to their typicality as a sport, they rank low in exemplariness for sports (hiking and hunting in Rosch 1975: 232, hiking in Armstrong, Gleitman and Gleitman 1983: 276, mountaineering, fishing, hunting and hiking in Hampton and Gardiner 1983: 513). The fact that activities or practices score low on such categorization judgements of prototypicality does not mean that they are automatically ruled out as sports. For example, in the Hampton and Gardiner study, karate is below mountaineering on the table of sport exemplariness, yet in this book karate would count as a sport. Rather, it means that if activities or practices like mountaineering, fishing, hunting and hiking are not prototypical sports, then they should be regarded as potential atypical fringe cases with regard to the category of sport. The reason for adding the modifier "potential" is that if Hampton and Gardiner had conducted their survey in Japan, karate might have been regarded as a better example of sport than mountaineering. Setting aside the observation of the need to calibrate this method using cross-cultural studies, we conclude that when activities or practices like hiking, mountaineering, fishing and hunting score low on judgements of goodness of category membership, to borrow a phrase from Rosch, then their status as sport can be contested. They can be seen as contested and controversial candidates for the category sports, and if our best theory of sport, which encompasses the prototypical sports, deemed them not to be sports, then we should conclude that they do not count as sports. Unless one is willing to count anything that someone or other calls "sport" as sport, or else accept the unhappy consequence of an undisciplined family resemblance method that everything in some sense is sport, then this is a theoretical strength of the line of thinking under consideration. Arguments and analysis bring discipline to the concept of sport and get to decide which of the fringe activities or practices under consideration count as sport and which do not. When settling on the borders of sport, theory and philosophical arguments are part of the equation. Analysis of prototypical sports like football and philosophical discussions about how to think about sports get to dictate the status of fringe or borderline cases with regard to belonging to the category of sport, and in our case that means that parkour, chess, non-competitive sailing, mountaineering, sport fishing, non-competitive surfing, hunting for sport, hiking, etc. are not sports.

At this point, one might wonder whether I have only paid lip service to prototype theory. Using analysis and philosophical arguments as the arbiters of membership inclusion for controversial fringe cases gives cut-off points between sports and non-sports, which seems contrary to Rosch and Mervis's idea that we should not think of category membership as an all-or-nothing phenomenon. An initial answer to this is that the problem of cut-off points in membership inclusion is everybody's problem, unless one thinks that everything is in some sense sport. Even if you insist on activities or practices being sports to various degrees, there will be cut-off points between that which is sports to varying degrees and that which is not. Membership in the category of what is sport to some degree or another in contrast to what is not depends on cut-off points. When thinking about the emergence of sport as a social historical kind, I wrote about sport-like stages and sport-like periods of that which preceded sport. It was argued that we might see a footrace at a certain stage of its existence as a rite, but also as a sport-like activity, i.e. a sport-like rite. Moving up to present-day activities or practices, regarding parkour, we followed Larsen in thinking that parkour is sport-like, but also in important respects closer to art and thus art-like. When discussing activities or practices like parkour, which is done for sport, we found that *lucha libre* is another activity or practice that is both sport-like and art-like. Thus, there are activities or practices that are close to or associated with sport and those we dub sport-like. Some sport-like activities or practices like parkour can easily become sports, whereas the practice of chess cannot. That which is done for sport need only add the competitive component and they become sports, whereas chess, and other board games like it, cannot become essentially physical, and thus will, according to the line of reasoning pursued here, remain outside the realm of sport.[22] Activities or practices that are sport-like are closer to sports than to ordinary everyday life activities, and we can play around with gradual closeness to sport without needing to encompass them in the realm of sport. In my view of things, you have a certain centre or centres of prototypical sports, which in the prescribed manner settle the domain of sport that includes non-prototypical, non-central or peripheral sports, whereupon you have a surrounding area of sport-like activities or practices. Among the activities or practices in the domain of sport, you find degrees of exemplariness with regard to certain features shared by all or most of the prototypical sports. Prototypical sports are athletic, thus involving strength, agility, speed and endurance. Put colloquially, you need to be physically fit to perform well in athletic sports. Stuart Rachels takes chess's lack of athleticism to be the reason why it should not be counted as a sport.

> [C]hess is not a sport, because physical exertion is inessential to chess. A great chess player could be paralyzed his whole life, but a sports star could not be. Note that sports practitioners are called *athletes*, but no one ever calls chess players athletes, presumably because "athlete" – even more than "sport" – connotes physical acumen.
>
> *(Rachels 2008: 221)*

However, consider curling and archery. Curling and archery are two good examples of non-prototypical sports, but they are not contested cases on the fringes of the sport domain. It would be misleading to describe these sports as involving athleticism. Both curling and archery involve physical skills and are sports according to the current line of thinking about sport. As for truly contested and controversial cases, the method under consideration settles those and notably regards various electronic sports as belonging to the sport domain. This I take to be a happy consequence, not because I intuitively take eSports like Super Mario Bros and Tetris to be sports, but because we demand of a theory that it somehow manage to draw some lines between sport and non-sport, and our way of doing that includes these. At the same time, our usage of prototype theory explains why such eSports remain on the outskirts of the sport domain. They would normally not be thought of as athletic endeavours, but they are essentially physical activities or involve centrally physical skills.

Furthermore, the domain of sport-like, but not sport activities or practices, is distinguished from domains that are neither sports nor sport-like. Our method could be used to settle questions of cut-off points between these domains, provided we have reliable data on categorization judgements of prototypicality or goodness of category membership regarding the category sport-like. I will leave it to others to ponder that issue, as this was not one of our theoretical tasks in this book. Building on the picture of social historical kinds developed in Chapter 2, we might also note that the question of whether a specific practice is a sport or merely sport-like, or sport-like or non-sport-like, might or might not be settled by a later stage of that social kind. We should remind ourselves that one of the take-home lessons from thinking about sport as a social historical kind was that we are dealing with a moving research target. Sport and sports evolve and so does our conception of them. With regard to social historical kinds like sports, we might further do well to ease up a little bit on the Lewis methodology. The Lewis line demands that theory agree with common sense, when common sense delivers a firm and uncontroversial answer about a not-too-far-fetched case, or according to the current take on it, that which is considered prototypical sports. However, if, say, chess at some future point in time moves into the centre or centres of our judgements of the prototypicality of sports, we might still withhold the status of sport from the practice of chess. Our philosophical arguments for why chess is so different from the activities or practices described as sport in this book still hold. We can, in such a scenario, refuse to be dictated by common sense or evaluations of prototypicality and instead argue that, with regard to chess, the subjects reporting on prototypical sports are conceptually confused.[23] Should a whole host of games that like chess are not essentially physical, or do not centrally involve physical skills, at one point all be seen as prototypical sports, then most likely one would argue that our concept of sport has changed to now also include non-physical sports. In that case, the divide between practices like football and chess will still be as deep and fundamental, only the word and concept of sport now seem to be applied to both types of activities or practices. Finally, consider a scenario in which chess and similar games occupy the centre or centres of prototypicality assessments, while practices like football, American football, tennis, badminton and basketball are pushed to the fringes as contested or controversial cases of what is now seen as sport. In that case, I believe that the natural thing to say is that we are dealing with a new and different concept of sport than the one we have at present. All these are live possibilities when thinking about social historical kinds like sport.

Objection: The author argues that Suits's Clause 2 – about there being means that limit the way by which the sport-specific intended state-of-affairs end-states can be achieved – is not a necessary condition for something being a sport. Limited means for achieving these sport-specific state-of-affairs end-states are, according to the author, a rational possibility, but not a requirement of sport. On the other hand, the author concurs with Suits and others that at the base of sports we find constitutive rules, which of course is the basic tenet of foundational formalism. However, constitutive rules of sport provide instructions on ways by which you do your sport, which in turn involves limiting the means by which you can reach the sport-specific state-of-affairs end-states you are aiming at. One cannot simultaneously reject Suits's Clause 2 and endorse Clause 3. Perhaps the fallout of that observation is that one should give up the distinction between constitutive and regulative rules and instead follow McFee, who argues that such a distinction is better viewed as "rules in their constitutive uses and rules in their regulative uses" and "that these are *uses* of rules, which different contexts bring to the fore" (McFee 2015: 129, McFee 2004: 44).

Reply: Let us consider the question of constitutive versus regulative rules first. One should concede to McFee that it is not always clear how we should think about a specific rule with regard to the constitutive versus regulative rules divide. For example, one might suspect that the handball rule in football is regulative given the way it is formulated. However, if anything is constitutive of football, it is some sort of rule prescribing that you are not allow to handle the ball or, in its positive equivalent, that only actions made with the feet, head, torso, thighs, etc., count as footballing actions, with the obvious exception of the goalkeepers inside the penalty box. That a rule is constitutive of the game does not mean that its actual formulation must follow the constitutive rule formula. Moreover, when playing football, constitutive rules like the handball rule will guide action. If one is a sport practitioner and has a lusory attitude when playing football, then rules like the handball rule will be behaviourally accommodated, because that is the best and most efficient way of winning football matches. These are the behavioural consequences of a constitutive rule like the handball rule, due to the limitations placed on the means by which you are allowed to play the game that the rule introduces.

However, a constitutive rule need not impose limitations on the sport one is playing, even though constitutive rules in sports played by humans mostly or always do. Our thought experiment of an open-style 100-metre race shows that you can have a sport without a set of means that limits the ways in which you participate in and finish the race. The open-style 100-metre race sport will have constitutive rules that tell you what counts as finishing the race and what counts as winning the race. These can all be formulated following the constitutive rule formula, and they state what counts as what in the open-style 100-metre race sport. You can have constitutive rules of a sport without limiting the means allowed in that sport. The rules of what counts as finishing and what counts as winning the race will influence the behaviour of the sport practitioners while racing. By no stretch of the imagination can one reasonably argue that there are regulative rules pertaining to this sport or that there is a regulative aspect or usage of any of the rules of the open-style 100-metre race sport. When you can have a sport with only constitutive rules, then the notion of a constitutive rule is conceptually anchored, even if there may be no human sports quite like our open-style 100-metre race sport. Regulative rules that have no constitutive element in them are easy to come by. No need for thought experiments here. We have already quoted one such rule. The FIFA rule that footballers, while playing football, are not allowed to flaunt any political, religious or personal slogans, statements or images is clearly regulative in nature. I cannot see that this rule as stated has a constitutive aspect or use. The constitutive versus regulative rules distinction seems to me to stand on firm philosophical ground together with the hybrid of reaction rules introduced earlier in this chapter, the latter showing that some rules do contain both a constitutive and regulative part.

Having said that, we do well to note that McFee's position on constitutive and regulative rules is motivated by his critique and rejection of reductive formalism (McFee 2004: 33–44). I will not enter into the details of McFee's line of argument on this issue, because the rejection of reductive formalism is common ground for McFee and the position defended in this book. Suffice it to say here that it is particularly the philosophical assumption of definiteness – a rule is definitely a constitutive rule or definitely a regulative rule – that McFee argues is untenable when it comes to thinking about sport. That, however, does not preclude one from arguing and demonstrating that some rules are clearly or definitely constitutive, while others are clearly or definitely regulative. Rejection of definiteness with regard to whether rules are constitutive or regulative rules only implies that not all of them are either one or the other. Setting aside reaction rules and concentrating on those traditionally viewed as either constitutive or regulative rules, there is no assumption in the arguments presented in this chapter that all of them are definitely only one or the other. The overall view argued for here is that sports are social historical kinds that change and evolve. I see no reason to exclude the rules of various sports, whether they are constitutive or regulative rules, from being subject to change. The blueprint of football – the football form – has not remained unchanged throughout the existence of the social historical kind of football. That means that one should accept that a rule, which perhaps at one stage was a core constitutive rule without any regulative use, could take on regulative uses at some later stage, possibly even becoming primarily or only a regulative rule. And vice versa for a regulative rule. As with social historical kinds that change and evolve, there will always be a question of whether the rule undergoing one change or another is still the same rule or at some later stage would be better seen as a new rule. What holds for social historical kinds like football also holds for its parts, among which we find the rules of the game.

Objection: Suits's logical incompatibility thesis should not be given up. You cannot break a constitutive rule of a sport like football and still be playing the game. However, you can break the sport's regulative rules without ceasing to be a player. The third kind of rule mentioned earlier in this chapter should be understood as regulative. Suits repeats this idea in the *Grasshopper*, and Morgan interprets this part of Suits to mean that regulative rules can be violated without the offender failing to play the game.

> Suits could not have been clearer on this point: "violating the [regulative] rule is neither to fail to play the game nor (necessarily) to fail to play the game well, since it is sometimes tactically correct to incur such a penalty for the sake of the advantage gained" [Suits 1978: 52].
>
> *(Morgan 1987: 3)*

The alleged counter-intuitiveness of Suits's logical incompatibility thesis is based on a misrepresentation of his view in this book. Suits uses the distinction between constitutive and regulative rules to distinguish constitutive rules from rules of penalties. The answer to the alleged problem of the logical incompatibility thesis is that, as Suits sees it, penalty-bearing rules are always of the regulative kind. You can break a regulative rule and pay the costs in terms of the penalty without breaking any of the constitutive rules. The author gets a lot of argumentative mileage out his *A Fistful of Fouls* case. Unfortunately, he fails to see that the rule violation of holding the opponents' shirts is an infringement of a regulative rule of the game and that it can, as such, be broken without the offender ceasing to be a player of the game. The logical incompatibility thesis stands on solid ground.

Reply: No. The rejection of Suits's logical incompatibility thesis is well-founded. Suits's spin on his so-called third kind of rule is that they are established by the constitutive rules and are simply extensions of them. Again, Suits does not have the theoretical resources necessary to make this claim, while maintaining that the logical incompatibility thesis holds. Certainly, there are regulative rules of football. I have already pointed to two such rules in this chapter. A player must wear shin guards while playing, and may not have any political, religious or personal slogans, statements or images on the compulsory football equipment (see *FIFA Laws of the Game* in the parts of *Law 4 – The Players' Equipment*, FIFA 2014). These are regulative rules. Indeed, Suits can accommodate violations of such regulative rules in his picture of things, though notably he fails to do so. In fact, when addressing these issues Suits never appeals to or uses the notion of regulative rules. One reason for this might be that regulative rules, like the ones mentioned above, clearly are not established by the constitutive rules or are simply extensions of them. True, I did fail to mention that Suits has the theoretical resources to deal with players who fail to wear shin guards or who have political, religious or personal statements or images on their compulsory football equipment, without these players thereby failing to be footballers. The reason is simply that I do not regard such regulative rules as particularly relevant to understanding sports like football.

Suits tells us that "two kinds of rule figure in games, one kind associated with prelusory goals, the other with lusory goals" (Suits 1978: 51). The kind associated with Suits's so-called prelusory goals are the constitutive rules, which "set out all the conditions which must be met in playing the game", whereas the other kind of rule "operates (...) *within* the area circumscribed by constitutive rules, and this kind of rule may be called a rule of skill" (Suits 1978: 51). Examples of such rules of skill, according to Suits, are "the familiar injunctions to keep your eye on the ball, to refrain from trumping your partner's ace, and the like" (Suits 1978: 51). Rules of skill, if it is correct to call them rules, are more like a heuristics that tells you how to play a sport well. If you think of these so-called rules of skill as something that could be written down in a manual on how to play football well, then there would be two ways to break them. Either by being an inept footballer who fails to play the game well, i.e. does not follow or is unable to execute the rules, or by being an innovative footballer who invents new ways of playing the game well, i.e. does not follow or is unwilling to execute the rules.[24] In either case, both inept and innovative footballers count as footballers, so these so-called rules of skill are irrelevant to the current discussion of the lusory attitude needed to play a sport and the so-called logical incompatibility thesis.[25] When Suits then goes on to claim that there is "a third kind of rule (...) the kind of rule whose violation results in a fixed penalty, so that violating the rule is [not] to fail to play the game", he fails to account for how the latter part follows given his logical incompatibility thesis (Suits 1978: 52). In a later work, Suits again addresses both constitutive rules and rules of skill, while telling us that "in football (...) the rules *rule out*, among other things, the use of machine guns by guards and tackles", though, again, there is no mention of regulative rules (Suits 1988: 5). The year after, Suits mentions regulative rules when referring to Meier's work, but does not use the term himself (Suits 1989: 12). The background for this reference is that Suits had argued that the offside rules in American football and ice hockey were constitutive rules, whereupon Meier claimed that "rules such as these, which specify the penalties to be applied when particular constitutive rules have been violated, may be more appropriately called 'regulative'" (Meier 1988: 20, Suits 1988: 5–6, see also Meier 1985). Suits does not accept this invitation. Instead, he merely modifies his view and admits to being mistaken when presenting the offside rule in American football and ice hockey "as illustrative of a constitutive rule per se, since such rules are extensions of, or derivations from, a game's basic constitutive rules" (Suits 1989: 11–12). In American football the offside rule yields yardage penalties, and according to Suits in the quote above, that offside rule is not *illustrative* of a constitutive rule *per se*, but is clearly still a constitutive rule. Suits is not at all clear on how his logical compatibility thesis is suppose to sit with the seemingly obvious observation that constitutive rules are broken when people play sports.

When I introduced Suits's requirement of constitutive rules for something to be a sport, contrary to Suits's approach, I contrasted them with regulative rules. I did this for a reason. From Chapter 2 we had the constitutive rule formula, which was instrumental in understanding social kinds. The way I set things up when we addressed Suits's constitutive rules requirement was meant to underscore that sports are social kinds created out of an acceptance that certain kinds of behaviours and events count as part of a sport, i.e. collective intentionality. Sports like football might differ from many other social kinds based on collective intentionality, in that many of their constitutive rules are often explicitly spelled out in rule books, but this difference in explicitness does not mark any ontological difference. The distinction between constitutive and regulative rules, as we used it, reminds us that while sports are constituted by their rules, unlike, e.g., various natural phenomena, we do well to note that not all of the rules are part of the sports' foundation, i.e. some rules are regulative, meaning they merely regulate already established sport behaviour.

Morgan argues that Suits's logical incompatibility thesis is correct, because the objection that it does not fit the sport landscape, as we find it in football, is based on a failure to understand that what can be violated in sports like football are regulative rules, not constitutive rules.

> For the unqualified claim formalism makes with respect to the observance of rules applies to only one kind of rule, namely the constitutive rules. It is only the latter kind of rule that defines what a game is in the sense of setting out all the conditions that must be met in the playing of the game. This kind of rule, upon which the very existence of the game is logically dependent, is to be distinguished from another kind which regulates antecedently or independently existing forms of behavior, and to which specific penalties are attached. Although the latter regulative rules presuppose the existence of constitutive rules (without which there would be nothing to regulate), and so count as extensions of the latter rules, it doesn't follow that the breaking of one of these rules invalidates the game as such.
>
> *(Morgan 1987: 3)*

The rules described by Morgan are what I have called reaction rules. Reaction rules or penalty-evoking regulative rules can be formulated as conditionals. If rule X is broken or violated, then penalty Y will be administered to the offending party.

Arguing that such penalty-evoking rules are regulative rules is not going to save the logical incompatibility thesis. Rather, it is only when regulative rules alone appear in the antecedent of the reaction or penalty-evoking regulative rule conditionals that Suits's logical incompatibility thesis can be upheld.

Let us consider *Law 12 – Fouls and Misconduct*, from FIFA's rule book 2015–2016 edition, concerning when fouls and misconduct are penalized by a direct free kick or penalty kick.

> A direct free kick is awarded to the opposing team if a player commits any of the following seven offences in a manner considered by the referee to be careless, reckless or using excessive force:
>
> - kicks or attempts to kick an opponent
> - trips or attempts to trip an opponent
> - jumps at an opponent
> - charges an opponent
> - strikes or attempts to strike an opponent
> - pushes an opponent
> - tackles an opponent
>
> A direct free kick is also awarded to the opposing team if a player commits any of the following three offences:
>
> - holds an opponent
> - spits on an opponent
> - handles the ball deliberately (except for the goalkeeper within his own penalty area)
>
> (…)
>
> A penalty kick is awarded if any of the above ten offences is committed by a player inside his own penalty area, irrespective of the position of the ball.
>
> (FIFA 2015: 37)

A penalty is given by way of a free kick or a penalty kick to the opposing team, when a certain offence has been committed, i.e. a rule has been broken or violated. Based on the offences listed in this part of *Law 12*, we can extract the following ten rules of football, with the addition for some of them of not being careless, reckless or using excessive force.

- Do not kick or attempt to kick an opponent
- Do not trip or attempt to trip an opponent
- Do not jump at an opponent
- Do not charge an opponent
- Do not strike or attempt to strike an opponent
- Do not push an opponent
- Do not tackle an opponent
- Do not hold an opponent

- Do not spit on an opponent
- Do not handle the ball deliberately (except for the goalkeeper within his own penalty area)

If you break or violate any of these ten rules of the game, i.e. commit any of the above-mentioned offences, then a free kick or a penalty kick will be awarded to the opposing team. Are all of these ten rules regulative rules? Certainly not.

In Chapter 2, in the discussion of football as a social historical kind, it was suggested that the year 1863 might mark the beginning of the social historical kind of association football. On December 1, 1863, at the fifth meeting of the Football Association, carrying the ball and hacking were banned and this, it was suggested, indicates that the fission of proto-football towards two distinct sports – association football and rugby football – had begun. The rules of not handling the ball and not kicking or tripping the opponent are at the centre of one of the most important stages in the life of the social historical kind of football, and those rules are clearly constitutive rules of the game. Things could have looked very different. Collins reports that "at the end of the fourth meeting on 24 November 1863, it seemed that a consensus had been arrived at (…) [r]unning with the ball in your hands would be allowed and hacking would be legal. In short, the meeting had agreed to play football along the lines played at Rugby School" (Collins 2017: 33). The rules of November 24, 1863 included the following:

> 9 "A player shall be entitled to *run with the ball* towards his adversaries' goal if he makes a fair catch, or *catches the ball* on the first bound; but in the case of a fair catch, he makes his mark, he shall not run."
> 10 "If any player shall run with the ball towards his adversaries' goal, any player in the opposite side shall be at liberty to *charge, hold, trip or hack* him, or to *wrest* the ball from him; but no player shall be held and hacked at the same time."
>
> (quoted in Harvey 2005: 140–141, my italics)

Compare rules 9 and 10 of the fourth FA meeting on November 24, 1863 with FIFA's rule book 2015–2016 edition *Law 12 – Fouls and Misconduct* on when fouls are penalized with a direct free kick or penalty kick to the opposing team. You will find that the latter almost looks like it was designed to refute and replace rules 9 and 10 of the November 24, 1863 rules. That is no accident. Harvey tells us that, at the fifth meeting of the FA, "laws 9 and 10 of the FA code were expunged and replaced by" the following (Harvey 2005: 143):

> 9 No player shall carry the ball.
> 10 Neither tripping [n]or hacking shall be allowed and no player to use his hand to push adversary.
>
> (quoted in Harvey 2005: 143)

At this point in history, it is reasonable to talk, at least, about the dawn of the social historical kind of association football. The rules of not handling the ball, not kicking opponents, not tripping opponents, not holding opponents, not charging opponents and the like, are woven into the football blueprint and are constitutive rules that are part of the foundation of football. This is part of the crossroad from which proto-football developed into association football and rugby football. These constitutive rules of the game are broken or violated on a regular basis by footballers, thus the need for reaction or penalty-evoking rules that instruct referees on how to deal with such rule violations. The idea that we can save Suits's logical incompatibility thesis by arguing that the often-seen violations of these rules of not handling the ball, not kicking opponents, not tripping opponents, etc., are mere violations of so-called regulative rules is clearly misguided. Suits's logical incompatibility thesis must be rejected.

The line of reasoning argued for here sidesteps the whole formalism versus anti-formalism debate in the philosophy of sport. On the question of what it takes to be a sport performer, we have already seen that both the formalism position, as stated by Suits, and the anti-formalism position, in the form of D'Agostino's ethos view, fail for fairly similar reasons. Sport participants endure, obey or accept the arbitration of a sport's rules, whereas practitioners also aim at fulfilling the sport's internal or intrinsic aim, while accepting the arbitration of the sport's rules. The line of enduring, obeying or accepting the arbitration of a sport's rules combines formalism's emphasis on rules in sport and the anti-formalism emphasis on rule interpretation in sport. The social historical kind of sports like football is held together by collective intentionality, which requires sport practitioners, while allowing mere participants. In sports like football, we find that the way players at times break or violate constitutive rules of the game are important for understanding how the sport changes and develops. Various other factors also play roles in the development of sports, for example, the fact that your typical spectator sports will take into account their audiences' reactions to the way the sports are played. The constitutive rules of a sport like football change, but regarding the picture of football as a social historical kind, that does not mean that the sport does not remain the same sport. Also, as previously mentioned, various versions of football – ranging from football as it is played in officially organized matches to kick-abouts or park games – might differ with regard to their constitutive rules, while all being versions of the same sport. There is no formula that will tell us how many rule changes a sport can undergo and still remain the same sport. Moreover, in a sport like football, some constitutive rules are more central than others. You might change many of the game's constitutive rules and still have football, but if you allow running with the ball, i.e. drop the rule prohibiting handling the ball, then we would most likely say that you were no longer playing association football, but something else. At the core of football is the constitutive rule of not being allowed to handle the ball. That does not mean that footballers who handle the ball are not playing football. When England's Jack Charlton, on the goal line, intentionally pushed the ball out with his hand keeper-style in the semi-final of the 1966 World Cup against Portugal, thereby robbing José Torres of a goal, only to see Eusébio convert the ensuing penalty, he was playing football.[26] The football community past and present has treated Charlton and others like him as part of the game, even though they broke or violated *one of the most central constitutive rules of the sport*. Our treatment of what it takes to be a sport participant or practitioner covers handballers like Charlton, while respecting the phenomenon of football as the footballing world perceives it. On the other hand, if Charlton, after his blatant handball, had picked up the ball and run towards the Portuguese half of the pitch, he would no longer have been playing football. Not because he yet again handled the ball, but because by doing so he would have been ignoring the referee's call to award a penalty kick to Portugal. In other words, he would no longer have been accepting, enduring or obeying the arbitration of the rules of football. Of course, should we find that episodes of carrying the ball Charlton-style are becoming increasingly common, when football matches are played, then we might possibly be witnessing the dusk of association football and the dawn of another kind of sport (under the assumption that, in this imaginary scenario, rugby football had not yet developed).

Conclusion

The human handgrips are key factors in our evolutionary success. On the face of it, it is an astonishing fact that the prime feature of our favourite sport is that you must forfeit your main means of manipulating objects and getting things done, and instead resort to other body parts. Once we learn that football belongs to the realm of the extra-ordinary and is not designed to solve everyday or ordinary world problems, the apparent oddness of this fact evaporates. Because nothing is at stake with regard to everyday ordinary world concerns, limiting the means by which you can play football is a rational possibility. People get together with the prelusory goal of having a sport or sport contest to play, and within the ensuing activity on the basis of the constitutive rules of the sport, certain sport-specific or lusory goals emerge as the way one wins the sport in question. Footballers need not necessarily understand the rules or even that the aim of playing is to win the game, but someone connected to the football match in question must. Those players are mere sport participants and can successfully play as long as they endure, obey or accept the arbitration of the rules of the game. More is required of footballers who are practitioners of the sport. Practitioners of football use the football form, and that means having the lusory attitude of aiming at winning football matches, while accepting the arbitration of the rules of the game. This lusory attitude does not mean that players cannot violate the rules of the game or the ethos of the game, while continuing to be footballers, only that while trying to win the game, they are willing to suffer the rulings of a referee. The role of such a referee is not only to implement the rules of the game, but also to maintain the character of the game and to mind or manage the game, the goal being to make it as enjoyable to play and watch as possible, given the framework of the football form. The first role points back to Chapter 1 and our argument that football is fictional in character, while the second concerns the aesthetics of football and will be addressed in the next chapter.

Notes

1 For a defence of Suits's notion of Utopia and its normative implications, see Vossen's work (Vossen 2016, 2017). Others who have defended Suits's notion of Utopia include Kretchmar 2006, Holowchak 2007, and Lopez Frias 2016, 2017, whereas Thompson 2004, Bäck 2008 and Yorke 2017 all question the intelligibility of Suits's Utopia. See Borge forthcoming for an argument for why Suits's Utopia is intelligible, but irrelevant for understanding human sports, i.e. sports that originate in and still thrive in the non-Utopian state of affairs we call our world. Among the human sports, of course, we find football.
2 See also Suits 1967a: 209–210, Suits 1967b: 148.
3 For a different critique of Suits on this issue, see Schneider and Butcher's arguments "that the notion of a 'pre-lusory goal' is incoherent as defined", and that "Suits does not define his sense of 'institution'" (Schneider and Butcher 1997: 39, 41, see Suits 2006 for a response).
4 Best suggested that we distinguish between purposive and aesthetic sports (Best 1974: 201–202, Best 1978: 103–105). Purposive sports are sports where "the aesthetic is relatively unimportant" and "the aim, purpose or end can be specified independently of the manner of achieving it as long as it conforms to the limits set by the rules or norms – for example, scoring a goal" (Best 1974: 201). Aesthetic sports are those where "the purpose cannot be considered apart from the manner of achieving it" (Best 1974: 202). Football is a purposive sport, and aesthetics is not woven into the football form. Aesthetic prescriptions are not part of football's constitutive rules. In football a goal is a goal, and regarding the result of a particular match, the manner in which it was scored does not matter. The goal-getter takes them any way he or she can – "the hallmark of a born goal-scorer – give them the merest hint of a goal and they'll pounce. They don't care what part of their anatomy the ball comes off, as long as it finishes in the back of the net" (Dalglish 1996: viii). Dalglish's sentiment is echoed by Barnes, who notes that "Ian Rush, Alan Shearer and Gary Lineker were not interested in being involved in the build-up to a goal, only in being in at the death. Those three would be ecstatic if the ball went in off their knee because they were real goalscorers, who lived to see the ball in the net" (Barnes 1999: 49). Among purposive sports we can distinguish between what Kupfer called quantitative/linear sports, and competitive sports, which is what I have dubbed measurement sports and constructive-destructive sports (Kupfer 1983: 114–124, Borge 2010a: 24–25).
5 For a critique of this move, see Meier 1988, 1989, Kretchmar 1989, 2008: 146–148.
6 Professionalism in sport will be addressed in Chapter 4.
7 *Metro on-line* reported that, in a 2010 greyhound race in Australia, a real hare crossed the track during a race, whereupon one of the dogs, Ginny Lou, promptly chased it. If reaching the goal line or winning the race had been on Ginny Lou's mind, she would not have chased the hare, but as trainer Scott Stefanos said: "she thought she was doing the right thing" (*Metro* 2010). From the perspective of Ginny Lou, she was involved in the time-honoured, well-appreciated dog activity of chasing stuff, not doing sport.
8 The greyhounds are furthermore cognitively closed to the concept of sport, whereas we are not.
9 Suits never managed to shake this *stalnaker*. *The Philosophical Lexicon*: "stalnaker, n. An *idée fixe* that brings a theory or theorist to a halt (www.philosophicallexicon.com). "He was going great until he got the idea that there was just one mathematical truth, and that stalnaker hung him up for years." "Einstein's stalnaker was that God does not play dice."
10 This does not entail that the rules are final or that, for a practice like football, you can in principle have a final set of rules. The rules, as written down, will not cover all eventualities. This is a Wittgensteinian point. Wittgenstein writes, "[i]t is not everywhere circumscribed by rules; but no more are there any rules for how high one throws the ball in tennis, or how hard; yet tennis is a game for all that and has rules too" (Wittgenstein 1967: §68).

11 Gullit notes, "[i]n my day, football was a lot less gentle: an elbow in the face, boots with massive aluminium studs to stomp on your foot, shirt tugging, groin grabbing, hair pulling ... you could expect anything and everything on the pitch. *It wasn't accepted*, it was against the rules, *but it happened*" (Gullit 2016: 69, my italics).

12 We also currently find examples of different or differing ethos as shown by Gullit's comment that "[t]hese days referees stop play for the slightest infringement. Less so in the Premier League perhaps (...) English referees are much more tolerant. Yet that often puts English clubs at a disadvantage when they play on the Continent. They are continually being penalized. In fact teams that compete internationally need two styles of play: one for the English league and one for the European competition" (Gullit 2016: 69).

13 I have made a distinction between park games that are self-refereed and competitive matches with appointed referees, and noted that with regard to the former "[i]t is not so much the decision to play a match *simpliciter* that confers obligations of fairness, but rather the decision to play a match of this self-refereed kind. It is the element of refereeing that confers obligations of fair play", whereas in the latter kind of matches "[e]ach player when deciding to play a competitive match *accepts* that there is a referee who decides which events or actions are to count as rightful or which are not to count as rightful" (Borge 2010b: 162, 163, my italics). In other words, *qua* a football player you must endure, obey or accept the arbitration of the rules of football by which the football form is implemented. Papineau adopts this position when he writes, "the crucial issue is whether you continue to *accept* the authority of the referee or other officials" (Papineau 2017: 67, my italics).

14 Which one you choose will depend on whether you think this sort of common knowledge of as-if playing the sport counts as a type of overtness or honesty, which gives you application of the football form, or as disregarding the internal or intrinsic aim of the sport, which gives you appropriation of the football form.

15 The reason for emphasizing the upper levels of the game in this observation is that I suspect that many games among amateurs around the world, even when there is an appointed referee, are played in a more cooperative manner than at the sport's upper levels. If this is correct, one reason might be that players at such levels are not willing to suffer the game behaviour that one finds at the upper levels. If enough prestige, identity, money, etc., are invested in particular matches, then one's level of tolerance for rule and ethos violations might be higher than if a game is played out more or less only for the entertainment of having a football match to play. Players tend to find a sense of proportion between their desire to win a match and the level at which a match is being played. With regard to this aspect of the game – how one chooses to enact the football conflict – it is important to see the appropriateness of talking about an uncooperative character. Note as well that the competitive spirit of the game, even when played uncooperatively, must be tempered in order to maintain the sport's fictional character.

16 Anyone who thought that video assisted refereeing (VAR) would remove controversial penalty decisions from the game by making it crystal clear when something counted as a handball foul in the box and when it did not was proven wrong by the last FIFA World Cup in Russia in 2018. The final itself contained a highly controversial penalty decision, which helped France beat Croatia.

17 Notwithstanding that humans can and do invent all kinds of fanciful games and sports, some in which the human ability and skill elements are slim or non-existent, while refraining from betting or having substantial prizes. If in the case of such animal sports the participants – which would be those who arranged it, the owners of the animals, etc. – and the spectators agreed that the sport performances did not reflect back on human abilities and skills, then my prediction is that such events, on closer inspection, would reveal relatively little engagement in who actually wins and that elements of the event, other than the event itself qua a game or sport, would explain their attraction.

18 In *FIFA Laws of the Game 2016–17. Law 05: The Referee. 2. Decisions of the referee*, we find that referees are making decisions not only "to the best of the referee's ability according to the Laws of the Game", but also according to "the 'spirit of the game'"

(FIFA 2016: 45). The open-ended and non-committal 'spirit of the game' might or might not be interpreted as including match minding, such as aesthetic considerations of ensuring the game has a good flow and maintaining game character.

19 If this latter impression has any truth to it, then we would expect players at the upper levels of the game to exploit this to their own advantage, given our argument that at these levels the game is often played in an uncooperative manner, and this is what they do. Savage tells us that "'Go and make your mark in the first few minutes. The ref won't do anything.' That's what Sparky [Mark Hughes] used to say to me. I did it to Juan Verón in the Argentina game, I did it to Ze Roberto of Brazil, and I did it to this guy in the Azerbaijan side. You knew if you clobbered someone early you'd probably get away with it" (Savage with Self 2011: 150–151). Similarly, Gullit notes that "[r]eferees often overlook infringements in the first minutes of the match since they are afraid of overusing their yellow and red cards" (Gullit 2016: 48).

20 The example of *Hardman's Referee* came up in the Q&A session of Hardman's presentation at the 36th IAPS conference in Tokyo, in September 2008. It is depicted from memory, but the general gist of it is as presented by Hardman during that session.

21 The two Rosch studies include the category "football", but that should be read as American football, not association football (Eleanor Rosch, personal communication).

22 One might possibly have a case for arguing that speed chess could become a sport and is more sport-like than ordinary chess. Rachels makes a similar observation when he notes that "[f]ast enough chess games might constitute sporting events" (Rachels 2008: 225).

23 In another work, Lewis strikes a similar note and admits, "[c]ommon sense has no absolute authority in philosophy. It's not that the folk know in their blood what the highfalutin' philosophers may forget. And it's not that common sense speaks with the voice of some infallible faculty of 'intuition'. It's just that theoretical conservatism is the only sensible policy for theorists of limited powers, who are duly modest about what they could accomplish after a fresh start. Part of this conservatism is reluctance to accept theories that fly in the face of common sense. But *it's a matter of balance and judgement*. Some common sense opinions are firmer than others, so the cost of denying common sense opinion differs from one case to the next. And the cost must be set against the gains. Sometimes common sense may properly be corrected, when the earned credence that is gained by making theory more systematic more than makes up for the inherited credence that is lost" (Lewis 1986b: 134, my italics).

24 According to Suits, "[t]o break a rule of skill is usually to fail, at least to that extent, to play the game well" (Suits 1973b: 52, see also Suits 1978: 51–52). I am not sure how Suits would view game or sport innovation and rules of skill, i.e. whether or not the former count as breaking rules of skill. However, if Johan Cruyff's innovative feign, aka the Cruyff turn, when it was performed for the first time, counts as following a rule of skill, then I fail to understand what rules amount to in this picture of things.

25 Seemingly, Suits would agree when he writes, "I propose to ignore the latter [rules of skill], since my purpose is to define not well-played games, but games" (Suits 1973b: 52, see also Suits 1978: 52). Elsewhere, Suits calls such rules "a rule of skill, or a tactical rule, or a rule of practice" and that if one violates such a rule, like "fail[ing] to keep my eye on the ball in golf when driving from the tee", then "no one accuses me of cheating, just of incredible incompetence" (Suits 1988: 6).

26 Notice the difference in Glanville's description of Charlton's handballing compared to that of Maradona's infamous hand-of-God handballing goal in 1986 (Glanville 2018: 151, 289–290).

4

THE AESTHETICS OF FOOTBALL

Football, bloody hell

Introduction

The 1999 Champions League final at Camp Nou in Barcelona was a welcome return to the biggest stage of European football for English champions Manchester United. Almost 31 years had passed since they last found themselves in this situation, but they were losing. German giant Bayern München had taken an early lead and had since controlled and patrolled the game with the nous of a team used to taking home big trophies. The 1–0 lead Bayern held did not properly reflect their dominance. The game was drifting away from Manchester United. With ten minutes left of the game, United's manager Alex Ferguson made his last throw of the dice. He introduced Norwegian striker Ole Gunnar Solskjær from the bench. A minute later United was saved by the woodwork. Carsten Jancker's overhead kick found the cross bar, not the net. As the match moved into the three allotted minutes of injury time, it was all but won for the Germans. Then came the turn around. In the 91st minute, another substitute, Teddy Sheringham, equalized for United and soon after Solskjær wrote his name in golden letters into the history of Manchester United. Latching onto a flick from Sheringham in the dying seconds of the game, Solskjær grabbed the winner. United were the champions of Europe. Ferguson's immediate reaction after the match said it all. "I can't believe it. I can't believe it" Ferguson told a reporter, "Football, bloody hell".

In this chapter, I will lay the groundwork for an aesthetics of football, which primarily springs from the sport as a competition and the drama it brings. First, however, we address ethical considerations of football and show that a meritocratic-fairness view of sports fails to capture the phenomenon of football. Fairness of result is not centre stage in football. Football is about the drama, about the tension and the emotions it provokes. This moves us to the realm of aesthetics. How we should understand the aesthetics of football, on the other hand, is not straightforward. I reject the idea of the aesthetics of football as disinterested aesthetic appreciation, which Immanuel Kant deemed central to aesthetics. Though football and any other phenomenon can be subjected to such a disinterested aesthetic gaze, it is neither the commonplace nor the central manner in which aesthetic engagement in football takes place. Instead, I argue that we should try to develop an agon aesthetics – a notion I introduce and will explain in due course – where our aesthetic appreciation is understood as involving and being embedded in our engagement in the game.

Fairness of result vs. the drama of football

There are various views on the nature and aim of sports competitions like football matches. One important strand in the philosophy of sport not yet addressed is the meritocratic-fairness view of sport. The meritocratic-fairness view of sport need not be at odds with the view that sports are unnecessary, autotelic, competitive, physical-skill activities involving rules. Followers of the meritocratic-fairness view of sports would add that, in sport competitions, the nature and aim of a sport is also to award the most skilful participant the victory. Loland tells us that "[t]he structural goal of sport competitions is to measure, compare and rank two or more participants according to athletic performance" (Loland 2002: 44). Similarly, Warren Fraleigh argues that sport competitions aim at revealing "the relative abilities of the participants to move mass in space and time" (Fraleigh 1984: 41). The structural aim of sport, or the knowledge sought in sport competition, is to determine who is the most skilful competitor and then rank him, her or them as the best or the winner, and so on and so forth for the various other competitors. Though few have described the meritocratic-fairness view as clearly as Loland and Fraleigh, the view that ethics and fairness are central to sport has a large following in the philosophy of sport. In particular, Robert Simon's influential view on the ethics of sport is at least a close cousin to the meritocratic-fairness view of sports (Simon 2004).

If fairness of result with regard to some well-defined definition of the sport-specific skills involved in playing football were at the heart of football as both a phenomenon and a sport, then one would expect matches with unfair results to be frowned upon and not held in high esteem. But that is not the case. Consider the 2005 Champions League final between Liverpool FC and AC Milan. The match ended 3–3 after extra time, and Liverpool won the penalty shoot-out 3–2. The match quickly entered football folklore as one of the most thrilling matches ever played, and as the greatest comeback in the history of football. Milan, led by their star midfielder Kaka and a deadly Hernán Crespo up front, went on a rampage as Liverpool got ripped apart in the first half. Liverpool, coming into the final as underdogs, were dead and buried by half-time, being 3–0 down against the top team of a country renowned for their ability to hang on to a lead. Milan also started the second half best, until Liverpool scored in the 54th minute and then, in what Milan manager Carlo Ancelotti appropriately dubbed "six minutes of madness", scored another two in the 56th and 60th minutes (BBC 2005). It took Milan some time to regain their composure, but they forced Liverpool to clear a ball off the goal line in the 70th minute. From there on, it was once again, more or less, Milan's match. In the extra time, Liverpool hung on for dear life, and with one minute remaining in the match, Milan striker Andriy Shevchenko forced Liverpool keeper Jerzy Dudek to pull off an amazing double-save. A vastly superior Milan had been held to a draw by Liverpool, and the latter promptly went ahead and won the penalty shoot-out. After the match, a stunned Diego Maradona exclaimed, "I have seen comebacks like that in football but never against a team that so clearly was superior as Milan were" (BBC 2005). Clearly, the result was not fair in the sense that defenders of the meritocratic-fairness view of sports would want results to be. However, that seemingly does not matter when we look at the reaction to Liverpool's defeat of AC Milan. The match is by common consensus considered a classic. The day after, the French newspaper *L'Equipe* declared that now "Liverpool are eternal", the Spanish newspaper *Diario AS* simply exclaimed "Liverpool. Olé!", the German newspaper *Bild* concluded "Giant final", and Portuguese newspaper *O Jogo* summed it up with the headline "Crazy crazy game" and sub-headline "Epic in the colour red".

If fairness of result were centre stage in football as a sport, and the main parameter by which we should judge the quality of the sport, then football would be a flawed game; games like the 2005 Champions League final would then show how deeply flawed the game is. But, of course, the reactions to the above-mentioned final demonstrate that football is not primarily about fairness.[1] Indeed, Maradona acknowledged that in an additional remark: "Liverpool showed that miracles exist. They proved that football is the most beautiful sport of them all" (*The Guardian* 2005). The beauty of football Maradona has in mind must be the seesaw qualities of drama that football matches like the 2005 Champions League final provide, and the unlikely and delightful (unless you supported AC Milan) underdog victory, which neutral football spectators often find so riveting. Football is about the drama – about the tension and the emotions it provokes. Indeed, if drama and emotions are at the centre of the phenomenon of football, then a certain amount of healthy unfairness and, perhaps, a dose of unethical conduct add to the spectacle of football.[2] As Nick Hornby pointed out, there is so much more to the match experience than is captured by a meritocratic-fairness approach to the game:

> For a match to be really, truly memorable (…) you require as many of the following features as possible (…) *Goals* (…) *Outrageously bad refereeing decisions* (…) Indignation is a crucial ingredient of the perfect footballing experience (…) I prefer to notice them, and howl at them, and feel cheated by them (…) *A noisy crowd*: In my experience, crowds are at their best when their team is losing but playing well (…) *Rain, a greasy surface, etc.* (…) you can't beat the sight of players sliding ten or fifteen yards for a tackle or in an attempt to get a touch to a cross (…) *Opposition missing a penalty* (…) *Member of opposition team receives a red card* (…) For fans, a sending-off is always a magic moment (…)

Some kind of "disgraceful incident" (aka "silliness", aka "nonsense", aka "unpleasantness"): We are entering doubtful moral territory here (...) Yet one has to conclude, regretfully and with a not inconsiderable degree of Corinthian sadness, that there is nothing like a punch-up to enliven an otherwise dull game (...) I am a fan, with no duty to toe the moral line whatsoever.

(Hornby 1992: 235–237)

However, before we set Hornby's observations and musings into the right theoretical framework of the agon aesthetics of football, we need to address the question of free beauty and football.

Free beauty and football

It is not clear who first introduced the phrase "the beautiful game". The choice seems to be between Brazilian footballer Waldyr Pereira, aka Didi (having first coined it in the guise of the Brazilian phrase "um jogo bonito"), and the English football reporter Stuart Hall (though others have also been said to be the originator).[3] Today, the phrase is very much associated with Brazilian football and their way of playing the game. No wonder it has caught on. Brazil is the biggest, most successful footballing powerhouse in the world, and who does not want to be able to play like them and have their success? The phrase is also quite remarkably marketable, but is perhaps misleading as it invites us to think of beauty in the beautiful game as "aesthetic judgement in Kant's analysis" (Kreft 2014: 366).[4] At the base of Kant's theory of aesthetics and aesthetic judgement lies the idea that to see or perceive something in an aesthetic way is to be disinterested (Kant 1790). The aesthetic gaze is disinterested and detached from an object or practice's standard/usual/prime function. Or, if one does not like talk of functions, the aesthetic gaze renders a take on an object or practice that disregards what the object or practice is. The gaze, if successful, yields a disinterested pleasure in the phenomenon in question. The Kantian line is that by aesthetically appreciating a phenomenon, one disengages from the context or the embeddedness of the phenomenon, and instead opens up a space where one can dwell on the phenomenon's pure perceptual qualities. As a mood, the tradition from Kant sees aesthetic appreciation as contemplative, not engaged. From the eighteenth century onward, the Kantian line has been the dominant view on aesthetic experience or appreciation, at least in the Western tradition. Alan Goldman sums up the tradition's basic tenets nicely:

> From the beginning the hallmark of the aesthetic attitude was held to be disinterest. (...) The common denotation in aesthetics is a lack of interest in the practical uses of the aesthetic object. We are to attend to the object as an object of contemplation only, to its phenomenal properties simply for the sake of perceiving them.

(Goldman 2005: 263)

Sometimes Kant calls the beauty that the aesthetic attitude avails free beauty, and he contrasts that with dependent beauty (Kant 1790: § 16). Free beauty is the beauty that is made possible by the disinterested aesthetic gaze for cool contemplation. Dependent beauty, on the other hand, is the beauty the phenomenon under consideration displays *qua* having a certain function or being of a certain kind. Free beauty is independent of function, while dependent beauty is not. It is a matter of controversy – as with all Kant's writings – just how we should understand his distinction between free and dependent beauty, and whether the perception of and attention to dependent beauty qualify as aesthetic experiences.

Leaving Kant scholarship aside, it is worth noting that Kant at least recognized that we talk of beauty that is connected with functionality, even though in the Western tradition free beauty became the assumed locus of the aesthetic experience.[5] One might furthermore note that contemporary aestheticians have worked on a related notion under the guise of functional beauty (see Parsons and Carlson 2008). It seems sufficient to say at this point that it would be surprising if there were no overlap or affinities between these theories and my agon aesthetics. I will introduce three examples of footballing interactions that are often deemed beautiful and elegant. The focus there is on how such aesthetic praise is connected to the (perceived) functionality of these interactions within the context of the competition, which a football match is. So functionality is clearly part of agon aesthetics, but there is more to it. In agon aesthetics, there is also a focus on the competitive setting, together with the drama that comes with that competitive setting. In short, agon aesthetics is a broader category than functional beauty.

In the Kantian tradition, aesthetic appreciation of something is the appreciation of the phenomenon as it appears to the subject, independent and regardless of its ontological status. What something is or is not – its ontological status – plays no role in the aesthetic appreciation of the phenomenon in question. Let us call this *disinterested aesthetics*. The aesthetics of Kant is, of course, a lot more sophisticated than this and covers vast fields of topics, but the disinterestedness of the aesthetic experience is the main *leitmotif* in his writings on aesthetics. Also, though I will not venture into a general critique of Kant and the Kantian line of reasoning, it is worth mentioning that there have been voices of dissent and more often than not it is the idea of disinterest and detachment being the hallmark of aesthetic appreciation that has come under scrutiny (see among others Carroll 2001, 2010, Danto 1996, 2003, Dickie 1964, Zemach 1997). Let us see how the disinterested aesthetics of Kant has played out when applied by scholars to the sport phenomenon.

In the philosophy of sport, Hans Ulrich Gumbrecht has advocated the virtues of the disinterested aesthetics when watching sport, in general, and football, in particular. Central to Gumbrecht's take on athletic beauty are the Greek notions of *agon* (Gr. ἀγών – competition) and *areté* (Gr. ἀρετή – striving for excellence). It is within the latter category that beauty emerges, and areté in sport takes precedence when, "with help from Immanuel Kant", Gumbrecht hopes to convince his reader that "watching sports may be a case of what philosophers call aesthetic experience" (Gumbrecht 2006: 48). In his praise of athletic beauty, Gumbrecht enlists Kant's help when he "by drawing on Kant's work (…) insist[s] that watching sports does indeed correspond to the most classical definitions of aesthetic experience" (Gumbrecht 2006: 39). The most classical definition of aesthetic experience that Gumbrecht builds his line of thought on is found in Kant's work, and here it is the disinterested aesthetics that takes centre stage.

> For Kant, the word *beautiful* comes from a "judgment of taste" performed in a situation of "pure disinterested satisfaction." The operative word here is *disinterested*, in its uncorrupted sense of "having no vested interest".
>
> *(Gumbrecht 2006: 40)*

Gumbrecht furthermore writes, "I opt for arete over agon (…) with the goal of praising athletic beauty" (Gumbrecht 2006: 71–72). It should be clear from the quotes above that the beauty in question is free beauty. According to Gumbrecht, "the central and conceptually most obvious explanation for the widespread popularity of sports" is "their aesthetic appeal" (Gumbrecht 2006: 40). Football's appeal, in Gumbrecht's view, lies in the realm of disinterested aesthetics – perhaps in a disinterested contemplation of the excellence of moving bodies. Quoting Kant, Gumbrecht tells us that the aesthetic experience of sport becomes sublime when it "threatens to overwhelm us" or else in the guise of the beautiful, where it "brings with it a feeling of the promotion of life" (Gumbrecht 2006: 47). Another philosopher of sport who explicitly endorses the Kantian line of disinterest and contemplation is Mumford. Mumford supports a way of watching sport, in general, and football, in particular, that "takes a deeper and more satisfying pleasure in the game", and he tells us we should become connoisseurs of sport who "are pleased by the finer things" (Mumford 2012a: 17, see also Vargiu 2010). Mumford recommends that we "watch sport (…) because it gives us aesthetic pleasure [and] release (…) in the contemplation of aesthetic value" (Mumford 2012a: 41). Mumford calls this "positive aesthetic value (…) beauty" (Mumford 2012a: 41). What sort of outlook on football, in particular, and sport, in general, does yield the beauty Mumford talks about? How should we understand the aesthetic attitude of the sport connoisseur? Mumford tells us, "[t]o answer this, there is a tradition in which the aesthetic perception is outlined in terms of disinterest. The notion is to be found in Kant" – i.e., disinterested aesthetics (Mumford 2012a: 60). The beauty of football – the beauty in the beautiful game – emerges or is made available to Mumford as a result of the disinterested and detached gaze of the Kantian football aesthete.

The pertinent question here is not whether the Kantian attitude of aesthetic disinterest is possible and a plausible description of the attitude at the root of aesthetic appreciation of various fine arts and beauty in nature. I will grant that possibility. Rather, the question of concern is how the disinterested aesthetics of the Kantian football aesthete connects with football and the aesthetic judgements people make when they deem a goal beautiful, an interchange on the pitch elegant and so on and so forth. Do the positive aesthetic values that people seem to find in football belong to the realm of disinterested aesthetics? The answer is no. This is not to suggest that football and similar sports cannot be appreciated in the disinterested aestheticizing manner of the detached Kantian aesthete in a contemplative mood. The non-fiction film *Zidane: A 21st Century Portrait* (Douglas Gordon and Philippe Parreno) about the French footballer Zinedine Zidane at times achieves this, or at least comes close. However, where the movie achieves this, the shimmering beauty of the movie is not dependent, in my view, on the movie consisting of documented scenes of a football match. It is telling that the movie mostly dwells on Zidane – in particular his face – and shows less of the interactions on the pitch between the footballers trying to win the match.[6] The film's aesthetic effects are largely achieved by preventing the audience from engaging in the football match going on around Zidane. Instead, the moviemakers force the audience to focus on Zidane's face and body, and the ambient surroundings with the dumbed-down sound of the terraces and Mogwai's experimental soundscapes and ambient noise. Of course, it is not lost on your average football supporter watching this film that it follows, (more or less) in real time, the mighty Zinedine Zidane as he plays a football match.[7] However, the beauty that emerges in the movie is more loosely connected to the fact that we are watching a football match. Recall that the disinterested aesthetics requires that the ontological status of the phenomenon in question – that it is a football match – play no role in the aesthetic appreciation of that phenomenon. The movie at times comes close to meeting that requirement. How the match we are watching in this film unfolds and ends is peripheral to our enjoyment of the movie. However, on the terraces or in front of our television screens when we follow a football match, we do not experience the aesthetics of a football match in the way that *Zidane: A 21st Century Portrait* avails itself of disinterested and contemplative pleasure. The aesthetic pleasure that football spectators invoke when they praise a goal by calling it beautiful is different. It is clearly connected to the actions on the pitch being actions in a football match. This shows that whatever aesthetic pleasures your average football spectator gets out of watching a game, it is not like the aesthetics of *Zidane: A 21st Century Portrait*. The two differ – that is, the actual match between Real Madrid and Villarreal CF, on the one hand, and the portrait of Zidane in that match in *Zidane: A 21st Century Portrait*, on the other – the former being a question of the nature of the game and how it connects with judgements of beauty, elegance and so on.

Gumbrecht and Mumford located the basis of the aesthetic sport experience in the Kantian notion of free beauty. We experience the pleasures of free beauty when we attend to an object or activity's phenomenal properties irrespective of what it is, i.e., of its ontological status. The ontological status of sports *qua* social activities is that they are competitions of a certain kind. It follows that, for these authors to appreciate sports aesthetically, they must be able to disregard them as competitions and to let the activity shine through in its mere phenomenal cloak. This is presumably why Gumbrecht opts for areté over agon and why Mumford calls for the contemplation of aesthetic value.[8] When you no longer see a particular football match as a competition between two teams trying to overcome each other – that is, when you no longer see the football match as a football match – the disinterested contemplative experience can give you a "feeling of the promotion of life" (Gumbrecht 2006: 47), or "an aesthetic insight into the nature of our embodied existence" (Mumford 2012a: 140).[9] It could be that, in certain measurement sports, it is easier to disregard the context in which an athlete's bodily movements take place, i.e. the sport competition, because, for example in long jump, there are no other competitors on the scene when each individual competitor performs his or her jump. Also, say, in watching a running event like the 100-metre race, a spectator can focus on one athlete's bodily movements and perhaps manage to achieve a disinterested detachment from the running event *qua* a competitive sporting event. However, in constructive-destructive sports like football, with its direct hindering or obstructing actions and body contact, the other competitor, i.e. members of the other team, is intrinsic to the football action. As a consequence, we find that the aesthetic praise of football actions is predominantly of actions *qua* actions in the game, and not connected to the so-called free beauty of Gumbrecht's and Mumford's philosophy of sport.[10] The best way to demonstrate this is to look at three famous footballing interactions that are often praised for their beauty and elegance.

First, consider Argentina's second goal scored by Esteban Cambiasso in Argentina's victory against Serbia and Montenegro in the 2006 World Cup. After an elaborate move of 24 passes, Hernán Crespo backheeled a return pass to Cambiasso, who emphatically put the ball past goalkeeper Dragoslav Jevrić. Why is this regarded in the football world as one of the most beautiful goals scored in a World Cup? Looking at the footage, we find that the interaction does not take place at breath-taking speed, though the move does speed up at the end of the interaction. The coherence and coordination of the goal are impressive and deemed beautiful by your average football spectator because he or she knows that it is taking place in a competitive setting where the Serbian players are chasing the ball, trying to destroy the move. The beauty of the goal lies deeply embedded in the context of agon; the Argentines seemingly effortlessly move the ball around the park as the Serbian players desperately try but fail to even get close to the Argentines, who crown their achievement with Cambiasso firing the ball into the net.[11] Would the move be beautiful if you were able to see its phenomenal properties simply for the sake of perceiving them and independently of what the move was, i.e., a finely weaved goal in a competitive football match? Perhaps. Perhaps someone would be able to see it like that. That latter beauty would resemble the beauty emerging in *Zidane: A 21st Century Portrait* and be similarly removed from the beauty of agon. The beauty within agon, however, is what your average football spectator sees. It is primarily a poster goal for the beautiful team goal in a football match.

Second, consider Johan Cruyff and his innovative feint, known as the Cruyff turn. The move was first performed in a 1974 World Cup match between the Netherlands and Sweden. This move is often seen as a fine representative of the aesthetic side of the game, but again the question is how we should understand that. The move started with Cruyff positioning his back against the opposition's goal and dropping his left shoulder, feigning a backward pass. This sent the defender forwards. Cruyff then dragged the ball backwards with his right foot behind his standing leg and turned 180 degrees. He was then free to head towards the opposition's goal. The chance Cruyff created in this match went begging, but the dummy was forever introduced into the football repertoire. Though I am sure some would claim that the move on its own was aesthetically beautiful, one does well to note that when Cruyff drags the ball backwards with his foot behind his standing leg, while twisting his body the other way, he looks rather awkward. You will not find this body posture among the statues exemplifying the antiquity conception of the beautiful body. This does not mean that someone with a disinterested aesthetic gaze could not find Cruyff's awkwardly twisted body beautiful, as I suspect one could argue that any body shape or form is open for the disinterested aesthetic gaze. Be that as it may. Again, the attraction of the move as football spectators see it is intrinsically tied to its functionality on the pitch – being a feint or a dummy does not even make sense outside the competitive setting. The elegance, audacity and novelty of the move are features that only emerge when seen as parts of a move in a competitive football match. Indeed, the beauty of the move is that it leaves the defender stranded, while the attacker is free to charge against the opposition's goal. It is a novel solution to a time-honoured problem in football – how to lose the defender while increasing your team's chance of scoring a goal. The aesthetic qualities of the move, which commentators and audiences alike praise, are closely tied to the constructive aim of footballers to score goals.

Last, but not least, consider Diego Maradona's famous solo goal for Argentina against England in the 1986 World Cup. In a dazzling display, Maradona took on the whole English defence, drove past defenders, ducked challenges and finally was able to lift the ball past an onrushing Peter Shilton in the England goal. If in a poetic mood, one might perhaps be tempted to say that Maradona danced through the English defence, but of course that is exactly what he did not do. Maradona's moves are not those of a dancer trying to express himself, but rather those of a footballer twisting his way through and slipping by defending bodies that are trying to close him down. The movements of his body bring with them a kind of aesthetic appeal, which is different than that of dance, precisely because it is conducted under the imminent threat of violence, aka the tackle, and is predicated on avoiding the flying bodies of the opponent's defence and targeting the opposition's goal. Listen to the crowd and how it roars as Maradona closes in and gets into the English box. No doubt, Maradona's opening move just around the halfway line, when he receives the ball and escapes two English players, is simply marvellous and stunning in its seemingly effortless effectiveness. Still, it is the movement up the pitch towards the English goal that gets the crowd going. If there ever was such a thing as footballing beauty, this should be a prime example. However, the appreciation and, dare we say, aesthetic experience of the sheer footballing beauty of Maradona in free flow is clearly not one characterized by the disinterested aesthetic contemplative mood of Gumbrecht's and Mumford's philosophy.[12] This does not mean that spectators were not left in awe by Maradona's goal, perhaps with an elevated feeling of just having seen something very special. Nevertheless, that appreciation is firmly placed within an understanding of the beauty and elegance of the goal as something that emerges within the competitive setting of the football match.[13] This is not an aesthetics of agon, where the aesthetic experience takes you away from engagement in the football drama, but rather an *agon aesthetics*, where the aesthetic experience is found within engagement in the football drama of competition.[14]

An agon aesthetics of football

Drama or the dramatic takes centre stage in football, not the fairness of the result or disinterested aesthetic contemplation. Kupfer noted, "[t]he complications introduced by human opposition multiply the aesthetic possibilities in competitive sports – dramatic possibilities due to social interaction", and I have argued that "[f]ootball is about the drama, about the tension and the emotions it provokes" (Kupfer 1983: 124, Borge 2010a: 28, see also Borge 2010b). Furthermore, Kreft has emphasized "[w]hen football is called a beautiful game, it is this universal dramatic character which is described, and not 'the aesthetic' used for 'aesthetic sports'" (Kreft 2014: 370, see also Kreft 2012, and Borge 2015c).[15]

The drama of football and football's dramatic possibilities must not be conflated with drama as theatre, fiction film, etc. Perhaps the reason why sport drama has remained a neglected field is because scholars working in mainstream aesthetics have a tendency to think of drama only in terms of theatrical art (including theatre and fiction film). After all, sport is, as Kreft puts it, "real action" where "athletes appear and perform as themselves" and not "dramatic personae" (Kreft 2012: 226, 228, 231). Best also emphasizes this when he writes, "it is a central convention of art (...) that the object of one's attention is an *imagined* object" (Best 1978: 118, see also Best 1974). In the normal case, actions on a theatre stage or in a fiction film are carried out by actors who we pretend are someone else – often non-existing persons – and the actions performed represent other actions carried out by these non-existing characters. We are aware that the actual actions belong to a type of action that is meant to induce this sort of pretence. The actor acts, while the character represented by that actor's acting is doing something else. Football and other spectator sports are not like that. The drama of football must not be equated with the drama of theatre or fiction film.

Why, then, would one identify (part of) our engagement in football as something belonging to the realm of aesthetics and not merely be satisfied with saying that sport engages us as spectators? We can speak about the dramatic and dramas with regard to the ordinary world. However, that per se does not necessarily justify assigning that which is dramatic or a drama to the realm of aesthetics. Granted. First, we have already seen in Chapter 1 how engagement in sport involves protopretence and that only then does a sport contest come alive engagement-wise – unless, as already noted, participants play for outcomes that matter simpliciter, like surviving. A further reason for thinking about a sport like football in aesthetic terms is the simple observation that people, sports pundits, commentators and spectators alike quite often use the language of aesthetic appreciation when describing events on a football pitch. These data give us motivation and are in need of explanation. We saw that aesthetic appreciation of football actions, like Argentina's second goal against Serbia and Montenegro, the Cruyff turn and Maradona's wondrous goal, relies on seeing them as part of a competitive sport. This is the basis for seeking to formulate an agon aesthetics. We are engaged in the teams' struggle to win – the social interaction between two teams locked in a competitive setting – and one way to understand that engagement is to say that we enjoy the drama as it unfolds before us. Exploring this line of argument is justified by the fact that appealing to drama and the dramatic is common in the world of football. Consider some examples of appeals to drama from the footballing world that do not fit the narrow conception of drama found in mainstream aesthetics:

> But, I guess, even those matches could not come close to the late drama of the 1966 final between England and Germany at Wembley – Germany's late goal in normal time, then Sir Geoff Hurst's wonderful strike at the end.
> (Phil McNulty, BBC 2014b)

> PENALTY! RED CARD! HANDBALL! PANIC! DRAMA! Ghana will have a penalty to win it! (…) Gyan missed it! And that's it. The penalty was the last kick of the match! Unbelievable stuff. Suarez is led off the pitch, weeping, before it's taken. (…) He's saved his team from certain defeat. Horrible cheating, on the other hand. (…) Amazing scenes: You should have seen Suarez's celebration when that penalty missed. Really, genuinely incredible drama (…) Sebastián Abreu wins it for Uruguay! A cheeky, lazy chipped penalty from the man they call El Loco.
> (Simon Burnton, The Guardian, 2010)

> Liverpool won great drama against Boro after 30 (!) penalties.
> (Thomas Haarstad, Dagbladet, 2014, my translation)

> [A] match full of everything, artistry, drama and courage which kept us on the edge of our seats to the last minute, when Red Star, with a final dazzling shot by Janković, settled the affair.
> (Geoffrey Green in The Times reporting on the second round in the European Cup between Liverpool and Crvena Zvezda at Anfield, November 6, 1973, quoted in Wilson with Murray 2013: 143)

Other examples are in abundance with regard to both football and other sports. This is an important basis for pursuing an agon aesthetics in relation to which drama and the dramatic have a central position. The fact that the disinterested aesthetics, which has traditionally been seen as the locus of the aesthetic experience, is ill-equipped to help us understand these data is no reason to think that football and other sports do not avail to their spectators some sort of aesthetic experience. Instead, this failure is an indication of the limited nature of disinterested aesthetics.

Best, on the other hand, dismisses talk of drama and the dramatic with regard to sports (Best 1978: 117–120). You can call sports drama just as you can call any other type of human interaction drama, but Best questions whether "'dramatic' is being used here in the same sense as when it occurs in the context of play" (Best 1978: 118). This dismissal, however, is too hasty. There are obvious and interesting similarities between drama as we find it in the theatre, fiction film, sports competitions and other places that are worth exploring. Best fails to notice them because he singles out the presence of fictional characters, i.e. representation of fictional characters, objects and events, as a necessary requirement for sensibly applying the notion of "drama" to some practice or social activity. Indeed, Best ties the notion of "drama" to fine art, and because Best does not consider sport art, it is also not drama proper. However, aesthetic value or appreciation and art are not coextensive. It is common in mainstream aesthetics to bring aspects of our natural environment into the realm of aesthetics and talk about, for example, the beauty of scenic nature. Best was well aware of this when he correctly distinguished between the artistic and the aesthetic (Best 1978: 113–114). Still, somehow, when Best dismisses talk of drama outside the art setting, he seems to relapse into identifying aesthetics with art, which is not his considered view. I will show that Best's narrow understanding of drama is wrongheaded.

The first thing to note is that it is far from clear that drama, in any original meaning of the word, denotes only fictional characters and their fictional actions. Kreft informs us that even though the word is often used to signify drama as theatre, on other occasions it is used "as signifier of any action, which is its original ancient Greek use. Historically, 'drama', similar to 'praxis', meant action" (Kreft 2012: 225). Obviously, neither the usage first described by Kreft nor etymology gets to be the final arbiter of what the word "drama" means. However, we can add to that the observation that there is a widespread practice of referring to football as drama – as the quotes above show – and Best's narrow understanding of drama seems more dubious. It is easy to find similar examples of other sports being called drama. Moreover, in ordinary usage, as we find it, for example, in various media outlets, the words "drama" and "dramatic" are often used to talk about what happens to real people and what real people do. Furthermore, documentary films – non-fiction – are usually also characterized by dramatic structure, once again showing how "drama" is not a special possession of fiction, but pervasive across many real activities.

Indeed, there are academic fields that are in line with such ordinary usage of the words "drama" and "dramatic". Famously, sociologist Erving Goffman borrowed a whole host of imagery from the world of theatre, including the notion of dramaturgy, when describing our ordinary world presentation of ourselves to others (Goffman 1959). Goffman was inspired by Kenneth Burke's *dramatism*. Burke considers human relationships to be dramas of living (Burke 1966). In the tradition of Burke and later as an important part of performance studies, anthropologist Victor Turner analysed human interaction as social drama. According to Turner, social drama is an unfolding of social events that constitute a "sequence of social interactions of a conflictive, competitive or agonistic type" (Turner 1987: 33, see also Turner 1981, 1982).

Conflict is the cornerstone of Turner's understanding of social drama. Turner's further analysis of the social drama, which depicts it as following certain stages, need not concern us here. Turner was interested in conflicts that arise in the ordinary world or in everyday life, whereas our focus is on sports like football. Conflict does not arise or emerge in a game of football. Conflict, in the form of competition, is part of the football blueprint. Football is by its very nature competitive — that is what it means to be a competitive sport — and sports that are constructive-destructive and involve direct hindering or obstructing actions have more and richer dramatic possibilities. To play a football match is to stage a sequence of social interactions — both cooperative actions on the game's creative side and conflictive actions on the game's destructive side — which renders football matches a sequence of actions and events of a conflictive, competitive and agonistic type. The two teams try to beat each other, or, minimally, not to be beaten by the other team. Sports, in general, and football, in particular, are subsets of Turner's category of social drama. In light of both ordinary usage of the word "drama" and various scholarly work, we can conclude that there is a clear sense in which drama is tied to actions and events as we find them in our world — both the ordinary world and the sport world — and not only to imagined actions and events.

Second, the art of theatre has in many ways moved away from the idea that the drama and the dramatic are identified or only associated with the theatrical arts. In his seminal work *Postdramatic Theater*, theatre researcher Hans-Thies Lehmann argues that theatre (or more appropriately theatrical art) need not be drama nor dramatic (Lehmann 2006). The postdramatic theatre, as identified by Lehmann, is often seen as a reaction to and critique of the representational aspect of traditional or dramatic theatre, and the structuring of time in such theatre. The first aspect of their critique concerns the representational aspect of traditional or dramatic theatre. This need not worry us here, because we have already conceded that this is one place where traditional theatre and sport come apart. When playing a sport like football, one does not normally represent dramatic personae, imagined objects or fictional characters. Also, as shown above, the word "drama" is widely used to describe more than just traditional theatre plays. It is interesting to note that Bertolt Brecht, who in his plays often explicitly challenges and problematizes the idea of represented characters in traditional theatre, endorses the sport spectacle. According to Kreft, the realness of action in sport, as opposed to the scripted representation of action in bourgeois theatre, is one of the things that caused Brecht to argue that theatre should be more like sports (Kreft 2011, Brecht 1995).

The second aspect of their critique concerns the temporal structuring of traditional or dramatic theatre. With regard to the second aspect, Lehmann writes, "[d]rama means a flow of time, controlled and surveyable" (Lehmann 2006: 40). Of course, postdramatic theatre, as described by Lehmann, aims at breaking away from the broadly Aristotelian understanding of drama as consisting of a beginning, a middle and an end, which are sequenced in linear time (Aristotle 1996). Moreover, Lehmann's understanding of drama might be read as excluding social drama, because real time is not controlled in the same way as the perceived time of traditional theatre. On the other hand, for us to call something in real life a drama, we would likely demand a certain level of surveyability. Furthermore, there is also reason to expect that the shorter the time span in which a sequence of social interactions of a conflictive, competitive or agonistic type occurs, the more dramatic these actions and events will seem to us. However, exploring the full ramifications of thinking of ordinary world sequences of actions and events as drama will have to wait for another day. Our detour through the theory of social drama was primarily aimed at showing that the notion of drama is used to denote more than theatre plays and fiction films, and not at providing a general defence of that theory.

Returning to Lehmann and the tradition of postdramatic theatre's critique of the temporal structuring of traditional or dramatic theatre, we might note that part of their critique of dramatic theatre is that "drama is a structure that gives a logical (namely dramatic) order to the confusing chaos and plenitude of Being" (Lehmann 2006: 40). Lehmann is far from clear on what Being is supposed to mean, though it certainly has a Heideggerian flavour to it. Here, I will assume that Lehmann's Being is something along the lines of Edmund Husserl's notion of a life-world or Martin Heidegger's Being-in-the-world (Husserl 1954, Heidegger 1927). The world as a lived experience is a confusing chaos of plenitude. The problem with the temporal structuring of traditional or dramatic theatre identified here is that by doing that – structuring so as to give logical order – drama does not reveal Being, but rather betrays it by presenting reality as it is not.

Whether this is a bad thing need not concern us here. Rather, the interesting part is that something similar happens in football and other sports. On the one hand, football is a type of conflict that we stage for our own enjoyment and the conflict, which a football match is, parallels many aspects of real-life conflicts. As I have argued elsewhere, "[t]he small margins and the element of chance keep football matches more open-ended and unpredictable than all other sports" and "[f]ootball matches involve many contingencies and it is like life's own uncertainties have been woven into the very fabric of the football fiction" (Borge 2010a: 32–33). Similarly, Kreft notes that the features of football "build a dramatic narrative (...) which simulates dramatic social dimension of lifeworld so quintessentially well" (Kreft 2014: 370).[16] On the other hand, football matches deliver unambiguous results – either one of the teams wins or else it is a draw – whereas conflicts in the ordinary world or in everyday life seldom have such clear and unambiguous outcomes. In this respect, football is very different from real life or life-world, which it parallels so well in many other ways. There is a transparency and unambiguousness to football, which makes it easier to deal with than the ordinary world outside the game. I suspect that this is an important reason why people find engagement in football and other sports so enjoyable. In football, we know what the conflict is about. It concerns winning the football match, or else, not losing it. We know who the relevant antagonists are: the two teams. We know there will be a result within 90 or 120 minutes (sometimes a little more). We even know which results are possible for the two teams: win, draw or lose. We can watch how the conflict unfolds on a pitch, a pitch that we can fully survey, thus keeping track of any development in the game. We know there will be an end result of the conflict by the end of the evening. Someone attracted to postdramatic theatre might argue that Brecht was too quick to propose the sport spectacle as a model for the theatrical arts. The sport drama shares with traditional or dramatic theatre the feature of making what in the ordinary world or everyday life is messy and often ambiguous into something orderly and unambiguous. In the ordinary world or everyday life, conflicts do not come in neat packages of clear-cut features like a set time span, highly predictable phases, a set location, clearly defined possible results, and so on and so forth, whereas they do in sports like football.

In football, the flow of time is both controlled and surveyable. Whereas theatrical drama is defined by being representational and structuring time in a certain manner, the football drama only structures time. However, football matches, like theatre plays, are staged. There is a decision to play a game of football. One finds a suitable place, a suitable time, players who are willing to participate and then the teams play the match – often in front of spectators. Unlike many everyday life events, which in a fairly clear sense sometimes just happen to people, football matches do not just happen. They are planned and executed. They are staged with a strict structuring of time. There is a beginning, a middle (which even contains a half-time break), and a second half, which when it is over marks the end of the match. Sometimes, there will be extra time and even a penalty shoot-out. Both players and spectators know all this beforehand. All parts are sharply punctuated by the referee officiating the match, blowing his or her whistle. Also, as already mentioned, for the spectator the football pitch can be seen and taken in all at once. As a football match unfolds, everything is there to be seen by the spectators and the players – all the action is there to be taken in. Again, the analogy to theatrical drama holds up pretty well. Performance studies scholar Richard Schechner makes a similar point when he writes, "[t]he spaces [great arenas, stadiums, churches and theatres] are uniquely organized so that a large group can watch a small group" (Schechner 2003: 14).

Football and other spectator sports share with the theatre and fiction film the feature of being an activity that is done in part for others to watch and enjoy. Football, the theatre and fiction film are staged, while most ordinary world interactions are not, though some are, e.g., court proceedings and public executions. In the latter types of cases, many are willing to speak of dramaturgy. One does well to note that such events also often go through quite predictable phases of events, towards a clearly defined conclusion. The same applies to football matches. Unlike most theatre plays and fiction films, football matches do not follow a script, though the constitutive rules of the game limit the actions that can occur within the practice of football. Football is *staged, but not scripted*. The football match, a staged competition, contains a kind of performance – improvised within certain parameters and according to certain rules. Within these limitations, there is also the presence of set pieces – corners, free kicks, penalties, throw-ins – which are moments in the game that can be more closely controlled and more precisely prepared for, though they are still unpredictable. Wolfgang Welsch makes the same observation when he writes, "[s]port is drama without a script. It creates its own drama" (Welsch 2005: 146).

The drama of football is unscripted and in this way importantly different from traditional or dramatic theatre. Mainstream aesthetics, with its focus on disinterestedness, is ill-equipped to understand our engagement in the football drama. For this reason, Kreft has suggested that when we wish "to develop aesthetics of sport" we should start with the "aesthetics of everyday life" (Kreft 2012: 219). This advice is sound, though there is a worry. Football and other sports are not part of everyday life or the ordinary world. Football is extra-ordinary. Doing something for sport, playing games and, furthermore, playing games that are sports are not everyday activities, and they are not generally undertaken for specific and useful purposes. Instead, the extra-ordinary world of football is something we voluntarily engage in even though the activity *qua* that activity does not have a specific purpose outside the sport itself.[17] Sport, including football, is an extra onto the ordinary, and its aesthetics is in that sense not of the same kind as the aesthetics of everyday life, aka the ordinary world. Kreft seems to agree when he concedes that "aesthetics of sport covers an activity which is not an ordinary aesthetic practice of everyday" and that "[t]he place of sport is a place under suspension of everyday reality, but still part of life" (Kreft 2012: 228–229).

The term, however, need not really worry us, though it is misleading with regard to football and other sports. Building on Tom Leddy and Yuriko Saito, Paisley Livingston reminds us that "the most basic motivations behind investigations in everyday aesthetics is the desire to explore *the aesthetic value of phenomena that were overlooked* as a result of an emphasis on the fine arts and certain aspects of the natural environment" (Livingston 2012: 259, my italics, see also Leddy 2005; Saito 1997, 2007). Livingston goes on, suggesting "this subfield of aesthetics should accordingly embrace *the aesthetic experience or aesthetic appreciation of things familiar or everyday, but not the aesthetics of the fine arts and scenic nature*" (Livingston 2012: 259, my italics). Along the same lines, Leddy suggests that if sports are not art forms, "then it [the aesthetics of sports] is part of everyday aesthetics" (Leddy 2012: 19). Football will, according to Livingston's operational demarcation of everyday aesthetics, fall within the scope of everyday aesthetics because it is familiar, even though it is not an everyday life or ordinary world matter. This is also appropriate, as Livingston identifies Kupfer's work as the first representative of everyday aesthetics. When thinking about the aesthetics of football, the Livingston line of thought liberates us from the theoretical straightjacket of always being forced to model our theorizing of aesthetic experiences on certain paradigmatic cases from the fine arts. The field opens up.

One worry for the aestheticians, whose focus is on the aesthetic experience of everyday objects and situations, is the question of whether that very process does not change the phenomenon at hand and remove it from the realm of the everyday or the ordinary. Saito worries that the aesthetic appreciation of everyday life renders "the ordinary extraordinary" (Saito 2007: 245, see also Leddy 2005: 17, Livingston 2012: 260–267). A leading idea in the thinking on everyday aesthetics is the possibility of and benefit associated with aesthetically appreciating a phenomenon of everyday life for its own sake. Does not that make one's experience of the everyday object or situation something other than an everyday experience, thus turning the ordinary into something extraordinary? This concern does not arise with regard to football, because football is already removed from the ordinary world; it is extra-ordinary. Furthermore, football and its drama are normally sought out and appreciated by spectators for their own sake, and not for some other practical purpose related to everyday dealings with the world.

It is here we find the basis of an agon aesthetics of football and similar sports. The aesthetics of competitions – the agon aesthetics – lies in engaging in the conflict that a competition is, while being aware that the conflict does not concern ordinary world issues, but is unnecessary and invented for the very purpose of having a conflict to enjoy. The pleasure of football and other sports is found in engaging oneself in the sport proceedings, not in distancing oneself. Whereas disinterested aesthetics demands refraining from any engagement in the functionality the object of aesthetic appreciation might have, agon aesthetics of football demands that the players and spectators invest interest and engagement in an activity that has no functionality outside its own realm. Winning a football match is not a matter of solving an ordinary world problem or otherwise being productive and trying to better one's own or others' life situation. As argued in Chapter 1, "football is fictional in character. The main fiction present in football is that winning football matches matters" (Borge 2010a: 28, Borge 2010b: 169).

As we have seen, the idea that football is fictional in character, in the sense that it involves some kind of make-believe or pretence, is a complex one. The make-believe or pretence in question is that winning football matches matters, when in truth it does not. That is, by winning a football match you are primarily achieving just that: winning a football match. This is not to suggest that you cannot find many matches where a great deal seems to be at stake, like the prestige of winning the World Cup or the salary of professional footballers. However, one must be careful to remember that to invest prestige in football matches is to pretend that it matters, thus making it matter. Many other things, on the other hand, matter simpliciter. Having the most beautiful or handsome spouse or partner – thus having sexual access to and breeding possibilities with someone whose looks are taken as a sign of good health and a reliable indicator of good genes – is prestigious in itself. Mating strategies involve, among other things, considerations of attractiveness, and one does not need to invest prestige in it for it to matter. Football is not like that. Football comes with no prestige in its own right, unless one invests prestige or interest in the game. Regarding professional footballers, they too depend on the football fiction in order to make football matches matter. A footballer like, say, Liverpool's Mohamed Salah is better off materially when his club wins football matches. However, the main reason for this is that spectators like me are willing to engage in the importance of Liverpool winning football matches. With the spectators' engagement comes income from ticket sales, TV rights, merchandise and various sponsorship deals – the sponsors being drawn to the game due to its large audience. Most spectators like me, however, do not gain materially from Liverpool's success, or, for that matter, lose based on their lack of success. When we admit that winning football matches matters economically for elite players like Diego Godín, Yaya Touré, Shinji Kagawa, and others who make their living playing football, we need to keep in mind that the factor enabling professionalism in football is the surrounding layer of make-believe or pretence on the part of audiences and spectators. Professional sports are only possible when spectators make the outcome matter and are willing to spend money on something that, in reality, makes little practical difference in their own life. Note also that we once more find a parallel to the art world. No one would doubt that, say, the James Bond movies should count as fiction. Still, Daniel Craig and others involved in the James Bond franchise make a living out of the James Bond make-believe, and thus it matters to them that Bond not be killed off in his fictional universe. For these people, the James Bond movies matter, and matter in the same way as other ordinary world concerns do, but this professionalism is enabled by the ticket-buying movie-going spectators' engagement in the fiction of James Bond.

Professional footballers are the football version of professional actors, just as amateur footballers are the football version of amateur actors. Professional actors and amateur actors are in the same business of make-believe for the entertainment of others and are basically doing the same thing. Presumably, the former are much better at what they do than the latter are. The same holds for professional and amateur footballers qua footballers. They are engaged in the same game. The former get to play on a bigger stage due to their superior footballing skills. These superior skills together with various other factors, such as the identity-making potential of football and football teams – make the rest of us willing to invest importance and money in the game. It is this investment that enables professionalism in the game. From this perspective, football matters to professional footballers the way ordinary concerns do. The rest of us, however, cannot say the same. The actors' ordinary world concerns for the plays and films they are in depend on the movie-going audiences' willingness to make these fictions matter. Without that there would be no theatre or film industry and professional actors. The footballers' ordinary world concern for the matches they play depends on the football-watching audiences' willingness to make these matches matter. Without that there would be no football industry or professional footballers. The analogy, however, does not carry all the way through. There are differences. Getting the football fiction going only requires the proto-pretence of social play, as we find it in rough-and-tumble play. That is presumably less demanding than whatever type of pretence transports an actor or actress into the mindset he or she needs to play a role. Furthermore, whereas an actor or actress is probably aware of engaging in make-believe, footballers as such are not. The proto-pretence of social rough-and-tumble play has a different phenomenology. Still, both activities need active engagement for the practices to come alive and be something we care about. Note again the contrast to the basic tenet of disinterested aesthetics. Whereas the latter demands disengagement for an object's or event's aesthetic qualities to shine through, the game of football does not come alive for spectators unless they are invested in the match mattering – something of importance is at stake. Recall our example of Cambiasso's goal against Serbia and Montenegro. Watch the footage and try to see it as a type of art performance, maybe a postmodern dance performance. What you get is something completely different than the thrill the spectators of this match got when watching it. For the interaction to come alive in an agon aesthetic manner, you must see it as a competition and furthermore think of it as something that is of importance. You must make it matter. Only then will you enjoy its agon aesthetic qualities.

On the other hand, it is important to our enjoyment that the sport conflict of football be unnecessary; there must be a fairly clear sense that nothing of importance is at stake. The latter makes it easier and more acceptable to enjoy participating in and watching such an event. This does not necessarily limit the *agon aesthetic attitude* towards such things as sporting events. One could take an agon aesthetic attitude towards ordinary world conflicts, but most would find that both distasteful and perhaps perverse. Imagine the reactions if a war correspondent, when reporting on a brooding conflict, said that he or she did not care who won the conflict and hoped it would be a good war with lots of casualties and dramatic situations. The outrage would have been justified. We are not supposed to enjoy participating in or watching conflict types like war. Why? One simple reason would be that war is a serious business that matters and that such things should not be enjoyed as a conflict spectacle. However, no one would raise an eyebrow if someone said of a football match that he or she did not care who won, as long as it was a good, hard-fought match with lots of drama and action.

Again, the parallel to the world of traditional theatre, but also fiction film and literature, is striking. Most enjoy these art forms primarily due to the drama and tension they provide and not due to a disinterested gaze at elements of style. The disinterested aesthetics of the Kantian aesthete is of course available when consuming these art products. The same applies to football – you can enjoy the spectacle in a disinterested fashion, but most spectators are drawn to the drama. Furthermore, in order to engage in fictional stories, one must pretend that the fate of the non-existing fictional characters matters. One might spin such *aesthetic engagement* as imagining that the fictional characters actually exist and because of that their fate matters, or suggest that aesthetic engagement is imagining that the fate of fictional characters matters. The latter, perhaps, sits better with the observation that even when we engage in fictional characters and events, we are still also aware that what happens is not real and in a fairly straightforward sense does not matter. Furthermore, when enjoying fiction we might sympathize with characters, hoping things will go well for them. Still, we might also want these characters to experience troubling situations, because that makes for interesting drama and narrative developments. Gregory Currie calls these two types of attitude character desire and narrative desire (Currie 1999). One might be shocked and saddened if a character in a fiction drama dies, while at the same time delight in the narrative possibilities this creates. However, if one were to take this attitude towards bad things that befall other people in real life, then I suspect one would be met with condemnation. Narrative desires are acceptable when they have fictional dramas as their objects, whereas they are not if their objects are the dramas of real life.[18] The same applies to football – to desire conflict because it provides us with a good drama is acceptable when the object is a competitive sport like football, whereas it is not if the object is a real-life conflict.

As noted in the beginning of this section, the aesthetic qualities that sports like football bring to the table involve the drama of social interaction that follows from the sport being a constructive-destructive sport that allows for direct hindering or obstructing actions. Competitions without such direct actions allow for less social interaction between participants and, thus, fewer ways in which the competition in question can unfold – fewer action-reaction sequences – making the sport more predictable than constructive-destructive sports like football. A football match might be ugly, but also action packed, and that can still be engaging. Furthermore, a tight game is often perceived as more action packed and tense than a one-sided game, where one of the teams has run up the score. This is not to suggest that, in the ordinary case, beautiful play is not to be preferred over ugly play, but rather that playing ugly is not necessarily an aesthetic flaw in football. The prime aesthetic flaw of a football game is not being ugly, but being boring. If that is the case, one might argue that spectators could sometimes prefer that one of the teams play ugly, negative football – if the two teams are very unevenly matched. Consider a case in which the much weaker team tries to play positive, perhaps even aspiring to play beautiful football, and by doing so finds itself at the receiving end of a rout being, say, 6–0 down before half-time. From an agon aesthetic point of view, one might very well argue that it would have been preferable if that team had instead played ugly, niggling and negative football, if that approach had resulted in a tenser game with more interesting action-reaction sequences. Moreover, to exploit the analogy between football and the theatre, fiction film and literature, one should not underestimate the pleasure of having teams and footballers that function for some as footballing anti-heroes whom one loves to hate. One would hope that everyone understands, deep down, that it is not actually morally despicable to play negative football – it is, after all, a sport. Still, the pleasures of vilifying the opposing team when one has forged an allegiance to either a team or a playing style should not be underestimated. It adds to the spectator's own engagement in the football drama and makes his or her experience even more emotional. The slogan might be that football feeds on emotions, not sound reasoning. And as with all good slogans, it oversimplifies. It evokes an overtly simplistic account of the relationship between reason and emotions. It underplays the extent to which fans and other football-world denizens do engage in (broadly) rational arguments about tactics, selection, player quality, etc. Moreover, emotion informs such arguments, as it does almost any topic about which we reason and argue. The presence of emotion does not make such arguments "unsound". All this is true. Still, the slogan captures something central to the football experience. Emotional engagement is in the driver's seat with regard to most football spectators' enjoyment of the game. Furthermore, when watching football, many, perhaps most, of us feel little compulsion to remain reasonable with regard to our reaction to whatever happens on the pitch.

One might expect that defending this line of agon aesthetics, with its emphasis on action in the form of action-reaction sequences, means committing oneself to the position that offensively minded teams, e.g., FC Barcelona of latter years, are aesthetically more pleasing or preferable compared to more defensively minded teams, e.g., José Mourinho's Chelsea. After all, do not matches with the former type of teams give spectators more action-reaction sequences to enjoy? No such thing follows. The first thing to note is that the main phenomenon for agon aesthetic appreciation in football is the match, not the individual teams. Viewing pleasure and our engagement are tied to what happens in matches. Still, one might reiterate this question as follows. Is it not the case that the agon aesthetics presented in this section predicts that a match between two fairly evenly matched, offensively minded teams that play well and serve up a 4–4 result, with loads of clear goal-scoring opportunities, is aesthetically superior to a match between two evenly matched, defensively minded teams that play well and serve up a 0–0 result with no clear goal-scoring opportunities? No. One could imagine a football aesthete of the agon aesthetics school who thinks that high-scoring games, which are loaded with goal-scoring opportunities, are vulgar and only aesthetically pleasing to the untrained, unsophisticated football eye. Real beauty, such a football aesthete might claim, lies in tight matches where the scoring is low and few chances are created, not because the teams are inept at creating chances, i.e. bad at the creative side of the game, but because both teams are equally brilliant at defence. Whereas the untrained eye sees a dull football match where the teams cancel each other out thereby creating no chances, according to the football aesthete, the connoisseur of football sees a more subtle ebb and flow of action-reaction patterns of creative and destructive football moves. The beauty lies in how both teams brilliantly close down the windows of potential goal-scoring opportunities. The constructive moves of each side open up such windows, which several moves down in the sequence of potential actions would have resulted in a goal-scoring opportunity and perhaps a goal. Those venues of action are then closed down by the defending team's reactions to the initial constructive moves.[19] Then, new constructive football moves initiate new such sequences of creative and destructive moves and countermoves, and so on and so forth. It is in the joy of good defending, which entails good constructive moves to defend against, our football aesthete exclaims, that the football connoisseur may glimpse the sublime.[20]

The importance of our imagined football aesthete is not whether his or her theory of football beauty is correct, but rather to see that the agon aesthetics of football suggested in this section does not render such questions – concerning which playing styles, match developments, scores, etc. are most aesthetically pleasing – foregone conclusions. This, I think, is one advantage of the theory of agon aesthetics. First, we must settle on a framework for how to understand the aesthetics of football. The agon aesthetics gives us that. Only then can we fill that framework with substantial arguments about questions such as what types of matches, playing styles, football moves, etc., are more or most aesthetically pleasing. Moreover, there is something clearly correct about the line pushed by our imagined football aesthete, which is that the more you understand and know the game, the more you get out of it. The agon aesthetics of football as presented explains what the trained football spectator enjoys, when he or she finds pleasure in matches that the novice football spectator might find boring. As with the three examples of football beauty at the end of the last section, it all comes down to action-reaction patterns set within the context of an unnecessary conflict staged for our enjoyment, which is what a football match is. The agon aesthetics makes sense of the drama of football, while the disinterested aesthetics of sport fails to make proper contact with the phenomenon at hand.

The football match setting provides a social drama of an agonistic kind – action-reaction patterns set within the context of an unnecessary conflict staged for our enjoyment – which can be explored further within an agon aesthetics as football themes, storylines or narratives. There is no script for the football match as such. Still, a game will go through various fairly predictable phases. There is an agon aesthetic basis for identifying re-emerging football themes, storylines or narratives. This is because the staging of football involves constitutive rules and a time limit. The staged social drama of the football match is resolved within 90 or 120 minutes. The aim of the antagonists is to win the match, or minimally, not to lose it. Due to the competitive nature of the proceedings, certain manners of acting and interacting will suggest themselves. They provide a room for footballers to manoeuvre in. These action prescriptions will be based on the constitutive rules of the game together with other, more informal considerations about what and how to do things. To put it bluntly, if you use the football form with a view to fulfilling the sport's internal or intrinsic aim, then you will try to score and avoid conceding goals. You will try to do that in a manner that is acceptable to the referee, thus paying careful attention to the constitutive rules and their interpretations. This, together with the strict structuring of time within the context of competition, will result in easily recognizable football themes, storylines or narratives.

Here are a few of them:

> The Hammering: A hammering occurs when one team is superior to the other team in all or most aspects of the game and is able to capitalize on that superiority by winning the match with a wide score line.

The most thrilling hammerings are those handed out in important games where the spectators expected the game to be close. Examples are Real Madrid's 7–3 demolition of Eintracht Frankfurt in the European Cup final in 1960 (later known as the Champions League). Another is the football lesson received by Johan Cruyff's so-called Dream Team in 1994, when AC Milan outplayed FC Barcelona 4–0 in the Champions League final.

> The Escape: An escape occurs when a team, though dominated in all aspects of the game by the other team, still manages a draw or a win. The team gets away with a result (so to speak) against the run of play.

A classic example of an escape was the 1–1 draw between England and Poland in a World Cup qualifier at Wembley in 1973. The English laid siege in the Polish half only to find that, behind a packed Polish defence, their goalkeeper Jan Tomaszewski was having a legendary match. On Poland's only attack of the evening, Grzegorz Lato scored. It did not matter that England afterwards equalized on a penalty. The result meant that Poland had qualified for the World Cup in West Germany the following year and England was out. Another escape was Norway's 0–0 draw away against the Netherlands in a World Cup qualifier in 1993. The Dutch swept over a Norwegian team clearly out of their depth, but Norway was helped out by the woodwork three times and also by the Dutch strikers' inclination to backheel absolute sitters, instead of merely scoring them.

> The Comeback: Any equalizer is, in one sense, a comeback. However, for a match to earn this title, the team making the comeback must have looked deflated and beaten at one point in the match, which usually means being down by two or more goals.

Examples are the already mentioned 2005 Champions League final between Liverpool FC and AC Milan. Another is the epic 1982 World Cup semi-final between West Germany and France, where France led 3–1 early in extra time, whereupon the West German substitute Karl Heinz Rummenigge orchestrated a staggering comeback ending with a 3–3 score line. The West Germans won the penalty shoot-out 5–4. Eusébio's Portugal also staged a comeback classic in the 1966 World Cup quarter-final when they went down 3–0 against North Korea, but ended up winning the match 5–3. Some comebacks like Liverpool's Champions League victory in 2005 also count as escapes.

> The Upset: An upset is when an underdog, a team left no chance of winning by experts and others, defies those odds and wins.

Examples of big upsets are North Korea's 1–0 win over Italy in the group stages of the 1966 World Cup and England's 1–0 loss to the USA in the group stages of the 1950 World Cup, which also was England's first World Cup appearance. Upsets might also be comebacks and quite often are escapes, though they need not be. We might also talk of upsets with regard to tournaments. Greece's victory in the European Football Championship in 2004 is perhaps the biggest of them all.

> The Rollercoaster: A rollercoaster is a match where the character of the match changes more than once and where there is an oscillation between which team is favoured by the score line at any given point.

Tournaments like Copa Libertadores (from 2005 and with the exception of the final) and the Champions League (with the exception of the final) are well designed for rollercoaster matches. Due to their design of home-away matches in the knockout rounds and with away goals counting double should the score be tied after two matches, the return matches often provide good rollercoasters. A fine example from the World Cup is Italy's 3–2 victory over Brazil in the World Cup second group stages in 1982. The premise of the game was that Brazil would go through to the semi-final with a draw, while Italy needed to win. With a goal from Paulo Rossi in the fifth minute Italy was in pole position, then Brazil was back in the semi-final with an equalizer in the 12th minute by Sócrates. Shortly thereafter, the semi-final beckoned for Italy (25 Rossi), then Brazil (68 Falcão) and finally Italy (75 Rossi) to book their place in the next round. Another rollercoaster classic was the 1970 World Cup semi-final between Italy and West Germany, which ended 4–3 to the Italians. The match came alive when West Germany forced extra time with a 1–1 equalizer three minutes into stoppage time. The 30-minute extra time rollercoaster resulted in five goals. First, West Germany was in the lead 2–1, then the score was 2–2, then Italy was in the lead 3–2, then West Germany equalized to 3–3 and, finally, nine minutes before full-time, Gianni Rivera settled the score 4–3 to Italy. Another famous one is the Merseyside Derby, which was the Football Association (FA) Cup final of 1989. Liverpool FC was up 1–0 for most of the match, thanks to a John Aldridge goal in the fourth minute, until the substitute for Everton, Stuart McCall, equalized with one minute remaining. In extra time, it went 2–1 Liverpool (95 Rush), then 2–2 (102 McCall), then 3–2 (104 Rush) for Liverpool.

> The Robbery: The robbery is a close cousin to the escape. In the escape the team winning or drawing the match against the run of play gets away with being the inferior team. In a robbery, on the other hand, the match is prized away from one of the teams owing to the referee's mistake or mistakes.

One of the clearest robberies in the history of the World Cup was South Korea's 5–3 penalty shoot-out win against Spain in the 2002 World Cup. The match ended 0–0. Spain had two perfectly good goals disallowed – where the second one in extra time would have counted as a golden goal – together with some, at best, highly disputable off-side decisions going against Spain. There is no doubt Spain got robbed. Another robbery, at least according to the supporters of AS Roma, is the case of Turone's goal (*Gol di Turone*). In a 1981 Serie A match between Juventus FC and AS Roma, with the match at a 0–0 stalemate and only ten minutes remaining, Roma's Maurizio Turone headed the ball into the net behind Juventus keeper Dino Zoff. The goal was controversially disallowed. Had Roma won the match, they would have been in the driving seat of the Serie A with two matches remaining, but the *Scudetto* ended up in Turin. To this day, Roma supporters will insist that they were robbed that day, which ever since has added special flavour to the clashes between the two teams.

Obviously, there are more football themes, storylines or narratives to be found. One example would be the *Smash and Grab*, and the match we started this chapter with is a good example of that football theme, storyline or narrative. Not only did Manchester United escape with the victory, they snatched it at the very end, leaving little or no time for a comeback from Bayern München. The better team lost that day, and that would hardly have been possible in sports where the scoring was higher and less was left to chance. Apart from the more complex interaction and drama of a constructive-destructive sport and the violence of a contact sport, football brings to the sport table its low scoring due to the mechanics of the game. Much of football's attraction, with its football themes, storylines or narratives, is made possible by the sport's relatively low scoring.

> Sometimes in football the margins between scoring a goal and a near miss are so slim that it seems reasonable to say that it could have gone either way. This is most vivid in escape-type matches. To acknowledge such slim margins in escape-type matches is to acknowledge that there can be an element of chance or luck when it comes to winning football matches. Indeed, one of the important elements of football is the real possibility of upset and escape matches (...) The small margins and the element of chance keep football matches more open-ended and unpredictable than all other sports.
>
> (Borge 2010a: 32–33)[21]

Among the various constructive-destructive sports, football is special owing to the dynamics of the game, where the hindering or obstructing actions, the destructive side of the game, are easier to master than scoring goals, the constructive side of the game. That turns football into a low-scoring affair, where the margins between scoring and a near miss, between winning and losing are slim, and chance plays a greater role than in similar sports. The mechanics of football, i.e. the way the sport is set up, leaves much to chance, though as already argued, football is a game of physical skill.

Why is it that football is by far the most popular team sport, when it is also highly unusual with regard to the very few goals scored compared to other sports with a wide following? In the esoteric wall game played at Eton College, scoring is even rarer than in football; in fact, David Winner reports that "[g]oals are staggeringly rare" and that "no goal has been scored in the St. Andrew's Day match since 1909" (Winner 2006: 260–261). Compared to the Etonians' wall game, football is a free-scoring romp, but compared to all other team sports with a global reach, it is a remarkably low-scoring business. Unless one thinks that practitioners and spectators are by nature more drawn to a game played with one's feet, than say with one's arms and hands, sticks, etc., then there is reason to believe that one of the main reasons for football's success is its low scores – that and the simplicity of the game. It is easy to see how football's simplicity could contribute to the game's spread and success. On the other hand, the idea that the low scores in football matches are a major contributor to the sport's success should strike one as curious. Look at a football match and its audience. The highlight of the game is the goals. It is the scoring of a goal that makes the crowd erupt in celebration and sends the goal scorer screaming and gesticulating in joy and wonder – think about Marco Tardelli losing it after scoring the second goal against West Germany in the World Cup final in 1982 or any Filippo Inzaghi goal. One would think this would be a case of the more goals, the better. Why then does the audience stick to football, when there are other ball games and team sports out there with more goals – with the higher score, more excitement? That which is lost by having fewer moments of scoring is regained in the sweeter uncertainty of outcome.[22] As the clock runs down, a seemingly safe lead in no way guarantees victory, as Gillingham fans found out in their 1999 Football League Second Division play-off final (third level) against Manchester City. Gillingham was up 2–0 as the match entered its last minute and still Manchester City drew level with goals in the 90th and 95th minutes and clinched promotion in a penalty shoot-out. Other team sports can also have dramatic endings, but none quite like football, with matches like the 1999 Champions League final, where a team that had been dominated for most of the match pulled back from the edge of defeat and won with two injury-time goals.

The drama of football is not only about which teams are the most skilful and will win, but also about which football theme, storyline or narrative will play itself out on a particular day. Is this the day the underdog comes out on top? Will the superbly skilful and attack-minded team dazzle the crowd and win the day, or self-implode due to lack of defensive rigour and discipline? Will the ultra-defensive team with a by-hook-or-by-crook attitude be able hold their line and steal the victory? Football by no means guarantees either a fair or happy ending to the show on display. It is this that distinguishes football as a spectator sport from other sports and, one might suggest, that is responsible for its worldwide success. Football has two outstanding features among the constructive-destructive contact team sports. The first feature is the simplicity of the game, which makes it easy to play without many resources. The other outstanding feature is that there are very few goals in football compared to similar sports. The fact that football is a low-scoring sport, the lowest-scoring sport with a substantial following, is not a disadvantage, but rather it is what explains its worldwide success. It gives its spectators a more unpredictable game and a darker, more complex and denser drama to enjoy.

Real values and fictional values

The drama of football as themes, storylines or narratives sits well with the idea that football involves proto-pretence of social play as found in rough-and-tumble play. The proto-pretence of social play in football accounts for the game's fictional character. This proto-pretence takes place within the confines of usage of the football form, where the latter gives rise to re-emerging action-reaction patterns and the former gives credence to thinking of these along the lines of themes, storylines or narratives. When engaging in sports like football, we have specific activations at the alief level – my suggestion being "Physical struggle/fight! D-a-n-g-e-r …! Activate fight-or-flight adrenaline now" – and this accounts for our excitement, though we do not act on these as if they were a reliable guide to the situation we are in – we do not actually end up displaying fight-or-flight behaviour. The essential pretence or make-believe, i.e. the fictionality of football, lies in the fact that we get excited and act that out in certain ways – continue to play, cheer for the teams from the terraces, shout in front of the television set, etc. – while we also know that this does not matter, as evidenced by the lack of actual fight-or-flight behaviour. Alief grounds the phenomenon of engagement in football and similar sports in human psychology, but there are also other factors that contribute once the alief activation is in place. Other props of the football spectacle pull in the same direction. Anthems and supporter songs, the easily accessible us-against-them feel that team sports like football provide (which, I believe, make us prone to pick sides), the banners, etc., together with the previously mentioned identity-making aspect of football, all intensify and heighten our engagement.

Another and complementary way to approach the question of football's fictional character is by thinking about it in terms of values. It is against a background of make-believe or pretence that winning football matches becomes important. The value of winning football matches is part of football's fictional character. We can call that a *fictional value*. Any interactive fiction or pretence, like football, takes place against the background of the non-fictional, non-pretence world, i.e. the ordinary everyday world. In the ordinary world, there are values that do not depend on fiction or pretence. These include that which we deem valuable per se (intrinsic value), like love, children, life, companionship, ourselves, happiness, etc., and that which we deem valuable as a means of getting or securing that which we deem valuable per se (instrumental value), like food, shelter, money, etc. Things that are intrinsically valuable make sense simpliciter, and relative to both instrumental values and fictional values, they constitute primitives of some sorts. Instrumental values are constitutively connected to intrinsic values, whereas fictional values are not, and we can call the former two values *real values*. We can further divide real values up into vital real values – which would include such things as staying alive, not seriously damaging one's health, having companionship, reproducing, etc. – and non-vital real values – such as having civil liberties, not being subject to discrimination, etc.[23] While vital real values are probably intimately related to the types of beings we are, and thus ahistorical and non-cultural, one could argue that non-vital real values are at least partly historical and cultural, which suggests they could change over time. Non-vital real values could, of course, also be merely personal. The fictional values depend on the real values being secure and unaffected by the proceedings of a sporting event like a football match in much the same way as instrumental values depend on intrinsic values.[24] Real values take precedence over, or trump, fictional values. In particular, they take precedence over or trump those fictions (including works of fiction and fictional activities like football) that are not perceived as directly or indirectly influencing the ordinary world in a positive manner. The loss of a real value destroys the value of the fiction, unless the work of fiction or fictional activity is perceived as directly or indirectly influencing the ordinary world in a positive way that outweighs the loss of a real value.

Given the fictional character of football and the fictional value of winning football matches, we should expect that if real values are threatened on the pitch, the game will cease to matter. This is what we find in footballers' voluntary suspension of play when other players are seriously injured (a player's health being a vital real value). When people are seriously injured or die on the pitch or the terraces, football no longer seems to matter.[25] This sentiment was given clear expression when Britain's biggest newspaper, *The Sun*, ran the headline "When football no longer matters" on its front page in response to the much-publicized event of Bolton Wanderers player Fabrice Muamba's collapse and cardiac arrest on the pitch in a match against Tottenham Hotspur in March 2012 (*The Sun*, March 18, 2012). Similarly, 41 years earlier, when things took a tragic turn in a match between the two Glasgow sides Rangers and Celtic in January 1971 and 66 spectators were crushed to death and 145 injured (at the Rangers end), the *Celtic View* appropriately ran the headline "BLACK SATURDAY: The Old Firm Match that Didn't Matter" (quoted in Murray 1984: 224–225). These kinds of events do not make football matches less important, rather such losses of real value destroy the fiction of football and with it the fictional value that winning football matches matters. With regard to other football tragedies, there are also cases when people have died in the stadium, but the match has been played or finished. In such cases, the justification tends to be a concern for avoiding more people getting injured, not an appeal to the relative importance of the match at hand. This was the case when it was decided that the 1985 European Cup final between Liverpool FC and Juventus FC at Heysel stadium should not be abandoned, even though 39 spectators (32 of them Italian) had been crushed to death as a result of English hooliganism.

> Italian commentator Bruno Pizzul (…) stated, boldly, that "the game is of no more importance". (…) At around 20.50, Pizzul gave the shocking news which, at the time, was very hard to believe. *Thirty-six people were dead* (…) German television refused to show the match at all. (…) Once the match started, Pizzul's commentary was dignified. He followed the game without raising his voice and often repeated that the game was not a real game, but was being played only for "reasons of public order".
>
> *(Foot 2007: 368–369)*[26]

After the match at the press conference, Liverpool's retiring manager Joe Fagan told the press that "What is a game of football when so many are dead? The match itself just fades into insignificance" (Fagan and Platt 2011: 311).[27]

We should also expect that (in some cases) the loss of a non-vital real value would make players and spectators unwilling to participate in the make-believe or pretence of football. The most obvious case would be racism. Racist utterances from either the spectators or participants destroy the non-vital real value of not being subjected to racial intolerance. Currently, the non-vital real value of not being subjected to racial intolerance takes precedence over or trumps the fictional value of winning a particular football match. Today, racist utterances are regarded by most (i.a., the ruling bodies of football) as something that is unacceptable during matches. Racist utterances thus destroy the fictional value of winning football matches and can be game- or sport-destroying in the sense that they quell our willingness to participate and furthermore engage in the game as spectators. This shows why it was wholly appropriate for Barcelona's Cameroon striker Samuel Eto'o to threaten to walk out of a Spanish La Liga away game against Real Zaragoza in February 2006, as the racist taunts directed at Eto'o were clearly game- or sport-destroying for him. Eto'o's reaction is not unique among footballers today. Brazil's Roberto Carlos, playing for FC Anzhi Makhachkala away against FC Krylia Sovetov Samara in the Russian Football Championship (first level) in June 2011, not only threatened to walk out of the game, but when a banana was thrown on the pitch close to Carlos, he actually did. For Eto'o, Carlos and other footballers who are subjected to racial abuse, these types of acts destroy the fiction of football, i.e., the notion that winning the game matters.

On other occasions, it is not what happens on the pitch or the terraces that destroys, trumps or otherwise diminishes the fictional value of winning football matches, but events in the surrounding everyday, ordinary world. Sport activities came to a standstill after the horrors of the 2011 attacks in Norway, when a lone right-wing terrorist blew up parts of the Norwegian executive government quarters (resulting in eight deaths) and murdered 69 people (mostly youth) at the yearly summer camp held by the youth organization of the then ruling party on the island of Utøya. The Norwegian FA cancelled the up-coming football round in Norway's top divisions and most other sport arrangements were also cancelled. This is not accidental. Why would one cancel a whole football round because of an event like July 22? Why were all sporting events in Paris cancelled after the November 2015 Paris attacks? I think the answer is to be found in the massive cognitive dissonance that would have occurred had football and other sports not been abandoned in the days following these attacks. How could one allow oneself to become emotionally involved in the unnecessary artificial conflict of football being staged as entertainment when real, everyday, ordinary world conflict had just taken lives on the doorsteps of the sport stadiums? How can you make football matter in the direct aftermath of such serious and traumatic events? The answer seems to be that you cannot. Of course, it is not given that this is how everyone will react. I can easily see a scenario in which a full round of football takes place as an act of defiance in reaction to a terrorist attack thought to be aimed at thwarting public assembly. Here, of course, it would be the act of arranging a full round of matches that would be of importance and the reason why one went ahead with the sporting event, not the football itself. When the two realms collide, the everyday or ordinary world takes precedence over sports like football. Granted, in the case of the attacks in Norway, other arrangements like music festivals were also cancelled, but art in various forms was used actively in the subsequent process as Norwegian society tried to come to terms with what had happened that day, whereas sport was not. That too is not accidental. As pointed out in Chapter 1, sports like football are not about anything and are therefore ill-suited to dealing with traumatic events, like those taking place on July 22, 2011 in southern Norway.

Things might also come to a head when the outside, everyday, ordinary world disturbance threatening to undermine the fictional value of football is not public or communal, but merely personal. Consider Norway's opening match against Mexico in the 1994 World Cup in the USA. This was Norway's first appearance on the world stage since 1938. It was a big deal for the minnows from the north. The match was a tightly fought affair, and in the 78th minute Norwegian player Kjetil Rekdal came on from the bench. Rekdal had been a stable fixture in the Norwegian team and instrumental in their qualification to the tournament. However, a recent slump in form had seen him dropped to the bench. It should have been his moment given that he scored the winner in the 84th minute. Instead, inexplicably for the Norwegian audience and media, Rekdal found it difficult to participate in the joyous scenes after the final whistle. He walked off the pitch refusing to talk to the press apart from a comment about always coming back. Here is Rekdal's own account of what happened.

> I know of course that I scored the winner just a few minutes after I came on, and that I first celebrated, and then turned ice-cold, but I can't say much about the atmosphere in the stands or what happened in the last minutes of the match. I was upset and not quite myself, all because of what Reidun [Rekdal's partner] and I had lost (...) In the dressing room I was unable to celebrate with the lads, but sat and cried with a towel over my head (...) Jan Åge put his head under the towel, and then I told him what had happened. That we had lost what could have been our baby, and that I was completely out of it (...) Despite victory and goal, I sat and sobbed in the dressing room. In reality, I was probably close to a breakdown. In a way I realized that football was no longer everything.
>
> *(Rekdal with Østrem 2012: 127, my translation)*

I suggest that what led to Rekdal's breakdown was the massive cognitive dissonance between the hysterical reaction of a stadium of 52,000 people erupting at the goal and the fact of it perhaps being the most important goal in Norway's footballing history, on the one hand, and his quiet, private sadness and despair over the miscarriage of a longed-for baby, on the other. The contrast could not have been starker. The two realms of the everyday, ordinary world and the extraordinary, unnecessary world of football came to a head for Rekdal that day, and his reaction is quite understandable. Under such circumstances, it is hard to make football matter, or, as the fiercely competitive Rekdal would have it, be all-important.[28]

Aesthetic engagement resistance

Eto'o's, Carlos's and other footballers' reactions to racial abuse are the football equivalent of the phenomenon known in aesthetics as imaginative resistance. When engaging in fictions like literature, fiction film, etc., we pretend that all sorts of fanciful things are true – like there being unicorns, superheroes with complicated love lives, various supernatural beings, etc. – but we baulk at accepting a fictional world in which it is supposedly true that "[i]n killing her baby, Giselda did the right thing; after all, it was a girl" (Walton 1994, p. 37). Gendler dubs this *"the puzzle of imaginative resistance"*, and as she sees it, the crux of the puzzle is "our comparative difficulty in imagining fictional worlds that we take to be morally deviant" (Gendler 2000: 180). Brian Weatherson argues that there are in fact four puzzles in this area: the alethic puzzle (we refuse to accept the sentence above as true), the imaginative puzzle (we cannot imagine a world where this is the case), the phenomenological puzzle (the sentence above makes the reader uncomfortable in a special manner), and the aesthetic puzzle (the work containing such a sentence is aesthetically compromised) (Weatherson 2004: 2). Still, there seems to be one overarching phenomenon (with different subparts à la Weatherson) that we can call *aesthetic engagement resistance*. That is, we resist the fiction or artwork – our engagement (including all shades of aesthetic appreciation) is destroyed, hindered or lessened by, for instance, deviant morality, viewpoints we find problematic, impossibilities that defy credibility or coherence, pure factual errors, and so on and so forth. At the root of it, what happens in the Giselda example is that we baulk at engaging in a fiction where being a baby girl justifies being killed, as opposed to, we must assume, being a baby boy. The reason for this might be a failure to accept the above sentence as true, because it contradicts our belief that boys and girls have equal value, a failure to imagine a world where this is the case or either of Weatherson's other two categories. Though the debate in this literature is rather complex and rich in detail, this need not worry us here, as our focus is on the parallel between what is fiction destroying – what destroys or hinders engagement in and other sorts of aesthetic appreciation of works of fiction – and what is sport destroying – what destroys or hinders engagement in and other kinds of aesthetic appreciation of sporting events.

What is worrying, though, is the unfortunate tendency in the literature to focus on "only puzzles that arise from a particular sentence in a story" and, furthermore, to limit the debate to sentences that are "intentionally presented in the voice of an authoritative narrator" (Weatherson 2004: 7). The latter brings problems of its own concerning how we should understand the function of a fictional narrator, while the former seems to exclude fiction film, or at least fail to appreciate the differences in mode of presentation between fiction film and literature. This is unfortunate, because fiction film proves a better parallel when thinking about football, for the simple reason that real people play the fictional characters. Furthermore, like football and many other sports, many works of fiction (both literature and fiction film) have no authoritative or explicit fictional narrator, but that does not in any way preclude a spectator from experiencing aesthetic engagement resistance. The basis of aesthetic engagement resistance need not be the claims made by an authoritative narrator.

Consider the following example:

> Western Movies: Nancy loves tales of the old west and western movies. Being an animal lover, however, Nancy is unable to sit through a whole viewing of some of the old western classics, like *Stagecoach* (John Ford, 1939) and *Jesse James* (Henry King, 1939), knowing that numerous horses were killed or crippled in the filming of those movies.[29]

Nancy's aesthetic engagement resistance is not alethic; scenes in a western are not in the business of being true or false. It is also not imaginative: Nancy is not reacting to the images of falling horses per se, but to animal cruelty. Nancy would be happy to watch (for her) perceptually indistinguishable remakes of both *Stagecoach* and *Jesse James* as long as they had disclaimers (that she trusts) like "No animals were harmed in the filming of this movie". That leaves us with Weatherson's phenomenological and aesthetic resistance. Surely, Nancy is uneasy watching real horses fall to their death (phenomenological resistance) and anything that makes you resist a fiction compromises, in a straightforward sense, the work aesthetically (aesthetic resistance). However, the categories of phenomenological and aesthetic resistance underplay the similarity between the *Western Movies* case and Muamba-type episodes as well as voluntary suspension of play in football.

We see a similar structure in the resistance to enjoying the spectacle of football as we see in Nancy's aesthetic engagement resistance to *Western Movies*. The excitement of living through the stagecoach's wild ride to safety, caring about the faith of the Ringo Kid and his love affair with Dallas, etc., which are fictional values, are trumped or destroyed by the fact that Nancy's real value – that one should avoid (unnecessary) cruelty to animals – is destroyed in the making of that movie. A sport-like case that parallels *Western Movies* is bullfighting. Although bullfighting is dramatic, athletic and skilful, and involves colourful uniforms and other props, all of which are the ingredients of a watchable spectacle, many fail to enjoy this spectacle due to the animal cruelty that is part of bullfighting. The similarity between football and fiction film would be even more glaring if this were a world in which (some) moviemakers were willing to let humans die to make a movie – in relation to which one could imagine disclaimers like "No humans were harmed in the filming of this movie". If someone like Nancy, in such a world, could not enjoy movies where humans died or were crippled, but would be happy to watch movies with the above-mentioned disclaimer, then we have an example that very much matches our football cases. As for other sports, I suspect that the reason why many people find it difficult to enjoy fight sports like western boxing, Muay Thai kickboxing, silat or bare-knuckle prize-fighting, to mention a few, is that the practitioners actually get seriously injured in these unnecessary fights. In this case, a vital real value, practitioners not damaging their health, takes precedence over, trumps or destroys the value of enjoying watching such fights. However, not managing or being willing to enjoy sports like the ones above does not prevent one from enjoying seeing the exact same activities depicted in a fiction film.

Gendler argues, "that the primary source of imaginative resistance is not our *inability* to imagine morally deviant situations, but our *unwillingness* to do so" (Gendler 2000: 180–181, see also 196 and 201). Some philosophers have thought otherwise (see Gendler 2006: 204–205 for a list of some of the critical voices). However, Gendler's line is obviously correct with regard to the kind of aesthetic engagement resistance we find in *Western Movies* and the engagement resistance we find in football and similar sports. In football there is ample evidence that we resist the make-believe that football matters whenever a life is threatened on the pitch, but that must be due to our unwillingness to remain engaged, not our inability. After all, not only did humans enjoy violent games like the gladiatorial combat of ancient Rome, but today as well we find sports, particularly the before-mentioned fight sports, for which the vital real value of practitioners not dying or getting seriously injured does not prevent audience members from being engaged in these sporting events. Humans are fully capable of enjoying sports that are not fictional in character, but when watching football we are not willing to continue enjoying when vital real values are in danger, thus revealing football's fictional character.

With regard to football and the loss of a non-vital real value such as not being subjected to racial discrimination, it is even clearer that the Gendler view is correct with regard to that sort of aesthetic engagement resistance. Going back to the late 1970s and 1980s, you will find that racist chanting on the terraces was common in, for example, England, and that black players simply tried to ignore this hostile environment and get on with their game. Cyrille Regis of West Bromwich Albion and Coventry City fame tells us that:

> There were monkey chants whenever we touched the ball. It would become commonplace over the next few seasons (...) I never allowed racism to affect me personally. (...) You couldn't pretend you didn't hear it, but equally it didn't put me off. Quite the contrary – it made me try harder. It was the same for years afterwards. Focus on the game.
>
> *(Regis with Green 2010: 77–78)*

Regis reports that his black teammate at West Bromwich, Brendon Batson, shared this sentiment: "We knew the grounds where we'd get abuse and bananas thrown at us (...) We just puffed out our chests and got on with it" (Regis with Green 2010: 96). For Regis, Batson and their other black teammate at West Bromwich Albion, Laurie Cunningham, racial discrimination was not sport destroying. Today, things look different.[30] Clearly, both Eto'o and Carlos were able to continue playing football while being subjected to racist taunts or having bananas thrown at them, but they were unwilling to do so. We should expect that a correct diagnosis of the phenomenon of aesthetic engagement resistance (including imaginative resistance) would cover engagement in literary fiction, fiction films, etc., as well as engagement in football and similar sports. This then is in line with Gendler's take on things, at least with respect to the types of aesthetic engagement resistance that are displayed when engaging in sports like football, where it is clearly not our inability, but our unwillingness that makes us abandon the game or give up our engagement in the sporting event.

Silly questions and the football fiction

Closely related to the phenomenon of aesthetic engagement resistance (including imaginative resistance) is the phenomenon that Walton dubbed "silly questions". Though neither Walton nor others have explored this connection, asking silly questions (in Walton's technical sense of it) is, in a very clear sense, a matter of resisting or falling out of one's engagement in the fiction. For example, the fictional character Othello in William Shakespeare's play of the same name speaks in superb verses as if he had "an almost unbelievable natural literary flair", though it is, when we think about it, odd for "a Moorish general (...) to come up with such superb verse on the spur of the moment" (Walton 1990: 175). Questions like "Why do other characters take no notice of his particular manner of discourse, or of his astounding literary talent?" are, according to Walton, silly questions (Walton 1990: 175). Walton explains:

> They are pointless, inappropriate, out of order. To pursue or dwell on them would be not only irrelevant to appreciation and criticism but also distracting and destructive. The paradoxes, anomalies, apparent contradictions they point to seem artificial, contrived, not to be taken seriously. We don't take them seriously. Ordinarily we don't even notice them.
>
> *(Walton 1990: 176)*

Someone asking a silly question is a person who does not quite want to play the game of make-believe; he or she is not quite willing to suspend disbelief with regard to a work of fiction in order to engage with the fiction. Furthermore, Othello's style of speaking might result in aesthetic engagement resistance on the part of a spectator or reader. Walton remarks that Othello speaking in verse does not constitute "an irritating intrusion on the appreciator's experience" (Walton 1990: 176). However, that does not mean that it cannot, and for some people probably does, constitute an irritation that causes them to fail to appreciate the play, i.e., to not get engaged. Whatever you can ask a silly question about can also potentially lead to aesthetic engagement resistance, even though silly questions, as understood by Walton, concern the details of the fiction and are, thus, internal to the fiction. We can call these questions *internal silly questions*.

Consider the scenario of someone who asks a spectator who has just been moved to tears by Shakespeare's *Othello* why he or she cares about characters that are not real, i.e. fictional characters. This is also a type of silly question. We can call these kinds of questions *external silly questions*. Such a question is external to the fiction; it is not concerned with the fiction *qua* fiction (about consistency, realism, etc. of the fiction), but with our very willingness to engage with fiction. It is also silly because it is pointless, inappropriate and out of order for the person being asked, i.e. the one engaging with the fiction. There is no proper answer to this sort of external silly question from the perspective of a spectator who is moved by a fiction, when he or she is moved. Either you engage with fictions or you do not. External silly questions surely have answers that can be found in sociology, psychology, philosophy (as is apparent from the alief line with regard to engagement in fiction), etc., but these are not the reasons ordinary spectators would give. But again, nudging someone who is currently being moved to tears by the faith of Romeo and Juliet and informing them that these two young people do not really exist constitutes the kind of external silliness just explained. Similarly, to ask a football fan who is upset because his or her team has just been relegated why he or she cares so much – given the relegation's absolute material unimportance to that person's ordinary world or everyday life concerns – is to ask a silly question. There and then, this question is pointless, inappropriate and out of order for the person being asked. There are, of course, philosophical questions to be posed about these matters, and this book is about them, but that does not prevent them from also being silly when addressed to someone who is engaged in football, while under the spell.

Are there internal silly questions in football that parallel the kind of internal silly questions we have considered so far? Not quite. The reason is that such questions pertain to the fictional nature of plays like *Othello* and the artistic presentation of the fiction. Football, on the other hand, is only fictional in character and has no artistic function. We should therefore not expect these kinds of silly questions to exist. Questions that are internal to the game of football – such as "Why do the defenders all run away from their own goal in such-and-such situations?", "Why does the keeper behave like that in such-and-such situations?", "Why doesn't the team with possession pass the ball to the player who is alone in front of the opposing team's goalkeeper instead of passing it sideways?" – are all sensible for someone who is trying to understand the mechanics of the game. They are not pointless, inappropriate or out of order, and most of us have asked similar questions when watching an unfamiliar sport. The answers given to such questions typically involve a reference to the actions being conducive to winning the sport contest in question. There are related questions that might feel silly because they display complete lack of understanding of the game, but that nevertheless are similar in form to the questions above. The answer to the question, "Why doesn't the team with possession pass the ball to the player who is alone in front of the opposing team's goalkeeper instead of passing it sideways?" is that it is not conducive to winning the game, because the player in question is in an offside position and any goal scored would most likely not count. Similarly, the question, "If preventing the other side from scoring is vital, why not use an invisible force field to make this impossible" is answered by pointing out that such a tactic would be ruled out and punished by a referee, and so on and so forth for similarly fanciful suggestions for how to play the game. Should an interlocutor who asks such questions about fanciful ways of defending and attacking finally wonder why there are any limitations at all on what one is allowed to do in football, then that seems like an external silly question – one that shows a lack of understanding that sports are activities or practices in which having limited means to achieve sport-specific goals is a rational possibility.

When thinking about potential internal silly questions regarding football and other sports, one needs to consider whether the felt silliness of such questions stems from them coming from a place of ignorance of the whole institution or tradition of football and other sports, which would account for why one is somewhat taken aback by them. Consider the case of a person who is watching a football match and who has got the hang of why players commit so-called professional fouls. Sometimes it is better to intentionally foul an opposing player than to stay within the boundaries set by the rules of the game. Imagine that this spectator at one point asks, with regard to a team that has trouble containing, say, the opposing team's star striker, why they do not simply commit the ultimate professional foul by killing that player. That, our imagined spectator could argue, would in certain circumstances be worth a sending off. Macabre as this question might be, we can think about it as a possible candidate for silly-question status, in Walton's technical sense. Just as asking about the style of Othello's speech counts as a silly question when considering fiction, asking why footballers do not go all the way in their struggle to win football matches seems equally silly, when considering sports like football that are fictional in character. To echo Walton, we do not take such questions seriously and ordinarily they do not arise. However, first there is an answer to this question, which is that murder is a crime and you will go to prison for it; second, one might view this question as merely externally silly because it displays a total lack of understanding of the type of activity and sport football is.

External silly questions with regard to football and other sports are easy to come by. Someone who asks the footballers playing a football match why they do not get a ball each instead of fighting over one ball is asking an external silly question. He or she simply does not understand that this is an artificial, unnecessary conflict staged for the purpose of having something to do battle over. Should he or she, after having been told what the purpose of the activity was, still insist that the players really would be better off if they all got their own personal ball to play and score with, then that person is simply not playing the game of making believe that the football match matters. As already mentioned, a spectator watching a football match who asks why the teams try to win the match, why the other spectators care about the result or engage in the match (given that they have no economic interest in the match result), etc., is asking external silly questions about football. For the agent engaged in football (either as a player or a spectator) and from the perspective of such engagement, there is no proper answer to such questions. This also explains and validates those people who just fail to see the point of football or any similar sports, because in one clear sense there is nothing to get or understand, unless you are to a certain extent willing to engage in the pretence or make-believe of football.

Objections and replies

Objection: The author mentions the Kantian notion of "dependent beauty". A notion related to and often developed in contemporary aesthetics under the guise of "functional beauty". However, noting the distinction between free and dependent beauty suggests that the Kantian football aesthete has an important additional tool for dealing with the aesthetics of football and similar sports. Or, if the Kantian line of reasoning cannot make proper contact with the phenomenon of football, perhaps an aesthetic theory about functional beauty like the one suggested by Parsons and Carlson can. The author needs to tackle the question of whether the Kantian notion of dependent beauty or Parsons and Carlson's notion of functional beauty has any traction with regard to football appreciation. Perhaps one of them or both can even be co-opted into the agon aesthetics account, for instance with Maradona's famous solo goal possessing beauty as exhibiting many of the key virtues — skill, strength, quick wittedness, determination, will-to-victory, etc. — needed in the game.

Reply: It is a tall order to delineate one's own theory from imagined developments of possible competitor theories. Perhaps too tall an order. The first thing to note is that the target is the disinterested aesthetics championed by Gumbrecht and Mumford, not Kant himself. Still, that does leave me with the question of what to say about the Kantian notion of dependent beauty or Parsons and Carlson's notion of functional beauty. Can any of these notions be developed to fit the phenomenon of aesthetic appreciation of football, or else become a part of a broadly agon aesthetic line of thought? One might suspect that with enough stage setting, scholarship can provide a version of Kant that fits the phenomenon of football and similar sports. The dangers of bennettiction will naturally loom large, and one might wonder why we should take such a detour through Kant.[31] Also, as with all of Kant's writing, there is controversy with regard to interpretation. Consider an interpretation of Kant that is in line with how I presented the Kantian concept of dependent beauty earlier in this chapter.

> For Kant, some beauties are dependent — relative to the sort of thing the object is — and others are free or absolute. A beautiful ox would be an ugly horse, but abstract textile designs, for example, may be beautiful in themselves without a reference group or "concept," and flowers please whether or not we connect them to their practical purposes or functions in plant reproduction (Kant 1790, section 16).
>
> *(Sartwell 2016)*

Dependent beauty is relative to what something is and how it is supposed to function or its practical purpose. The contrast between the possibility of free appreciation of flowers and their function is meant to establish the latter point. However, this is not the only interpretation. Paul Guyer, Stephen Davies, and Parsons and Carlson argue that Kant's notion of dependent beauty does not point towards aesthetic appreciation originating in the functionality of the phenomenon under consideration. Rather, dependent beauty is the aesthetic appreciation of something, when this appreciation is constrained by what that something is and how it is supposed to function (Guyer 2002b: 447–450, Davies 2006, Parsons and Carlson 2008: 120–123, 231–233).

> Kant allows that recognition of a thing's kind and function can constrain how or what about it can be beautiful, but the relevant qualities do not derive their beauty from the success with which they contribute to its discharging its function; that is, the item's functionality is not a source of its beauty.
>
> (Davies 2010: 316)

The latter understanding of the Kantian notion of dependent beauty implies, were we to employ the notion in the service of agon aesthetics, that our aesthetic appreciation of the moves on a football pitch is constrained, but not grounded in our knowledge of what we are watching and what works within that competitive setting. The root or origin of the beauty of Maradona's wondrous goal against England is not to be found in the fact that those moves work, are functional or fit the competitive context of a football match, but rather in their very phenomenological appearance. Aesthetically speaking, a shoot that misses the target by a country mile can be just as beautiful as, say, Marco van Basten's spectacular volley that sealed the Netherlands' victory over the Soviet Union in the 1988 final of the European Championship. The reason why we do not see it that way is because our aesthetic appreciation is constrained by our knowledge of what we are watching. The source of aesthetic appreciation of the van Basten goal does not originate in our understanding that we are watching a game of football. If the Guyer, Davies, Parsons and Carlson line of argument on Kant's notion of dependent beauty is correct, then it should not be incorporated into agon aesthetics. Looking back at our three examples of footballing beauty – Argentina's team goal, the Cruyff turn and Maradona's wondrous goal – it is clear that whatever aesthetic appreciation spectators derive from these footballing interactions, it lies within the realm of agon. Only someone in the grip of a theory would suggest that knowledge of the game of football and what is seen as working within that setting only constrained but did not contribute to the audience's aesthetic excitement. I will in any event leave it to Kant scholars to decide whether or not Kant's notion of dependent beauty is a species of functional beauty. I would not mind having the Sage of Königsberg on board the agon aesthetics bandwagon, though I doubt he fits the mould and would be comfortable in our company.

Functionality, on the other hand, in some form or another, is most obviously part of the agon aesthetics equation. The question is whether it should be associated with the notion of functional beauty. Let us consider Parsons and Carlson's theory of functional beauty, which is the most philosophically well-developed theory available. Dependent beauty (pace Kant) or functional beauty is the beauty or positive aesthetic value something has as a consequence (whether that consequence relation is intrinsic or extrinsic) of what that something is and how that something is supposed to function. The reason why a healthy tiger in its prime is beautiful is (at least partly) because its (perceived) aesthetic value displays, is grounded in or tied to the tiger being a well-functioning biological system. This would entail being good at what tigers do: stalking, killing, etc. Conversely, an injured, sick, etc., tiger does not invoke in us similar aesthetic pleasure. Related observations are supposed to hold *prima facie* for other phenomena that can be said to have functions, such as artefacts. Unfortunately, Parsons and Carlson's theory of functional beauty, as presented, does not sit very comfortably with the phenomenon of football and sports. The problem is Parsons and Carlson's so-called naturalism. Parsons and Carlson tell us that "to *naturalize*" is to provide a "non-intentional analysis" and that their approach to functional beauty is to "turn away from human intention, and towards the sort of 'naturalistic' approaches applied to function in biology" (Parsons and Carlson 2008: 70, 73). They aim at understanding the function of artefacts and their potential functional beauty independent of these artefacts having been produced by intentional creatures. If you hold that there are good reasons for thinking that humans are creatures that intend, believe, hope, fear, etc. when moving about in the world – i.e., that we are intentional creatures – then this naturalization project should give you pause. Why? *Prima facie*, what artefacts are for, i.e. their function, and them having been produced for reasons, i.e. by intentional creatures intending to use them for particular purposes, seem to be connected. Furthermore, it is not unreasonable to assume that further usage of such artefacts is somehow connected with the reasons those users have for using them, i.e., what the users aim at achieving. Both strands must be rejected as accidental and thus ignorable in the envisaged naturalization of functions of artefacts.[32]

As it turns out, Parsons and Carlson's best argument in favour of jettisoning the connection between the function of artefacts and what users aim at achieving by using them does not hold up. Their argument is a version of a well-known argument in the philosophy of language, which we can dub the *Humpty Dumpty argument*. When setting the stage, Parsons and Carlson's first observation is that someone might make an artefact intending it to be used in a certain manner, but "not all artefact functions correspond to the intentions of designers" (Parsons and Carlson 2008: 64). That is correct. In the philosophy of language, we would say that a speaker might intend to convey y by uttering x, but fail to achieve that goal. There is failure of uptake in both cases. Nothing much follows from that. For example, it would still be the case that a particular artefact was produced with the intention of functioning in a certain manner, even though it failed to do so. Furthermore, individual users of an artefact might use it for a non-standard purpose. In that case, we would not say that the non-standard usage was the function of that type of artefact. However, we would say that the function of the usage of the artefact on that particular occasion was a non-standard application of the artefact for solving the task at hand. Parsons and Carlson, on the other hand, want a theory of functionality of artefacts that crucially involves proper functions, where "[t]he most basic idea behind the notion of a proper function is the idea that it is the function that belongs to the object itself" (Parsons and Carlson 2008: 66). It is perhaps not surprising that Parsons and Carlson mostly address artefacts and steer clear of social kinds and practices like sport.[33] Owing to their physicality, artefacts enjoy an ontological independence from users that sports do not. I suspect that this makes a difference when approaching these topics. There would still be chairs around if we stopped using them, but there would not be any sports if we stopped practising them. Whereas artefacts can survive the intended functions of their creators and the first generations of users and take on new functions, social practices like sports cannot. The social practice of sport comes with a variety of aesthetic qualities, and it is difficult to envisage how these qualities can be divorced from practitioners' and audiences' awareness that what they are doing or seeing is a sport and not, say, a ritual. In Chapter 2, we saw that the transition of *danza de los voladores* from being a ritual to becoming something done for sport follows or is grounded in collective intentionality. Presumably, a change of function has taken place when a given practice goes from being a ritual to being done for sport. The form remains the same, while its internal aim changes and with it, we might expect, its external function. Awareness of the practice's internal aim is crucial to social kinds like football and other sports, i.e. collective intentionality, as this is the ontological arbiter that decides what sort of practice a practice is, i.e., how we individuate different social practices.

Now consider Parsons and Carlson's rejection of the intentionalist position on the functions of artefacts.

> The intentionalist might suggest (…) that intention gives rise to proper function, as opposed to function *simpliciter*, when it is sufficiently creative. (…) [T]his is not necessarily the case. Although some clever individual's inspired use of a frying pan as a satellite dish would be very creative, that would not change its proper function, which remains providing a portable hot surface for cooking.
>
> *(Parsons and Carlson 2008: 68)*

This is a Humpty Dumpty argument. In philosophy of language, the Humpty Dumpty argument was meant to show that communicative intentions do not play any role in understanding word and sentence meaning. What the argument managed to establish is that meaning conventions are not necessarily overturned by a single deviant or non-standard usage of a word or sentence. No one has, to my knowledge, actually argued for such a position. Not much follows from the Humpty Dumpty argument in the philosophy of language, and it does not fare better when transported into the debate on artefacts and their functions.[34] Aiming and succeeding at using an artefact in a non-established, non-standard manner does not immediately change the established or standard usage or the established or standard function.[35] However, should the usage of frying pans as satellite dishes catch on to the extent that one day all frying pans are used as satellite dishes, then surely the function has changed. The masters are the users. This shows the limited nature of Humpty Dumpty arguments.[36] If you admit a change in function in the frying pan case, then you seemingly allow human intentionality back into the equation, because at that point change in usage, i.e. function, is due to users aiming at something different when applying the artefact in question as a satellite dish. Parsons and Carlson, on the other hand, try to paint an alternative picture in which users do not aim at anything when using artefacts, and they do so by borrowing the notion of proper function from the life sciences.

> Trait X has a proper function F if and only if X currently exists because, in the recent past, ancestors of X were successful in enhancing fitness because they performed F, leading to reproduction of the genotype for trait X.
>
> (Parsons and Carlson 2008: 72)

This is a definition of proper function with regard to natural kinds in the life sciences. In order to translate this into a theory of functionality for artefacts, the following substitutions must be made. The phrase "ancestors of X" is replaced with "similar predecessors whose success in the market was a factor in the production of X" (Davies 2010: 318, Parsons and Carlson 2008: 76),[37] "enhancing fitness" with "meeting some need or want in the marketplace" (Parsons and Carlson 2008: 75, 148), and "reproduction of the genotype for trait X" with "leading to manufacture and distribution, or preservation, of Xs" (Parsons and Carlson 2008: 148).

> X has a *proper function* F if and only if Xs currently exist because, in the recent past, similar predecessors whose success in the market was a factor in the production of X were successful in meeting some need or want in the marketplace because they performed F, leading to manufacture and distribution, or preservation, of Xs.
>
> (Parsons and Carlson 2008: 75, 76, 148, Davies 2010: 318)

Before evaluating this, we do well to note that this definition comes after Parsons and Carlson's wholesale rejection of the intentionalist line. Having rejected the Humpty Dumpty argument presented by Parsons and Carlson, we should remind ourselves that their line is not the only game in town. In fact, an intentionalist could easily accept the definition above and argue that a natural interpretation of the market or marketplace would be as something involving intentions and collective intentionality. The market, among other things, contains intentional systems and how they go about negotiating the world, including aiming at end results, i.e. intending. Things look different with regard to biology and biologists' understanding of proper functions. Here the explanation of why a trait X came about and is maintained involves understanding how the trait functions and why it has been selected via the mechanism of natural selection. The first question to ask, when thinking about why a specific trait of a biological kind emerged and remained, is how it enhances or contributes to the biological system's fitness. The parallel question with regard to artefacts will very soon run into the question of whether needs and wants involve thoughts about how to satisfy those needs and wants, which again will give us intentions concerning usage. Merely alluding to the market does nothing to dispense with the intentional part of usage and application of most artefacts and, throwing our conceptual net wider, social kinds like football and similar sports. We would need to know the mechanism of the market, and intentions and collective intentionality will most likely enter the fray at some point. The mechanism of natural selection is blind, but the same does not necessarily hold for Parsons and Carlson's so-called marketplace.

This is not to suggest that intentions and collective intentionality are the be-all and end-all of social kinds. Our discussion in Chapter 2 shows that there is more to social kinds than intentions and collective intentionality. However, these are important aspects when trying to understand social historical kinds like football and similar sports. One way to think about social historical kinds is as spacetime worms that exist over time. These can and do change. The social historical kind is constituted by the participants and practitioners of the kind – how they behave and their attitude towards the kind itself. Furthermore, the practice survives by new members and generations being incorporated and assimilated into the practice. Obviously, the edges of such a social historical kind will be blurry or vague. We need not assume that the conscious choices of the participants and practitioners of the social historical kind drive all change. The way in which we individuated social historical kinds of sport in Chapter 2 was by using form and function, where the latter was understood as usage of the form in accordance with the kind's internal aim. Football *qua* sport will not survive a fundamental change of its internal aim, but the form can survive such a change. Another way of conceptualizing this part of our social world would be to not think in terms of social historical kinds and collective intentionality, but instead in terms of continuous causally connected stages of practices. This will be a different type of kind, which allows both change of form and function, i.e. internal aim. As long as the stages of the kinds are causally linked and remain as a reasonably well-defined practice – remain suitably discrete – then it seems we can identify what we might call a *mere causal social historical kind*. When a ritual becomes a sport, the social historical kind of that specific ritual ceases to exist and the social historical kind of that particular sport emerges, while encompassing both is the mere causal social historical kind. In the case of a ritual becoming a sport or something done for sport, the form remains, but one can also envisage the form changing (gradually) while the mere causal social historical kind survives. There is no reason to believe that the mere causal social historical kind and its development are only matters of intentions and collective intentionality. The lessons learnt from history and sociology tell us something different. In Chapter 1, we briefly mentioned the identity-making potential of sport. The identity-making potential of sport might be one factor that drives change, where the change can be explained without any detour through intentions and collective intentionality. One might furthermore imagine that the drive for identity can morph a sport into some other type of social historical kind that, at that point in history, better meets that need or want in the marketplace. Changes within a social historical kind and a mere causal social historical kind can originate outside the realm of the intentional systems *qua* intentional systems. However, the question of the social historical kind of football and similar sports is importantly also a question of intentions and collective intentionality. When the football form is not used and one is no longer playing according to the game's internal aim, then one is doing something different. If no one is any longer using the form, then football *qua* sport is gone. That was one of the main take-home lessons from Chapter 2.

At this point, it is useful to remind ourselves of the distinction, introduced in Chapter 1, between the internal or intrinsic purpose, aim or goal of sport, on the one hand, and the external or primary purpose or goal of sport, on the other: the inside and outside of sport. Why? We need to be clear on what sort of purpose, aim or goal the aesthetic side of sport is attached to. In Chapter 1, we suggested competition and domination as the external purposes of sports like football, especially because they connect conceptually with the internal aim of football, which is to win matches. However, identity making might also be an external purpose of football, or it must at least be considered when we ask the question of why a sport like football survives across generations and what human needs it fulfils. Let us assume that part of the answer to the latter question is how football functions to provide audiences and spectators with a social identity. I think that assumption is a good one, though it is not within the scope of this book to argue for this position. I also suggest that this identity-making function does not necessarily originate in collective intentionality. Certainly, individual football supporters may never consider the idea that one reason they attend matches is because it makes them feel like part of a larger social whole. When Saturday comes, football fans hardly think to themselves: "Time to go to the stadium and be part of the identity-making project of our local team." They might tell you, if asked, that camaraderie and being together with like-minded individuals is important, but I imagine that the identity-making potential of football, in its sociological sense, is not in the mind's eye of most football supporters when they show up at a match. That, however, does not prevent identity making from being an important part of the explanation for the practice of playing and watching football. Does our aesthetic appreciation of football attach to or originate in such external functions of the sport? Hardly. Football's function as an identity maker is not part of the aesthetics of football, though there is a connection. The easily available us-against-them feature of the football set-up, which facilitates engagement in the football drama and thus belongs to the agon aesthetics of football, paves the way for football's identity-making potential. The fact that the suggested external functions of football, like competition, domination and identity making, have counterparts on the inside of the sport gives further credence to the agon aesthetic line of reasoning.

But how are we to understand these external functions? I suspect we would do well to employ a pluralist approach and derive inspiration from various disciplines like biology, history and sociology. Such external purposes can be understood as overarching macro-movements that are not necessarily consciously considered by the individual members of a group, even though it is the needs of the collective that drive or maintain, say, a certain practice of a sport. The equation that can explain the needs and wants of the marketplace responsible for sports like football being selected as something worth doing and watching – and how surrounding circumstances favoured sport, in general, and football, in particular, in the historical periods when these came to occupy prominent places in the cultures they belonged to – certainly involves more than the individual intentions of participants and practitioners of sport, and the collective intentionality of the sporting community. However, as we saw in Chapter 2, sport, in general, and football, in particular, also involve intentions of participants and practitioners, and the collective intentionality of the sporting community. The macro- and micro-levels must be seen as working in concert. The macro-level function of identity making works in concert with the sport's inside. The mechanics of the game creates the social drama of conflict (competition), which spectators enjoy, while it also has an us-against-them quality, which pared with the physicality of a contact sport with direct hindering or obstructing actions (domination) is part of the reason why football, in particular, has proven to be a vehicle well suited to meeting the need for a social identity among its consumers (identity). When an identity-making function of football has taken effect, it then feeds back into engagement in the game both for players and spectators, which again reinforces the identity-making function of the proceedings. Parsons and Carlson's theory of functions of artefacts is of no help here for understanding the agon aesthetics of football and its connection to the game's external functions.

Instead, when thinking about the aesthetics of football, what does help is trying to understand how moves made in the game are predicated on the internal aim of the sport – winning the match by scoring goals and not conceding goals – and the mechanics of the sport – how one can best accomplish that in this particular sport. Movements in a football match are aesthetically appreciated because they are perceived as enhancing a team's chance of achieving the internal aim of the game, i.e. winning the match. Only when players and their moves are seen as aiming at winning does the game come alive agon aesthetically, which means that there seems to be little chance of naturalizing our enterprise. As I see it, there is no need to assume that a move that is lauded as, say, beautiful is necessarily the most effective, only that it is seen as improving one's chances of winning the match. Talk of graceful moves belongs to this part of the agon aesthetics. Gracefulness is often understood as involving being seen as somehow looking effortless, being seen as effective, though not necessarily using the most effective means of reaching a sport-specific goal. I suspect that evaluation of gracefulness and ungracefulness in movement quite often involves a certain conservative element. What we see as prime examples of graceful movements in a sport often coincide with whichever way of playing the sport was most effective in our formative years, when we were getting to know it. When a new way of playing a sport emerges, i.e. innovation in sport, it might at first be denounced as ungraceful. Then, perhaps only years later or perhaps after a generation, the same moves are lauded as beautiful or graceful, and few people recall what all the fuss was about in the beginning. Be that as it may. I will not explore this any further here. Note, however, that players of the sport generally drive game innovations – that is, new ways of playing within the parameters set by the rules. The key virtues – skill, strength, quick-wittedness, determination, will-to-victory, etc. – needed in the game of football are all connected with the aim of winning sport competitions. We find the same with regard to judging moves in a football match as beautiful, graceful, etc. These aesthetic qualities are predicated on agon, i.e. seeking to win the match, and seeking or aiming to win gives you intentionality. Footballers aim at winning by scoring goals and not conceding goals, and it is within that intentional sphere we judge moves as beautiful, graceful, etc. Things look somewhat different when we inquire into the sport drama of football.[38]

Footballers on the pitch do not intend to create a good drama, even if this is the fallout of their moves in football matches. Football matches create their own drama given the possible end results of winning, losing or drawing, and some matches are more dramatic than others. Whereas the aesthetic qualities of moves within the game are predicated on aiming at winning, the drama of the game is a result or an effect of pitching two opposing teams against each other to compete for the prize of being the winner. Unlike the various moves of bodies within the game, the game's dramatic qualities do not march in step with the players' intentions. Engagement in winning the game pertains to both participants and spectators, but the drama of sport comes more sharply into focus with regard to the spectators. The drama of sport, in general, and football, in particular, is likely the most important factor in the popularity of sport competitions as spectator events. As we saw in Chapter 2, exactly how sports emerged in antiquity from rituals, and how folk football emerged in the Middle Ages and later morphed into proto-football, is partly obscured by the fog of history. Presumably, their origin and emergence constitute a multifaceted historical development involving both macro- and micro-developments. I suspect that this is true of most social kinds and more or less all social historical kinds. One person's or group's choices did not straightforwardly create football, though its development into what we today know as association football also involved conscious choices. Furthermore, creating a good drama need not have been on the agenda in association football's formative years, but it certainly must be brought into the equation when explaining football's extraordinary worldwide success as a spectator sport. Today, the question of offering up a good drama is clearly on the agenda, when, for example, football authorities tweak the rules of the game.

Currently, football authorities – with their organizational pyramid where the Fédération Internationale de Football Association (FIFA) is at the top and the various regional confederations and national associations underneath – serve not only as keepers of the rules of the game, but also as sport-wrights who make occasional changes to the sport. Given the massive success of football in the latter part of the twentieth century and in the twenty-first century, these changes have mostly been quite conservative. Perhaps the biggest rule change that modern association football has experienced was the change in the offside rule in 1925, when it was decided that there only needed to be two players between the player who received a pass, as it was played, and the goal, not three. More goals were scored as a consequence of the rule change. There has been quite a lot of tinkering with the offside rule since then, but nothing has been as radical as the 1925 rule change. The best way to understand many of these rule changes is to see them as ways of making the game more exciting to watch, thus demonstrating football's receptiveness to audiences' appreciation of the game. This, for example, was the case with the introduction, in the 1990s, of the back-pass rule that prohibits goalkeepers from handling the ball when receiving a pass from a teammate, which later was expanded to include direct handling of throw-ins. Football displays what I, in a previous work, dubbed response sensitivity (Borge 2015a: 359).

> Sports can (...) exhibit a phenomenon called [response sensitivity]. If a rule change gets an approving response from those who watch, it is more likely to stay. If a rule change meets with disapproval, it is less likely to stay.
> (Mumford 2012a: 47)[39]

Mumford's emphasis is on football and football examples, and among these examples we find the already mentioned back-pass rule. Mumford concludes that "[t]he chief [response sensitivity] for the mass spectator sports (...) will be to the aesthetic reactions of those who watch" (Mumford 2012a: 47).[40] That aesthetic reaction, I would claim, pertains to the drama of football, i.e. the creation of interesting action-reaction patterns in the competitive and controlled setting of the football match. Introduction of the back-pass rule came in the slipstream of the disappointing 1990 World Cup in Italy. The tournament did contain the highly entertaining clash between the Netherlands and West Germany in the first knockout round, but it was otherwise seen as fairly stale and dull. It did not help that teams were allowed to have the goalkeeper throw the ball to the nearest defender, then to have him hold it, pass it back to the goalkeeper, who could pick up the ball, only to repeat the routine until the opposing team moved enough players up field to stop the numbing repetition. The back-pass rule eliminated a very unexciting method of running down the clock.[41] These changes, made by the football authorities to enhance the drama of football, are conscious decisions aimed at making football a more attractive sport to watch, i.e. involving organizational intentions. One might at this point reintroduce the idea of selection in a market, but this market will consist not only of players' and audiences' behavioural moves, but also the intentions of the sport-wrights, i.e. those changing the rules to enhance the watchability of the game. A naturalization project along the line of Parsons and Carlson's is bound to fail. This is not surprising, as social historical kinds like football involve intentions at ground level.

Objection: To what extent has the author managed to liberate his alternative picture from the disinterested aesthetics he criticizes? The author invokes the notion of pretence or make-believe and cashes this out in terms of "aesthetic engagement". The idea is that we pretend or make-believe that the outcome of a football match matters, while knowing that it does not really matter in any important sense. This suggests the following concern. A broadly Kantian perspective on art is that it is somewhat disconnected from real-world engagement. Aesthetic engagement might, in that sense, be described as disinterested, no matter how passionate. That looks quite similar to the author's take on your average football spectator who enjoys the football spectacle of an unnecessary staged conflict, while knowing that whatever the result is, it will not have any serious ramifications for his or her everyday life.

Reply: Again, we face the danger of being pulled into the battleground of Kant scholarship. I will resist entering the minefield. Having said that, there is still an interesting challenge here. Is my view, which I contrasted with disinterested aesthetics, at its core in fact also a type of disinterested aesthetics? If by "disinterested" you mean extra-ordinary and furthermore unnecessary for everyday concerns, then the answer is yes. If by "disinterested" you mean anything else, then the answer is no. I prefer writing about sports like football as extra-ordinary and unnecessary, instead of considering them along the lines of disinterested. The key question, as we saw in Chapter 1, is how we manage to engage in something that we must also be aware is irrelevant to our everyday ordinary world concerns. Why care about the fate of Leyton Orient, Deportivo Wanka, Grasshoppers Zurich, IL Skrim, Étoile Sportive du Sahel, and all those other football clubs gracing our planet? The answer was that it involves the activation of certain belief-like states that cause us to ready ourselves for a fight-or-flight situation. Those states are embedded in the proto-pretence of social play, as seen in rough-and-tumble play, and can give rise to enjoyment when engaging in a sport like football. This then was the suggested physiological basis of engagement in football: that which stirs us and enables engagement in the game, which after all has no consequences of importance for most players' and spectators' everyday life. This chapter has shown that such engagement can be trumped if real values are at stake. A natural consequence of the latter view is that we can resist the push towards engagement in sports like football. There could be various reasons why one would resist such a push, and I suspect that one reason might be a lack of taste for artificial unnecessary conflicts. Personality type might play a role here. The important thing is that engagement in sports like football can be resisted and also broken, i.e. when other concerns trump the fictional value of winning football matches. This means that talk about disengagement being necessary for the phenomenon's aesthetic character to shine through is misguided. Instead, there must be a positive movement for the phenomenon to come agon aesthetically alive. This movement can be active in the sense of actively seeking out the phenomenon to immerse oneself in it or else feeling the pull and allowing oneself to be transported inside the extra-ordinary world of the football drama. Once inside, one might then pull back to ponder the phenomenological character of the game, and that would indeed involve disengaging from the agon aesthetic interest in the football drama.[42] That is certainly a respectable activity for those so inclined. It should not, however, be equated with the aesthetic experiences afforded by football qua football. These are, as argued, found in the agon aesthetic realm.

Objection: The author gets a lot of mileage out of the result of the 2005 Champions League final between Liverpool FC and AC Milan, making it the centrepiece of the argument that fairness of result is not at the heart of the sport. Perhaps the result was not unfair, no matter what Maradona and other alleged experts say. In fact, after re-watching the game, sports writer Jonathan Wilson opines, "Liverpool weren't actually that bad in the first half" (Wilson with Murray 2013: 2). We need to pay careful attention to the matches themselves and not merely the general perception formed of them when the results are known. Perhaps agon aesthetics need not be opposed to the meritocratic-fairness view of sports. Why cannot agon aesthetics be paired with a meritocratic-fairness view of sports that sees sport as aiming at and often delivering fair results?

Reply: The latter question is easily answered. I see no reason why that could not be the case. However, the claim in this section is not conceptual, but empirical. It could be that audiences only enjoy watching sport competitions that give fair results and are appalled by unfair results. That could be true, but it is not. Furthermore, one does well to note that proponents of the meritocratic-fairness view of sports defend a very strong claim about the nature of sports – that the structural goal of sports is to deliver fair results – and I suspect that this line of argument is the mainstream or orthodox view in the philosophy of sport. The view is seldom challenged and more often than not taken for granted. To proponents of the meritocratic-fairness view of sports, a good game is one with a fair result. As a description of football audiences that is false. This is evidenced by the fact that there are football matches with unfair results that are still cherished by football audiences. The Liverpool FC vs. AC Milan match from 2005 is not the only example of a match with an unfair result that is held in high esteem. Manchester United's 2–1 victory over FC Bayern München in the 1999 Champions League final, which we opened this chapter with, is another. That match did not yield a fair result. The result did not accurately reflect the quality of athletic performance demonstrated by the two teams. It is not accidental that these two examples are cup matches. The general perception is that, due to the knockout format of cup tournaments, cup matches more easily lend themselves to outcomes in which the best team is not the winner (see Borge 2010a for further elucidation of the idea that the best team can lose). A league match might just as easily (or not) have an unfair result, but a team can still win the league even if it is massively unlucky in and loses a single match. Cup matches, due to the format of such competitions, bring this aspect of the game into sharper focus for the general public. Football audiences do not shy away from cup games or cup tournaments. Indeed, in some countries like England, the FA Cup is revered. The English talk about the romance of the FA Cup. Part of the romance is that, due to the knockout format, minnows can sometimes get lucky and knock out far better teams. One seldom hears complaints about cup upsets being unfair, i.e. about unfair results not properly reflecting the quality of play. Of course, cup upsets need not be unfair, though quite often they are. A good game of football, as perceived by your average football spectator, need not end in a fair outcome. The meritocratic-fairness view of sports does not fit the actual landscape of football spectatorship. The claim about the structural goal of sports made on behalf of the meritocratic-fairness view of sports is too strong.

One the other hand, it would be equally misguided to claim that there need not be any connection between how good someone is at a sport competition, i.e. the quality of athletic performance or the ability to perform a particular sport, and the results generally generated by such sport competitions. Although your average football supporter does not look down on the cup tournament format and cup matches, whether they be national or international tournaments, he or she also expects and demands that football to some degree deliver fair results. Most football fans will agree that the most prestigious trophy to win nationally is the league, not the national cup tournament. The reason for this is simple. The league is a more reliable guide with regard to deciding which team in the country is the best, i.e. most likely to generate a fair result. The question of a sport like football delivering fair results is not a question of either/or, but both/and. Football would not be a good sport if the results of football matches generally failed to reflect, to some degree, the quality of performance in football matches. The good in a good sport, however, is not a matter of ethics, but of aesthetics. If the results of football matches were utterly random, then I suspect the game would lose its attraction. It would be a bad sport, because it would be uninteresting both to play and to watch. Randomness per se in the context of extra-ordinary activities does not result in good drama. Without good drama, you do not have a good spectator sport. It is telling that no one stages, televises or otherwise watches games of chance like the lottery, unless one has made the game interesting by introducing betting into the equation. Lottery as a game of chance is itself uninteresting. Games of chance as such do not engage us. Still, the element of chance gives or contributes to, for example, the romance of the FA Cup and similar tournaments. There is a balance to be struck between the elements of chance and merit (see Borge 2010a). Thus, after having rejected the view that the structural goal of football is to deliver fair results, we must also concede to the defenders of the meritocratic-fairness view that part of the structure of football is to deliver fair enough results.

The possibilities of chance playing a role in a sport competition such that the sport competition can end with an unfair result gives you more unpredictability, thus making the sport experience more suspenseful. There must also be sufficient correspondence between quality of performance or ability and the results generated by the sport competition for us to find it engaging. Different sports strike the balance differently. As a football supporter, I tend to think that, among the sports we play, football strikes the balance best. However, I have no principled argument for why that is the case and on reflection I think it is better to say that the different ways of striking this balance in different sports have different appeal. It might also be the case that the mechanics of a sport is important with regard to the degree to which the possibility of chance playing a role in getting unfair results is seen as attractive or not. Perhaps this is more appealing, i.e. fun, in (some kinds of) constructive-destructive sports than, say, in your typical measurement sport. As to the question of whether the result of the match between Liverpool FC and AC Milan was unfair, it should be clear by now that the line of argument in this reply does not rely on that. Moreover, even if the result of that game was not unfair, the general perception is that it was and that it was a great game. That is all I need to defend my view. Wilson, in the passage quoted in the objection, goes on to concede that most remember "the miracle, the sheer implausibility of the whole thing", and he speculates that it "is the nature of memory: we remember the headline but not the detail" (Wilson with Murray 2013: 2). The game is perceived and remembered as a classic with an unfair result.

Perhaps Liverpool that night in Istanbul was not that bad. Still, the drama as it unfolded left a lasting impression of the miracle comeback and the struggling underdog team, holding on for dear life and finally lifting the trophy at the end of the match against all odds and the run of play. Perhaps a cool, more scientific analysis of the footage that day would yield a more nuanced and mixed picture. That just tells us that the cool-minded science of the game and the aesthetics of the game, which involves engagement in the drama, can and do sometimes come apart. It is a difference in interest and attitude. Few have given a better exemplification of this than Spanish coach Juanma Lillo when he scolded the football media's and fans' lack of understanding.

> That's one of the things I like to project to the players: the journey is the goal, the objective (...) [T]he objective is the journey, the process; the work matters (...) And it's far more complex than saying: win, good; don't win, bad (...) [W]hat enriches you is the game, not the result. The result is a piece of data (...) But the process that led to that? Now *that's* enriching. Fulfilment comes from the process. You debate the game not the results. (...) Do you go into a football stadium, in the last minute of a game, have a look at the scoreboard and leave? You watch 90 minutes, which is the process (...) You can't validate the process through the results. Human beings tend to venerate what finishes well, not what was done well. We attack what ended up badly, not what was done badly (...) Bayern Munich are a great team in the 90th minute [in 1999] when they are winning the Champions League and in the 92nd minute they're rubbish. How can that be? (...) The thing is, *después del visto todo el mundo es listo*: everyone's a genius after the event. I call them prophets of the past. And yet they are wrong to even evaluate the process in the light solely of how it came out in the end.
>
> (Lowe 2011: 60–61)

Lillo is talking as a practitioner of the art of building and leading football teams and, from this perspective, it is sensible to downplay the outcome – if and only if that is the best way to make players and teams perform better, thus enhancing their chances of winning games. Furthermore, football managers and coaches know that results do not always properly reflect performance. One must look behind the results, if one is looking to improve a team's performance. This is why it was perfectly sensible for Guariola to respond to that 4–0 loss, for his Bayern München against Real Madrid, by saying that he would not change his view on how to play football. Surely, others whose work is to manage or play football would agree.

However, for the rest of us at the terraces or in front of our television screens, things look different. We are indulging in the agon aesthetic pleasures of the social drama of the staged and confined conflict that football matches are. With regard to us, Lillo's disdain of the result is misguided. The result might not actually reflect the process properly with regard to athletic footballing abilities and skills, but it gives you something equally important. The final whistle and the end result deliver a verdict on which football theme, storyline or narrative that day's football drama consisted of. The time limitation on any game frames the drama of football and will also dictate any manager's tactical considerations as the process unfolds within the constitutive framework of the football form. Whatever the score is during a match influences the process, and the final score decides the football theme, storyline or narrative of the day. There is of course a balance to be struck between the scientific process-oriented evaluation of a football match and the agon aesthetic framing of the event as a certain kind of drama. In the latter, the saliency of certain match-defining moments and the result might obscure more sombre reflections on the match. Wilson reports that Ferguson himself was prone to point this out with regard to that famous night in Barcelona.

> A favourite ploy of Sir Alex Ferguson (...) is to remind [journalists] that he still has the first editions from 27 May 1999, the morning after Manchester United completed the Treble by winning the Champions League. In their running copy, journalists noted that Bayern Munich were much the better side, wondered why United had yet again failed to deliver in Europe (...) Only in the panicky seconds that followed those two match-turning goals in injury-time did they tack on a top and a tail hurriedly describing how, despite all that, United had somehow, once again, snatched an implausible victory. By the time of the re-writes that make up the later editions, the tone had changed to glory in United's success: Ferguson's finest hour, a courageous victory rooted in implacable self-belief.
>
> *(Wilson 2010: 3–4)*

Wilson goes on to note, "the truth is that it was the first editions, before knowledge of the result had coloured the perception, that more accurately reflected the match" (Wilson 2010: 4). This is true based on a process-oriented evaluation of the match, but most spectators came for the football drama, and from that agon aesthetic perceptive, everything changes in those action-packed injury-time minutes. Those two goals changed the whole story of the game and, rightly so, with it the perception of the game. In those few minutes, the story of Bayern's night went from a controlled superior victory to stumbling on the finishing line, while Manchester's went from lacklustre performance of folding with a whimper on the big stage to the unlikely comeback kings of stubborn, never-say-die resistance. What the British press did was to rewrite their report, in the light of which drama in fact ended up unfolding itself. That necessarily changes the perception of previous events in such a story. Had United not won, then the fact that they managed to keep the score down would still amount to actions seen within the overarching narrative of being dominated and finally losing. With the two goals, those actions are now part of a storyline of how United hung on to the possibility of turning the match around and finally did, and our perception of them is rightly coloured by that fact. The aesthetics of the agon of football gives you a drama that is closely tied to how a match ends. And note here how the analogy to fiction holds up quite well. Imagine you are watching a theatre production or a fiction film that bears all the genre hallmarks of a romantic comedy, but then at the tail end of the story it all unravels and the lovers die, Romeo-and-Juliet style. Certainly, theatre- or moviegoers will (often) reinterpret earlier events in the fiction in light of its ending. These events will be seen in a different light due to the tragic ending of the fictional proceedings, i.e. the result (the death of the lovers) colours our perceptions. Something similar is going on in football appreciation, and the agon aesthetics presented in this chapter explains why this is the case. With regard to the drama of the game, those three minutes of stoppage time at Camp Nou in 1999 changed everything.

Objection: The line of reasoning presented here fails to pay proper attention to the fact that football and similar sports are essentially games of skill. The main purpose of games of skill is that the outcome accurately reflect which competitor is the most skilful, i.e., award victory to the best competitor. As players we want to be as skilful as possible, not merely win whatever match we are playing, and as spectators we want to watch the most skilful players in action. This is what Gumbrecht was after when he proclaimed that he opted for areté over agon.

Reply: This is a good opportunity to revisit the question of skills in football, as it is important to understand that the theory argued for in this book makes ample room for skill to be central to the sport of football. Obviously, skill is part of the pleasure of both playing and watching football, and that fits the model presented here. Games of chance like lotteries, roulette, etc. only become interesting when real values are at stake (money being an instrumental real value). We might consider that such games, in the larger scheme of things, belong to the extra-ordinary side of things, but they're not fictional in character. There is no need for any make-believe to get excited about the prospects of winning large sums of money. Partaking in games of chance with nothing of significance on the line – no money, no social prestige, etc. – to make it deep will not excite us. Furthermore, it is unlikely to activate anything on the alief level, so that venue of excitement is also closed. The model presented here can explain why fictional games and sports, if they are to excite us, require that skill execution be part of their mechanics. Recall that the suggestion was that getting excited about playing or watching a game of football involves activation of some type of alief, along the lines of "Physical struggle/fight! D-a-n-g-e-r ...! Activate fight-or-flight adrenaline now". This activation of a very basic mental state or amalgam of mental states prescribes action alternatives. Whereas games of chance, if properly designed, entail randomness, games that trigger "Physical struggle/fight! D-a-n-g-e-r ...! Activate fight-or-flight adrenaline now" need (perceived) achievable action alternatives if they are to be psychologically satisfying. The latter entails skills. In this connection, something being a skill is minimally taken to mean that what you achieve action-wise is partly a result of your abilities and decisions, and not some random process. Not seeing any achievable action alternatives when in a fight-or-flight state leads to frustration and, lastly, resignation. It is a well-known fact in psychology that if you trigger typical fight-or-flight mental states in an animal, but deprive it of possible action alternatives, first frustration and then apathy will follow (Overmier and Seligman 1967, see also Seligman and Maier 1967, Seligman, Maier and Geer 1968, and Seligman 1972). If we assume that the same applies to humans, then not only can the model accommodate the idea that football is a sport of skill, but skill also gets into the model on the ground floor and explains why playing and watching football are exciting and not merely frustrating, leading to apathy. It also follows naturally that, measured using this parameter, the more skilful you get, the more action alternatives open up and the more pleasurable becomes the experience of both playing and watching football. This, however, must be calibrated with the parameter of drama and the questions of how well the teams are matched and how interesting the social drama provided by the match is.

Skills are necessary, but solely focusing on skill quality is misguided. Areté does not take precedence over the drama of agon. Much of the football played and watched around the world is not particularly well executed, at least not if your standard of comparison is the absolute best teams and players. Gumbrecht insists that "[s]pectators prefer to watch athletes as they test and push the absolute limits of human performance" and "desire to see the very best athletes", but there is more to constructive-destructive sports like football than this single-minded focus on skill quality (Gumbrecht 2006: 73). Even if one grants Gumbrecht that spectators would prefer to watch the very best athletes, that still leaves us with the task of explaining what all those spectators who show up year after year to watch football performances well below the elite level are getting out of the experience. Many lower-level division teams around the globe have enthusiastic and passionate followers who seem to care deeply about how their teams are faring, in whatever league or cup they might be playing, while not caring much or as intensely about how some top-level teams in the country are doing. The majority of football spectators who show up on the terraces are not watching the very best players and teams.

In short, we need to explain the euphoria that spread among the home fans at the Belmont Ground, home of Whitstable Town, when the home side won an all-important six-pointer in the battle to avoid relegation against local Kent rivals Chatham Town on April 9, 2011. For Whitstable Town it had been a poor match. They had a man sent off after 17 minutes, Chatham Town dominated the proceedings and had been able to capitalize on that dominance, being up one goal to nil. Things were not looking good and the threat of relegation loomed large. Then in the 81st minute, against the run of play, Gareth Cornhill equalized for the home side, and two minutes later Dan Wisker put Whitstable ahead. Thanks to a considerable amount of luck, Whitstable Town managed to hang on to the lead. Suddenly, with only two matches left to play, Whitstable Town was six points clear of the relegation zone. The atmosphere among the home supporters was of bemused disbelief at actually having won the match, and the sheer joy of being clear of the relegation threat. This was the Ryman Football League Division One (South) and a far cry from the Champions League, the English Premier League or any other high-profile competition. None of the 245 paying spectators was under any illusion that this match was a display of high-quality playing. In fact, it was a poor game, even by Ryman Football League Division One (South) standards. Still, I am sure that very many of us, who were there at the Belmont Ground that very special evening, would prefer this match over some run-of-the-mill Premier League match, while being painfully aware of the fact that the quality of Premier League matches is light years ahead of anything that ever goes on at the Belmont Ground. The football at the Belmont Ground that day was not top-notch, but the drama of the game was second to none.

There are good reasons to spend some time on this example and to try to get a feel for what it was like to be there. The joys and pleasures of watching a sporting event of very low quality will make or break any theory of football and similar sports. If you cannot explain and understand what goes on at the Belmont Ground and similar venues around the world, then you have not explained or understood sports like football. Whereas spectator engagement in the Whitstable Town–Chatham Town match and similar matches is easily accommodated and explained in the general theoretical framework of this book, it becomes an anomaly, almost perverse, in theories of sport that put exclusive emphasis on high skill, quality and sporting prowess. Indeed, Gumbrecht, at one point, realizes that something might be amiss with the idea that sport appreciation is primarily about appreciating excellence, because this idea entails that sport spectators always want to see the best athletes.

> So how can college football [American football] and college basketball be so very popular, you may ask, if we know that those teams would not stand a chance to win against their professional counterparts? There is certainly no other sport that I watch with more passion than college football. (...) [W]hat matters above all, I believe, is knowing that the best college players in football and basketball will be tomorrow's professional stars.
>
> *(Gumbrecht 2006: 74)*

There is something desperate, almost sad, about the above passage. As a philosopher, Gumbrecht has identified the attraction of sport in the excellence of bodily movement, and from that it follows that we prefer the very best, but his heart does not follow. His argument that you prefer something over what you deem to be better, because that something will one day become that better thing, is analogous to arguing that you prefer to eat at a restaurant you consider less good than the restaurant next door, because the best chefs in the restaurant you eat at now tend to get better and land a job at the restaurant next door. The view argued for in this book can explain Gumbrecht's love for the Stanford Cardinal, though he himself cannot.

Objection: Consider a group of friends who decide to play a football match against each other. Because their continuous friendship is more important than the outcome of the match, there is a tacit understanding among them that the match should end in a draw, and so it does. Here there is no pretence that winning the football match matters, but the friends still seem to be playing a football match. This challenges the whole understanding of football as it has developed throughout the book.

Reply: Not really, but this is a fine occasion to elaborate on the gliding transitions between social historical kinds and how they are employed in this area. Regarding the friends tacitly playing for a draw, we might appeal to the distinction made in Chapter 2 between usage of the football form and application of the football form. Under the assumption that tacit understanding is understood as something that falls within the scope of the overtness or honesty requirement of application of the football form, then the friends are applying the football form, but not using it. We might complicate the case by saying that the players in such a pick-up game begin by using the football form, trying to win, but are at the same time willing to adjust and move into application mode should the game not yield the desired result. In such a case, there might be a mixture of elements of usage and application of the football form, or else the application mode of the football form might remain in the mix only counterfactually. Similarly, in a case where adults and children play together, one will most likely find the children in usage mode, while the adults will temper their game staying in application mode most of the time – or if one prefers, abuse mode. Taking it a step further, does kicking the football about when there is no game on count as football? Again we find that it is misguided to view this question as a polar question that makes a yes-no answer relevant. The players kicking the ball about are not using the football form fully, but instead they are applying elements of the football form in a training or leisure activity, and we might say their kicking the ball about is done for football.

In Chapter 2, we saw that the world of football already has in place an institution of football matches that relies on application of the football form, not usage of it, which is the institution of testimonial matches. Football remains a sport, as most matches are not enacted as testimonials. Also, the world of football has no equivalent to basketball's Harlem Globetrotters, who have one foot in the world of sport and the other in what we might call the world of sport entertainment.[43] We might define sport entertainment as an athletic activity that is not competitive, but performed as if it is competitive, thus yielding predetermined winners and losers. The fairly similar practices of professional wrestling and *lucha libre* are more loosely connected to their sport counterpart Greco-Roman wrestling, and come across not only as mere sport entertainment, but even as sport theatre. Commenting on professional wrestling, Barthes concurs and comments, "[w]hat is thus displayed for the public is the great spectacle of Suffering, Defeat, and Justice" (Barthes 2009: 8).[44]

Such loosely scripted good-versus-evil drama is perhaps given an even clearer expression in *lucha libre*, where the masked wrestlers are either *técnicos*, who rely on technical skills and fairness, or *rudos*, who rely on trickery and cheating. Such sport entertainment is more like art with elements of athleticism and improvisation, than it is like competitive sport. Testimonial matches in football share elements with professional wrestling and *lucha libre*. In all these activities, there is normally a shared rough understanding of how things should play out. In testimonials, the play should be fairly open and yield goals; it should be tempered and the result should be a draw or a fairly narrow victory for one of the sides. On the other hand, testimonials remain part of the sport of football, because such matches are institutionally linked to the sport. The teams that play testimonials are sport teams. However, one could easily imagine how those sorts of matches became popular not merely as tributes to certain players, but as show pieces of footballing skills, and how teams that only played such matches emerged. In that case, the football form would have been appropriate for sport entertainment purposes, and we would have a football equivalent to the Harlem Globetrotters.

The group of friends that tacitly agree to play for a draw pretend they are playing a football match that is fictional in character, i.e., they pretend to pretend that winning the football match matters. We have make-believe within the make-believe. One might argue that we can find elements of such make-believe within make-believe in regular football matches. A familiar, but misinformed, view among philosophers of sport is that all athletes (unless they are corrupt) want and should want to win every competition they are in. Loland gives voice to that view when he writes, "there seems to be a more or less tacit understanding among sports people and the public that single competitions are of primary importance" (Loland 2002: 103). *Au contraire*, everybody in football knows and in general accepts that, in games played in the context of a league, group play or home-away fixtures, teams sometimes play for a particular result and will be more concerned with not losing or not losing by too many goals, than with actually winning that particular match. Something quite interesting can happen in, say, the last round of the World Cup group stages, when in a particular match both teams find themselves favoured by the score line. Both teams will go through to the knockout stages if the score line does not change. Say, the score line is 1–0. The team that is down will probably at some point be more interested in not conceding a second than in actually trying to win the match or salvaging a draw. Such matches have a tendency to die out towards the end. Neither of the teams is willing to risk much, and both teams seem to be waiting for the final whistle. What are we then to say of games where 0–0 would ensure both teams a place in the knockout stages, or in a league setting, where a draw would ensure both teams' safety from relegation? Why do not such matches die on their feet? I suggest it is because teams usually have the good sense to pretend (to some degree) to want to win the match, even though both actually would take a draw any time. The teams make token or very guarded efforts to win the match. Of course, such pretence within the pretence of these kinds of football matches is a much tenser affair than the type of pretence within pretence that exists between friends in a pick-up game, as described in the objection. There is always the odd chance that one of the teams will actually score, even though both teams are more or less only trying to put on a show that makes it look like they are willing to attempt to score. If one team scores, then the game is on. It happens sometimes. The pretence within the pretence and the tension that ensues from the possibility that a goal could be scored, though it might not be very likely, are what make such games bearable to watch.

This gives us a whole new perspective on the infamous last group stage match between West Germany and Austria in the World Cup in Spain 1982. West Germany needed to win and mounted attacks in the beginning of the game. In the 10th minute Horst Hrubesch put the Germans in front, and a 1–0 win to West Germany would see both teams through to the knockout stages at the expense of Algeria. After ten minutes of football the match died. Loland correctly remarks, "[t]he second half became a parody in which neither team even tried to score", but mistakenly views this as "violat[ing] both the structural goal of competitions and the intentional goals of other parties concerned" (Loland 2002: 103). Given that playing for a particular result is a widespread phenomenon in football that is generally both accepted and expected, something else was amiss in the West Germany versus Austria match. The problem with the match was not that the two teams played for a particular result, but that they put on a bad show, or more correctly, no show at all. The two teams could not even be bothered to pretend they were trying to score after West Germany had got their goal, and that kind of arrogance is deplorable.[45] As mentioned earlier, the main aesthetic flaw of football is being boring, and this particular match was by far the most boring one ever to disgrace a World Cup tournament. In such matches, we expect and demand of teams that they at least pretend to try during most of the match, before they let the match die out at the very end of the game.[46]

Objection: Morality matters. Sport is and ought to be about more than just winning competitions, exerting dominance and competing. The line pushed in this book, however, describes the football spectacle as one seemingly deprived of moral considerations. Instead, we could follow McNamee and draw an analogy to Europe's medieval "morality plays", in which "good and evil were played out on a stage where what was at stake was the very soul of the principle character: Everyman" (McNamee 2008: 1). McNamee's contention is that "sports (…) now fulfil this role or function on a global scale (…) sports offer a cognitively simple canvas of good and evil writ large in the everyday contexts of the arena, the court, the field and, of course, the back pages of our newspapers and the screens of our televisions" (McNamee 2008: 1).

Reply: McNamee's idea that sport is a modern-day version of morality plays is very much in keeping with the general aesthetic line taken in this book, but at least when it comes to football, admitting that morality matters does not force us to give it centre stage. Arguing that morality or ethical considerations are not central to football does not leave it spinning in a morally frictionless void. Real values impose clear restrictions on the way we play football. Football, due to its fictional character, rests or supervenes upon real values. If what happens in a match threatens or destroys real values, then the fictional value of winning a football match is therewith also destroyed. Furthermore, when real values change, the game is generally forced to change with them. As for the analogy to medieval morality plays, I suspect that football is not really your ideal candidate. In fact, football is a rather unholy mixture of aggression and deceitful behaviour (cheating, shameless gamesmanship, anger, dominance, etc.), but also cooperative and honest conduct (fair play, respectful sportsmanship, friendliness, goodwill, etc.). It is a multifaceted spectacle that outruns any ethical theory I have seen on the market. Note, however, that football's foundation is cooperation. There is no game unless footballers either cooperate to self-referee matches according to the rules of the game (with whatever deviation of conduct each occasion allows) or cooperate by agreeing to let matches be refereed according to the rules of the game by a non-player and to endure, obey or accept this referee's decisions.

McNamee's idea of sports' potential as a morality play invites some final reflections on the drama of football. Instead of the medieval morality plays of Everyman, let us consider the legend of Robin Hood. Doing so seems appropriate given the clear moral lessons to be learned from the story (as we know it today) and the fact that one can trace references to a Robin Hood character all the way back to medieval times. What would football look like if it were to become more like a Robin Hoodish morality play and less like the game we know today? The first thing to note is that the game would probably have to transition from being a sport to becoming sport entertainment, the goal being to ensure that football dramas, i.e. matches, actually had morally appropriate or happy endings. The worry then would be whether much of the dense drama that football provides would be diminished, if the possibility for morally inappropriate or unhappy endings were eliminated. Consider the World Cup in South Africa in 2010. The tournament's absolute most dramatic moment was the quarter-final between Uruguay and Ghana, when in the very dying seconds of extra time Ghana looked destined to score the winning goal, only to see Uruguay's Luis Suárez clear the ball off the line with his hand. A penalty was given, and Suárez got his marching orders. Asomoah Gyan missed it with the last kick of the match. Ghana lost the penalty shoot-out. Larger parts of the footballing world howled at the injustice and heaped scorn and moral indignation on the cheating Suárez – who had the audacity to celebrate Gyan's penalty miss and later cheekily exclaimed, "The hand of God belongs to me". It is difficult to see how football as sport entertainment could in practice match such a gripping real-time drama of uncertainty of outcome. Furthermore, and perhaps most importantly, in order to achieve a moral drama like Robin Hood, you actually need a Luis Suárez. This is because, for every Robin Hood (real or fictional), there must be a Sheriff of Nottingham.[47]

If one wished to liken the dense drama of the football spectacle to a fictional genre, football looks a lot more like a soap opera than morality plays, Shakespeare plays, or any other kind of fictional narrative.[48] Despite the occasional unfair results and blatant rule breaking that go unpunished, audiences keep coming back to watch matches. Perhaps the unfair results, the rule breaking, the bad behaviour, etc. and the moral outrage they allow spectators to vent at players and teams – together with the feeling of moral superiority that goes with such moral outrage – are really part of the charm of watching football matches. Let us take another look at Suárez. He is currently plying his trade in La Liga for FC Barcelona, and before that he was in the English Premier League for Liverpool FC. Suárez's stay in the English Premier League started some months after his very own hand-of-God incident and, given the English's troubled relationship with small handballing South Americans and Suárez's own volatile nature, it is no wonder the relationship had its ups and downs. During his time in England, Suárez was as adored by the Liverpool supporters as he was despised by the rest of the spectators. Throughout the 2012 summer Olympic Games in London, when playing for Uruguay, the English audience booed Suárez whenever he got the ball. Similar reactions followed him as a Liverpool player on the team's travels in England. English audiences treated him like a soap opera baddie: a pantomime villain – a player they love to come out and see so they can shower him with moral indignation and scorn. In a telling episode in January 2013, Suárez once again handled the ball and as a result scored Liverpool's winning goal in the FA Cup third-round tie against the minnows of Mansfield Town. As it happened, the referee had seen the ball touching Suárez's hand, deeming it to not be a handball, thus making Suárez's actions and goal perfectly legitimate. Still, the English were having none of it. The public was outraged. James Lawton of the British newspaper *The Independent* called it "a diabolical act from Luis Suarez" (Lawton 2013). Take a second to consider what manner of actions you would, under normal circumstances in the ordinary world, possibly think of as diabolical. I suspect that, whichever actions you think deserve the label diabolical, Suárez touching the football that afternoon at Mansfield is not even in the same ballpark. In light of the fact that Suárez did not injure anyone, but merely scored a goal in a football match after the ball had touched his hand, calling that a diabolical act definitely has the feel of soap opera moral outrage, as did the perpetual booing Suárez received in England whenever he went down on the floor at away games.[49] Of course, one should keep in mind that, as with McNamee's suggested morality play analogy, the soap opera analogy is also just an analogy. On the other hand, I urge readers to give the analogy some serious consideration, because if you look at football in that way, while keeping in mind that the game is fictional in character, the phenomenon and all its surrounding noise suddenly make a lot more sense.

Conclusion

Football gives its participants and spectators a drama to engage in, which, because the sport is extra-ordinary and fictional in character, allows us to let our emotions run freely. Football is not only a game; it is because it is a game that it captivates us the way it does. The phenomenon of football outstrips the theoretical resources of the meritocratic-fairness view and the disinterested aesthetics of sport. These theories do not make proper contact with what is going on in sports like football. Instead, we need to build an agon aesthetics of football and similar sports that puts drama and the dramatic centre stage. I have shown why I think that is the way to proceed when thinking about football and how the agon aesthetics presented in this chapter is well equipped to help us understand the phenomenon at hand.

Notes

1 Some philosophers of sport would argue that football ought to be about fairness and that, because it is not, the game is flawed. Here, I will be concerned with how things are, not how they ought to be.
2 This is not to suggest that football and similar sports are exempt from all ethical considerations or critique, only that neither ethics, in general, nor fairness of result, in particular, is at centre stage of the sport. See Borge 2010b: 169–171, for a further discussion of football and ethics.
3 As Goldblatt tells us, "[t]he phrase was popularly credited to Pelé after he published his memoirs with the title *My Life and the Beautiful Game* in 1977. Others with a prior claim include H.E. Bates, Didi and Stuart Hall" (Goldblatt 2014: 251).
4 For the question of whether sport is art or could be art, see Best's (1974, 1985, 1986a) and Reid's (1970) arguments against the sport-art association, Wertz's arguments against the Best-Reid conclusion (Wertz 1984, 1985), together with Best's response (Best 1985, 1986b, see also Wertz 1977). Recently, Mumford has attempted to forge or bolster the link between sport and art, while I have shown why Mumford's attempt fails (Mumford 2012a, Borge 2012). Edgar gives a different take on the question and argues that the two share a common ground (Edgar 2013).
5 On Kant's distinction between free and dependent beauty, see i.a., Crawford 1974, Schaper 1979, Scarre 1981, Lorand 1989, 1992, Stecker 1990, Lord 1991, Dutton 1994, Guyer 1997, 1999, 2002a, 2002b, Wicks 1997, 1999, Eaton 1999, Allison 2001, Mallaband 2002, and McAdoo 2002.
6 This movie has a precursor in Costard's documentary *Fussball wie noch nie* from 1970, which in a similar manner followed Manchester United's George Best through a match against Coventry City.
7 This does not quite do justice to the film, as it shows quite a lot of football action in a variety of modes. However, it is quite telling that when Zidane creates the equalizer, you are shown that not in a game mode – how Zidane's moves are effective in achieving the aim of scoring with regard to defenders and fellow players – but rather with close-ups on Zidane's bodily movements. Only then, and more as an afterthought, is the goal shown as it was scored and as you would see it on television. The focus throughout the game is on Zidane in the game, not a game with Zidane.
8 It is far from clear that Gumbrecht can opt for areté over agon, when he at the same time considers athletic beauty to be part of disinterested aesthetics. Areté or excellence in sport or a sport seems intrinsically linked to the ontology of sport, in general, and the mechanics of individual sports, in particular, i.e. being a competition with certain standards for quality performance, which enables a participant or practitioner to win or do well. Disinterested aesthetics, on the other hand, prescribes a gaze that ignores or looks past what something is, thus enabling the phenomenal character of the phenomenon to speak uninterrupted. The two do not seem compatible. I doubt whether Gumbrecht can escape this dilemma, which in effect means that his position fails to get off the ground.
9 The quote from Gumbrecht is Gumbrecht quoting Kant with approval.
10 I write "predominantly" and not "always", because I do not want to rule out that somewhere out there, there might be someone who has praised a football action, interaction or game at the level of disinterested aesthetics.

11 Davis gives this goal special attention, arguing that "[t]he goal displayed harmony, fluency, balance, rhythm, purity, integrity, wholeness and even a metaphorical narrative, complete with supremely satisfying closure", and that we can "have 'traditional' aesthetic qualities such as grace, elegance, harmony or the sublime, yet reject or remain noncommittal on the category of beauty" (Davis 2015: 144–145). The agon aesthetic line is compatible with Davis's observation, although here I freely appeal to beauty. One might view talk of beauty in reference to football interactions as a shorthand for two or more of the aesthetic qualities mentioned by Davis.
12 We find a subtler defence of a Kant-, Merleau-Ponty- and Bachelard-inspired aesthetics of football in Edgar's view: "[s]port too is pleasurable in the Kantian sense, not least in that it is open to a depth of appreciation that draws upon a subtle and complex knowledge of the game, its rules, tactics and even history (…) pleasure is yielded insofar as players and spectators alike strive to appreciate the ways in which the movements of players about the pitch articulate a complex experience of space (…) pleasure in football exemplifies 'topophilia' (…) the spatial experience of play in terms of an understanding of the manner in which the flow of play allows or inhibits the player's exercise of sporting competence" (Edgar 2015: 153–154). If the knowledge referred to in the first part of this quote and the love of space talked about in the latter part are set within the framework of agon, then Edgar's line of thought can be subsumed within the agon aesthetics. That is, it will be one theory in the realm of agon aesthetics, or a theory that emphasizes a certain aspect of the agon aesthetic pleasures of playing and watching football.
13 A good example of how aesthetic appreciation of football interactions is buried deep within agon – where there is no compartmentalization of the aesthetics of the experience, on the one hand, and taking in the ramifications of the interaction qua an event in a competition, on the other – was reported in a conference presentation by Davis. Davis observed the reactions of English football supporters to that famous second solo goal Maradona made against England in the 1986 World Cup: "I watched this goal in a crowded television room with many avid England fans. When the goal went in, many – at the least – took on a very precise facial expression which they held for a long time. The expression palpably intimated a melancholy awe, a perception that something awesome but crushing had just been witnessed. There was, again, no impression of switching between rival states – no display of 'Oh no, we're two down' followed by a display of 'What a wonderful goal', followed by reversion to the first. There was, instead, every impression of one, quite lasting, intrinsically ambiguous state" (Paul Davis conf. presentation, BPSA, Gloucester 2013). Davis's observation serves as a good antidote to Mumford 2012b.
14 This agon aesthetic line of Borge 2015c seems to be endorsed by Ryall 2018: 38, and Kadlac 2018: 53.
15 Mumford 2012a and 2014 acknowledges drama as an aesthetic category when appreciating football, but fails to square this with his endorsement of Kant's view of aesthetics as disinterested and his own line regarding finding release in contemplating the aesthetic value of football interactions. The latter seems anathema to appreciating the football drama and the engagement it brings.
16 The title of Gebauer's work *Das Leben in 90 Minuten* suggests something similar, but does not make contact with this line of thought (Gebauer 2016).
17 Notwithstanding that football is a multifunctional and multidimensional phenomenon that people engage in for a variety of reasons and that some such reasons, like primarily playing football to stay fit and healthy, belong to the realm of ordinary everyday life. However, if someone cites exercise as the main reason for playing football, then that does not explain why that person has chosen to play football instead of merely exercising in other ways. Exercise and heath explain why someone engages in some sort of activity that involves bodily movement, but not why so many are drawn to sports as a way of exercising. Football *qua* football is not undertaken for any specific purpose outside the game itself, but football *qua* exercise most obviously is.

18 On narrative desires being inappropriately applied to real-world situations, see also Smith 2010: 237–238.
19 This bears some affinity with Kreft's idea of "aesthetic imagination (…) as a necessary condition for playing the game of football" (Kreft 2015: 124).
20 Xabi Alonso exemplified the thinking behind such an agon aesthetic attitude, when he said, "I can't get into my head that football development would educate tackling as a quality, something to learn, to teach, a characteristic of your play (…) How can that be a way of seeing the game? I just don't understand football in those terms. Tackling is a [last] resort and you will need it, but it isn't a quality to aspire to, a definition" (quoted in Anderson and Sally 2014: 127). Our imagined football aesthete would add that the beauty in, say, Paulo Maldini's game lies not in the tackles made, but in those not made, because Maldini already occupied the space in which a pass could have found an opponent had Maldini not closed down that possible venue of action: moves and countermoves, actions and reactions. However, aesthetically speaking, your hand is not forced. You might recognize the supreme footballing qualities of a Maldini and still prefer games with less talented defenders in which there is a healthy dose of tackles and the occasional reducer. Each to one's agon aesthetic own – or there is at least a discussion to be had about which method of playing is the most pleasing, agon aesthetically speaking.
21 This latter observation has been confirmed by empirical research; "[c]hance is a central element of any given football match (…) how often do favourites, across these different countries and disciplines, end up winning any given game? In football, it's only a slight majority: a little over half. In handball, basketball and American football the favourites win around two-thirds of their games while in baseball it's a solid 60 per cent (…) [t]he idea that football's favourites only win about 50 per cent of the time clashes with everything we think we know about the game" (Anderson and Sally 2014: 51, 52, 54). The latter is obviously an overstatement, but the statistical evidence wheeled out by Anderson and Sally supports the conclusion that "football is the most uncertain of the team sports" (Anderson and Sally 2014: 57). One can use playing formations and tactics to exploit the possibility of chance. The long-ball tactic of Wimbledon FC in their prime is perhaps the clearest example of this. Put the ball in the mixer, fill up with bodies and hope for the best. Occasionally the ball will fall favourably in the box, and the lesser team might snatch a goal or two from a superior opponent. Success based on organizational and tactical simplicity can on occasion overcome much more skilled opposition.
22 Football fans know this. Supporters of small teams go to cup matches against superior teams with the hope that today might be the day when all the margins go their way; today the ball will bounce off the post and out onto the pitch, not into the net, and so on and so forth. "You never know", they tell themselves. The so-called romance of knock-out tournaments relies on the element of chance or luck being big enough for giant killings to actually happen, and not merely being remote but never-actualized possibilities.
23 In this section, I concentrate on real values belonging to the realm of the ordinary world and contrast them with fictional values. That does not mean that values connected to the extra-ordinary realm cannot count as real values. In my view, religion belongs to the extra-ordinary side of things and, to religious practitioners, religious values count as real values. This complication need not worry us here. Whenever I write "real values" that should be understood as ordinary world real values.
24 If an assumed instrumental value in fact turns out not to be valuable for acquiring intrinsic values, perhaps it even hinders or destroys them, in which case it is no longer of value.
25 For a fairly recent debate on the phenomenon of voluntary suspension of play, see Russell 2007, Hardman 2009, and Mumford 2010. All of these philosophers see voluntary suspension of play as an example of fair play, as constituting a fair play norm, whereas in my theory of football, voluntary suspension of play, when players are (seriously) injured, is an anticipated consequence of football's fictional character. At least tacitly, players demonstrate an understanding of the character of the game they are playing. At the same time, if I am correct in arguing that football is a niggly game – where players constantly seek game advantages and generally show little concern about

26 fair play, unless such concerns give them a game advantage – then we should expect to find exploitation of the practice of voluntary suspension of play, where players either overplay their injury or fake it to get the opposing team to stop playing. Mumford shows that the latter is the case (Mumford 2010: 258–263).
26 Foot gives a good account of the reasoning leading up to the match being played and the controversy surrounding the playing of the match and its aftermath in Italy (Foot 2007: 360–372). Foot also tells us, "[l]ater, however, Pizzul became carried away. He finished his 'commentary' with the oft-criticized phrase: 'this is a glorious day for Italian sport'", and Hornby admits, "I am still embarrassed by the fact that I watched the game; I should have turned the TV off, told everyone to go home, made a unilateral decision that football no longer mattered, and wouldn't for quite a while (...) nobody really cared who won the European Cup any more, but there was still a last, indelible trace of obsession left in us" (Foot 2007: 369, Hornby 1992: 157).
27 Reactions to crowd disasters throughout the history of football have varied. The historical and sociological background is complex. There is no room in this chapter to enter into this debate, but for a further discussion see, e.g., Johnes 2004. However, as the quotes show, the philosophical understanding pursued here is mirrored in both current reactions and reactions that go back quite some time.
28 Anyone familiar with Rekdal's fiercely competitive nature will understand the gravity of his concession that football was no longer everything.
29 In *Stagecoach* they used the Running W technique to create the spectacular chase scene, where various horses and riders fall to the ground. Mitchum and Pavia describe the device as follows: "[w]ires attached to a horse's forelegs were threaded through a ring on the cinch and secured to buried dead weights. When the horse ran to the end of the wires, his forelegs were yanked out from under him" (Mitchum with Pavia 2005: 63).
30 This is not meant as a critique of Regis, Batson, Cunningham and other pioneering black footballers in English football, such as Nottingham Forest's Anderson and Watford's and Liverpool's Barnes. I merely record how things have changed and show how that fits into my theoretical framework. Anderson recalls an early career match at St. James' Park in Newcastle and how "what I experienced that night went way beyond the boundaries of acceptable behaviour", while he echoes the sentiment of the West Bromwich Albion players that one just has to get on with it: "Nowhere was free from the scourge. I suffered as much as anyone from the hate but most of the time I was able to shut it out and concentrate on my game. Perhaps it even spurred me on to be a better player. There was no room for complacency (...) The next away game could bring the most disgusting chants by the crowd and racist comments from individual supporters" (Anderson with Guest 2010: 10–11). Currently, we do not accept racial abuse and other bigoted behaviour on our terraces, but as Barnes notes, "[r]acists may have to stay silent for ninety minutes, but they remain racist (...) Just because the public suddenly do not hear racist remarks does not mean racism has been eradicated. Society is too racist for the intolerance to disappear simply through a few pamphlets pleading with fans to stop calling John Barnes a nigger. Before racism can be tackled in football, rugby or cricket it has to be addressed in society" (Barnes 1999: 95).
31 bennettiction, n. Praise for a philosopher for solving a problem that was not invented until several hundred years after his death. "His study of Kant concludes with a bennettiction of Kant for solving the problem of a private language" (*The Philosophical Lexicon*: www.philosophicallexicon.com).
32 The labels of "naturalism" and "naturalization" are unfortunate. Those of us who believe that the intentional part of intentional creatures is part of the furniture of the world, and that the world is physical, are forced to reject naturalism and naturalization projects. For us, naturalism and naturalization constitute the project of denying that a part of the natural world exists. The labels are the philosophical heritage of the behaviouristic heydays of Quine and Sellars. We seem to be stuck with them.
33 They briefly discuss sport, but do not really give the phenomenon any serious consideration (Parsons and Carlson 2008: 96–97).

34 When claiming that some philosopher of language occupies a Humpty Dumpty position, it is argued that it is entailed in that philosopher's position on meaning, that what a speaker intends to mean by a word or sentence is what that word or sentence means. However, as the Humpty Dumpty argument goes, even if a speaker intends to mean that grass is green by uttering the sentence "snow is white" that does not make the sentence "snow is white" mean that grass is green, because the sentence "snow is white" means that snow is white. The background for the Humpty Dumpty association is Carroll's *Through the Looking-Glass, and What Alice Found There*, where the character Humpty Dumpty claims that uttering the sentence "There's glory for you!" means that there's a nice knock-down argument for you, and when Alice questions whether you can make words mean so many different things, Humpty Dumpty replies that the question is, which is to be master. Grice's theory of meaning is probably the theory most often charged with Humpty Dumptyism (Grice 1957, 1968, 1969, 1982, 1991). For a discussion on how to deal with this objection within a broadly Gricean picture and why nothing much follows in general from this type of argument, see Borge 2010c: 383–393.

35 Established or standard usage, or established or standard function, covers the same ground as the notion of "proper function", but comes without its theoretical baggage.

36 Davies sees this when he writes, "if we accept the examples Parsons and Carlson offer in favor of their anti-intentionalist stance, it can be argued that their conclusions are too strong. More attention to the social context of intending, to the roles of intenders, and to how both of these affect what intentions can be realized might explain why not everyone who expresses an intention about an item's proper function can confer that function or can supersede a proper function that was established earlier" (Davies 2010: 323).

37 This is Davies's formulation. Parsons and Carlson instead write "[w]e will take an artefact X's ancestors to be those objects that are (1) similar to X and (2) whose success in the marketplace was a causal factor in the production of X" (Parsons and Carlson 2008: 76).

38 Football has a variety of playing styles, and spectators' aesthetic appreciation might vary with regard to what they count as beautiful and graceful, all depending on which football culture they have grown up in and become accustomed to. Furthermore, taste in football style might change over time. Mumford seems to beg to differ when he writes, "there is a rough consensus as to which athletes are graceful and which are not" (Mumford 2012a: 28). History, however, is a harsh judge with regard to questions concerning beauty and grace. For example, when considering two female tennis players, who today are regarded as all-time greats, Cordner tells us that Navratilova "lacks grace" (Cordner 1984: 305) and "does not herself warm to and flow with the game", but leaves an "impression of clinical detachment" (Cordner 1984: 309), while Evert-Lloyd played "as if she played without feeling, without *herself* being part of, or confluent with her play", both players lacking "a 'human' dimension" (Cordner 1984: 308). These comments tell us more about Cordner and the general cultural and political climate of his time than about Navratilova's and Evert-Lloyd's styles and achievements. Even though Mumford believes there is a rough consensus as to which athletes are graceful and which are not, I doubt that you will find many who agree with Cordner's harsh judgement of the playing styles of Navratilova and Evert-Lloyd. There is a further question of whether beauty and grace in sport are consequences of being part of a competition or whether they are more or less independent of that. According to Mumford, "we have natural dispositions to respond to types of properties or features of the world with particular types of aesthetic judgment" (Mumford 2012a: 29–30). That claim seems dubious with regard to events in a football match, like a beautifully taken free kick that curves over the wall into the top corner of the goal, the graceful slicing up of a defence by a brilliant through ball, the majestic and well-timed last-ditch slide tackle that prevents a clear goal-scoring chance, and so on and so forth, because these are all constitutively dependent on the invention of the practice of football. It would be odd to say we have natural pre-set dispositions – independent of our understanding of the game and these actions' role in the competition – to regard the curve of the ball that hits its target as beautiful or

graceful, as opposed to a free kick with a similar curve that ends up by the corner flag. Talk of beautiful or graceful play in football is intrinsically tied up to our understanding and perception of football as a competition.

39 Mumford's original label for this phenomenon in the quote above is "response-dependency". That label is unfortunate. According to Haukioja "[t]he term 'response-dependence' made its entrance into the philosophical vocabulary in the late 1980's" and "[i]n general, to say that a concept or a property *F* is response-dependent is to claim that there is an a priori connection between *F* and our responses (with respect to *F*) in normal, favourable, or ideal conditions" (Haukioja 2013: 167–168). Given the established usage of the term to describe a priori connections between the extension of a term/concept/ property and the responses of speakers/thinkers using the term/concept, or the responses of the agents who have a concept that expresses that property, I have introduced the term "response sensitivity" for the phenomenon Mumford describes.

40 Again, Mumford uses the word "response-dependency" not "response sensitivity".

41 Any argument that running down the clock is always dull, unexciting and should be vetted out of any sport by changing the rules does not hold true for football. A team in the lead or otherwise with a result they are pleased with, which passes the ball around with the other team chasing them, while the *olés* go round the stadium, can be an awe-inspiring sight. This is, of course, because this tactic both takes impressive footballing skills and comes with a risk.

42 With regard to disinterested aestheticization of a phenomenon like football, will it make a difference whether one first had to disengage from an engagement in the game or not? Will the disinterested aesthetic experience in those two cases differ or be the same? Similarly, will it make a difference to such aestheticizing, whether one had a prior understanding of the phenomenon counting as a sport or not? Will the disinterested aesthetic experience in those two cases differ or be the same? If, regarding both of these questions, it does not make a difference, then it is irrelevant for the disinterested aesthetic mode that it is a sport and the mode cannot be said to give us an aesthetics of sport, in general, and football, in particular. The aesthetic qualities of the movements of bodies and interaction between them would have been the same if, say, the football form were appropriated, not used. If it does make a difference, then with regard to the first question, the disinterested aesthetics is secondary to the agon aesthetics, and with regard to the second question, the concept of the sport would guide the disinterested aesthetics, which again makes the aesthetic experience dependent on the agon of the activity. I leave it to philosophers who are sympathetic with a disinterested aesthetics approach to sport and football to answer these important questions.

43 My reason for saying that they have one foot in each camp is that they apply the basketball form for entertainment purposes. The sport entertainment basketball team "starting life in 1927, the Harlem team, comprising extrovert African American players, evolved from a playful yet competitive outfit to a virtual circus, complete with clownish antics, accompanying music and all sorts of gimmicks" (Cashmore 2000: 308).

44 Cashmore tells us that the British wrestler Shirley Crabtree "became synonymous with the hybrid sport that we now associate with the World Wrestling Federation: half combat sport and half circus act, and totally showbusiness (...) Wrestling at this stage had become less a competitive sport and more a staged mock conflict (...) Heroes and villains were soon established, with villains typically snarling and threatening at the braying crowds. It was as if the spectators suspended belief for the duration of a fight (...) wrestling fans in all probability knew that the matches were rehearsed and managed, but still enjoyed the spectacle. Not that the wrestlers were devoid of skill or athleticism" (Cashmore 2000: 35).

45 No doubt much of the outrage over this match must be understood in a broader context. It was noticed around the world that two European nations so blatantly cooperated, the end result being preventing an African team from reaching the knockout stages of a World Cup for the first time. Matters were not helped by these nations being West Germany and their former World War II Anschluss compatriots Austria. The

publicity catastrophe was not lost on the West German media and general public, who were livid. Though "[s]ome politely chose to dub the drama a 'non-alignment pact' (...) most observers didn't mince words. West Germany's largest tabloid spat Shame on you!, former international Willi Schulz labelled all 22 players 'gangsters' and the TV commentator covering the match, or whatever it was, lapsed into the murmur of a funeral speech. 'What's happening here is disgraceful and has nothing to do with football,' he whispered in a broken voice. 'You can say what you want, but not every end justifies every means'" (Hesse-Lichtenberger 2003: 248–249).

46 Even though Algeria was at the receiving end of the debacle in Gijón, they themselves were happy to play for a particular result in the Africa Cup of Nations in Angola 2010. In the last two games of Group A, Angola met Algeria, while Mali faced Malawi. Within three minutes of the Mali–Malawi game, Mali led the game 2–0, courtesy of goals from Kanouté and Keita (the match ended 3–1). This meant that both Angola and Algeria would go through to the quarter-finals, if their match ended 0–0 (given that Mali won their match). The players from both Algeria and Angola were informed of the score in the other match and, not surprisingly, put on a rather subdued performance, though nothing like the horror show presented by West Germany and Austria in 1982. The match predictably ended 0–0. Algeria's midfielder Ziani explained that "we knew the score (of the Mali v Malawi), we knew a draw would be enough and against a strong side like Angola it was safer to stay behind and in control" and because both teams at least pretended to try, there was no *Schande von Gijón* in Luanda (Pretot 2010).

47 Great football teams tend not to be made up of choirboys or moral saints. Ferguson recalls his experiences as Aberdeen manager when meeting the great Liverpool team of the late 1970s and 1980s in the second round of the European Cup in 1980: "We lost the first leg at Pittodrie 1–0, but learned a lot, not just in terms of skill, but also in the psychological warfare stakes and the fact that, for all their quality, Liverpool had a bit of grit and nastiness about them that you need from time to time" (Ferguson 2011: 4). Similarly, Cruyff assembling his FC Barcelona dream team of the 1990s recalls that it was not complete until he had Bulgarian striker Stoichkov on the books: "Hristo was someone I needed not only because of his footballing qualities, but also because of his character. He was a fighter, and obstinate in a good way (...) he was the type who would shake things up. Not only in the changing room, but also on the pitch" (Cruyff with de Groot 2016: 134). Stoichkov was a confrontational character with grit and nastiness who would go the extra mile and foul to win games. As Lowe reports, "Carrasco described him as '(...) he's got *mala leche*'. *Mala leche* literally means bad milk; edge, a fearsome temper, aggression, competitiveness, a touch of madness. It is also exactly the point. Cruyff had focused on Stoichkov as much for his temperament as his talent. 'We needed him. We had too many nice guys'" (Lowe 2013: 282). Cruyff protégé Guardiola had Busquets to shake things up for his Barcelona. And the list goes on.

48 Tomlinson in passing writes of football that "[i]t is soap opera on grass, providing main narratives, sidelines, unlikely diversions, wonderful arrays of character" (Tomlinson 2013: 2).

49 Suárez sometimes plays the role to perfection, such as when he absurdly and inexplicitly bit Chelsea's Ivanović at the end of the 2012–2013 season, and then a year later, beyond belief, re-enacted the feat by making a meal out of Italy's Chiellini in the group stage meeting between Uruguay and Italy at the 2014 World Cup in Brazil. Obviously, one can do a lot worse things on a football pitch than having a little nibble of an opponent – careers are not ended by what Suárez did – but still, there is something untoward about Suárez biting other players. See Martínková and Parry 2015.

CONCLUSION
They think it's all over

This is not the end. Our topic is not exhausted. There are still questions left to be asked and answered regarding football, in particular, and sport, in general. Perhaps most pressingly, we have not addressed the question of whether, and subsequently how, football and sport and engagement in them among adults contribute to or enhance our biological fitness both as individuals and as a species. More precisely, what adaptive advantages are gained, if any, by adult human beings expending large amounts of resources on sports like football? We have addressed the internal question of why humans engage in sports like football and how we engage, as well as the external question of what needs and wants a sport like football fulfils. These explain what drives our participation in sport in the first place and why we continue to see it as worth pursuing. The suggested external or primary purposes of football – competition, domination and identity making – are mirrored on the inside of the sport. This is not surprising. If there were external or primary purposes that drove the process of which the emergence of the sport of football was the end result, then the football form would be designed to meet such needs and wants. The external or primary purposes of football, however, may or may not also contribute to our fitness as individuals or a species.

Sadly our time is up. I leave it to other authors to guide us through this area of research and give it the full treatment it deserves. We might note, however, that answering the question of potential adaptive advantages of adults spending energy on sports represents no small theoretical hurdle. In Chapter 1, we saw that pinpointing exactly the role of play in enhancing various species' fitness has turned out to be difficult. There is no general consensus among researchers on the question of how play contributes to the fitness of the various biological systems that engage in play. Most researchers in the field think that, given the fact that the animal kingdom at a certain level of cognitive sophistication is ripe with play, the activity or mode of activity must somehow contribute to fitness. The theory of evolution, with its mechanisms of natural selection, demands this. Given that sport is a more complex phenomenon than play – especially because play is one of the roots or origins of sport – it is perhaps no wonder that no one has yet attempted to subject sport to such general considerations of its possible adaptive function of promoting fitness. Research has shown us that most play in nonhuman animals takes place in the formative period leading up to adulthood. This indicates that whatever it is that play activity contributes to a species, both phylogenetically and ontogenetically, it is reasonable to think that it concerns the development of certain cognitive and behavioural traits of the creature in question. Football and many similar sports, on the other hand, are primarily adult entertainment, both in origin and in their present incarnation. The main hypothesis of play research does not seem to be available to us when thinking about football and fitness. That does not mean we should not address or think about this question, but that we need to be patient, because this is a dark corner of our topic as far as theory development goes. Moreover, we need to allow ourselves to explore other aspects of sports like football, even if this aspect remains obscure to us.

Of course, it might be that asking about football's and similar sports' adaptive function is the wrong question, or that we have framed the question in the wrong way. Looking directly at the complex social and historical phenomenon of football and similar sports, and asking about their adaptive advantages in a story of how properties and practices are evolutionarily selected, might be the wrong way to go about it. Perhaps there are no adaptive advantages to be gained by sports like football *qua* sport. To borrow a metaphor from the Marxist tradition, football and similar sports might belong to the superstructure of human development and existence. The real action that drives and shapes us as a species might take place on a more basic level of everyday interactive dealings with issues that influence survival and reproduction and, on the individual level, during our formative years of becoming well-functioning individuals adapting to various environmental pressures and to reproduce. The adult entertainment that is football, whether we amuse ourselves as players or spectators, might not directly enter into that equation. But that does not mean these kinds of questions do not enter into our understanding of football and similar sports. Instead, we might frame the question differently, asking whether there are mechanisms that are selected because they contribute to our fitness, and whether this also underpins our ability and willingness to engage in sports like football. The picture I have painted of football and similar sports involves mechanisms such as alief activation and the proto-pretence of social play. Activation of aliefs is advantageous in an evolutionary perspective, because it gives a quicker response time to, say, threats than if the individual in question would have to go all the way to the level of belief before deciding what to do. Furthermore, from the perspective of cognitive economy, the alief hypothesis makes sense, because we humans are cognitive misers in that our minds are designed to minimize effort when processing input from the world around us. The theory of football presented in this book has little problem fitting in with a general evolutionary view of humans and human development. The alief mechanism is selected and gives us the evolutionary underpinning for understanding why we get excited about football actions and interaction. We get and remain excited even though we clearly, on some level, know we are not in any real danger. This is explained by showing how social play involves proto-pretence – social play having been selected for its various adaptive advantages – and the suggestion is that this type of proto-pretence is also part of our engagement in sports like football. Football engagement is triggered by aliefs and sustained by the proto-pretence of social play, thus giving us the fictional character of football.

The nature of football is that it is a social historical kind based on direct collective intentionality, which allows stage type exceptions with regard to collective intentionality. Being a social historical kind means that the sport is in movement, changing as it goes along. Any analysis of football qua sport must take that fact into consideration, which gives us foundational formalism as the correct way to think about the relationship between the constitutive rules of the game, its ethos (including rule interpretation), and the sport itself. Sports like football are not static entities – neither are their rules, interpretation nor ethos more broadly understood – though they are kinds that avail themselves to analysis and arguments about what falls within the scope of sports and football and what does not. Football is a specific social historical kind in relation to which we can talk about the football form. Once we have that in place, we can show the various relations the form can enter into. Not all of them will be cases of playing football *qua* sport, but these other cases provide us with an important understanding of how we should deal with the various scenarios and the question of whether or not someone is playing a game of football. In order to play the sport of football, the football form must be used.

When analysing the sport phenomenon, we find that the following picture holds. Sports like football are rule-based physical skill activities or practices in which one cooperates in order to have an unnecessary competition one aims at winning. Within the sport logic, one can introduce less efficient ways of reaching the sport-specific goals of the competition and carry or support uncooperative conduct of play, including breaking the rules of the game and violating any ethos that may or may not be in place. Sport participants endure, obey or accept the rulings of an arbiter or arbiters of the rules of the game concerning what counts as what in the game. Practitioners of the game accept these rulings and aim at winning the sport by achieving the game's lusory goal. Practitioners ensure that the football form is used and that a game of football counts as a sporting event. Carefully studying the social historical kind of football, as it has been played and is currently played, shows us that we must settle for a rather minimal requirement for how footballers related to the rules of the sport and its ethos, if there even is a shared ethos in a particular footballing encounter. We cooperate to get our game going, but within the game, we aim at defeating each other and can be uncooperative with regard to both the game's rules and its prevailing ethos. Footballers will typically adapt their behaviour to the way a referee practises the rules of the game. Players adapting to refereeing practices gives us convergence on rule interpretation, not necessarily because they respect the rules of the game or are swayed by any particular ethos, but because this is the best way to win football matches. The referee sets a standard, the players follow suit. Apart from implementing the rules of the sport, referees also play a role in maintaining the game's fictional character and guarding game development, the goal being to make it a better playing and viewing experience.

The football viewing experience of the average sport spectator is a question of engaging in the game as it unfolds. When we take our starting point in engagement in the unnecessary staged conflict that football matches are, an agon aesthetics emerges, and within that perspective we find that footballing actions deemed beautiful, elegant and so on, are normally considered as such due to their functionality within the game. Aesthetic praise of footballing actions is predominantly anchored in the understanding that they are part of a competitive setting and are conducive to achieving the aim of the sport, which is to win football matches. Moving from individual football actions and interactions to the competition of the football match, which involves two teams battling for victory, we find that from an aesthetic point of view drama or the dramatic takes centre stage. The football drama is a staged social conflict, where participants not only strive to do their best to win the sport competition, but also actively try to prevent the other team from doing the same. The agonistic nature of constructive-destructive contact sports like football – that has limitations on the means by which one can play the sport together with space and time limitations on the match – sets the stage for a dense and sometimes dark drama, where players frequently stretch or break the rules of the game in order to win. Adding to this density is the fact that football is a low-scoring sport, where chance plays a greater role than it does in most other sports. Superiority on the pitch need not be reflected properly in whatever the score is at any given time in a game. Part of the enjoyment of watching sport is the uncertainty of outcome. In football this uncertainty is amplified by the game's 'chanciness' and low scoring, which means that even with a safe score line as the clock runs down, supporters of a team cannot be quite sure they will win, because dramatic turnarounds happen fairly often in football. Within the game's given parameters, matches go through various fairly predictable phases, and we can identify re-emerging football themes, storylines or narratives. The average football spectator knows these football themes, storylines or narratives well – but not which one of them will come to fruition on any particular match day. Indeed, in a single match, a few minutes of stoppage time can completely change the dramatic structure of a game, turning those who looked like the victors into losers and elevating the dominated side to the status of champions. They thought it was all over, but that is football.

REFERENCES

Ackerman, Diane. 1999. *Deep play*. New York: Random House.
Aggerholm, Kenneth and Signe Højbjerre Larsen. 2017. Parkour as acrobatics: An existential phenomenological study of movement in parkour. *Qualitative Research in Sport, Exercise and Health*, 9, 1: 69–86.
Allison, Henry E. 2001. *Kant's theory of taste: A reading of the critique of aesthetic judgment*. Cambridge: Cambridge University Press.
American Academy of Pediatrics Committee on Sports Medicine and Fitness. 2001. Medical conditions affecting sports participation. *Pediatrics*, 107, 5: 1205–1209.
Anderson, Chris and David Sally. 2014. *The numbers game: Why everything you know about football is wrong*. London: Penguin Books.
Anderson, Viv with Lynton Guest. 2010. *First among unequals: The Autobiography*. Datchet: Fullback Media.
Andrews, Kristin. 2011. Animal cognition. In *Stanford Encyclopaedia of Philosophy*: 1–46.
Appiah, Kwame Anthony. 1995. The uncompleted argument: Du Bois and the illusion of race. In L.A. Bell and D. Blumesfeld (eds.) *Overcoming race and sexism*. Lanham, MD: Rowman & Littlefield: 59–78.
Appiah, Kwame Anthony. 1996. Race, culture, identity: Misunderstood connections. In K. A. Appiah and A. Gutmann (eds.) *Color conscious: The political morality of race*. Princeton, NJ: Princeton University Press: 30–105.
Aristotle. 1996. *Poetics*. London: Penguin Books.
Armstrong, David M. 1997. *A world of states of affairs*. Cambridge: Cambridge University Press.
Armstrong, Sharon Lee, Lila R. Gleitman and Henry Gleitman. 1983. What some concepts might not be. *Cognition*, 13: 263–308.
Austin, John. 1956. A plea for excuses. *Proceedings of the Aristotelian Society*, 57: 1–30.
Bäck, Allan. 2008. The paper world of Bernard Suits. *Journal of the Philosophy of Sport*, 35, 2: 156–174.
Bakowski, Gregg. 2016. Bastian Schweinsteiger and the great handball dilemma: Was it intentional? *The Guardian*, 8 July.

Ball, Phil. 2003. *Morbo: The story of Spanish football*. London: WSC Books.
Barnes, John. 1999. *The autobiography*. London: Headline.
Barthes, Roland. 2007. *What is sport?* New Haven, CT: Yale University Press.
Barthes, Roland. 2009. *Mythologies*. London: Vintage Books.
Bartoš, Luděk, Barbora Fričová, Jitka Bartošová-Víchová, José Panamá, Pavel Šustr and Eva Šmídová. 2007. Estimate of the probability of fighting in fallow deer (Dama dama) during the rut. *Aggressive Behavior*, 33: 7–13.
Bateson, Patrick. 2011. Theories of play. In A.D. Pellegrini (ed.) *The Oxford handbook of the development of play*. Oxford: Oxford University Press: 41–47.
BBC. 2005. Ancelotti shattered after defeat, 25 May.
BBC. 2014a. Bayern Munich's Pep Guardiola 'will not change philosophy', 2 May.
BBC. 2014b. World Cup 2014: Goals, drama & that bite – is Brazil the best? 11 July.
Beach, Frank A. 1945. Current concepts of play in animals. *The American Naturalist*, 79, 785: 523–541.
Bekoff, Marc. 1995. Play signals as punctuation: The structure of social play in canids. *Behaviour*, 132, 5–6: 419–429.
Bekoff, Marc. 2004. Wild justice and fair play: Cooperation, forgiveness, and morality in animals. *Biology and Philosophy*, 19: 489–520.
Bekoff, Marc, Colin Allen and Gordon M. Burghardt (eds.). 2002. *The cognitive animal: Empirical and theoretical perspectives on animal cognition*. Cambridge, MA: MIT Press.
Bekoff, Marc and John A. Byers. 1981. A critical reanalysis of the ontogeny and phylogeny of mammalian social and locomotor play: An ethological hornet's nest. In K. Immelmann, G.W. Barlow, L. Petrinovich and M. Main (eds.) *Behavioral development: The Bielefeld interdisciplinary project*. Cambridge: Cambridge University Press: 296–337.
Bekoff, Marc and Jessica Pierce. 2009. *Wild justice: The moral lives of animals*. Chicago, IL: The University of Chicago Press.
Bentham, Jeremy. 1894. *Theory of legislation*. London: Trüber & Co.
Best, David. 1974. The aesthetic in sport. *British Journal of Aesthetics*, 14, 3: 197–213.
Best, David. 1978. *Philosophy and human movement*. London: George Allen & Unwin.
Best, David. 1985. Sport is not art. *Journal of the Philosophy of Sport*, 12, 1: 25–40.
Best, David. 1986a. Sport is not art: Professor Wertz's Aunt Sally. *Journal of Aesthetic Education*, 20, 2: 95–98.
Best, David. 1986b. The limits of 'art'. *Philosophy*, 61, 238: 532–533.
Bignasca, Andrea. 2009. Mito e realtà alle origini del'agonismo. In E. Dozio, C.M. Fallani and S. Soldini (eds.) *Gli atleti di Zeus: Lo sport nell'antichità*. Milan: Silvana Editoriale Spa: 85–103.
Black, David R. and John Nauright. 1998. *Rugby and the South African nation: Sport, cultures, politics and power in the old and new South Africas*. Manchester: Manchester University Press.
Blecker, Robert. 1984. Bobby Fischer: A great future behind him. *Computer Chess Digest Annual*: 137–145.
Blumer, Herbert. 1969. Fashion: From class differentiation to collective selection. *The Sociological Quarterly*, 10: 275–291.
Borge, Steffen. 2007. A modal defence of strong AI. In D. Moran and S. Voss (eds.) *Epistemology. The proceedings of the twenty-first world congress of philosophy. Vol. 6*. Ankara, Turkey: The Philosophical Society of Turkey: 127–131.
Borge, Steffen. 2010a. May the best team win! In T. Richards (ed.) *Soccer and philosophy*. Chicago, IL: Open Court: 23–35.
Borge, Steffen. 2010b. In defence of Maradona's hand of god. In A. Hardman and C. Jones (eds.) *Philosophy of sport: international perspectives*. Cambridge: Cambridge Scholars Publishing: 154–179.

Borge, Steffen. 2010c. *Speaker's meaning. An essay in the philosophy of language*. Syracuse: Syracuse University.
Borge, Steffen. 2012. Watching sport: Aesthetics, ethics and emotion. *Sport, Ethics and Philosophy*, 6, 3: 401–406.
Borge, Steffen. 2013. Questions. In M. Sbisà and K. Turner (eds.) *Pragmatics of speech actions, vol. II of the handbooks of pragmatics*. Berlin: De Gruyter Mouton: 411–443.
Borge, Steffen. 2015a. Sport records are social facts. *Sport, Ethics and Philosophy*, 9, 4: 1–12.
Borge, Steffen. 2015b. Epistemology and sport. In M. McNamee and W.J. Morgan (eds.) *Routledge handbook of the philosophy of sport*. London: Routledge: 115–130.
Borge, Steffen. 2015c. An agon aesthetics of football. *Sport, Ethics and Philosophy*, 9, 2: 97–123.
Borge, Steffen. Forthcoming. Suits' Utopia and human sports. *Sport, Ethics and Philosophy*.
Borge, Steffen and Mike McNamee. 2017. Football and philosophy. In J. Hughson, K. Moore, R. Spaaij and J. Maguire (eds.) *Routledge handbook of football studies*. London: Routledge: 245–254.
Brecht, Bertolt. 1995. *Der Kinnhaken und andere Box- und Sportgeschichten*. Frankfurt am Main: Suhrkamp.
Breueggeman, Judith Ann. 1978. The function of adult play in free-ranging Macaca mulatta. In E.O. Smith (ed.) *Social play in primates*. New York: Academic Press: 169–191.
Brohm, Jean-Marie. 1989 [1978]. *Sport: A prison of measured time*. Reprinted, London: Pluto Press.
Brown, Heywood Hale. 1979. *Tumultuous merriment*. New York: Richard Marek Publisher.
Burghardt, Gordon M. 1998. The evolutionary origins of play revisited: Lessons from turtles. In M. Bekoff and John A. Byers (eds.) *Animal play: Evolutionary, comparative, and ecological perspectives*. Cambridge: Cambridge University Press: 1–26.
Burghardt, Gordon M. 2005. *The genesis of animal play: Testing the limits*. Cambridge, MA: MIT Press.
Burghardt, Gordon M. 2010. Play. In M.D. Breed and J. Moore (eds.) *Encyclopedia of animal behavior*, vol. 2. Oxford: Academic Press: 740–744.
Burghardt, Gordon M. 2011. Defining and recognizing play. In A.D. Pellegrini (ed.) *The Oxford handbook of the development of play*. Oxford: Oxford University Press: 9–18.
Burghardt, Gordon M. 2015a. Creativity, play, and the pace of evolution. In A.B. Kaufman and J.C. Kaufman (eds.) *Animal creativity and innovation*. Amsterdam: Elsevier: 129–159.
Burghardt, Gordon M. 2015b. Integrative approaches to the biological study of play. In J.E. Johnson, S.G. Eberle, T.S. Henricks and D. Kuschner (eds.) *The handbook of the study of play, vol I*. London: Rowman & Littlefield: 21–39.
Burke, Kenneth. 1966. *Language as symbolic action. Essays on life, literature, and method*. Berkeley: University of California Press.
Burnton, Simon. 2010. World Cup 2010: Uruguay v Ghana – as it happened. *The Guardian*, 2 July.
Caillois, Roger. 2001 [1961]. *Man, play and games*. Reprinted, Urbana and Chicago: University of Illinois Press.
Call, Josep. 2006. Descartes' two errors: Reason and reflection in the great apes. In S. Hurley and M. Nudds (eds.) *Rational animals?* Oxford: Oxford University Press: 219–234.
Call, Josep and Michael Tomasello. 1996. The effect of humans on the cognitive development of apes. In A.E. Russon, K.A. Bard and S.T. Parker (eds.) *Reaching into thought: The minds of the great apes*. Cambridge: Cambridge University Press: 371–403.
Carroll, Noël. 2001. *Beyond aesthetics: Philosophical essays*. Cambridge: Cambridge University Press.
Carroll, Noël. 2002. The wheel of virtue: Art, literature, and moral knowledge. *Journal of Aesthetics and Art Criticism*, 60, 1: 3–26.

Carroll, Noël. 2010. *Art in three dimensions*. Oxford: Oxford University Press.
Cashmore, Ellis. 2000. *Sports culture: An A-Z guide*. London: Routledge.
Chown, John 1994. *A history of money: From AD 800*. London: Routledge.
Christesen, Paul. 2012. *Sport and democracy in the ancient and modern worlds*. Cambridge: Cambridge University Press.
Clayton, Nicola S., Timothy J. Bussey and Anthony Dickinson. 2003. Can animals recall the past and plan for the future? *Nature Reviews Neuroscience*, 4, 8: 685–691.
Clutton-Brock, Tim H., Steven D. Albon, Robert M. Gibson and Fiona E. Guinness. 1979. The logical stag: Adaptive aspects of fighting in red deer (Cervus elaphus L.). *Animal Behaviour*, 27: 211–225.
Collins, Tony. 2005. History, theory and the 'civilization process'. *Sport in History*, 25, 2: 289–306.
Collins, Tony. 2017. Association football and rugby football: Two codes, one historiography. In J. Hughson, K. Moore, R. Spaaij and J. Maguire (eds.) *Routledge handbook of football studies*. London: Routledge: 30–39.
Collins, Tony. 2019. *How football began: A global history of how the world's football codes were born*. London: Routledge.
Cordner, Christopher D. 1984. Grace and functionality. *British Journal of Aesthetics*, 24, 4: 301–313.
Crawford, Donald W. 1974. *Kant's aesthetic theory*. Madison: University of Wisconsin Press.
Critchley, Simon. 2017. *What we think about when we think about football*. London: Profile Books.
Cruyff, Johan with Jaap de Groot. 2016. *My turn: The autobiography*. London: Macmillan.
Currie, Gregory. 1990. *The nature of fiction*. Cambridge: Cambridge University Press.
Currie, Gregory. 1999. Narrative desire. In C. Plantinga and G.M. Smith (eds.) *Passionate views: Film, cognition, and emotion*. Baltimore, MD: The Johns Hopkins University Press: 183–199.
Currie, Gregory. 2006. Rationality, decentring, and the evidence for pretence in non-human animals. In S. Hurley and M. Nudds (eds.) *Rational animals?* Oxford: Oxford University Press: 275–290.
Currie, Gregory. 2013. Does great literature make us better? *The New York Times*, 1 June.
Currie, Gregory and Anna Ichino. 2012. Aliefs don't exist, though some of their relatives do. *Analysis*, 72, 4: 788–798.
Curry, Graham and Eric Dunning. 2015. *Association football: A study in figurational sociology*. London: Routledge.
D'Agostino, Fred. 1981. The ethos of games. *Journal of the Philosophy of Sport*, 8, 1: 7–18.
Dalglish, Kenny. 1996. Foreword. In Ian Rush with Ken Gorman, *Ian Rush: An autobiography*. London: Ebury Press: vii–x.
Danto, Arthur C. 1996. From aesthetics to art criticism and back. *Journal of Aesthetics and Art Criticism*, 54, 2: 105–115.
Danto, Arthur C. 2003. *The abuse of beauty: Aesthetics and the concept of art*. Chicago, IL: Open Court Publishing Company.
Darwin, Charles. 1872. *The descent of man, and selection in relation to sex*. New York: D. Appleton and Company.
Davies, Glyn. 1994. *History of money*. Cardiff: University of Wales Press.
Davies, Stephen. 2006. Aesthetic judgment, artworks and functional beauty. *The Philosophical Quarterly*, 56, 223: 224–241.
Davies, Stephen. 2010. Functional beauty examined. *Canadian Journal of Philosophy*, 40, 2: 315–332.
Davis, Paul. 2015. Football is football and is interesting, very interesting. *Sport, Ethics and Philosophy*, 9, 2: 140–152.

Dawkins, Richard. 2006. *The god delusion*. London: Bantam Press.
Decker, Wolgang. 2004. Vorformen griechischer Agone in der Alten Welt. *Nikephoros*, 17: 9–25.
Decker, Wolgang. 2010. Theorien zum Ursprung des Sports. In M. Krüger and H. Langenfeld (eds.) *Handbuch Sportgeschichte*. Schorndorf: Hofmann-Verlag: 62–68.
Delaney, Trevor. 1984. *The roots of Rugby League*. Keighley: Trevor Delaney.
De Waal, Frans. 2007 [1982]. *Chimpanzee politics: Power and sex among apes*. Baltimore, MD: The Johns Hopkins Press, reprint.
De Waal, Frans B.M. and Peter L. Tyack (eds.). 2003. *Animal social complexity: Intelligence, culture and individualized societies*. Cambridge, MA: Harvard University Press.
Dickie, George. 1964. The myth of the aesthetic attitude. *American Philosophical Quarterly*, 1, 1: 56–66.
Dickie, George. 1974. *Art and the aesthetic: An institutional analysis*. Ithaca, NY: Cornell University Press.
Dickie, George. 1984. *The art circle: A theory of art*. New York: Haven Publications.
Dietschy, Paul. 2012. Football imagery and colonial legacy: Zaire's disastrous campaign during the 1974 World Cup. *Soccer & Society*, 13, 2: 222–238.
Doggett, Tyler. 2012. Some questions for Tamar Szabó Gendler. *Analysis*, 72, 4: 764–774.
Downing, David. 2003. *England v Argentina: World Cups and other small wars*. London: Portrait.
Dunning, Eric. 1971. The development of modern football. In E. Dunning (ed.) *The sociology of sport: A selection of readings*. London: Frank Cass: 133–151.
Dunning, Eric. 1997. Sport in the quest for excitement: Norbert Elias's contributions to the sociology of sport. *Group Analysis*, 30, 4: 477–487.
Dunning, Eric. 1999. The development of soccer as a world game. In *Sport matters: Sociological studies of sport, violence and civilization*. London: Routledge: 80–105.
Dunning, Eric and Kenneth Sheard. 2005. *Barbarians, gentlemen and players: A sociological study of the development of rugby football*, second edition. London: Routledge.
Dutton, Denis. 1994. Kant and the conditions of artistic beauty. *British Journal of Aesthetics*, 34, 3: 226–241.
Eaton, Marcia Muelder. 1999. Kantian and contextual beauty. *Journal of Aesthetics and Art Criticism*, 57, 1: 11–15.
Edgar, Andrew. 2013. Sport and art: An essay in the hermeneutics of sport. *Sport, Ethics and Philosophy*, 7, 1: 1–171.
Edgar, Andrew. 2015. Football and the poetics of space. *Sport, Ethics and Philosophy*, 9, 2: 153–165.
Egan, Andy. 2011. Comments on Gendler's, 'the epistemic costs of implicit bias'. *Philosophical Studies*, 156: 65–79.
Elias, Norbert. 2008. Introduction. In Norbert Elias and Eric Dunning, *Quest for excitement: Sport and leisure in the civilising process*. Dublin: University College Dublin Press: 3–43.
Elias, Norbert. 2012. *On the process of civilisation: Sociogenetic and psychogenetic investigations*. Dublin: University College Dublin Press.
Elias, Norbert and Eric Dunning. 2008a. The quest for excitement in leisure. In Norbert Elias and Eric Dunning, *Quest for excitement: Sport and leisure in the civilising process*. Dublin: University College Dublin Press: 44–72.
Elias, Norbert and Eric Dunning. 2008b. Folk football in medieval and early modern Britain. In Norbert Elias and Eric Dunning, *Quest for excitement: Sport and leisure in the civilising process*. Dublin: University College Dublin Press: 174–188.
Elleray, David. 2004. *The man in the middle*. London: Time Warner Books.
Emeritus Pope Benedict. 2013. Letter to Piergiorgia Odifreddi. *La Repubblica*, Sept.

Fagan, Andrew and Mark Platt. 2011. *Joe Fagan: Reluctant champion. The authorised biography*. London: Aurum.
Fagen, Robert. 1981. *Animal play behavior*. New York: Oxford University Press.
Fagen, Robert. 2011. Play and development. In A.D. Pellegrini (ed.) *The Oxford handbook of the development of play*. Oxford: Oxford University Press: 83–100.
Ferguson, Alex. 2011. The manager's column. *United Review: Manchester United v Liverpool. Official Matchday Programme 2010/11 Season*, 72, 16: 4–5.
FIFA (Fédération Internationale de Football Association). 2014. *Laws of the Game 2014/2015*. Zurich: Fédération Internationale de Football Association.
FIFA (Fédération Internationale de Football Association). 2015. *Laws of the Game 2015/2016*. Zurich: Fédération Internationale de Football Association.
FIFA (Fédération Internationale de Football Association). 2016. *Laws of the Game 2016/17*. Zurich: Fédération Internationale de Football Association.
Foot, John. 2007. *Calcio: A history of Italian football*. London: Harper Perennial.
Fraleigh, Warren P. 1984. *Right actions in sport: Ethics for contestants*. Champaign, Ill: Human Kinetics.
Freeland, Cynthia A. 1997. Art and moral knowledge. *Philosophical Topics*, 25, 1: 11–36.
Friedman, Milton. 1994. *Money mischief: Episodes in monetary history*. San Diego, CA: Harcourt Brace & Company.
Friend, Stacie. 2011. Fictive utterance and imagination II. *Proceedings of the Aristotelian Society*, Supplementary Volume, 85, 1: 163–180.
Friend, Stacie. 2012. Fiction as a genre. *Proceedings of the Aristotelian Society*, 112, 2: 179–209.
Funkhouser, Eric. 2014. *The logical structure of kinds*. Oxford: Oxford University Press.
Gallese, Vittorio, Luciano Fadiga, Leonardo Fogassi and Giacomo Rizzolatti. 1996. Action recognition in the premotor cortex. *Brain*, 119, 2: 593–609.
Gebauer, Gunter. 2016. *Das Leben in 90 Minuten: Eine Philosophie des Fußballs*. München: Pantheon Verlag.
Geertz, Clifford. 1972. Deep play: Notes on the Balinese cockfight. *Daedalus*, 101, 1: 1–37.
Gendler, Tamar. 2010 [2000]. The puzzle of imaginative resistance. Reprinted in *Intuition, imagination, and philosophical methodology*. Oxford: Oxford University Press: 179–202.
Gendler, Tamar. 2010 [2006]. Imaginative resistance revisited. Reprinted in *Intuition, imagination, and philosophical methodology*. Oxford: Oxford University Press: 203–226.
Gendler, Tamar. 2010 [2008a]. Alief and belief. Reprinted in *Intuition, imagination, and philosophical methodology*. Oxford: Oxford University Press: 255–281.
Gendler, Tamar. 2010 [2008b]. Alief in action (and reaction). Reprinted in *Intuition, imagination, and philosophical methodology*. Oxford: Oxford University Press: 282–310.
Gendler, Tamar. 2012. Between reason and reflex. Response to commentators. *Analysis*, 72, 4: 799–811.
Gessmann, Martin. 2011. *Philosophie des Fußballs: Warum die Holländer den modernsten Fußball spielen, die Engländer im Grunde immer noch Rugby, und die Deutschen den Libero erfinden mußten*. München: Wilhelm Fink.
Gibson, Alfred and William Pickford. 1906. *Association football and the men who made it*, vol. 4. London: Caxton.
Glanville, Brian. 2018. *The story of the World Cup: The essential companion to Russia 2018*. London: Faber & Faber.
Goffman, Erving. 1959. *The presentation of self in everyday life*. New York: Doubleday.
Goldblatt, David. 2014. *Futebol nation: A footballing history of Brazil*. London: Penguin Books.
Golden, Mark. 1998. *Sport and society in ancient Greece*. Cambridge: Cambridge University Press.

Goldman, Alan. 2005. The aesthetic. In B. Gaut and D.M. Lopes (eds.) *The Routledge companion to aesthetics*, 2nd edition. London: Routledge: 255–266.
Goodall, Jane. 2000 [1971]. *In the shadow of man*. Boston, MA: Mariners Books, reprint.
Goodman, Nelson. 1955. *Fact, fiction, and forecast*. Cambridge, MA: Harvard University Press.
Goulstone, John. 2001. *Football's secret history*. Upminister: 3-2 Books.
Greenland, Walter. 1965. *The history of the Amateur Football Alliance*. Harwich: Amateur Football Alliance.
Grice, H. Paul. 1991 [1957]. Meaning. Reprinted in *Studies in the way of words*. Cambridge, MA: Harvard University Press: 213–223.
Grice, H. Paul. 1991 [1968]. Utterer's meaning, sentence-meaning and word-meaning. Reprinted *Studies in the way of words*. Cambridge, MA: Harvard University Press: 117–137.
Grice, H. Paul. 1991 [1969]. Utterer's meaning and intentions. Reprinted in *Studies in the way of words*. Cambridge, MA: Harvard University Press: 86–116.
Grice, H. Paul. 1991 [1982]. Meaning revisited. Reprinted in *Studies in the way of words*. Cambridge, MA: Harvard University Press: 283–303.
Grice, H. Paul. 1991. Retrospective epilogue. In *Studies in the way of words*. Cambridge, MA: Harvard University Press: 339–385.
Groos, Karl. 1898. *The play of animals*. New York: D. Appleton and Company.
Groos, Karl. 1919. *The play of man*. New York: D. Appleton and Company.
Grundlingh, Albert. 1998. From redemption to recidivism? Rugby and chance in South Africa during the 1995 Rugby World Cup and its aftermath. *Sporting Traditions*, 14, 2: 67–86.
The Guardian. 2005. Before the game, what they said: ... and the world's post-match verdicts as well as five great games from this season's Champions League, 29 May.
Gullit, Ruud. 2016. *How to watch football*. London: Viking.
Gumbrecht, Hans Ulrich. 2006. *In praise of athletic beauty*. Cambridge, MA: Harvard University Press.
Guttmann, Allen. 2004a. *From ritual to record: The nature of modern sport*. New York: Cambridge University Press.
Guttmann, Allen. 2004b. *Sports: The first five millennia*. Amherst and Boston: University of Massachusetts Press.
Guyer, Paul. 1997. *Kant and the claims of taste*. Cambridge: Cambridge University Press.
Guyer, Paul. 1999. Dependent beauty revisited: A reply to Wicks. *Journal of Aesthetics and Art Criticism*, 57, 3: 357–361.
Guyer, Paul. 2002a. Free and adherent beauty: A modest proposal. *British Journal of Aesthetics*, 42, 4: 357–366.
Guyer, Paul. 2002b. Beauty and utility in eighteenth-century aesthetics. *Eighteenth-Century Studies*, 35, 3: 439–453.
Haarstad, Thomas. 2014. Liverpool vant stordrama mot Boro etter 30 (!) straffer. *Dagbladet*, 23 September.
Hämäläinen, Mika. 2013. Two kinds of sport records. *Sport, Ethics and Philosophy*, 7, 4: 378–390.
Hampton, James A. 1987. Inheritance of attributes in natural concept conjunctions. *Memory & Cognition*, 15, 1: 55–71.
Hampton, James A. and Margaret M. Gardiner. 1983. Measures of internal category structure: A correlational analysis of normative data. *British Journal of Psychology*, 74: 491–516.
Hardman, Alun R. 2009. Sport, moral interpretivism, and football's voluntary suspension of play norm. *Sport, Ethics and Philosophy*, 3, 1: 49–65.
Harris, Max. 2000. *Aztecs, moors, and christians: Festivals of reconquest in Mexico and Spain*. Austin, TX: University of Texas Press.

Harvey, Adrian. 1999. Football's missing link: The real story of the evolution of modern football. In J.A. Mangan (ed.) *Sport in Europe: Politics, class and gender*. London: Frank Cass: 92–116.
Harvey, Adrian. 2001. 'An epoch in the annals of national sport': Football in Sheffield and the creation of modern soccer and rugby. *The International Journal of the History of Sport*, 18, 4: 53–87.
Harvey, Adrian. 2002. The curate's egg put back together: Comments on Eric Dunning's response to 'An epoch in the annals of national sport'. *The International Journal of the History of Sport*, 19, 4: 192–199.
Harvey, Adrian. 2004a. *The beginnings of a commercial sporting culture in Britain, 1793–1850*. Aldershot: Ashgate.
Harvey, Adrian. 2004b. Curate's egg, pursued by red herring: A reply to Eric Dunning and Graham Curry. *The International Journal of the History of Sport*, 21, 1: 127–131.
Harvey, Adrian. 2005. *Football: The first hundred years. The untold story*. London: Routledge.
Harvey, Adrian. 2013. The emergence of football in the nineteenth-century: The historiographic debate. *The International Journal of the History of Sport*, 30, 18: 2154–2163.
Haslanger, Sally. 2000. Gender and race: (What) are they? (What) do we want them to be? *Noûs*, 34, 1: 31–55.
Hatfield, Elaine, John T. Cacioppo and Richard L. Rapson. 1992. Primitive emotional contagion. In M.S. Clark (ed.) *Emotion and social behavior (Review of Personality and Social Psychology)*. Thousand Oaks, CA: Sage: 151–177.
Hatfield, Elaine, John T. Cacioppo and Richard L. Rapson. 1994. *Emotional contagion*. Cambridge: Cambridge University Press.
Haukioja, Jussi. 2013. Different notions of response-dependence. In M. Hoeltje, B. Schnieder and A. Steinberg (eds.) *Varieties of dependence: Ontological dependence, grounding, supervenience, response-dependence*. Munich: Philosophia Verlag: 167–190.
Hawkey, Ian. 2010. *Feet of the chameleon: The story of African football*. London: Portico Books.
Heidegger, Martin. 1963 [1927]. *Sein und Zeit*. Tübingen: Max Niemeyer Verlag, reprint.
Hesse-Lichtenberger, Ulrich. 2003. *Tor! The story of German football*, third edition. London: WSC Books.
Holowchak, M. Andrew. 2007. Games as pastimes in Suits's Utopia: Meaningful living and the 'metaphysics of leisure'. *Journal of the Philosophy of Sport*, 34, 1: 88–96.
Holt, Richard. 1988. Football and the urban way of life in nineteenth-century Britain. In J.A. Mangan (ed.) *Pleasure, profit, proselytism: British culture and sport at home and abroad 1700–1914*. London: Frank Cass: 67–85.
Holt, Richard. 1989. *Sport and the British: A modern history*. Oxford: Clarendon Press.
Hornby, Nick. 1992. *Fever pitch*. London: Victor Gollancz.
Huggins, Mike and Jack Williams. 2006. *Sport and the English, 1918–1939*. London: Routledge.
Huizinga, Johan. 1950. *Homo ludens: A study of the play-element in culture*. Boston, MA: The Beacon Press.
Huntingford, Felicity A. and Angela K. Turner. 1987. *Animal conflict*. London: Chapman and Hall.
Husserl, Edmund. 1970 [1954]. *The crisis of European sciences and transcendental phenomenology*. Evanston, IL: Northwestern University Press, reprint.
Iacoboni, Marco. 2008. *Mirroring people: The new science of how we connect with others*. New York: Farrar, Straus and Giroux.
Ilundáin-Agurruza, Jesús. 2014. Skillful striving: Holism and the cultivation of excellence in sports and performative endeavors. *Sport, Ethics and Philosophy*, 8, 3: 221–342.
James, Mark. 2002. The trouble with Roy Keane. *Entertainment Law*, 1, 3: 72–92.

Johnes, Martin. 2004. 'Heads in the sand': Football, politics and crowd disasters in twentieth-century Britain. *Soccer & Society*, 5, 2: 134–151.

Kadlac, Adam. 2018. Appreciating the not-obviously-beautiful game. In R. Askin, C. Diederich and A. Bieri (eds.) *The aesthetics, poetics, and rhetoric of soccer*. London: Routledge: 44–61.

Kant, Immanuel. 2008 [1790]. *Critique of judgment*. Oxford: Oxford University Press, reprint.

Keane, Roy with Eamon Dunphy. 2002. *Keane: The autobiography*. London: Michael Joseph.

Khalidi, Muhammad Ali. 2013. *Natural categories and human kinds: Classification in the natural and social sciences*. Cambridge: Cambridge University Press.

Khalidi, Muhammad Ali. 2015. Three kinds of social kinds. *Philosophy and Phenomenological Research*, 90, 1: 96–112.

Kreft, Lev. 2011. Hook to the chin. In F. Dorsch, J. Stejskal and J. Zeimbekis (eds.) *Proceedings of the European Society for Aesthetics*, 3: 154–166.

Kreft, Lev. 2012. Sport as a drama. *Journal of the Philosophy of Sport*, 39, 2: 219–234.

Kreft, Lev. 2014. Aesthetics of the beautiful game. *Soccer & Society*, 15, 3: 353–375.

Kreft, Lev. 2015. Aesthetic imagination in football. *Sport, Ethics and Philosophy*, 9, 2: 124–139.

Kretchmar, R. Scott. 1988 [1975]. From test to contest: An analysis of two kinds of counterpoint in sport. Reprinted in W.J. Morgan and K.V. Meier (eds.) *Philosophic inquiry in sport*. Champaign, IL: Human Kinetics Publisher: 223–229.

Kretchmar, R. Scott. 1989. On beautiful games. *Journal of the Philosophy of Sport*, 16, 1: 34–43.

Kretchmar, R. Scott. 2001. A functionalist analysis of game acts: Revisiting Searle. *Journal of the Philosophy of Sport*, 28, 2: 160–172.

Kretchmar, R. Scott. 2005. *Practical philosophy of sport and physical activity*, second edition. Champaign, IL: Human Kinetics.

Kretchmar, R. Scott. 2006. The intelligibility of Suits's Utopia: The view from anthropological philosophy. *Journal of the Philosophy of Sport*, 33, 1: 142–155.

Kretchmar, R. Scott. 2007. The normative heights and depths of play. *Journal of the Philosophy of Sport*, 34, 1: 1–12.

Kretchmar, R. Scott. 2008. Gaming up life: Considerations for game expansions. *Journal of the Philosophy of Sport*, 35, 2: 142–155.

Kretchmar, R. Scott. 2015. Formalism and sport. In M. McNamee and W.J. Morgan (eds.) *Routledge handbook of the philosophy of sport*. London: Routledge: 11–21.

Kretchmar, Scott and Tim Elcombe. 2007. In defense of competition and winning: Revisiting athletic tests and contests. In W.J. Morgan (ed.) *Ethics in sport*, second edition. Champaign, IL: Human Kinetics: 181–194.

Kupfer, Joseph. 1983. *Experience as art: Aesthetics in everyday life*. Albany: State University of New York Press.

Kyle, Donald G. 1990. Winning and watching the Greek pentathlon. *Journal of Sport History*, 17, 3: 291–305.

Kyle, Donald G. 1995. Philostratus, repêchage, running and wrestling: The Greek pentathlon again. *Journal of Sport History*, 22, 1: 60–65.

Kyle, Donald G. 2007. *Sport and spectacle in the ancient world*. Oxford: Blackwell.

Kyle, Donald G. 2014. Greek athletic competitions: The ancient Olympics and more. In P. Christesen and D.G. Kyle (eds.) *A companion to sport and spectacle in Greek and Roman antiquity*. Oxford: Wiley-Blackwell: 21–35.

Lamarque, Peter and Stein Haugom Olsen. 1994. *Truth, fiction, and literature*. Oxford: Claredon Press.

Larsen, Signe Højbjerre. 2015. *Parkour: Institutionalisering af en ny bevægelseskultur i Danmark*. Odense: University of Southern Denmark.

Larsen, Signe Højbjerre. 2016. What can the parkour craftsmen tell us about bodily expertise and skilled movement? *Sport, Ethics and Philosophy*, 10, 3: 295–309.

Lawton, James. 2013. The hand of God? No, this was a diabolical act from Luis Suarez that cast a shadow over the FA Cup. *The Independent*, 6 January.

Leal, Luis. 1982. Los voladores: From ritual to game. *New Scholar*, 8: 129–142.

Leddy, Tom. 2005. The nature of everyday aesthetics. In A. Light and J.M. Smith (eds.) *The aesthetics of everyday life*. New York: Columbia University Press: 3–22.

Leddy, Tom. 2012. *The extraordinary in the ordinary: The aesthetics of everyday life*. Peterborough, ON: Broadview Press.

Lee, James F. 2008. *The lady footballers: Struggling to play in Victorian Britain*. London: Routledge.

Legerstee, Maria. 2005. *Infants' sense of people: Precursors to a theory of mind*. Cambridge: Cambridge University Press.

Lehmann, Hans-Thies. 2006. *Postdramatic theatre*. London: Routledge.

Lester, David. 2004. A possible suicide epidemic after Weininger's 'Sex and Character': A comment on Thorson and Oberg. *Archives of Suicide Research*, 8, 3: 293–294.

Lewis, David. 1969. *Convention: A philosophical study*. Cambridge, MA: Harvard University Press.

Lewis, David. 1975. Languages and language. In K. Gunderson (ed.) *Minnesota studies in the philosophy of science, vol. VII*. Minneapolis: University of Minnesota Press: 3–35.

Lewis, David. 1978. Truth in fiction. *American Philosophical Quarterly*, 15, 1: 37–46.

Lewis, David. 1986a. Postscripts to 'Causation'. In D. Lewis, *Philosophical papers, volume II*. New York: Oxford University Press: 172–213.

Lewis, David. 1986b. *On the plurality of worlds*. Oxford: Blackwell.

Livingston, Paisley. 2012. New directions in aesthetics. In A.C. Ribeiro (ed.) *The Continuum companion to aesthetics*. London: Continuum: 255–267.

Loizos, Caroline. 1966. Play in mammals. *Symposia of the Zoological Society of London*, 18: 1–9.

Loland, Sigmund. 2000. The logic of progress and the art of moderation in competitive sports. In T. Tännsjö and C. Tamburrini (eds.) *Values in sport: Elitism, nationalism, gender equality and the scientific manufacture of winner*. London: Taylor & Francis: 39–56.

Loland, Sigmund. 2001. Record sports: An ecological critique and a reconstruction. *Journal of the Philosophy of Sport*, 28, 2: 127–139.

Loland, Sigmund. 2002. *Fair play in sport: A moral norm system*. London: Routledge.

Lopez Frias, Francisco Javier. 2016. The reconstructive and normative aspects of Bernard Suits's Utopia. *Reason Papers*, 38, 1: 51–64.

Lopez Frias, Francisco Javier. 2017. A Kantian view of Suits' Utopia: 'A kingdom of autotelically-motivated game players'. *Journal of the Philosophy of Sport*, 44, 1: 138–151.

Lorand, Ruth. 1989. Free and dependent beauty: A puzzling issue. *British Journal of Aesthetics*, 29, 1: 32–40.

Lorand, Ruth. 1992. On 'free and dependent beauty' – a rejoinder. *British Journal of Aesthetics*, 32, 3: 250–253.

Lord, Catherine. 1991. A note on Ruth Lorand's 'Free and dependent beauty: A puzzling issue'. *British Journal of Aesthetics*, 31, 2: 167–168.

Lorenz, Konrad. 1970. *Studies in animal and human behaviour. Volume 1*. London: Methuen & Co Ltd.

Lorenz, Konrad. 2002 [1966]. *On aggression*. Reprinted, London: Routledge.

Lowe, Sid. 2011. The brain in Spain: Juanma Lillo, mentor to Pep Guardiola, explains his thinking on clubs, coaching and why society is sick. *The Blizzard*, 1: 55–64.

Lowe, Sid. 2013. *Fear and loathing in La Liga. Barcelona vs Real Madrid*. London: Yellow Jersey Press.

Mallaband, Philip. 2002. Understanding Kant's distinction between free and dependent beauty. *The Philosophical Quarterly*, 52, 206: 66–81.
Mallon, Ron. 2006. 'Race': Normative, not metaphysical or semantic. *Ethics*, 116, 3: 525–551.
Mallon, Ron. 2016. *The construction of human kinds*. Oxford: Oxford University Press.
Maradona, Diego Armando with Daniel Arcucci and Ernesto Cherquis Bialo. 2007. *Maradona: The autobiography of soccer's greatest and most controversial star*. New York: Skyhorse Publishing.
Martin, Paul. 1984. The time and energy costs of play behaviour in the cat. *Zeitschrift für Tierpsychologie*, 64: 298–312.
Martin, Paul and Tim M. Caro. 1985. On the functions of play and its role in behavioral development. In J.S. Rosenblatt, C. Beer, M.-C. Busnel and P.J.B. Slater (eds.) *Advances in the study of behavior*, 15: 59–103.
Martínková, Irena and Jim Parry. 2015. On biting in sport – The case of Luis Suárez. *Sport, Ethics and Philosophy*, 9, 2: 214–232.
Matravers, Derek. 2014. *Fiction and narrative*. Oxford: Oxford University Press.
Matsuzawa, Tetsuro (ed.). 2001. *Primate origins of human cognition and behaviour*. Hong Kong: Springer.
Maynard Smith, John and David Harper. 2003. *Animal signals*. Oxford: Oxford University Press.
Maynard Smith, John and George R. Price. 1973. The logic of animal conflict. *Nature*, 246: 15–18.
McAdoo, Nick. 2002. Kant and the problem of dependent beauty. *Kant-Studien*, 93, 4: 444–452.
McCourt, Ian. 2013. Clattenburg plays the right cards. *The Guardian*, 4 March.
McFee, Graham. 2004. *Sport, rules and values: Philosophical investigations into the nature of sport*. London: Routledge.
McFee, Graham. 2015. *On sport and the philosophy of sport: A Wittgensteinian approach*. London: Routledge.
McNamee, Mike. 2008. *Sports, virtues and vices: Morality plays*. London: Routledge.
McPherson, Barry D., James E. Curtis and John W. Loy. 1989. *The social significance of sport: An introduction to the sociology of sport*. Champaign, IL: Human Kinetics.
Meier, Klaus V. 1985. Restless sport. *Journal of the Philosophy of Sport*, 12, 1: 64–77.
Meier, Klaus V. 1988. Triad trickery: Playing with sport and games. *Journal of the Philosophy of Sport*, 15, 1: 11–30.
Meier, Klaus V. 1989. Performance prestidigitation. *Journal of the Philosophy of Sport*, 16, 1: 13–33.
Metro. 2010. Clever greyhound chases real hare off track during races, Wednesday 21 July.
Mey, Jacob L. 2007. *Pragmatics: An introduction*, second edition. Oxford: Blackwell.
Midgley, Geoffrey C.J. 1959. Linguistic rules. *Proceedings of the Aristotelian Society*, 59: 271–290.
Midgley, Mary. 1974. The game game. *Philosophy*, 49: 231–253.
Mills, Richard. 2009. 'It all ended in an unsporting way': Serbian football and the disintegration of Yugoslavia, 1989–2006. *The International Journal of the History of Sport*, 26, 9: 1187–1217.
Mitchum, Petrine Day with Audrey Pavia. 2005. *Hollywood hoofbeats: Trails blazed across the silver screen*. Irvine, CA: Bowtie Press.
Morgan, William J. 1987. The logical incompatibility thesis and rules: A reconsideration of formalism as an account of games. *Journal of the Philosophy of Sport*, 14, 1: 1–20.
Morgan, William J. 1994. *Leftist theories of sport: A critique and reconstruction*. Urbana and Chicago: University of Illinois Press.
Morris, Desmond. 1981. *The soccer tribe*. London: Jonathan Cape.

Mumford, Stephen. 2010. Breaking it or faking it? Some critical thoughts on the voluntary suspension of play and six proposed revisions. *Sport, Ethics and Philosophy*, 4, 3: 254–268.
Mumford, Stephen. 2012a. *Watching sport: Aesthetics, ethics and emotion*. London: Routledge.
Mumford, Stephen. 2012b. Moderate partisanship as oscillation. *Sport, Ethics and Philosophy*, 6, 3: 369–375.
Mumford, Stephen. 2014. The aesthetics of sport. In C.R. Torres (ed.) *The Bloomsbury companion to the philosophy of sport*. London: Bloomsbury: 180–194.
Murray, Bill. 1984. *The old firm: Sectarianism, sport and society in Scotland*. Edinburgh: John Donald Publishers Ltd.
Murray, Sarah C. 2014. The role of religion in Greek sport. In P. Christesen and D.G. Kyle (eds.) *A companion to sport and spectacle in Greek and Roman antiquity*. Oxford: Wiley-Blackwell: 309–319.
Murray, Sarah C. 2015. Sport and education in ancient Greece and Rome. In W.M. Bloomer (ed.) *A companion to ancient education*. Oxford: Wiley-Blackwell: 430–443.
Nakano, Shigeru and Yuko Kanaya. 1993. The effects of mothers' teasing: Do Japanese infants read their mothers' play intentions in teasing? *Early Development and Parenting*, 2, 1: 7–17.
Newsham, Gail J. 1994. *In a league of their own! Dick Kerr Ladies Football Club, 1917–1965*. Chorley: Pride of Place Publishing.
Nielsen, Thomas Heine. 2014. Panhellenic athletics at Olympia. In P. Christesen and D.G. Kyle (eds.) *A companion to sport and spectacle in Greek and Roman antiquity*. Oxford: Wiley-Blackwell: 133–145.
Nussbaum, Martha C. 1990. *Love's knowledge: Essays on philosophy and literature*. New York: Oxford University Press.
Nussbaum, Martha C. 1995. *Poetic justice: The literary imagination and public life*. Boston, MA: Beacon Press.
Overmier, J. Bruce and Martin E.P. Seligman. 1967. Effects of inescapable shock upon subsequent escape and avoidance responding. *Journal of Comparative and Physiological Psychology*, 63, 1: 28–33.
Palagi, Elisabetta. 2006. Social play in bonobos (Pan paniscus) and chimpanzees (Pan troglodytes): Implications for natural social systems and interindividual relationships. *American Journal of Physical Anthropology*, 129, 3: 418–426.
Palagi, Elisabetta, Gordon M. Burghardt, Barbara Smuts, Giada Cordoni, Stefania Dall'Olio, Hillary N. Fouts, Milada Řeháková-Petru, Stephen M. Sivity and Sergio M. Pellis. 2016. Rough-and-tumble play as a window on animal communication. *Biological Review*, 91: 311–327.
Papineau, David. 2017. *Knowing the score: How sport teaches us about philosophy (and philosophy about sport)*. London: Constable.
Parker, Sue Taylor and Constance Milbrath. 1994. Contributions of imitation and role-playing games to the construction of self in primates. In S.T. Parker, R.W. Mitchell and M.L. Boccia (eds.) *Self-awareness in animals and humans: Developmental perspectives*. Cambridge: Cambridge University Press: 108–128.
Parry, Jim. 1988. Olympism at the beginning and end of the twentieth century. *Proceedings of the International Olympic Academy*, 28 July: 81–94
Parry, Jim. 2006. The idea of the record. *Sport in History*, 26, 2: 197–214.
Parsons, Glenn and Allen Carlson. 2008. *Functional beauty*. Oxford: Clarendon Press.
Pellegrini, Anthony D. 2009. *The role of play in human development*. Oxford: Oxford University Press.
Pellegrini, Anthony D. 2013. Play. In P.D. Zelazo (ed.) *The Oxford handbook of developmental psychology, volume 2*. Oxford: Oxford University Press: 276–299.

Pellegrini, Anthony D. and Peter K. Smith. 2005. Play in great apes and humans. In A.D. Pellegrini and P.K. Smith (eds.) *The nature of play: Great apes and humans*. New York: The Guilford Press.

Pellis, Sergio M. and Andrew N. Iwaniuk. 2000. Adult-adult play in primates: Comparative analyses of its origin, distribution and evolution. *Ethology*, 106, 12: 1083–1104.

Pellis, Sergio M. and Vivien C. Pellis. 1996. On knowing it's only play: The role of play signals in play fighting. *Aggression and Violent Behavior*, 1, 3: 249–268.

Penn, Derek C., Keith J. Holyoak and Daniel J. Povinelli. 2008. Darwin's mistake: Explaining the discontinuity between human and nonhuman minds. *Behavioral and Brain Sciences*, 31: 109–178.

Pepperberg, Irene M. 2002. *The Alex studies: Cognitive and communicative abilities of grey parrots.* Cambridge, MA: Harvard University Press.

Pepperberg, Irene M. 2006. Intelligence and rationality in parrots. In S. Hurley and M. Nudds (eds.) *Rational animals?* Oxford: Oxford University Press: 469–488.

Porter, Dilwyn. 2006. Revenge of the Crouch End Vampires: The AFA, the FA and English football's 'great split', 1907–1914. *Sport in History*, 26, 3: 406–428.

Power, Thomas G. 2013 [2000]. *Play and exploration in children and animals.* Reprinted, New York: Psychology Press.

Pretot, Julien. 2010. Mali lodge complaint over Angola vs Algeria draw. *Reuters*, 19 January.

Putnam, Hilary. 1975. Brains and Behaviour. In *Mind, Language and Reality: Philosophical Papers, vol. 2.* Cambridge: Cambridge University Press: 325–341.

Rachels, Stuart. 2008. The reviled art. In B. Hale (ed.) *Philosophy looks at chess.* Chicago, IL: Open Court: 209–225.

Rawls, John. 1955. Two concepts of rules. *The Philosophical Review*, 64, 1: 3–32.

Reddy, Vasudevi. 1991. Playing with others' expectations: Teasing and mucking about in the first year. In A. Whiten (ed.) *Natural theories of mind: Evolution, development, and simulation of everyday mindreading.* Cambridge, MA: Blackwell: 143–158.

Regis, Cyrille with Chris Green 2010. *My story: The autobiography of the first black icon of British football.* London: Andre Deutsch.

Reid, Louis Arnaud. 1970. Sport, the aesthetic and art. *British Journal of Education Studies*, 18, 3: 245–258.

Rekdal, Kjetil with Olav Østrem. 2012. *Mitt liv som I.* Oslo: Aschehoug.

Rendell, Luke and Hal Whitehead. 2001. Culture in whales and dolphins. *Behavioral and Brain Sciences*, 24, 2: 309–382.

Rizzolatti, Giacomo and Laila Craighero. 2004. The mirror-neuron system. *Annual Review of Neuroscience*, 27: 169–192.

Rizzolatti, Giacomo, Luciano Fadiga, Vittori Gallese and Leonardo Fogassi. 1996. Premotor cortex and the recognition of motor actions. *Cognitive Brain Research*, 3, 2: 131–141.

Rosch, Eleanor H. 1973. On the internal structure of perceptual and semantic categories. In T.M. Moore (ed.) *Cognitive development and the acquisition of language.* New York: Academic Press: 111–144.

Rosch, Eleanor H. 1975. Cognitive representations of semantic categories. *Journal of Experimental Psychology: General*, 104, 3: 192–233.

Rosch, Eleanor H. 1977. Human categorization. In N. Warren (ed.) *Advances in cross-cultural psychology I.* London: Academic Press: 1–49.

Rosch, Eleanor H. 1978. Principles of categorization. In E. Rosch and B.B. Lloyd (eds.) *Cognition and categorization.* Hillsdale, NJ: Lawrence Erlbaum: 27–48.

Rosch, Eleanor and Carolyn B. Mervis. 1975. Family resemblance: Studies in the internal structure of categories. *Cognitive Psychology*, 7: 573–605.

Rosch, Eleanor, Carolyn B. Mervis, Wayne D. Gray, David M. Johnson and Penny Boyes-Braem. 1976. Basic objects in natural categories. *Cognitive Psychology*, 8: 382–439.

Rosch, Eleanor, Carol Simpson and R. Scott Miller. 1976. Structural bases of typicality effects. *Journal of Experimental Psychology: Human Perception and Performance*, 2, 4: 491–502.

Rozin, Paul, Linda Millman and Carol Nemeroff. 1986. Operation of the laws of sympathetic magic in disgust and other domains. *Journal of Personality and Social Psychology*, 50, 4: 703–714.

Russell, Dave. 2013. Kicking off: The origins of association football. In R. Steen, J. Novick and H. Richards (eds.) *The Cambridge companion to football*. Cambridge: Cambridge University Press: 13–26.

Russell, John S. 2007. Broad internalism and the moral foundations of sport. In W.J. Morgan (ed.) *Ethics in sport*, 2nd edn. Champaign, IL: Human Kinetics: 51–66.

Rutter, Jeremy. 2014. Sport in the Aegean bronze age. In P. Christesen and D.G. Kyle (eds.) *A companion to sport and spectacle in Greek and Roman antiquity*. Oxford: Wiley-Blackwell: 36–52.

Ryall, Emily. 2018. Good games as athletic beauty: Why association football is rightly called 'the beautiful game'. In R. Askin, C. Diederich and A. Bieri (eds.) *The aesthetics, poetics, and rhetoric of soccer*. London: Routledge: 27–43.

Sack, Allen L. and Zeljan Suster. 2000. Soccer and Croatian nationalism: A prelude to war. *Journal of Sport and Social Issues*, 24, 3: 305–320.

Saito, Yuriko. 1997. The aesthetics of unscenic nature. *Journal of Aesthetics and Art Criticism*, 52, 2: 101–111.

Saito, Yuriko. 2007. *Everyday aesthetics*. Oxford: Oxford University Press.

Sansone, David. 1988. *Greek athletics and the genesis of sport*. Berkeley: University of California Press.

Sartwell, Crispin. 2016. Beauty. In *Stanford Encyclopedia of Philosophy*: 1–17.

Savage, Robbie with Janine Self. 2011. *Savage! The Robbie Savage autobiography*. Edinburgh: Mainstream Publishing.

Savage-Rumbaugh, Sue, Stuart G. Shanker and Talbot J. Taylor. 1998. *Apes, language, and the human mind*. New York: Oxford University Press.

Scanlon, Thomas. 2009. Contesting ancient Mediterranean sport. *The International Journal of the History of Sport*, 26, 2: 149–160.

Scarre, Geoffrey. 1981. Kant on free and dependent beauty. *British Journal of Aesthetics*, 21, 4: 351–362.

Schaper, Eva. 1979. Free and dependent beauty. In *Studies in Kant's Aesthetics*. Edinburgh: Edinburgh University Press: 78–98.

Schechner, Richard. 2003. *Performance theory*. London: Routledge.

Schiller, Friedrich. 2005 [1801]. Letters on the aesthetic education of man. Reprinted in W. Hinderer and D.O. Dahlstrom (eds.) *Essays*. New York: Continuum.

Schneider, Angela J. and Robert B. Butcher. 1997. Pre-lusory goals for games: A gambit declined. *Journal of the Philosophy of Sport*, 24, 1: 38–46.

Seabright, Paul. 2010. *The company of strangers: A natural history of economic life*. Princeton, NJ: Princeton University Press.

Searle, John R. 1964. How to derive 'ought' from 'is'. *The Philosophical Review*, 73: 43–58.

Searle, John R. 1965. What is a speech act? In M. Black (ed.) *Philosophy in America*. Ithaca, NY: Cornell University Press: 221–239.

Searle, John R. 1969. *Speech acts: An essay in the philosophy of language*. Cambridge: Cambridge University Press.

Searle, John R. 1995. *The construction of social reality*. London: Penguin Books.

Searle, John R. 1998. *Mind, language and society: Philosophy in the real world*. New York: Basic Books.
Searle, John R. 2008. Philosophy in a new century. In *Philosophy in a new century: Selected essays*. Cambridge: Cambridge University Press: 4–25.
Searle, John R. 2010. *Making of the social world. The structure of human civilization*. Oxford: Oxford University Press.
Seligman, Martin E.P. 1972. Learned helplessness. *Annual Review of Medicine*, 23: 407–412.
Seligman, Martin E.P. and Steven F. Maier. 1967. Failure to escape traumatic shock. *Journal of Experimental Psychology*, 74, 1: 1–9.
Seligman, Martin E.P., Steven F. Maier and James H. Geer. 1968. Alleviation of learned helplessness in the dog. *Journal of Abnormal Psychology*, 73, 3: 256–262.
Shankly, Bill. 1977. *Shankly*. London: Book Club Associates.
Sharpe, Lynda L. 2005. Play does not enhance social cohesion in a cooperative mammal. *Animal Behaviour*, 70: 551–558.
Shout Factory. 2001. Origins and soccer cultures. In *History of soccer: The beautiful game*. New York: DVD.
Simon, Robert L. 2004. *Fair play: The ethics of sport*, 2nd edition. Boulder, CO: Westview Press.
Smith, J. David, Wendy E. Shield and David A. Washburn. 2003. The comparative psychology of uncertainty monitoring and metacognition. *Behavioral and Brain Sciences*, 26, 3: 317–373.
Smith, Murray. 2010. Engaging characters: Further reflections. In J. Eder, F. Jannidis and R. Schneider (eds.) *Characters in fictional worlds: Understanding imaginary beings in literature, film, and other media*. Berlin: De Gruyter: 232–258.
Smith, Peter. 2016. We explain the 'grappling' law which has caused controversy in the Premier League. *Sky Sports*, 29 August.
Souness, Graeme with Bob Harris. 1985. *No half measures*. London: Willow Books.
Spurling, Jon. 2010. *Death or glory: The dark history of the World Cup*. Kingston upon Thames: Vision Sport Publishing.
Stecker, Robert. 1990. Lorand and Kant on free and dependent beauty. *British Journal of Aesthetics*, 30, 1: 71–74.
Steenveld, Lynette and Larry Strelitz. 1998. The 1995 Rugby World Cup and the politics of nation-building in South Africa. *Media, Culture & Society*, 20, 4: 609–629.
Sugden, John. 2005. Sport and community relations in Northern Ireland and Israel. In A. Bairner (ed.) *Sport and the Irish: Histories, identities, issues*. Dublin: University College Dublin Press: 238–251.
Suits, Bernard. 1967a. Is life a game we are playing? *Ethics*, 77, 3: 209–213.
Suits, Bernard. 1967b. What is a game? *Philosophy of Science*, 34, 2: 148–156.
Suits, Bernard. 1973a. The grasshopper; A thesis concerning the moral ideal of man. In R. G. Osterhoudt (ed.) *The philosophy of sport: A collection of original essays*. Springfield, IL: Charles C. Thomas Publisher: 198–219.
Suits, Bernard. 1973b. The elements of sport. In R. G. Osterhoudt (ed.) *The philosophy of sport: A collection of original essays*. Springfield, IL: Charles C. Thomas Publisher: 48–64.
Suits, Bernard. 1988. Tricky triad: Games, play, and sport. *Journal of the Philosophy of Sport*, 15, 1: 1–9.
Suits, Bernard. 1989. The trick of the disappearing goal. *Journal of the Philosophy of Sport*, 16, 1: 1–12.
Suits, Bernard. 2005 [1978]. *The grasshopper: Games, life and utopia*. Reprinted, Peterborough, ON: Broadview Press.

Suits, Bernard. 2006. Games and their institutions in *The Grasshopper. Journal of the Philosophy of Sport*, 33, 1: 1–8.
The Sun. 2012. When football no longer matters. Front page, 18 March.
Sutton-Smith, Brian. 1997. *The ambiguity of play*. Cambridge, MA: Harvard University Press.
Tamboer, Jan W.I. 1992. Sport and motor actions. *Journal of the Philosophy of Sport*, 19, 1: 31–45.
Tamburrini, Claudio M. 2000. *The 'Hand of God'? Essays in the philosophy of sports*. Göteborg: Acta Universitatis Gothoburgensis.
Taylor, Matthew. 2008. *The association game: A history of British football*. Harlow: Pearson Longman.
Thomasson, Amie L. 2003a. Foundations for a social ontology. *ProtoSociology*, 18–19: 269–290.
Thomasson, Amie L. 2003b. Realism and human kinds. *Philosophy and Phenomenological Research*, 67, 3: 580–609.
Thompson, Keith. 2004. Sport and Utopia. *Journal of the Philosophy of Sport*, 31, 1: 60–63.
Thorson, Jan and Per-Arne Öberg. 2003. Was there a suicide epidemic after Goethe's Werther? *Archives of Suicide Research*, 7, 1: 69–72.
Tomasello, Michael, Josep Call and Brian Hare. 2003. Chimpanzees understand psychological states – the question is which ones and to what extent. *Trends in Cognitive Science*, 7, 4: 153–156.
Tomlinson, Alan. 2013. 'And did those feet …': Introduction. In R. Steen, J. Novick and H. Richards (eds.) *The Cambridge companion to football*. Cambridge: Cambridge University Press.
Tranter, Neil. 1998. *Sport, economy and society in Britain 1750–1914*. Cambridge: Cambridge University Press.
Trezza, Viviana, Petra J.J. Baarendse and Louk J.M.J. Vanderschuren. 2010. The pleasures of play: Pharmacological insights into social reward mechanisms. *Trends in Pharmacological Sciences*, 31, 10: 463–469.
Truslove, Ben. 2016. The Leicester City fans gambling on a winning finish. *BBC*, 10 March.
Turner, Victor. 1981. Social dramas and the stories about them. In W.J.T. Mitchell (ed.) *On narrative*. Chicago, IL: University of Chicago Press: 137–164.
Turner, Victor. 1982. *From ritual to theatre: The human seriousness of play*. New York: Performing Art Journal Publications.
Turner, Victor. 1987. *The anthropology of performance*. New York: PAJ Publications.
Ulf, Christoph. 2006. Elemente des Utilitarismus im Konstrukt des 'Agonalen'. *Nikephoros*, 19: 67–79.
Ulf, Christoph. 2008. Antiker Sport und Wettbewerb – ein sozio-kulturelles Phänomen. In P. Mauritsch, C. Ulf, R. Rollinger, et al. (eds.) *Antike Lebenswelten: Konstanz, Wandel, Wirkungsmacht: Festschrift für Ingomar Weiler zum 70. Geburtstag*. Wiesbaden: Harrassowitz Verlag: 5–23.
Ulf, Christoph. 2011. Ancient Greek competition: A modern construction? In N. Fisher and H. van Wees (eds.) *Competition in the Ancient World*. Swansea: The Classical Press of Wales: 85–111.
Vamplew, Wray. 1988. Sport and industrialization: An economic interpretation of the changes in popular sport in nineteenth-century England. In J.A. Mangan (ed.) *Pleasure, profit, proselytism: British culture and sport at home and abroad 1700–1914*. London: Frank Cass: 7–20.
Vanderschuren, Louk J.M.J. 2010. How the brain makes play fun. *American Journal of Play*, 2: 315–337.

Van Lawick-Goodall, Jane. 1968. The behaviour of free-living chimpanzees in the Gombe Stream Reserve. *Animal Behaviour Monographs*, 1, 3: 161–311.
Vargiu, Luca. 2010. Kant at the Maracanã. In T. Richards (ed.) *Soccer and philosophy*. Chicago, IL: Open Court: 172–184.
Vasili, Phil. 1996. Walter Daniel Tull, 1888–1918: Soldier, footballer, black. *Race & Class*, 38, 2: 51–69.
Vasili, Phil. 1998. *The first black footballer: Arthur Wharton 1865–1930: An absence of memory*. London: Frank Cass.
Vasili, Phil. 2000. *Colouring over the white line: The history of black footballers in Britain*. Edinburgh: Mainstream.
Vossen, Deborah P. 2016. Utopia is intelligible and game-playing is what makes Utopia intelligible. *Journal of the Philosophy of Sport*, 43, 2: 251–265.
Vossen, Deborah P. 2017. The paradoxes of Utopian game-playing. *Journal of the Philosophy of Sport*, 44, 3: 315–328.
Wacker, Christian. 2006. Antike Sportgeschichte versus Geschichte des Agon. In J. Court (ed.) *Jahrbuch 2005 der Deutschen Gesellschaft für Geschichte der Sportwissenschaft*. Berlin: LIT Verlag: 39–43
Walton, Kendall L. 1978. Fearing fictions. *The Journal of Philosophy*, 75, 1: 5–27.
Walton, Kendall L. 1990. *Mimesis as make-believe: On the foundations of the representational arts*. Cambridge, MA: Harvard University Press.
Walton, Kendall L. 1994. Morals in fiction and fictional morality. *Proceedings of the Aristotelian Society*, Supplementary Volume 68: 27–50.
Walton, Kendall L. 2015. 'It's only a game!' Sports as fiction. In *In other shoes: Music, metaphor, empathy, existence*. Oxford: Oxford University Press: 75–83.
Warneken, Felix and Michael Tomasello. 2006. Altruistic helping in human infants and young chimpanzees. *Science*, 311: 1301–1303.
Weatherford, Jack. 1997. *The history of money*. New York: Three Rivers Press.
Weatherson, Brian. 2004. Morality, fiction, and possibility. *Philosopher's Imprint*, 4, 3: 1–27.
Weiler, Ingomar. 2014. Recent trends in the study of Greek sport. In P. Christesen and D. G. Kyle (eds.) *A companion to sport and spectacle in Greek and Roman antiquity*. Oxford: Wiley-Blackwell: 112–129.
Welsch, Wolfgang. 2005. Sport viewed aesthetically, and even as art? In A. Light and J.M. Smith (eds.) *The aesthetics of everyday life*. New York: Columbia University Press: 135–155.
Wenz, Peter S. 2006. Human equality in sports. In J. Boxill (ed.) *Sport ethics: An anthology*. Oxford: Blackwell: 230–239.
Wertz, Spencer K. 1977. Toward a sports aesthetic. *Journal of Aesthetic Education*, 11, 4: 103–111.
Wertz, Spencer K. 1984. A response to Best on art and sport. *Journal of Aesthetic Education*, 18, 4: 105–107.
Wertz, Spencer K. 1985. Sport and the artistic. *Philosophy*, 60, 233: 392–393.
Whiten, Andrew. 1996. Imitation, pretence, and mindreading: Secondary representation in comparative primatology and developmental psychology? In A.E. Russon, K.A. Bard and S.T. Parker (eds.) *Reaching into thought: The minds of the great apes*. Cambridge: Cambridge University Press: 300–324.
Wicks, Robert. 1997. Dependent beauty as the appreciation of teleological style. *Journal of Aesthetics and Art Criticism*, 55, 4: 387–400.
Wicks, Robert. 1999. Can tattooed faces be beautiful? Limits on the restriction of forms in dependent beauty. *Journal of Aesthetics and Art Criticism*, 57, 3: 361–363.
Williams, Jean. 2003. *A game for rough girls? A history of woman's football in Britain*. London: Routledge.

Williams, Jean. 2007. *A beautiful game: International perspectives on woman's football*. Oxford: Berg Publishers.
Williams, Jean. 2014. *A contemporary history of woman's sport, part one: Sporting woman, 1850-1960*. London: Routledge.
Williamson, David. 1991. *Belles of the ball: Early history of woman's football*. Devon: R & D Associates.
Williamson, Timothy. 1994. *Vagueness*. London: Routledge.
Wilson, Jonathan. 2010. *The anatomy of England: A history in ten matches*. London: Orion.
Wilson, Jonathan. 2016. *Angels with dirty faces: The footballing history of Argentina*. London: Weidenfeld & Nicolson.
Wilson, Jonathan with Scott Murray. 2013. *The anatomy of Liverpool: A history in ten matches*. London: Orion.
Winner, David. 2006. *Those feet: An intimate history of English football*. London: Bloomsbury.
Winsemius, Pieter. 2004. *Je gaat het pas zien als je het doorhebt: Over Cruijff en leiderschap*. Amsterdam: Balans.
Wittgenstein, Ludwig. 1967. *Philosophical investigations*. Oxford: Blackwell.
Yorke, Christopher C. 2017. Endless summer: What kinds of games will Suits' utopians play? *Journal of the Philosophy of Sport*, 44, 2: 213–228.
Young, David C. 1984. *The Olympic myth of the Greek amateur athletics*. Chicago, IL: Ares.
Young, David C. 1988. Professionalism in archaic and classical Greek athletics. In J.O. Segrave and D. Chu (eds.) *The Olympic Games in transition*. Champaign, IL: Human Kinetics: 27–36.
Young, Percy M. 1968. *A history of British football*. London: Stanley Paul.
Zack, Naomi. 1993. *Race and mixed race*. Philadelphia, PA: Temple University Press.
Zack, Naomi. 2002. *Philosophy of science and race*. New York: Routledge.
Zemach, Eddy M. 1997. *Real beauty*. University Park, PA: Pennsylvania State University Press.
Zillmann, Dolf. 2013. Moral monitoring and emotionality in responding to fiction, sports, and the news. In R. Tamborini (ed.) *Media and the moral mind*. New York: Routledge: 132–151.

INDEX

Abreu, Sebastián 200
AC Milan 115, 191–192, 212, 237, 239
adaptive function 257
aesthetic appreciation 193–194, 227, 250n13
aesthetic engagement 191, 208–209, 235–236
aesthetic engagement resistance 167, 220–223
aesthetic gaze 193
aesthetic judgement theory 193
aesthetic puzzle 220
aesthetic sports 126, 187n4
Africa Cup of Nations 255n46
agon aesthetics: areté vs. 196, 241, 249n8; attitude toward ordinary world conflicts 208; basis for 200; drama and 199–202, 250n15; emotional engagement 209–210; engaging in conflict of competition 206; everyday aesthetics 205–206; fairness and 237; football themes and 211–214; functionality as part of 227–228; gracefulness 233–234; rule violations and 161; social drama 202; ugliness of 209; *see also* aesthetic engagement
agonistic fighting 36–37
Ajax 115
Aldridge, John 213
alethic puzzle 220
Algeria 255n46
aliefs 9–10, 23–27, 162, 216, 247–248 *see also* fight-or-flight aliefs, Physical struggle/fight! D-a-n-g-e-r …! Activate fight-or-flight adrenaline now

Alonso, Xabi 251n20
Ancelotti, Carlo 191–192
ancient Olympics 89–92, 112, 114
 see also modern Olympics, pre-modern sport
Anderson, Chris 251n21, 252n30
Anfield 9, 147
Angola 255n46
animal sports 137, 158
anti-formalism 184–185
areté vs. agon 196, 241, 249n8
Argentina 197, 198
Aristotle 1
Armstrong, Sharon Lee 174–175
Arsenal vs. Tottenham derby 164
art: *Duchamp's urinal in the gallery* 88–89; epistemic value 59n6; as extra-ordinary 17; Nussbaum-Freeland view on 11–12, 59n7; as a social kind 88
artefacts, functions of 228–230, 233
as-if proto-pretence 32
AS Roma 147, 213–214
association football: British folk football and 94, 96; diversity in 98; folk football 94–96; folk football transition to proto-football 96; history of 111–113; internal evolution of 145; offshoots of 100; origin of 94–95; proto-football 95–96, 98–100, 106; rugby vs. 95, 100; Sheffield FC codification of 1858 97; as social kind 98–99; stages of 95; traditional histories of 94–95
athleticism 110, 176–177

Austin, John 15
Austria 246

Bachelard, Gaston 250n12
back-pass rule 235
Baggio, Roberto 157
Balinese cockfights study 50–51, 53
Ball, Phil 104
Barcelona *see* FC Barcelona
bare-bones formalism 101
Barnes, John 187n4
Barthes, Roland 21, 244
Bartoš, Ludek 55–56
Bates, Herbert Ernest 249n3
Bateson, Patrick 35
Batson, Brendon 222
Battle of Highbury 149
Battle of Santiago 148
Bayern München *see* FC Bayern München
"beautiful game, the" 193
beauty of football 193–199
behaviour: emotional engagement 21–23; non-serious vs. serious 42–43; valve theories of 29–30
Bekoff, Marc 43
Belmont Ground 242
Benayoun, Yossi 164
Benedict, Pope 10
Bentham, Jeremy 50–51
Best, David 12, 187n4, 201
Best, George 249n6
betting 51, 157–158
bodily movement 17–18, 149–150, 197, 243, 249n7, 250n17
Bosingwa, José 164
Brazil 167–168, 213
Brecht, Bertolt 202, 204
British folk football 94, 96
Brohm, Jean-Marie 159
Brown, Heywood Hale 20
bullfighting 221
Burghardt, Gordon 34–35, 37–38, 41, 65n31
Busquets, Sergio 255n47

Cacioppo, John 49
Caillois, Roger 18–19
Call, Josep 47
Cambiasso, Esteban 197
Cameron, David 81
Cancer Game case 132, 138
Carlos, Roberto 218
Carlson, Allen 226–230, 233
Caro, Tim M. 37–38

Carrasco, Francisco José 255n47
Carroll, Lewis 253n34
Cashmore, Ellis 254n44
Champions League: 1999 final 190, 215; 2005 final 191–192, 237–241; rollercoaster matches 213
Chance; football 203, 214, 251n21; sport 158, 238–239; ratio between skills and 158, 238–239
character desires 209
Charlton, Jack 185–186
Chatham Town 242–243
cheating 139–140
Chelsea 164
chess 126, 159, 170, 177–178
chess boxing 121n17
Chiellini, Giorgio 255n49
Chile 148, 157
Christesen, Paul 91, 111–112
civilizing process theory 29–30
Clattenburg, Mark 164–165
Coin Minting Machine case 79, 84
collective intentionality: of being at war 85–86; constitutive rules and 137–138, 182; rule changes and 146; social kinds held together by 73–76, 185, 231; stage-type exception 145–146; token exceptions 79; *see also* direct collective intentionality, intentionalism
Collins, Tony 99, 184
collision sports, contact sports vs. 64–65n27 constitutive rule formula 72
constitutive rules: breaking 139–140; of chess 134; collective intentionality and 137–138; dependent on prelusory goals 126–127; enabling aspect of 133–134; FIFA rules as 184–185; footballers and 136; foundational formalism and 258; framing aspect of 134; limited means and 133–135, 179; limiting action of game 204–205; obedience to 138–139; regulative vs. 134–135, 178–180; spectators and 136; staging of football requiring 211; Suits's requirement of 139, 182; *see also* regulative rules, rule violations
constructive-destructive sports 25–26, 115
constructive rules 70–71
contact sports 23, 26–27, 32, 259
contact sports, collision sports vs. 64–65n27
contests, tests vs. 127–128
conventions 55, 60–61n10
Copa Libertadores 213
Cordner, Christopher D. 253n38

corner flagging 163–164
Cornhill, Gareth 242–243
corrupt players 152
Costard, Hellmuth 249n6
Crabtree, Shirley 254n44
creativity, play and 35–36
Crespo, Hernán 197
Croatia 188n16
crowd disasters 252n27
Cruyff, Johan 69, 189n24, 197–198, 212, 255n47
Cruyffism 120n1
Cruyff turn 189n24, 197–198
Cunningham, Laurie 222
Curious Incident of Mwepu Ilunga Kicking the Ball Away case 167–170
Currie, Gregory 25, 47, 59n6, 209
Curry, Graham 96, 97–98

D'Agostino, Fred 144, 146–147, 185
danza de los voladores (dance of the flyers) 93, 106, 229
Darwin, Charles 2
Davies, Stephen 226–227, 253n36
Davis, Paul 250n11
Dawkins, Richard 10
decentring 47
Deep Blue 107
deep play 49–51, 53–54, 66–67n45, 157
dependent beauty 194, 226–227
De Rossi, Daniele 139
Dinamo București 147
direct collective intentionality 78–81, 86, 129, 134, 140, 150, 258 *see also* collective intentionality
direct free kick 183–184
disgust experiments 24
disinterested aesthetics 190–191, 194–196, 206, 235–236, 249n8, 254n42
diving 126–127
Doggett, Tyler 24
domination: as feature of human condition 29–30, 70; identity-making and 116–117; no material consequences in 54; as primary purpose of sport 30, 65n32, 102, 129, 232–233, 264
Donohue, Alex 67n46
drama: definition of 201; Lehmann on 202–203; as logical order to chaos 203; social 202; usage of 201–202
drama of football 199–201, 204–205, 234, 250n15
Drogba, Didier 164
Duchamp, Marcel 18
Duchamp's urinal in the gallery 88–89

Dudek, Jerzy 192
Dunning, Eric 29, 95, 96, 97–98

Edgar, Andrew 250n12
Eintracht Frankfurt 211–212
electronic sports 177
Elias, Norbert 29, 54, 112
Elleray, David 156, 166
Elyot, Thomas 94
emotional engagement 21–23, 209–210
end-states 45, 57–58, 82, 107–108, 113, 126–127, 129–133, 138–139, 178
England 149, 185–186, 198, 212, 213
English FA (Football Association) 95, 141–142, 143, 155, 184, 213
English Football Association *see* Football Association (FA)
error theory of sports 140–141
escape-type football matches 214
ethics of sport 191, 246–247 *see also* morality
ethos: conflicting 148–149; D'Agostino's view of 144–148, 185; shared 152–153
Eton Field Game 96, 99, 214
Eto'o, Samuel 218
European Cup 211–212, 217, 227, 255n47
Eusébio 185, 212
Evert-Lloyd, Chris 253n38
everyday aesthetics 205–206
evolution 256–257
external purpose of sport 232
external silly questions 223–225
extra-ordinary 15–19
extreme sports 109–110

Fagan, Joe 217
Fagen, Robert 33, 35
fairness view of sport 191–193
fashion/fashionableness 74–76
FC Anzhi Makhachkala 218
FC Barcelona 210, 212, 255n47
FC Bayern München 115, 190, 214, 237, 239–240
FC Krylia Sovetov Samara 218
Ferguson, Alex 190, 255n47
fictionality of football: activating belief-like states 30–31; character of 11; description of 9–10; fictional value 216; fiction-non-fiction divide 10–11; intentionalist view of 14; ordinary world undermining 217–219; preliminaries 10–13; representations 13–14
fictional value 216
fiction films 31

fiction-non-fiction divide 10–11
fictions: definition of 14–15; filling in 14–15; myths vs. 14
field sports 108
FIFA (Fédération Internationale de Football Association) 82, 135, 179 see also World Cup
FIFA rule book 143–144, 162–163, 183–185
FIFA World Cup: Argentina vs. England (1986) 198; Argentina vs. Serbia and Montenegro (2006) 197; Battle of Santiago (1962) 148; Brazil vs. Zaire (1974) 167–168; Chile vs. Italy (1962) 148; Chile vs. Italy (1998) 157; Comeback, The 212; Cruyff turn 197–198; England vs. Poland (1973, qualifer) 212; England vs. Portugal (1966) 185–186; England vs. USA (1950) 212; Escape, The 212; fictionality of football and 14; France vs. Croatia (2018) 188n16; Iranian team of 1978 148, 153; Italy vs. Brazil (1982) 213; Italy vs. West Germany (1970) 213; knockout stages of 254n45; Maradona goal against England (1986) 198, 250n13; Netherlands vs. West Germany (1990) 235; Netherlands vs. Norway (1993, qualifier) 212 ; North Korea vs. Italy (1966) 212; Norway vs. Mexico (1994) 219; Portugal vs. North Korea (1966) 212; prestige of winning 206; Robbery, The 213–214; Rollercoaster, The 213; Spain vs. South Korea (2002) 61, 213–214; Upset, The 212; Uruguay vs. Ghana (2010) 247–248; Uruguay vs. Italy (2014) 255n49; West Germany vs. Austria (1982) 246; West Germany vs. France (1982) 212; World Cup qualifier eligibility 82
fighting 36–37, 39–40 see also play fighting
fight-or-flight aliefs 26–27, 30–31, 58–59, 65n32, 162, 216, 242 see also aliefs
fine art see art
Fischer, Bobby 170
Fistful of Fouls case 139, 140, 154, 180
folk football 94–96, 111
Foot, John 252n26
football: building dramatic narrative 203–204; as constructive-destructive sport 25–26, 28; as cooperative effort 154; externalist approach to 116–117; fiction films compared to 204–205; identity-making aspect of 22–23; limited means and 129–133; pick-up games 4, 244, 245–246; played as if outcome matters 45–46; rule breaking in 141–147; as a sport 11; as staged, but not scripted 204–205; wide following of 160; see also games
Football and the Bust case 151, 152
Football and the Natives case 79–80, 91, 101, 106
Football Association (FA) see English FA (Football Association)
football authorities 234–235 see also referees/refereeing
football engagement 48
footballers: actors compared to 207; adapting to refereeing practices 258–259; alief impulses of 28; breaking rules 259; constitutive rules and 136; corrupt 152; dependence on spectators 207; depending on football fiction 206–207; drive game innovations 233–234; game statistics and 115; performance measurements 115–116; professional 207; understanding rules 186; see also football practitioners
football form: abuse case 151; abuse of 103–105; application of 105–106; appropriation of 106; corrupt player 152; description of 7; evaluation parameters 103; of football practitioners 186; as identity maker 232; match fixing 103–104, 152; parroting 107, 136; providing audiences with social identity 232; ritual vs. 229; usage of 103; usage vs. application of 244
football matches: beginnings of 122; crowd swaying footballers at 49; drama in 234; engagement in 25; escape-type 214; as fiction 13–15, 20; as fine art 11–12; highlight of game as goal 215; low scoring 214–215; lusory goal of 124–125; as make-believe 15, 22; parallels aspects of real-life conflicts 203–204; ritual-like elements of 22–23; scoring in 5; settling conflict 56; social hierarchies and 53; spectators reaction at 28–30; unpredictability of 7; winning and 4, 9, 11, 20, 46
football parroting 107
football practitioners 102–103, 146–147, 151, 160–161, 186, 239 see also footballers, sport practitioners
football supporters 21 see also spectators
football teams, as symbols of pride and identity 22 see also individual team names
football themes, storylines and narratives 7, 211–215, 240, 259; Comeback, The 212; Escape, The 212; Hammering, The

211–212; Robbery, The 213; Rollercoaster, The 213; Smash and Grab, The 214; Upset, The 212 *see also* football form
Footrace and the Professors case 91–92, 106
footraces: developmental periods of 92–93; as initiation rites 90–92; limited means of 130; marathon race runners 128; *stadion* race 90–92
formalism: anti-formalism vs. 184–185; bare-bones 101; *Football and the Natives* case 79–80; foundational 70, 133, 171; Kretchmar on 70–71; *see also* reductive formalism
Fountain (Duchamp) 18
Fraleigh, Warren 58, 191
France 188n16, 212
free beauty of football 193–199, 227
free kick 183–184
Freeland, Cynthia 12
Friedman, Milton 120n3
Fully Fixed Match case 104
functional beauty 227–228
functionality 227–228

game character maintenance 162
game playing, prelusory goals 123–124
games: criteria 123; obedience to rules 138–139; overcoming unnecessary obstacles 16–17; as ritualized conflicts 49–50; Suits's position on 70; as unnecessary activities 16; *see also* play, sports
games of chance 157–158, 238, 241–242
games of skill 241–244
Gardiner, Margaret 174
Geertz, Clifford 49–51, 53, 157
Gendler, Tamar 9, 23–27, 220, 222
Ghana 247
Gillingham FC 22, 215
Gleitman, Henry 174–175
Gleitman, Lila R. 174–175
goal-getter 187n4
Goffman, Erving 201
Goldblatt, David 249n3
Golden, Mark 92
Goldman, Alan 193
Goodall, Jane 2, 39
Goodman, Nelson 145
Goulstone, John 97
gracefulness 233–234, 253n38
Grand Canyon Skywalk case 24
Grasshopper: Games, Life and Utopia, The (Suits) 123–124, 180
Grice's theory of meaning 253n34

Groos, Karl 32–33, 111
Guardiola, Pep 3, 255n47
Gullit, Ruud 122, 188n11, 189n19
Gumbrecht, Hans Ulrich 194–197, 241, 242, 249n8
Guttmann, Allen 90, 98, 111–113, 117–118, 121n27
Guyer, Paul 226–227
Gyan, Asomoah 247
gymnastics 126

Håland, Alf-Inge 165–167
Hall, Stuart 193, 249n3
Hampton-Gardiner study 174–175
Hampton, James 173, 174
handball rule 156–157, 184–186
Hardman, Alun 163
Hardman's Referee case 163–164
Harlem Globetrotters 105
Harvey, Adrian 95, 97
Hatfield, Elaine 49
Holt, Richard 96–97, 121n14
Holyoak, Keith 2
Homo Ludens (Huizinga) 18
Hornby, Nick 192–193
house building as sport 83, 108–109
Huggins, Mike 149
Hughes, Mark 189n19
Huizinga, Johan 18–19, 63n16, 111
human pretence play 33–34
humans: competition and domination of 29; extra-ordinary side of life 17; as pack animal 48; as rational animals 1; as sporting animals 2; uniqueness of 1–2
Human Stampede case 76, 86–87
Humpty Dumpty argument 228–230, 253n34

Ichino, Anna 25
identity-making aspect of sport 22–23, 64n24, 111, 116, 207, 216, 231–233
IL Skrim 236
Ilunga, Mwepu 167–169
imaginative puzzle 220
imaginative resistance 220–223
inclusive theory of play 41–42
incompatibility thesis 139, 165–170, 180–186
ineffective means, as necessary condition for sport 130
institutional theory of sport 28–29, 59n5
instrumental values 216
intentionalism 14, 228–231, 233 *see also* collective intentionality
internal purpose of sport 83, 232

internal silly questions 223–225
internal vs. intrinsic purpose 116
Inzaghi, Filippo 215
Italy 148, 149, 157, 212, 213, 255n49
Ivan and Abdul's Ultimate Game case 131–132, 133
Ivanović, Branislav 255n49

Jahani, Ghafoor 148
James, Mark 166
Jancker, Carsten 190
Jancović, Slobodan 200
Jevrić, Dragoslav 197
Juventus FC 213, 217

Kanouté, Frédéric 255n46
Kant, Immanuel 191, 193, 227, 250n12
Keane, Roy 166–167
Keita, Seydou 255n46
Kendall, Walton 9
Khalidi, Muhammad Ali 73–74, 79, 81, 85
kick-about 69
knockout tournaments 213, 235, 237, 245–246, 251n22, 254n45
Kreft, Lev 10, 62n11, 199, 201, 203, 205
Kretchmar, R. Scott 63n18, 70–71, 127–128
Kupfer, Joseph 11–12, 20, 28–29
Kyle, Donald 89, 114

Lamarque, Peter 15
Larsen, Signe Højbjerre 109–110
Lato, Grzegorz 212
Lawton, James 248
Leddy, Tom 205
Lee, Rob 168–169
Lehmann, Hans-Thies 202–203
Lewis, David 55, 60–61n10, 88–89, 189n23
Lewis methodology 88–89, 174
Lillo, Juanma 239
limited means: achieving prelusory goals 129; agreed-upon starting times 132; as necessary condition for sport 130
Liverpool FC 9, 115, 164, 191–192, 212–213, 217, 237, 239, 255n47
Livingston, Paisley 205
logical incompatibility thesis (Suits) 139–140, 180–183
Loland, Sigmund 58, 191, 245
Lorenz, Konrad 41–42
lucha libre 244–245
lusory attitude for playing sports 138, 151
lusory goal of sport 124–125, 181
lusory state of football 150–151

make-believe: emotional engagement 22, 27, 31–32; fictional character of football as 18–22; foundation of 32–33; make-believe in 245; mimic play 18; in nonhuman animals 33; phenomenological feel of 34; proto-pretence of 40, 42, 45–47; psychological basis of 4–5; silly questions and 223, 225; social prestige in 52–54; spectators participation in 217–218; types of 13–15; winning matches matter 9, 20, 170, 206–207; *see also* fictionality of football
Malawi 255n46
Maldini, Paulo 251n20
Mali 255n46
Manchester City 165–166, 215
Manchester United FC 64n22, 165–166, 190, 214, 237, 240–241
Maradona, Diego 192, 198, 227, 250n13
marathons 128
Marta 17
Martin, Paul 37–38
Matadar, Mo 164
match fixing 103–104, 152
McCall, Stuart 213
McCourt, Ian 164
McFee, Graham 16, 59–60n8, 141, 158, 165, 166, 179
McNamee, Mike 16, 170, 246
McPherson, Barry D. 159
measurement sports 25–26
Meier, Klaus 158, 181
membership inclusion 176
mental mechanisms 42, 47, 58
mere causal social historical kind 231
meritocratic-fairness view of sport 191–193, 237–241
Merleau-Ponty, Maurice 250n12
Mexico 219
Midgley, Mary 49–50, 54, 67–68n51, 135
Mimesis as Make-Believe (Walton) 19–20
mimic play 18–19
mind archery 159
mind football 160
Mind Games case 159, 170
mind ice hockey 159–160
Mobutu Sese Seko 168
modernity as civilizing process 54
modern Olympics 112 *see also* ancient Olympics
modern sport 26, 89, 111–118 *see also* pre-modern sport, sports
Montenegro 208
morality 16, 59–60n8, 246–248
Morgan, William 16, 180, 182

Mourinho, José 210
Movilă, Lică 147
Muamba, Fabrice 217
Mumford, Stephen 13, 28–29, 59n5, 195–197, 235, 250n15, 253n38, 254n39
Murphy, Danny 139–140
Murray, Sarah 90–91
myths 14

narrative desires 209
naturalism 228, 252n32
natural kinds philosophy 71–72
Navratilova, Martina 253n38
negative rules of conduct 141
Netherlands 197–198, 212, 227, 235
new riddle of induction (Goodman) 145
no-limitations-on-available-means feature 133
nonagonistic fighting 36–37
nonhuman animals: decentring capability of 47; engaging in pretence 46–47; play in 32–33, 38–39; self-handicapping among 45; social play and 162; tool use 2
non-prototypical sports 177
non-sport sport-like 110
non-vital real values 216
North Korea 212
Norway 212, 219
Norwegian FA 218
Nussbaum-Freeland line of thought on art 11–12, 59n7

offside rule 181–182, 235
Olsen, Stein Haugom 15
Olympics see ancient Olympics
outcome uncertainty 7, 52–53, 58, 215, 247, 259

Panhellenic athletes 113
parkour 109–110, 176
parroting 107, 136
Parsons, Glenn 226–230, 233
Pellegrini, Anthony D. 40, 66n40
Pellis, Sergio M. 42
Pellis, Vivien C. 42
penalties: direct free kick 183–184; free kick 183–184; penalty kick 141–142, 183–184
penalty kick 183–184
Penn, Derek 2
Pepperberg, Irene 2
Pereira, Waldyr 193
phenomenological puzzle 220
phenomenological resistance 221
Phillippides 128
phoney wars 87–88, 120n10

physical ordinary world challenges 127–128
physical skills of football 157–160
Physical struggle/fight! D-a-n-g-e-r ...! Activate fight-or-flight adrenaline now 26–27, 31, 65n32, 162, 216, 241–242 see also aliefs, fight-or-flight aliefs
pick-up games 4, 244, 245–246
Pizzul, Bruno 217, 252n26
platonism about sport 101
play: aesthetic connections between 32–33; as autotelic 38; benefits of 38; biological function of 35; definition of 18, 37–38; enhancing creativity 35–36; evolutionary account of 31; football separate from 45–46; functional theories of 34–36; inclusive theory of 41–42; make-believe in 33; metabolic resources of 34–35; as more primitive than games/sports 19; non-human 38–39; as purposeless behaviour 37–38; social inhibition in 41–42; types of 32; see also deep play, games, play behaviour, social play
play behaviour 34, 36, 37–38, 41, 63n18
play bite 43
players see footballers
play fighting 36–37, 39–40, 44–47, 66n37 see also fighting
play signal 43
Plymouth Argyle 18
Poland 212
Portugal 185–186, 212
positive rules of conduct 141
Povinelli, Daniel 2
Power, Thomas 35, 46–47, 66n37
practitioners see football matches, religious practitioners, sport practitioners
prelusory goals of sport 124–129, 181
pre-modern sport 114–118 see also modern sport
pretence play 46–48 see also proto-pretence
problem of rule following (Wittgenstein) 145
professional fouling 145
professional fouls 143, 168
professional wrestling 244–245
proper function, definition of 230
proto-football 95–96, 98–100, 106, 111
proto-pretence: definition of 32; as-if proto-pretence 32; mental mechanism of 42, 47; of rough-and-tumble play 208; social play 32, 34, 40–41, 42, 46–48, 199, 215–216
prototype theory 172–174, 175–178
prototypical sports 174–176
Pryke, John 67n46

Index 285

purposive sports 187n4
puzzle of imaginative resistance 220

quantification of performance 113–115

Rachels, Stuart 177
racism/racist chanting 73–74, 218, 222
rainmaking ritual 79–80
randomness in extra-ordinary activities 238
Rapson, Richard 49
rational thought 1–2
reaction rules 142, 182–183
Real Betis 104
Real Madrid 115, 196, 211–212, 240
real values 216–219, 251n23
recessions, social kinds and 73–74
reductive formalism 71, 101–102, 141–146, 169, 179
referees/refereeing: appointed 188n13; controlling a match 162–163; footballers and 186, 258–259; interpretation view of 144, 145; mechanical view of 144–145; minding/managing the game 161–165; rule interpretation 153–154; self-refereeing 153, 188n13; shared ethos 153; video assisted refereeing (VAR) 188n16
Regis, Cyrille 222
regulative rules: constitutive vs. 134–135, 178–180; definition of 135; *see also* constitutive rules, rule violations
Rekdal, Kjetil 219
religion/religious practice 17–19, 63n16
religious practitioners 19
representations 13–14
response-dependency 235, 254n39
Riley, Mike 164
risk sports 52
rites and rituals 88, 110–111, 229
rites of passage 90
ritualized fights 49–50, 55–56
Rivera, Gianni 213
Robot Football case 107
Robson, Bryan 165–166
Ronaldo, Cristiano 120n1
Rosch, Eleanor 172–173, 175
Rossi, Paulo 213
rough-and-tumble play 32, 33, 39, 42, 57–58, 66n40, 208
Ruentes, Ronaldo 157
rugby football 95, 100
Rugby School football 96
rule of skill 181
rules of penalties 141–142

rules of the game: acceptance of 151, 153, 186; arbitration of 160–161; back-pass rule 235; breaking 258; changes within 234–235; definiteness of 179–180; FIFA as keeper of 234; flexibility of 4; football authorities setting 234–235; implementing 155–156; lusory attitude for 144, 149; modifying 234; offside rule 181–182, 235; playing with sport knowledge 136; positive rules of conduct 141; referees and 6, 28, 160–164, 247; self-refereeing and 247; *see also* constitutive rules, rule violations
rule violations: corner flagging 163–164; corrective penalty 142–143; handball rule 156–157, 185–186; interpretation view of refereeing 144; negative rules of conduct 141; penalties from 183–184; penalty kick 141–142; positive rules of conduct 141; professional fouls 143, 168; reaction rules 142; shirt pulling/tugging 155–156, 161; time wasting 168–169; unacceptable behavior 146; widespread in football 139; *see also* constitutive rules, penalties, regulative rules
Rummenigge, Karl Heinz 212
Running Race case 76
running races *see* footraces
Running W technique 252n29
Rush, Ian 187n4, 213
Russell, Dave 95
Ryman Football League Division One 243

Saito, Yuriko 206
Salah, Mohamed 207
Sally, David 251n21
San Francisco Chinese Basketeers 105
Searle, John R. 72–73, 74, 79, 85, 134–135
Searle's Cocktail Party case 80–81, 84, 85
self-refereeing 153, 188n13
Serbia 197, 208
Serbia and Montenegro 197
Sevilla 104
shallow betting 51
Shankly, Bill 9, 59, 67–68n51
Sheard, Kenneth 95
Sheffield FC codification of 1858 97, 121n16
Sheringham, Teddy 190
Shevchenko, Andriy 192
Shilton, Peter 198
shirt pulling/tugging 155–156, 161
Shoreline Runners case 76–77, 86–87, 134

silly questions, football fiction and 223–225 *see also* aesthetic engagement resistance
Simon, Robert 191
Smith, Peter 155
social drama 202
social historical kind: association football and 98, 184–185; changes within 231–232; collective intentionality and 134, 185, 231, 258; emergence of sport as 176–178; ethos view of sport and 145–146; evolution of 145; football form and 102, 119, 180; gliding transitions between 244; intentionalism and 235; monocultural practices and 147–148; naturalism and 174; participants and practitioners of 231; referees/refereeing and 123; ritual and 231; rule changes and 180, 184
social identity 22
social kind of sport 72–73, 83–94
social kinds: association football as 98–99; collective acceptance of 72; with collective intentionality 78–80; collective intentionality dependent 73–76; collective intentionality with token exceptions 86–87; constitutive rules defining 70–73; construction of 73; *danza de los voladores* (dance of the flyers) 93; fashion/fashionableness 74–76; by fiat 81; fringe cases of 88–89; natural vs. 71; racism and 73–74; recessions 73–74; self-referentially dependent 74–75; transparency and 135–136; types of 76; without collective intentionality 76–78; without token exceptions 80–82
social play: as autotelic 117; of chimpanzees 39; as-if proto-pretence in 32; nonhuman 162; play mode intrinsic to 58; as proto-contest 40; proto-pretence of 40–41; reward systems for 41; sportifying 57–58; *see also* play
Sócrates 213
Solskjær, Ole Gunnar 168, 190
Souness, Graeme 147
Souness-Movilă incident 147
South Korea 61, 213–214
Soviet Union 227
Spain 61, 213–214
spectators: aggression vs. fighting 27; aggressive behaviour of 26–27; constitutive rules and 136; emotional contagion of 49, 65n28; exploiting alief impulses 27–28; footballers dependence on 207; football viewing experience of 259; intentionalism and 233; make

professional sports 207; neutral 48–49; partisanship among 48–49
sport by fiat 82
sport competitions, structural goal of 191
sport drama 199–201
sport entertainment 244
sport form, primacy of 150
sporting events 87
sport-like domain 176, 177
sport participants, collective intentionality of being 136–138
sport performers 136–137
sport practitioners 23, 26, 63n16, 67n48, 100, 109–110, 136–137, 156 *see also* football practitioners
sports: adaptive function of 257; aesthetic insight 11–13; definition of 15–16, 123–124; determining something as 171–172; everyday world taking precedence over 218–219; as extra-ordinary 15–19, 54–55; extreme 109–110; in Greek antiquity 89–90 *see also* ancient Olympics; house building as 83; involving pretence 20; to let off steam 29; moral education and 16, 59–60n8; non-sports vs. 107–110; in Panhellenic world 89–90 *see also* ancient Olympics; parkour 109–110; as part of everyday life 56–57, 62n11; performance quantification 113–115; psychological setting of 102; purposes of 29; as real action 10; as ritualized conflicts 55–56; as social kind 71–72, 110–111; social setting of 102; stage token exceptions 87; Suits's position on 70; turning physical ordinary world challenge into 128; as unnecessary activities 16; as vehicles for identity making 48; *see also* football, games, modern sport, pre-modern sport
sport-specific state-of-affairs end-states 132–133, 138–139, 178–180
sport spectacle as model for theatrical arts 204
stadion race 90–92
state-of-affairs end-states 129, 130 *see also* sport-specific state-of-affairs end-states
status rivalry hypothesis (Dunning) 96
Stefanos, Scott 187n7
Stoichkov, Hristo 255n47
Stowe, Harriet Beecher 17
Strategic Yellow Card case 162–163
Stubbes, Philip 94
Suárez, Luis 247–248, 255n49
Sugden, John 63n14

Suits, Bernard: analysis of sport 123–124; on chess 126; on constitutive rules 182; on end-state goal 107–108; on game criterion 123; on games 70; *Grasshopper: Games, Life and Utopia* 123–124, 180; on judged sports that aren't games 126–127; logical incompatibility thesis 139–140, 180–183; on mechanical view of refereeing 144–145; on reaction rules 142–143; on rule of skill 189n25; on sport's physical requirements 158–160; technical activities notion 129; Utopia, notion of 187n1
surplus energy theory of play 32, 65n31
Sutton-Smith, Brian 63n15
Sweden 197–198
symbolic play 47

Tardelli, Marco 215
Taylor, Matthew 95
technical activities (Suits) 129
tests, contests vs. 127–128
Thai kick-boxing 118
theatrical arts 204
Thomasson, Amie 73–74
thought experiments 7, 91–92, 159–160, 170, 179
token exceptions 79, 80–82, 86–87
tokens of war 84–85
Tolstoy, Leo 10
Tomasello, Michael 47
Tomaszewski, Jan 212
Tomlinson, Alan 255n48
tool use 1–2
Torres, José 185
transparency, to social kind of sport 135–136
Turner, Victor 202
Turone, Maurizio 213

Uncle Tom's Cabin (Stowe) 17
uniqueness of humans 1–2
unnecessary obstacles 16–17, 125–126
Uruguay 247, 255n49
USA 213
Utopia (Suits) 187n1

van Basten, Marco 227
Verón, Juan 189n19
video assisted refereeing (VAR) 188n16
Villarreal CF 196
voluntary suspension of play 217, 221, 251–252n25

Walton, Kendall 13–14, 19–20, 21, 63n20, 223
war/warfare: as armed conflict between societies 86; codified conventions of 86; collective intentionality of being 85–86; phoney wars 87–88, 120n10; started by fiat 87
Washington Generals 105
Weatherson, Brian 220, 221
Welsch, Wolfgang 205
Weiler, Ingomar 121n13
we-intentionality 77–78
Werther effect 27
Western Movies case 221, 222
West Bromwich Albion 222, 230
West Germany 212, 213, 215, 235, 246
Whiten, Andrew 66n43
Whitstable Town 242–243
Williams, Jack 149
Wilson, Jonathan 237, 240
Wilson, Steve 139–140
Wimbeldon FC 251n21
Winner, David 214
Wisker, Dan 243
Wittgenstein, Ludwig 145, 171–172, 187n10
World Cup *see* FIFA World Cup
World Cup qualifier 82
wrestling, professional 244–245
Wycombe Wanderers 18

Zaire 167–168
Zé Roberto 189n19
Ziani, Karim 255n46
Zidane, Zinedine 196, 249n7
Zidane: A 21st Century Portrait (film) 196, 197
Zoff, Dino 213